Broadcast Journalism
IN THE 21ST CENTURY

Broadcast Journalism
IN THE 21ST CENTURY

K. M. Shrivastava

NEW DAWN PRESS, INC.
UK • USA • INDIA

NEW DAWN PRESS GROUP

Published by New Dawn Press Group
New Dawn Press, Inc., 244 South Randall Rd # 90, Elgin, IL 60123
e-mail: sales@newdawnpress.com

New Dawn Press, 2 Tintern Close, Slough, Berkshire, SL1-2TB, UK
e-mail: ndpuk@newdawnpress.com

New Dawn Press (An Imprint of Sterling Publishers (P) Ltd.)
A-59, Okhla Industrial Area, Phase-II, New Delhi-110020
e-mail: info@sterlingpublishers.com
www.sterlingpublishers.com

Broadcast Journalism in the 21st Century
©2005, K. M. Shrivastava
ISBN 1 932705 45 7

All rights are reserved. No part of this publication may be reproduced, stored in a retrieval system or transmitted, in any form or by any means, mechanical, photocopying, recording or otherwise, without prior written permission of the publisher.

PRINTED IN INDIA

Preface

More than a decade has passed since I wrote *Radio and TV Journalism*, which was published in 1989. The world of broadcasting has changed since then, not only because of technology but also because of major political changes that have taken place in the Eastern Europe and Central Asia.

The convergence of technology had started changing the world broadcast scene at the time of the first edition of this book. We are now in the era where telecommunication, satellite, computers and broadcasting have come together with some such results that were not imaginable at that time.

Internet was not heard of then. Now it has emerged as one of the important factors in the global media environment. Internet radio is a reality while Internet TV is not very far once bandwidth problem is solved. Most broadcasters already have their presence on the Internet. Cable TV has taken new strides and can now provide not only TV but also Internet and telephony. In fact, another kind of digital divide is emerging – those who have broadband access and those who do not have it.

The global media scene is now more dominated by the western media. By mergers, acquisitions and strategic alliances, fewer companies now decide what the world listens and sees around the world. Though there is a search for alternatives like community media, the impact of such alternatives is not significant.

This book is an attempt to fill a felt need in developing countries, for most books on the subject are still from the West and are becoming less affordable due to increase in price. With globalisation, the West cannot afford to ignore the rest of the world. Thus, this book will have relevance even in the West.

K. M. Shrivastava

Contents

	Preface	v
1.	Evolution	1
2.	Indian Scene: Prasar Bharati	11
3.	Private and Foreign Channels	36
4.	Some Technical Aspects	79
5.	Some Tricks of the Trade	113
6.	Broadcast News – Radio	143
7.	Television News	184
8.	Trends and Issues	221
9.	Glossary	273

Appendices

1.	MacBride Commission Report: Conclusions and Recommendations	311
2.	RTNDA Code	334
3.	Airwaves Are Public Property (SC Judgement)	338
4.	The Prasar Bharati (Broadcasting Corporation of India) Act, 1990	344
5.	Programme and Advertising Codes	367
6.	DTH Guidelines	371
7.	Foreign Investment and Uplinking Policy	374
8.	Community Radio Guidelines	384
9.	The Cable Television Networks (Regulation) Act, 1995	389
10.	Index	397

1

Evolution

During the course of the twentieth century, humankind has marched from the "Gutenburg Galaxy" to the "Global Village" ushered in by information technology. In the first half, we had radio and then television and the second half took us to the space age, as the first international communication satellite systems, Intelsat and Intersputnik were in place by the mid-sixties. Since then innovations have brought convergence of mass media, telecommunication, informatics and optical electronics leading to a wide variety of communication tools like cellular telephones, satellite television and Internet. The Internet has revolutionised the communications world as never before. The invention of the telegraph, telephone, radio and computer set the stage for this unprecedented integration of capabilities. In fact, the Internet has soon become a worldwide broadcasting capability, a mechanism for information dissemination, and a medium for collaboration and interaction between individuals and their computers without regard for geographic location.

    Our world has been changing and communications are central to this change. The digital media has revolutionised the information society. Multi-channel television will soon be available to all who have the purchasing power. More and more people can gain access to the Internet through personal computers, televisions, mobile phones, and even games consoles. The choice of services available is greater than ever before. High-speed phone lines give households access to a whole new range of communications services and experiences. Using their TV sets people are able to e-mail, shop from home, and devise their own personal viewing schedules.

The communications revolution has arrived and in fact, radio, television and Internet are fruits of the evolution of communication technology. Telegraphy was invented around 1840 by Sir Charles Wheatstone and Samuel Morse. The first telegraph message was transmitted in 1844. In 1876, Bell sent the first telephone message by wire. Around 1895, Marconi and Popoff succeeded independently of one another in transmitting and receiving wireless messages. In 1906, Fessender transmitted the human voice by radio. In 1839, Daguerre devised a practical method of photography. The first film was screened in 1894. Already in 1904, the first photographs were transmitted by phototelegraphic apparatus (Belin system), while the first picture was televised in 1923. The first radio broadcasting networks were installed in the 1920s, television broadcasting began in the 1930s and regular transmission of colour television began in 1954. Rapid intercontinental communication was initiated with the underwater telegraph cable between America and Europe, laid in 1857. While the first transatlantic telephone cable entered into service only in 1957, the intercontinental radio telephone and telegraph systems were already functioning regularly by the 1920s; teleprinting became operational at the start of the 1930s. Finally, Early Bird, the first commercial communication satellite was launched in 1962. Two big international satellite systems, Intelsat and Intersputnik, were launched respectively in 1965 and 1971. The world's first domestic synchronous orbit satellite system for telecommunication purposes and for distribution and reception of television programmes, through low-cost earth stations and low-power transmitters was inaugurated in 1973 in Canada. (USA launched WESTAR I in 1974 with capacity of 8 m words/second). In 1977, the satellite system could carry voice facsimile and data directly to the end user. A gallium araenide laser which may enable numerous television programmes to be transmitted along a fiber, no thicker than a human hair, was tested in 1970. Optical fibre cables were field-tested in 1976.

In these analog technologies, the missing ingredient was processing. Digital systems, in contrast to analog, allowed one to work with and manipulate content. Information processing thus needed another ingredient that arrived in 1958 when Robert Noyce and Gordon Moore created the integrated silicon chip, following on the work of William Shockley, who had invented the transistor in 1948. The invention of the silicon chip has reduced the space required to minute proportions. Binary codes of transmission have created a new language, virtually eliminating delays. The company they founded was Intel, that really broke the computing barrier in 1974 with the 8080 chip. It was virtually an entire computer on a single chip. In 1977, Apple produced the Apple II, and the desktop computer was born. All this unleashed a chain reaction of faster and cheaper chips embodied in the now famous principle of Moore's Law.

To all these developments, add memory (which evolves even faster than the microchip) and the software and you have the final ingredients of the Information Age.

A fibre optic interactive computer-controlled network was designed in Japan to carry two-way video information, to and from households. In another field, videocassettes were invented in 1969, audiovisual cassettes became a marketable reality in 1971 and a first videodisc system was available to consumers in 1979.

Computer systems working in parity with communications have spawned the Internet and the advanced networks we see today that fully integrate satellites, telephones, wireless devices, broadcasting and cable over fiber-optic, broadband, and wireless networks. The result is what we now call convergence.

Convergence is not just a technological phenomenon. We see the collapsing of previously distinct markets and competitors. Convergence is radically altering economic assumptions underlying cost structures and altering business models. This challenges the policy makers to make a similar leap from analog-rooted regulations to ones that are applicable and relevant to the digital environment.

This new mediasphere has greatly increased our communication choices. Narrowcasting, interactive, educational and other networks now respond to hundreds of different needs, interests and tastes. Multimedia systems are broadening the horizons of artistic and intellectual creativity through video art, holography and virtual reality. Electronic images are replacing traditional forms of sharing and recording memory.

Satellite technology has brought about major changes in broadcasting since the transoceanic relay of TV programmes between the US and Europe in the early 1960s. This was basically a point-to-point relay using large and expensive earth stations at both the ends and further distribution through existing terrestrial TV network. The use of Intelsat system for international distribution of TV signals in this mode made it possible for a very large international audience to see the first step of a man on the moon.

A major quantum leap in satellite technology was marked by the US satellite ATS-6 (Applications Technology Satellite, also called ATS-F) launched in 1974 that enabled the direct reception of satellite-relayed TV signals by simple, low-cost receiving systems. In effect, it replaced the high cost earth stations with cheap Direct Reception System (DRS) consisting of a 3 m parabolic mesh antenna and an electronic converter attached to a conventional TV set. The ATS-6 was thus able to bypass the coverage constraints imposed by the need to have a TV transmitter. The Satellite Instructional Television Experiment (SITE) in 1975-76 was a field demonstration of the capabilities of this system in India and the same technology is now an integral part of the Indian Satellite System (INSAT). It is important for a television network to gather programme material at a central location specially for the purposes of news and current affairs programmes. Satellite News Gathering (SNG) has made this possible. The SNG system is a highly portable satellite uplink of such small size and weight that it is capable of being transported in a scheduled airline, helicopter, automobile or even carried by hand to the site of a fast-breaking news event. Such an equipment can be set up and operated by two persons within an hour. A fly-away SNG system can be packaged in shock-resistant flight cases within the parameters of IATA regulations on scheduled flights.

India has tried Direct Broadcasting Satellite (DBS) service during SITE and it was expected that direct broadcast TV service to very small rooftop/home dish antennae will be cost-effective in India in the 90s. The key to large scale introduction of DBS lies in establishing viable number of viewers (about one million). The concept is now called Direct-to-Home (DTH).

Evolution

High Definition Television (HDTV) looked a certainty few years ago. Before the world could decide whether to follow the Japanese standard or the American standard, it has been overtaken by digital broadcasting. Needless to say that the Japanese were the first to develop HDTV and the Americans insisted on developing their own standard. HDTV is now talked about as a part of ISBD (Integrated Services Digital Broadcasting) which integrates it with conventional television, enhanced teletext, audio services and new forms of interactive multimedia services.

Digital Video Broadcasting (DVB) is being implemented for satellite, cable and terrestrial transmission. At the end of 1995, the European DVB project finalised the specifications for channel coding and modulation of the broadband, digital TV transmission channels.

Digital satellite broadcast systems are in operation in the US since 1995 and the digital cable delivery has started in late 1996.

Digital television service was launched in the US on 1 November 1998, and more than 50 per cent of the US population had access to terrestrial DTV signals within one year. As of May 15, 2001 there were 195 DTV stations on the air in the US. Within the next 10 years all the existing analog systems were likely to be replaced by the digital systems with added capabilities like HDTV, interactive programmes, full Internet access and telephone services. DVB promises great expectations: pay TV, pay-per-view TV (PPV), near video on demand (NVOD), interactive video on demand (IVOD), video games (supply of software and downloading, services on demand (SOD) including anything from teleshopping, telebooking, telebanking, telelearning and true interactive TV with teleworking.

Cooperative corporate efforts at standardisation need mention here. The Advanced Television Systems Committee, Inc. (ATSC), is an international, non-profit membership organisation developing voluntary standards for the entire spectrum of advanced television systems. ATSC was formed in 1982 by the member organisations of the Joint Committee on Intersociety Coordination (JCIC): the Electronic Industries Association (EIA), the Institute of Electrical and Electronic Engineers (IEEE), the National Association of Broadcasters (NAB), the National Cable Television

Association (NCTA), and the Society of Motion Picture and Television Engineers (SMPTE). Currently, there are approximately 170 members representing the broadcast, broadcast equipment, motion picture, consumer electronics, computer, cable, satellite and semiconductor industries. ATSC has been incorporated on January 3, 2002.

Another group, called the Advanced Television Enhancement Forum (ATVEF), has defined protocols for television programming enhanced with data, such as Internet content. Members of this group included CableLabs; CNN; DIRECTV, Inc.; Discovery Communications, Inc. (DCI); The Walt Disney Company; Intel Corporation; Microsoft Corporation/WebTV Networks, Inc.; NBC Multimedia, Inc.; Network Computer, Inc. (NCI); NDTC Technology; Public Broadcasting Service (PBS); Sony Corporation; Tribune Company and Warner Bros. The goal is to allow content creators to design enhanced programming that may be delivered over any form of transport (analog or digital TV, cable, or satellite) to all types of broadcast receivers that comply with the proposed specification. Enhanced television offers new entertainment and commerce opportunities, such as: sports events with complementary information on players and teams, news with additional details and related stories, and ads that allow consumers to order merchandise with the click of a button. The ATVEF is working with other industry groups and standards bodies to incorporate the specification as part of those bodies' standards, in order to provide a consistent international blueprint for enhanced products and services. Those bodies include: OpenCable, Digital Video Broadcasting (DVB), Advanced Television Systems Committee (ATSC), World Wide Web Consortium (W3C) and the Society of Motion Picture and Television Engineers (SMPTE)

Until 1980s most broadcasting and telecommunications were state monopolies and with a very few exceptions. They were seen as the vehicles to ensure that national culture was properly reflected by delivering information, education and quality entertainment for all. In 1980 most European states, whether through state-controlled or public service broadcasting, held monopoly. In Africa national broadcasting was strictly government owned and operated. Countries such as Australia, Brazil, Canada, Finland or the United Kingdom had mixed systems. Community broadcasting was rare.

In most of Europe, state-controlled or public service broadcasting prevailed until the beginning of the 1980s. In the United Kingdom commercial television was admitted side by side with the BBC in 1959; commercial radio was accepted in Italy in the 1970s and commercial television in the 1980s. France and the Federal Republic of Germany followed suit in 1984. By the end of the decade, all the European countries were admitting private providers to the market, while the government continued to facilitate infrastructure development. In the Central and Eastern Europe less well supported state media had to compete with private companies. The movement to deregulate broadcasting was strong in sub-Saharan Africa. Mali had more than 15 operational private radio stations, Burkina Faso had more than nine licensed stations. The National Broadcasting Commission of Nigeria had granted licences for one radio and six television stations as well as eleven cable/satellite retransmission stations. The media in the Arab world is characterised by state control but there is a wide availability of regional and international media channels. International viewing is pervasive in the Gulf states which may provide the world's biggest videocassette market and pirated television programmes.

There was increasing privatisation and foreign investment in telecommunication networks – Singapore and South Korea in 1993, Hungary, Pakistan, Peru and Russia in 1994, Bolivia, Cote d'Ivoire, Czech Republic, India, Turkey and Uganda in 1995.

Even in the US, the Telecommunications Act of 1996, was a remarkable and important shift in telecommunications policy. Its purpose was to move from a regulated monopoly model of telecommunications to a deregulatory competitive markets model. The Act's preamble declares that its purpose is to "promote competition and reduce regulation in order to secure lower prices and higher quality services for American telecommunications consumers."

This 1996 Act is focused principally on deregulation and the move to markets. There are parts of the statute that recognise the growing technological convergence, but they offer only modest guidance for regulation in the converged digital era. For example, the statute opens up some previously prohibited cross-market competition and Section 706 commands to "encourage the deployment on a reasonable and timely basis of advanced telecommunications capability to all Americans."

Deregulation or the relaxation of government controls in the operation of markets, which has been one of the means to promote competition, may also promote concentration of ownership. Recent giant mergers claiming the merits of synergy are evidence of this trend. The convergence of interlocking technologies and the positioning of domestic market leaders abroad have favoured the international concentration of ownership. An unprecedented round of alliances, mergers and acquisitions has affected every sector: consumer electronics, media production, television, cable, publishing, computer and telecommunications are all striving to position themselves in the global market.

New alliances are being forged between owners of content and owners of infrastructure. In May 1995, MCI, the American long-distance telecommunication carrier announced a two billion dollar investment in Rupert Murdoch's News Corporation, bringing the fibre optic pipeline hardware and the software content together. A vast array of films, television programmes, publishing and multimedia were henceforth distributed through a fibre-optic telecommunication network with access to the Internet. The Time Warner agreement to buy Turner Broadcasting System for US $7.5 billion has been trumpeted as the creation of the world's largest media company. The $19 billion merger of Capital Cities/ABC with the Disney empire led to what the Disney's Chairman Michael Eisner saw as "the world's greatest entertainment company in the next century".

But when 'the next century" arrived, all this paled to insignificance in front on US $106 billion AOL and Time Warner

Evolution

merger. The deal was announced on 10 January 2000 and AOL Time Warner came into existence on 11 January 2001, duly approved by regulators, despite opposition from rivals. It described itself as, "AOL Time Warner (NYSE:AOL) is the world's first Internet-powered media and communications company, whose industry-leading businesses include interactive services, cable systems, publishing, music, cable networks and filmed entertainment." *The Wall Street Journal* expressed its astonishment that a company "not old enough to buy beer" had essentially swallowed a mature media conglomerate that took most of a century to construct.

Besides AOL Time Warner, which has CNN and HBO in its fold, the other big multi-interest players that lead the media world are: Disney, Viacom, Vivendi, General Electric (GE), News Corporation, Sony, Bertelsmann, AT&T and Liberty Media. These groups own a large number of media properties off-line and on-line. They have no problems even in having strategic alliances with each other to capture a particular segment of market. For good or for ill, as the MacBride Commission pointed out, the mass media have a vast responsibility, because they do not merely transmit and disseminate culture but also select or originate its content. The current trend is diversification and expansion, alone or in cooperation with others, and all the above giants have followed this trend of mergers, acquisitions and strategic alliances.

The future is broadband, a lightning fast means of data transmission that could revolutionise the way we all send and receive information. For broadband digital world the rush has already begun. Much of the rush is prompted by the promise of greener pastures. Companies are seeking the benefits of cheaper and more efficient infrastructures, though deployment comes at great cost. The markets are in search of greater material gain from that infrastructure by offering more services over it and by bundling those services for consumers. Moreover, it also holds out hope for entirely new markets and new innovative services.

The presence of radio on the Internet should also be noted here. Radio-Locator, formerly MIT list of radio stations on the

Internet, is a comprehensive radio station search engine on the Internet. It claims to have links to over 10,000 radio station Web pages and over 2500 audio streams from radio stations in the US and around the world. But another future is community radio. This might become great means of empowerment for local communities. It is cheap. It may find a niche not considered profitable by big media.

2
Indian Scene: Prasar Bharati

In the beginning broadcasting in India was in private hands. The first radio programme in India was broadcast by the Radio Club of Bombay (now Mumbai) in June 1923. When the private enterprise failed, the government took it over very reluctantly. But since then till 1997, broadcasting remained a government-owned monopoly. The Government of India had been running monopoly broadcast organisations, All India Radio and Doordarshan as part of the Ministry of Information and Broadcasting.

Even when broadcasting was in private hands the government had wide ranging powers to fully control it. In a press communique issued on March 27, 1925 it was announced that the government was prepared to grant a license to private enterprise "for the provision of broadcasting by means of stations to be erected in British India".

In this communique it was made very clear that the government reserved the right "to inspect broadcasting stations, take over or operate these or impose a complete censorship, or partial prohibition or pre-censorship, either generally or specially at any time, issue any special or general restrictions as regards matter which may or may not be broadcasted, or as to the persons who may or may not broadcast, specify sources from which news and information in the nature of news may be obtained and the times of broadcasting the same, terminate the license at any time in the event of improper or inefficient use of broadcast station, require a broadcasting station to broadcast free of cost government weather reports, forecasts, government notice and communique and educational propaganda or other government matter, provided the time taken out of the ordinary programme did not exceed 10 per cent". An agreement was signed on September 13, 1926 and provided for a government nominee on the board of directors of the Indian Broadcasting Company.

The first government nominee, Mr. P. J. Edmunds in his note on censorship (May 5, 1927) expressed the hope that eventually the procedure in India would become similar to that in England where the broadcasting company had earned the entire confidence of the (British) government and was allowed to use its own discretion on the understanding, that it would refer all doubtful points to the Post Master General.

However, this private enterprise did not last long and on the night of February 28, 1930 the IBC broadcast carried the last message for its listeners, "As already announced, the Indian Broadcasting Company was unfortunately compelled to decide to close down the service from tonight. You are probably aware, however, that certain negotiations are going on with the Government of India for carrying on the broadcasting service. Pending final settlement of these arrangements the liquidator has decided to continue the service without interruption, as he hopes these negotiations will materialise and the public will continue to enjoy the benefits of broadcasting".

It also said, that there was an "unusual demand for government action" in the matter, from receiver license-holders and dealers of wireless equipment. The leaders and deputy leaders of the main political parties in the Assembly requested the Hon'ble Member In-charge of Industry and Labour that immediate steps be taken to ensure that the service should be carried on without interruption; the government if necessary should itself take over and continue the service. The government took it over reluctantly initially for two years and then decided to own it as a monopoly for good.

Lionel Fielden analysed the sorry end of IBC about ten years later, and felt that the company had been under-capitalised; capital reserve and revenue had been insufficient from the start, very high price of receiving sets (Rs.500 for a four valve set); there had also been no effort to popularise this medium among the masses, with the emphasis being on programmes meant for western-oriented Indians and Europeans only.

During his tenure as the first governor of broadcasting, Fielden faced a lot of problems because the bureaucracy treated broadcasting as any other function of the government. When in London in July 1937, he wrote two anonymous articles in *The Times*, which he owned in his autobiography later, he wrote, "Whether in India broadcasting was to remain a subsidised and uneconomic activity of government or whether, it might be treated as a semi-independent body were and are matters undecided. This has had a direct effect on development since, if broadcasting is to pay its way and stand on its own feet, the urban population from whom alone revenues can come must first be served. If on the other hand broadcasting is to be treated as a social and educational subject subsidised by the government, it is clearly more important to concentrate on the 83 per cent of India's population who live in villages".

He went on to argue, "Broadcasting did not fit happily into the slow machinery of the government, and therefore delays almost fatal to the development of broadcasting in India were bound to occur. Apart from this, broadcasting in India, though needing, of course, the most careful control must always be suspect while it is entirely in government hands. It is true that the government has given an undertaking in the Legislative Assembly that broadcasting shall not be used for political propaganda, but this is more easily said than done... In India especially these days politics is the breath of life and there is scarcely a subject on which it does not intrude."

The Government of India issued a formal communique stating that they were not in agreement with the views of the writer.

National Planning Committee

In 1938, Congress President Subhas Chandra Bose set up the National Planning Committee for Independent India with Jawaharlal Nehru as its chairman. It appointed 29 subcommittees, the one headed by Sir Rahimatuallah Chinoy looked into communications. This subcommittee of the National Planning Committee passed a resolution about communication and broadcasting policy in independent India. It said, "Communication and broadcasting are public utility services affecting the well-being of the community and are at present under state control. They should be public monopolies and should be run on commercial lines and developed intensively, subject to the paramount consideration that they are social services and as such powerful agents in the task of national development." It recommended the setting up of a statutory corporation for radio broadcasting with an advisory council consisting of representatives of the public and experts attached to it.

On March 15, 1948, Prime Minister Jawaharlal Nehru said that he was in favour of a broadcasting set up similar to BBC but felt that the time was not ripe for that yet.

Chanda Committee

After Nehru's death when his daughter Mrs. Indira Gandhi became minister of information and broadcasting in Lal Bahadur Shastri's Cabinet, she appointed a committee on broadcasting and information media with A. K. Chanda, a former auditor general, as chairman. Members of this committee were Nath Pai, M. S. Gurupadaswamy, Dr. L. M. Singhvi, Smt. Kamala Chandhuri, Vidhya Charan Shukla, Hasan Zaheer, Ashok Mitra, M. Chalapathi Rau and Dr. Hazari Prasad Dwivedi. A senior director of AIR's programme staff Miss Mehra Masani was secretary of this committee.

The Chanda Committee opined. "It is not possible in the Indian context for a creative medium like broadcasting to flourish under a regiment of departmental rules and regulations. It is only by an institutional change that AIR can be liberated from the present rigid financial and administrative procedures of government."

The committee recommended that separate public corporation should be set up for Akashvani and Doordarshan to evolve new methods of recruitment, financial management, and conditions of service suitable for special requirements of creative media. The committee clearly pointed out that though, "theoretically it (AIR) has the freedom of a national newspaper to present objectively topics of current interest but in practice it has failed to do so mainly for two reasons. First, successive ministers have usurped the policy-making functions of the director-general and started interfering even in matters of programme planning and presentation, and second, the selection of the directing staff was so made as to ensure unquestioning compliance. As a result the public image of AIR has become tarnished, its objectivity destroyed, and its initiative gradually whittled away."

These recommendations were considered by the cabinet headed by Prime Minister Indira Gandhi in December 1969, and the Parliament was told in April 1970 that the government did not think that the time was ripe for conversion of AIR into an autonomous corporation. The opposition criticised this decision to continue AIR and Doordarshan under government control, and felt that the Indira Gandhi government was utilising the powerful media to further its own narrow political interests.

Verghese Working Group

After the March 1977 elections, the Janata Party government declared that it would make AIR and Doordarshan "genuinely autonomous", and constituted a working group on autonomy of Akashvani and Doordarshan on August 17, 1977 with B.G. Verghese as chairman. The members were V.G. Rajyadhyaksha, Dr. Malcolm S. Adiseshiah, Chanchal Sarkar, P. L. Deshpandea, Uma Shankar Joshi, A. G. Noorani, J. D. Sethi, P. L. Fernandes, C. R. Subramanium and Dr. Ishwar Das (member secretary). Mrs. Nayantara Sehgal was appointed member of this group on November 7, 1977. The working group submitted its report to the government on February 24, 1978.

It recommended that "Akash Bharati" a National Broadcast Trust, be set up as an autonomous body to look after both Akashvani and Doordarshan. It should have a board of trustees consisting of 12 persons (but not to exceed 21); of these three were to be full-time trustees and should look after (i) current affairs (ii) extension and (iii) culture. The trustees should be appointed by the president on the recommendation of the prime minister from out of a list of names submitted by a nominating panel, consist of the chief justice of India, the chairman of the Union Public Service Commission, and the Lok Pal (Ombudsman). For the office of the chairman, the above nominating panel would recommend two or at the most three names out of which one would be forwarded by the prime minister to the president. The controller general of broadcasting, the chief executive of the trust was to be appointed by the board of trustees. The other directors on the Central Executive Board would look after Radio (Akashvani), T.V. (Doordarshan), news and current affairs, engineering, finance, personnel and audience research. The service was to be a four-tier structure – national, zonal, regional and the local stations. This decentralisation was to facilitate quick decisions-making and to deal with regional and local sensitivities.

The working group also recommended the auditing of accounts by a duly qualified company of auditors, setting up of a licensing board for permitting other, mainly educational, 'franchised' stations to function under specified terms, and a complaints board consisting of a chairman and two other members appointed by the chief justice of India. The annual report of the trust along with the reports of the auditors, the licensing board and the complaints board was to be laid on the tables of both the Houses of Parliament.

This report of the working group was discussed in the Rajya Sabha on May 18, 1978 and in the Lok Sabha on November 30 and December 1, 1978. The government promised that it would bring up a bill on the future set up of broadcasting in the next Budget Session of the Parliament.

Prasar Bharati Bill 1979

On May 16, 1979, L. K. Advani, the Janata Party minister of information and broadcasting introduced the Prasar Bharati Bill in the Parliament, which envisaged that an autonomous corporation 'Prasar Bharati' would be responsible for radio and television. It provided for a board of governors of 11 to 15 members with a full time chairman and a full time director-general. The broadcasting wing of the Ministry of Information of this ministry and the secretary, Ministry of Finance, were to be the ex-officio members of the board of governors of Prasar Bharati.

Indian Scene: Prasar Bharati

The Bill in fact rejected the concept of trusteeship and provisions of constitutional safeguards recommended by the working group. Decentralisation and 'franchise stations' did not find a place in it. Financial control was to be maintained by the government through the Comptroller and Auditor General of India. Modifications in the procedure for the selection of the chairman of the corporation in effect meant that it would become a political appointment. Further made clause 23 of the Prasar Bharati Bill empowered the government to issue directives to the corporation from time to time, as it considered necessary. A copy to these directives was to be laid before each House of Parliament.

Mr. B.G. Verghese and five members of the working group expressed their dissatisfaction with the Prasar Bharati Bill in a joint statement issued on May 23, 1979, and said that it offered "something emasculated and confined with the executive continuing as the dominant influence." They argued, "when the reason why the people want an independent corporation is because the executive, abetted by a captive Parliament, shamelessly misused broadcasting during the Emergency, that is what has to be prevented for all time. Democracy is not something based on the pillar of only one institution, such as the Parliament or the judiciary, however important it may be. It is a tapestry woven out of many institutions of which a free, responsible and creative broadcasting system is one of the most significant."

In his rejoinder issued on June 2, 1979, the minister L. K. Advani said that the Verghese Working Group had conceived of "not just an autonomous corporation but an independent constitutional status for AIR. The government is unable to accept this independent entity concept, but so far as the concept of autonomy is concerned it has gone far beyond the Chanda Committee's recommendations". The press in general was against this Bill and so were the broadcasters. Sentiments of those days could be best summed up in a phrase from Kartar Singh Duggal who spent a lifetime with AIR, "Autonomy seems to have given broadcasting the slip."

However, the Bill was referred to a joint-select committee of the two Houses of Parliament and was to come up for discussion during the monsoon session of the Parliament in July 1979. But the Lok Sabha was dissolved before that and the Bill lapsed. Though a non-starter, the Bill represents the farthest point to which the urge for autonomy has been able to reach in India. The Ministry of Information and Broadcasting in its annual report for 1979-80 said that the government had decided not to set up an autonomous body of AIR and Doordarshan as recommended by the Verghese Group because such an organisation was not considered necessary to enable these mass media to discharge their basic objectives of serving the people who were not served by other media.

Joshi Working Group on Software

On December 6, 1982, the government appointed a working group on software for Doordarshan with Dr. P. C. Joshi, Director of the Institute of Economic Growth as its Chairman and Manzurul Amin, Additional Director-General, Doordarshan as its Member Secretary. The other members were Sai Paranjpe, Alyque Padamsee, GNS Raghavan, Rami Chhabra, Binod C. Agrawal, Rina Gill, Yogendra Singh, Mohan Upreti, Bhupen Hazarika, K. S. Gill and R. B. L. Srivastava. This working group submitted its report to the government on April 2, 1984, which was placed on the table of the Lok Sabha on August 12, 1985.

In the opinion of the Joshi Working Group, "the issue of reforms in structure and in management style is much more complex and subtle than is captured by the fashionable cliche, "government control vs. autonomy". A structure may be fully autonomous from the government control and yet still be formidable constraint on the release of creativity. This is confirmed by numerous examples of highly bureaucratised and hierarchically organised autonomous structures which seriously thwart creativity and elude social accountability. On the other hand, an institution may continue to be within the government framework and yet be so structured as to provide powerful support to creativity and innovation as in the case of the Atomic Energy and Space Research Centre".

The working group quoted Vikram Sarabhai for distinguishing two types of tasks which governments had to undertake. "At one end of the spectrum, are certain administrative services acting on past precedents and traditions providing security and continuity, impersonalised to the extent that if one person is substituted by another, everyone knows how the successor will behave and operate under a given set of circumstances. At the other end, there are organisations based on research and development, involving individuals who act on insights and hunches, non-conformists, questioning assumptions, innovating and learning. The two extremes require organisations and working cultures which are rather different. Many tasks encountered in the contemporary world call for organisations where creative thinking and innovation are essential ingredients of survival as well as growth. The diversity of tasks to be performed within the government framework require individuals who are not only sensitive to the needs of the two cultures but can provide a dynamic leadership to the conflicting systems."

According to the Joshi Working Group, from this angle one can see how, software planning and production are being hampered by the obsolete hierarchical structures whose principal function is to ensure conformity, to rigidly laid down procedures, and established pattern of norms. What planning and production require at every step is a structure and management style which consciously promotes break from conformity, from routinisation and standardisation in the direction of creative self-expression, both by an individual and collectively. But instead of creative freedom for the communicator within the framework of accountability to social objectives, we have conformity to directives from above, inhibiting the communicator's creative response and initiative. Instead of the interactive type of leadership which promotes creative orientation, we have the hierarchical boss-subordinate relationship which inhibits creative thinking and produces either 'Yes-men' or 'No-men'. Structural reforms, therefore, are indispensable which recognise that the role of administration is to support and facilitate work rather than to exercise outside controls.

The Joshi Working Group pointed out that though the government has not accepted the Verghese Group's recommendation of statutory autonomy for Akashvani and Doordarshan, its spokesmen have said that they are for functional freedom for the two organisations. It observed, "From our study of the working of Doordarshan we are convinced that it does not enjoy functional freedom, the lack of such freedom is having a detrimental effect on the planning and quality of its programmes ... We are of the view that it is possible and desirable even while the Indian television continues to be run by the government as a departmental undertaking, to effect a substantial delegation of powers to Doordarshan, and within it from the level to level, and to insulate the organisation's day-to-day functioning within the parameters of clearly spelt-out policy, from non-professional pressure and interference."

The Joshi Working Group suggested that the Ministry of Information and Broadcasting should be reorganised on the lines of the Railway Board and like it, should be manned by officers who have grown up in TV and not by birds of passage drawn from the IAS. The minister should have the benefit of advice not only from the proposed Information Board but additionally from a National Doordarshan Council. The minister would be the chairman of the council and the director-general, the convener. The chief engineer of Doordarshan would also be a member. Six or eight other members of the council would be non-officials drawn from various fields such as education, science and technology, agriculture and rural development, communication research, advertising and sports. The council would meet once a quarter and its life would be three years.

The council would discharge three functions: to review the performance of Doordarshan, to guard its professional and functional autonomy, and to function as Ombudsman in matters concerning news and current affairs. The director-general should be a person appointed on contract, with a proven record of excellence in social communication as well as leadership qualities necessary for attracting and utilising creative talent. His status should not be less than a secretary to the Government of India.

The group also suggested that each Doordarshan *Kendra* should have a programme advisory council comprising members with expertise in different subjects. Other structural changes suggested in Doordarshan include "the cutting of the umbilical cord that keeps it tied to All India Radio despite the formal separation of television from sound broadcasting in 1976". The group feels that there is no justification any longer for the continuing movement back and forth of programme and engineering staff between AIR and Doordarshan and they should be provided with legitimate prospects of career advancement within Doordarshan.

Namedia Feedback

Namedia, the Media Foundation of the nonaligned took up in 1986 a feedback project on Indian Television funded by the Planning Commission and the Ministry of Information and Broadcasting. This project envisaged a series of five regional seminars which were held in Calcutta (January 4-5) Bangalore (January 17-18), Bombay (February 7-8), Ahmedabad (February 8-9) and Guwahati (February 18-19), and the national colloquium was held in New Delhi from March 22 to March 24, 1986. On the basis of this feedback exercise Namedia published its report "A Vision for Indian Television".

It recommended that "a Television Authority of India as a public trust set up by and under the benign scrutiny of the Parliament and governed by experienced professionals and broadminded persons of national stature with acclaimed scientific, technical, cultural, artistic and aesthetic backgrounds, was thought to be ideal. Such an Authority would per se adopt neither an adversary nor a conformist attitude towards the government at the centre or the states but have a positive, healthy working relation with them. The domain of the Television Authority should be: 1. central-decentral in organisation, 2. independent in area operation and 3. autonomous in field function all the way down so that initiative, innovation and excellence are at their highest."

The area operational bodies recommended were the Agency for Educational Television, the Agency for Rural Television, Television News and Television Entertainment Programme Organisation (TEPO). It was clarified that the TEPO would deal with pure entertainment, sports and such other activities which do not fall within the purview of the other agencies. There would be a national network and state and regional networks with a system of interchange between all the networks. If a national centre for dubbing is established the interchange would be even more meaningful.

It was further recommended that the Television Authority should have jurisdiction over associated areas like public television and cable television. "There was strong opinion in favour of franchise stations for universities and public bodies. The universal desire articulated was that many more channels should be commissioned as soon as possible to permit specialised programmes, and a choice for the viewers. In a vast country like India, it is impossible to do justice with one or two channels and this should be remedied with utmost rapidity."

Sarkaria Commission

The issue of autonomy of AIR and Doordarshan also came up before the Sarkaria Commission on the Centre-State relations. These systems fall within the scope of the words "wireless, broadcasting and other like forms of communication" in Entry 31 of the Union List in the Seventh Schedule to the Constitution. The legislative and executive powers with respect to these subjects vest exclusively in the Union and both the systems are controlled and owned by the Union.

The Sarkaria Commission said in its report that most state governments had not proposed any change in the existing constitutional arrangements, though some of them had suggested that broadcasting should be transferred to the State List. The general tenor of replies from the intelligentsia was that the two systems must be run in such a way that they have a substantial autonomy in the type of information or entertainment disseminated. They also desired that direct interference, in either the content or the quality of dissemination, should be minimised. The Commission observed that it is implied therefore that there is too much interference from the bureaucratic system at present.

It is alleged that the states, particularly those governed by parties other than the one ruling at the centre, do not get reasonable access to these media. While large number of states have not questioned the placement of broadcasting in the Union List, there is a general complaint of over-centralisation of both these systems which has led to the denial to some states, of the legitimate use of these media for putting across their views to the public. One state government suggested that a law be made or the present law be amended to enable the state governments, wherever feasible, to set up their broadcasting stations subject to such conditions or restrictions as necessary in the national interest. Another state government has suggested a special channel in the existing systems to be placed at the disposal of the states so that the listeners of radio and viewers of television may have a choice and come to their own conclusions. Two state governments have even urged autonomy for AIR and Doordarshan.

The Sarkaria Commission pointed out that the control over frequencies for broadcast is exercised by the International Telecommunications Union. There is no criticism on the working of the international agreements in replies received by the commission. "What the states seek is control over the message or the entertainment disseminated by the system and freedom to air their views through the system."

The Sakaria Commission further argues that in a country where a substantial part of the citizenry is illiterate or semi-literate and the population, particularly in the rural areas is not very mobile and have few opportunities to get information of men and affairs in the other parts of the country, the radio and TV are powerful media for influencing thinking attitudes and options of the citizenry. Hence, every political party seeks to have access to the media. In the more educated and enlightened countries with several systems of mass communication to which people have access, the citizen has some means of comparing notes and differentiating between propaganda and fact. In this country where parochialism, chauvinism, casteism and communalism are pervasive and are actively made use of by powerful groups, if uncontrolled use of these media is allowed, it may promote centrifugal tendencies endangering the unity and integrity of the nation.

The Sakaria Commission agreed with the views of the Verghese Working Group that "the propagation of a national approach to India's problems creating in every citizen an interest in the affairs, achievements and culture of other regions, and helping them to develop a national consensus on issues which concern the country as a whole is of such supreme importance that any structure which inhibits this cannot be accepted." The Commission observed that the message of unity and integrity, and the basic cultural links of the various parts of the country, has to be carried to all, especially to the backward areas. From a purely economic angle, if other reasons are not conclusive, a devolution to the states to have their own broadcasting and control will help largely the richer states only. The poorer states will not have the resources to avail of the freedom and their areas will continue to develop without any understanding of the basic unity, further strengthening centrifugal forces. If autonomous state level broadcasting corporations are set up, a coordinated approach to many inter-state linkages will become far more difficult. The telecommunication and space facilities which are vital for radio and television networks are also under the control of the Union. "For all these reasons and particularly the need to control centrifugal tendencies we cannot support the demand for either a concurrent or an exclusive power to the states with respect to broadcasting," the Commission concluded.

The Sakaria Commission also rejected the demand for autonomy of these media. After considering the pleas of the states, intellectuals, and suggestions of the Verghese Working Group the Commission observed, "We have given careful consideration to these suggestions. These powerful media have to be used in our country in the public interest to further the cause of development with social justice and strengthen the impulses of modernisation. These audiovisual media are for educating the people. Their immense potential should be exploited to foster national unity and integrity and to fight effectively fissiparous tendencies. Keeping in view these objectives and their enormous potential for making India a strong modern nation (or harming it, if improperly used), we are of the view that there can be no total autonomy for such powerful media. They must continue to be under the control of the Union government which will be responsible for their proper functioning to the Parliament. We have no hesitation in saying that, till national integrity and unity become more firmly rooted than what is obtaining today and the pulls of regionalism, parochialism, casteism and communalism are substantially reduced, it will be premature to consider the grant to uncontrolled functional freedom to these powerful media. We do recognise the need for reasonable decentralisation and freedom in the day-to-day operations of these media in a vast country like ours, so rich in diversity. To play an effective role these systems must, in their working constantly strive for a harmonious adjustment between the imperatives of national interest and the varied needs and aspirations of the states and their inhabitants."

The Sakaria Commission expressed satisfaction over AIR code and ground rules for political broadcasts. It suggested that all broadcasting stations should have their own programme advisory committees and state governments should be consulted while appointing the non-official members and the chairman. The Commission expressed satisfaction over the fact that in these committees non-official members predominate and a quorum requires at least one-third of the non-official members to be present. However, it said, "But there will be an advantage if a non-political competent is made chairman and the station director is made deputy chairman of these committees."

Regarding complaints from states, the Commission recommended that if any state had any serious complaints about the use of the media, an approach to the Inter-Governmental Council, (a new body suggested by the Sarkaria Commission) would be the solution.

The Prasar Bharati Act

During the 1989 Lok Sabha election the autonomy of electronic media became a major issue. The Indian National Congress (Indira) under the leadership of Rajiv Gandhi said in its manifesto that the two media would remain under the control of the government but for functional autonomy and better profession standards. All India

Radio and Doordarshan would be converted into corporations. The National Front manifesto promised that, "One of the first acts of the National Front government will be to liberate the electronic media from the governmental stranglehold and convert them into autonomous corporations."

The left front almost ignored the issue and the Communist Party of India (Marxist) did not include it among the 16-point programme of demands in the manifesto. However, the Bhartiya Janata Party manifesto promised to "Revive the Prasar Bharati Bill of 1979, which sought to convert AIR and Doordarshan into an autonomous corporation, sui generis. The Corporation would have greater autonomy than that enjoyed by the BBC today." It further promised to "Implement the P. C. Joshi Report on TV software to improve the quality of the TV programmes."

As soon as the new government came to power with the Janata Dal leader V. P. Singh as the prime minister in its first session of the Parliament, the Prasar Bharati Bill 1989 was introduced. The Bill was put to the nation for a debate and the Indian Institute of Mass Communication organised seminars in various parts of the country in which people of all shades of opinion were being invited to express their opinion on the Bill.

Professionals outside these media welcomed the move and felt that it was only the first step towards full autonomy and therefore should have been welcomed. Many felt that autonomy may emerge finally just as eyewash and some even feared that the government would be free to do whatever it would like to do but would enjoy freedom from responsibility under the cover of so called autonomy.

B. G. Verghese, who was chairman of the working group on autonomy of Akashvani and Doordarshan which was appointed in 1977 was of the opinion that the Prasar Bharati Bill 1989 was better than the Prasar Bharati Bill 1979 as in this Bill the procedure of the selection and appointments was relatively more independent of the government.

The main complaint was that the proposed corporation would not have financial autonomy and had to look at the Ministry of

Information and Broadcasting for the purpose and the one who controlled the purse also controlled the strings.

The Bill did ignore the News and Current Affairs Wing completely and it was criticised on this account as this department is the real bone of contention. Many professionals within the organisations felt that the situation in the news rooms did not change in V. P. Singh's regime and some even complaint that the government interference had increased.

It had been observed that when a political party was in power it wanted to continue the government control over the electronic media, and when it went out of power it wanted autonomy for radio and television. Finally the Prasar Bharati Bill, with amendments for scope of additional channels and possibilities for partial privatisation of broadcasting, was passed by the Parliament and became Act no. 25 of 1990 on September 12, 1990. However, it was not implemented by the successive governments even at the beginning of 1997. The possible impact of international satellite broadcasting and a Supreme Court judgement (February 1995) that airwaves are not monopoly of the Union Government but "public property" created new issues on the subject. A subcommittee of members of Parliament with Mr. Ram Vilas Paswan looked into the media policy and prepared a working paper.

Paswan Committee

The working paper on national media policy prepared by the subcommittee of the consultative committee of members of Parliament attached to the Ministry of Information and Broadcasting with Mr. Ram Vilas Paswan as its chairman finalised its report on March 29, 1996. The Paswan Committee recommended that the broadcasting should observe a greater degree of responsibility and sensitivity to the Indian culture and ethos and cater to the development requirement of the country. It should achieve an Indian personality in telecasting / broadcasting. It recommended that there should be an independent and autonomous regulatory body to oversee both public and private telecasting / broadcasting but no recourse should be taken by the government to dilute the provisions of the Prasar Bharati Act, 1990.

It recommended that adequate care should be taken to enable the setting up of non-commercial broadcasting stations to be run by universities, educational institutions, panchayats / local bodies, state governments, etc. Direct or indirect foreign equity participation in companies entering the field of private broadcasting should not be permitted.

Paswan Committee recommended that appropriate provisions must be made to ensure that the control of private broadcasting did not fall in the hands of companies having major stake in the print medium or vice versa. Cross-media ownership restrictions must, therefore, be considered. The foreign satellite channels must have been brought within the ambit of the regulatory body in order to make them amenable to the Indian laws.

Sengupta Committee

Another experts' panel was constituted to look into the issues with Mr. N. K. Sengupta as its chairman. The Sengupta Committee on Prasar Bharati submitted its report on August 1996 and suggested a creation of Radio and Television Authority of India, an independent body which was not part of the Prasar Bharati. The Prasar Bharati being one of the many players in the Indian broadcasting arena, would also be overseen by the authority as far as complaints function were concerned.

The authority would perform the following functions: (i) Licensing of (a) satellite uplinking, (b) terrestrial analog transmission of radio and television, (c) terrestrial digital transmission of radio and television, and (d) multiplex providers. (ii) Prescribing programming obligations and programming standards to ensure quality and diversity. (iii) Making arrangements for ascertaining and monitoring public opinion about the programmes and services and ascertaining the needs, interests and tastes of members of the public. (iv) Determining the maximum limit for the quantum of advertising content so that the advertisements were not obtrusive or jarring. (v) Receive complaints of violation of norms of decency and of the programming and advertising codes and adjudicate them after hearing the parties concerned.

Indian Scene: Prasar Bharati

The Sengupta Committee also recommended extending of uplinking facilities to domestic and foreign satellite channels as it would be beneficial to the nation economically and bringing them under the purview of the Indian laws. While granting licences the Radio and Television Authority of India would compel them to adhere to the prevalent programming and advertising codes. Sengupta Committee pointed out that the 1885 Telegraph Act aimed at checking the misuse of airwaves had become outdated and required to be recasted. Before providing uplinking from the Indian soil to a foreign party, the credentials of the party would have to be scrutinised.

The Sengupta committee recommended some changes in the Prasar Bharati Act to accommodate these provisions and also suggested, "It is necessary to split Akashvani and Doordarshan into two completely separate wings under the corporate umbrella of the Prasar Bharati Corporation with close coordination in areas clearly defined and delineated by the corporation. For all practical purposes they should operate as separate entities. Steps should be taken to demarcate the hardware and assets between Akashvani and Doordarshan and bifurcate the personnel across all disciplines."

A draft broadcasting bill was discussed by the Indian cabinet on January 27, 1997 and was given to a cabinet subcommittee with a brief to examine its legal and constitutional aspects and give its opinion within a fortnight. The comprehensive bill was intended to bring some order to the chaotic electronic media scene by prescribing norms for uplinking, cable services and digital Direct-to-Home (DTH) transmission. An independent authority was proposed to be set up to regulate the use of airwaves by broadcasting companies in the light of the Supreme Court judgement that airwaves are public property and should be freed from state monopoly. The draft bill restricts granting of uplinking facility to domestic private TV companies. The Bill proposed cross-media restrictions to prevent monopolies and restrict foreign equity to 49 per cent. The Bill also provided for an autonomous broadcasting corporation to run All India Radio and Doordarshan. Cable regulations were also being fine-tuned through the provision of licensing of cable operators.

On 22 July 1997, the government in a Gazette notification appointed 15th September 1997 as the day on which the Prasar Bharati Act, 1990 took effect. However, the committee to select the Prasar Bharati Board members could not be appointed as the election for the post of vice-president was under way. On 29 October 1997, some changes were made in the Prasar Bharati Act through an Ordinance and on 23 November 1997, the Prasar Bharati Board with Chairman Nikhil Chakravartty, a senior journalist, took control of the All India Radio and Doordarshan.

On 6 May 1998, the Prasar Bharati Ordinance of 1997 lapsed but the Board continued. On 27 June 1998, the Chairman of Prasar Bharati Nikhil Chakravartty (85) died. On 31 July 1998, the Lok Sabha passed the Prasar Bharati (Amendment) Bill 1998 to restore all the provisions of the 1990 Act. On 29 August 1998, an Ordinance was promulgated to give effect to the Bill passed by the Lok Sabha. Member (executive) S. S. Gill, a former secretary, Information Broadcasting, became ineligible to hold the post as he was over age. There were several officiating member executive, all members of bureaucracy, until the appointment of a regular one, also a member of Indian Administrative Service, in 2002.

All India Radio

When India attained Independence in 1947, All India Radio (AIR) had a network of six stations located at Delhi, Bombay, Calcutta, Madras, Lucknow and Tiruchirapalli. There were only 18 transmitters – six on the medium wave and the remaining on short wave. The coverage was 2.5 per cent of the area and just 11 per cent of the population. AIR today has a network of 208 broadcasting centres with 150 medium frequency (MW), 48 high frequency (SW) and 128 FM transmitters. The coverage is 89.51 per cent of the area, serving 98.82 per cent of the people in the largest democracy of the world. AIR uses 24 languages and 146 dialects in home services. In external services, it broadcasts in 26 languages; 16 national and 10 foreign languages. As against a mere 2,75,000 receiving sets at the time of Independence, now there are about 111 million estimated radio sets in about 105 million homes in the country. There are in all 198 broadcasting centres, including 74 local radio stations.

AIR thus has a three-tier system of broadcasting, namely, national, regional and local.

The national channel of All India Radio started functioning on May 18, 1988. It caters to the information, education and entertainment needs of the people, through its transmitters at Nagpur, Mogra and Delhi, beaming from dusk to dawn. It transmits centrally originated news bulletins in Hindi and English, plays sports, music, newsreel, spoken word and other topical programmes, to nearly 76 per cent of the country's population fully reflecting the broad spectrum of national life.

The regional stations in different states form the middle tier of the broadcasting including the North-Eastern Service at Shillong which disseminates the vibrant and radiant cultural heritage of the North-Eastern region of the country.

Local radio is comparatively a new concept of broadcasting in India. Each of the station serving a small area provides utility services and reaches right into the heart of the community, which uses the microphone to reflect and enrich its life.

What distinguishes the local radio from the regional network is its down to earth, intimate and uninhibited approach. The programmes of the local radio are area specific. They are flexible and spontaneous enough to enable the station to function as the mouthpiece of the local community.

FM service is available at All India Radio stations in Delhi, Mumbai, Calcutta, Madras and Panaji and time slots are also allotted to private parties for broadcasting programmes. The content is mainly popular Indian and Western music, compered in a vivacious and contemporary style and therefore highly popular with the urban youth.

External Services

The external services of All India Radio acts as a bridge between India and the world. The External Services Division (ESD) broadcasts programmes for 69 hrs. and 45 mts. every day in 26 languages – General Overseas Service in English and 16 other foreign languages (Arabic, Baluchi, Burmese (Myanmar), Chinese (Pu-Tonghua), Dari, English (GOS), French, Indonesian, Nepali, Persian, Pushtu, Russian, Sinhala, Swahili, Thai and Tibetan) and in 8 Indian languages (Bengali, Gujarati, Hindi, Punjabi, Sindhi, Tamil, Telgu and Urdu) for our listeners in different parts of the globe.

The external broadcasts project the Indian point of view on world affairs and acquaint the overseas listeners with the developments in India along with the information on the myriad facts of Indian life, thought, culture, tradition and heritage.

The target areas of ESD span almost all the countries and include the areas of West, North, East and South Asia, North West and East Africa, Australia, New Zealand, United Kingdom and Europe and the Indian subcontinent.

In addition to foreign languages, ESD also broadcast in Indian languages for Indian people settled in different parts of the globe. The services in Hindi, Tamil, Telugu and Gujarati are directed to Indians overseas, while those in Urdu, Bengali, Punjabi and Sindhi are meant for the listeners in the subcontinent's adjoining countries.

The broadcasts follow a composite pattern and generally comprise news bulletins, commentary on current events and a review of the Indian press. Besides this, newsreels, magazine programmes on sports and literature, talks and discussions on socioeconomic, political, historical and cultural subjects, features on developmental activities, important events and institutions, classical, folk and modern music of the India's diverse regions form a major part of the total programme output.

The External Service Division brings out independently a monthly programme journal entitled *India Calling*, providing advance information of the programme broadcast in external service. The journal supplied free of cost to overseas listeners also carries selected excerpts from the talks, letters from listeners and other information.

Doordarshan

Doordarshan, the national television service of India, devoted to public service broadcasting is one of the largest terrestrial networks in the world. The flagship of Doordarshan – DD-1 – operates through a network of 1308 terrestrial transmitters of varying powers reaching over 89 per cent of the population. There are 107 additional transmitters giving terrestrial support to other channels. Doordarshan uses a large number of transponders on the Insat and other satellites to network its terrestrial transmitters and also to provide additional satellite channels. Doordarshan has established programme production facilities in 56 cities across the country. Doordarshan programmes are watched in India by 362 million viewers in their homes. Doordarshan earned around Rs.4 billion during the last financial year through commercial advertisements.

The first telecast on Doordarshan originated from a makeshift studio at Akashvani Bhavan, New Delhi on 15th September, 1959. A transmitter of 500 W power carried the signals to areas within a radius of 25 km from Delhi. There were only 21 community TV sets. All India Radio provided the engineering and the programme professionals.

A regular one hour service with a daily news bulletin was started in 1965. Television went to a second city, Mumbai, only in 1972, and by 1975 Calcutta, Chennai, Srinagar, Amritsar and Lucknow also had television stations.

The first experiment with satellite technology in India, known as the Satellite Instructional Television Experiment (SITE), was conducted in 1975-76. This was, incidentally, the first attempt anywhere in the world of using the sophisticated technology of satellite broadcasting for social education. It brought TV to 2,400 villages in the most inaccessible and the least developed areas for one year.

The year 1982 witnessed the introduction of a regular satellite link between Delhi and other transmitters, the starting of the national programme and also heralded the era of colour television in the country. The Asian Games held in Delhi that year acted as the major impetus for bringing out these changes. After 1982, television facilities have been rapidly expanding and during certain periods the country got an additional transmitter everyday. In the decade 1981-90 the number of transmitters increased from 19 to 519.

Doordarshan has tried to establish a three-tier primary programme service—national, regional and local. In the national programmes the focus is on events and issues of interest to the whole nation. The regional programmes originating from the state capitals and relayed by all transmitters in the respective states have programmes of interest at the state level, in the language and idiom of that particular region. The local programmes are area specific and cover local issues featuring local people. At each tier there is a mix of information, education and entertainment programmes.

On the national network, news bulletins are telecast in Hindi and English on the hour. All major TV stations telecast news bulletins in the evenings in their respective languages where regional events are covered in greater detail. Some stations telecast regional news in Urdu also. Doordarshan has a number of programmes on current affairs where topical issues are discussed in-depth, bringing out various viewpoints. Information programmes also include telecasts on agriculture, rural development, health, family welfare, consumer's rights, environment, etc. There are programmes specially targeted to women, children and youth.

Doordarshan brings to its viewers all the major national and international sports and games through live telecasts. There are other programmes on sports, including interviews with eminent sports persons, sports education, etc.

The educational programmes range from basic health education for the not-so-well-educated to the higher education programmes for university students.

In 1961, India's first school television service was commissioned at Delhi for the instititutions run by the Delhi municipal corporation. ETV programmes for school children are telecast from a number of regional *kendras* in different languages covering both formal and informal education.

To put quality education within the reach of students residing even in small villages and towns, the University Grants Commission, the authority responsible for university education in India, has 'a countrywide classroom' telecast on the national network. Besides this, syllabus-based programmes for the students of Indira Gandhi National Open University are also being telecast on the national network

There is a wide range of entertainment programmes on Doordarshan including serials, sitcoms, soaps and game shows. Feature films and programmes based on excerpts from feature films are also telecast on the national network and also from regional *kendras*.

In 1984 a second channel was added in Delhi to provide alternative viewing to the heterogeneous metropolitan population. Later it was extended to viewers in Mumbai, Kolkata and Chennai. In 1993, these four terrestrial transmitters were linked through satellite to provide an exclusive entertainment channel for the urban audience. This service, DD-2 Metro Entertainment Channel, was available terrestrially in 56 cities and could be received through dish antennas or through cable operators. It was closed before the 2004 General Elections to make way for a 24-hour news channel. Doordarshan also has a sports channel.

To provide programmes in the major regional languages Doordarshan has 11 regional language satellite channels. Doordarshan-India, the international channel, is in operation since 1995 and reaches about 50 countries in Asia, Africa and Europe, USA and Canada. In 2004 its 40-channel DTH platform DD Direct Plus has been launched carrying several free-to-air private channels along with 14 Doordarshan and three educational channels. Doordarshan also has Internet presence at www.ddindia.com and www.ddinews.com.

3

Private and Foreign Channels

Today more than a hundred television channels are available in India. However, until about the end of 1980s, like most of the world the television was not in private hands in India. In the news production area there were some stringers of Doordarshan. That was the only private enterprise. They were given assignments to cover news and later they were also involved in current affairs programmes and documentaries. Some of them opened their own private production houses which initially catered to Doordarshan and later when foreign satellite channels needed Indian programmes they produced programmes for them. The Indian news agency, Press Trust of India (PTI) was the first news agency in the world to start a television wing in 1983, but this did not develop much and soon became insignificant. A similar attempt by its rival the United News of India had similar fate. But there were success stories also.

NDTV

New Delhi Television (NDTV) is one such Indian company. In 1988, NDTV started producing *"The World This Week"*, a weekly newsmagazine covering world news and entertainment for Doordarshan. In 1989, NDTV produced India's first live televised coverage of the country's general elections results with analysis. In 1995, NDTV became the country's first private producer of the national news with the telecast of *"Tonight"* on Doordarshan. In 1998, NDTV set up the STAR News Channel, India's first 24-hour news channel as part of Rupert Murdoch's STAR Network.

NDTV now has 19 offices and studios across the country with modern and sophisticated production facilities. In 1999, NDTV launched its website www.ndtv.com. With live video streaming of NDTV's news bulletins, ndtv.com claimed of average 55,000 hits a day within a month of its launch. In the year 2000, NDTV expanded into regional news with an half-hour daily Tamil news programme which airs every evening on Vijay TV, a channel owned by STAR network. On 31 March 2003, the contract for producing content for the Star News Channel ended and in April 2003, NDTV launched its own news channels in English and Hindi. While NDTV World runs Hindi news channel, the English news channel is under NDTV Ltd. Both have a distribution tie-up with One Alliance, a joint venture of Sony Entertainment Television and Discovery Networks that already distributes Sony, Set MAX, Discovery, Animal Planet, HBO, AXN and CNBC India.

Besides providing national news, the two channels can give region or city-specific news to its viewers in the local language. This is possible by the IRDs (integrated receiver decoders) NDTV has got from Irideto. "With the help of these addressable boxes we will introduce the concept of 'break away' news broadcasting for the first time in India. The concept is quite popular among the news networks in the US," said Prannoy Roy, president NDTV while announcing the new channels.

TV Today Network

Another important private news producer which first worked for Doordarshan already has an independent 24-hour news channel of its own, "Aaj Tak". It is part of India Today Group, which had its foray into the electronic medium was marked by the incorporation of TV Today Network (TVTN) in 1988. The success story of TVTN started with the launch of the first video newsmagazine titled *Newstrack*. TV Today Network made for Doordarshan the first privately produced Hindi news and current affairs programme, "Aaj Tak" in the year 1995. It was aired at 10.00 pm daily on Doordarshan Metro channel first on 17 July 1995. On January 14, 1999 'Aaj Tak' became the only news and current affairs programme by a private producer on Doordarshan to cross the 1000 episode mark.

Another programme 'Subah Aaj Tak' was launched on 10 August 1998 for telecast at 7.15 a.m., Monday to Friday on DD Metro. This feel-good show of 45 minutes covered a wide range of issues like business, politics, sports, entertainment and human interest. Subah Aaj Tak also featured interviews and studio discussions

Using the brand value of its programme "Aaj Tak" on Doordarshan, the India Today group launched a 24-hour Hindi news and current affairs channel Aaj Tak on 31 December 2000. It claims to have a team of over 300 professionals devoted to news gathering and production across the country with an additional network of stringers. It also claims to have state-of-the-art technology that includes lightweight cameras, on-line editing, newsroom automation and 3D-graphics. It has also launched an English language news channel 'Headlines Today' in April 2003.

ANI

Asian News International (ANI) grew out of an Indian documentary film production company, Asian Films launched in the year 1975 by Prem Prakesh, a cameraman with business and news sense. He initially served Visnews and after it was taken over by the Reuters. He and ANI worked for Reuters TV. Today ANI is present all over South Asia. It has over fifty camera crews and journalists covering Afghanistan, Pakistan, India, Nepal, Bangladesh, Sri Lanka, Bhutan, Maldives and Burma. When it comes to covering South Asia, ANI goes across the globe to bring news of and from South Asia wherever it takes place. ANI's TV subscribers everyday receive twelve to fifteen edited, ready to use video news clips, each of ninety to one hundred and twenty seconds with shot list, commentary and natural quality audio. ANI also has a text service – ANI Wire – that delivers nearly 20,000 words a day covering South Asia. The service is delivered via e-mail or the traditional methods of teleprinters now turned online.

ANI also has a Multimedia News Service. Web Enabled Multimedia News Content (WEMNC) consists of: video clips of about one minute each which cover the day's major happenings in India and the Indian subcontinent, audio bytes of major news events,

Private and Foreign Channels

text news items covering important events with a focus on South Asia. This content offering is ideally suited for horizontal and vertical portals, corporate websites, niche websites, websites of newspapers and magazines, TV channel websites, and other websites wanting to provide their visitors, a rich multimedia experience in news and general interest features.

Gulf War and After

In the early 1990s, perhaps the first foreign satellite channel which was seen with interest in India was CNN during the Gulf War. The CNN coverage was supplied free to Doordarshan as a propaganda measure by the USIS, but those with resources and some five star hotels put dishes to watch the original CNN fare. Star TV followed. But the foreign programmes did not have a long term interest among Indian audiences. Zee TV came up using the same satellite as Star and Doordarshan launched DD Metro to counter it effectively. The success of Zee led to the establishment of a large number of other Indian channels and many foreign channels also beamed their signals to India. Prior to this satellite invasion the Indian viewers had to make do with DD's chosen fare which was non-commercial in nature, directed towards only education and socioeconomic development. Entertainment programmes were few and far between and were mainly based on the Indian film industry and some were imported. When a family soap 'Hum Log' (1984) and mythological dramas: like 'Ramayan' (1987-88) and 'Mahabharat' (1988-89) were broadcasted on Doordarshan, millions of viewers stayed glued to their sets. This sentiment is still exploited by large number of channels, some exclusively devoted to religious fare.

The Indian viewers were exposed to more than 50 channels by 1996. Here is some information that may give an idea of current status and trends:

STAR

STAR TV: A wholly-cwned subsidiary of the Rupert Murdoch's News Corporation was launched in 1991 with five television channels. Addressing the News Corporation shareholders on 9

October 2002 Murdoch said, " In Asia, STAR was profitable for the second half of the fiscal year, a first-time achievement for our pan-Asian television platform. STAR Plus in India was broadcasting an average of 19 of the top 20 cable shows every week by the end of fiscal 2002 and STAR is now making significant inroads in Southern China and Taiwan. We expect STAR to be modestly profitable for the current fiscal year, a sign that our faith in this platform is about to be rewarded."

STAR broadcasts 40 services in eight languages and offers a comprehensive choice of entertainment, sports, movies, music, news and documentaries. It claims to reach more than 300 million viewers in 53 countries across Asia.

Covering movies, entertainment, sports, music, documentary and news, each brand carries its own distinctive content and brand personality while collectively providing audiences a range of choice. The launch of India's first 24-hour commercial FM radio network and the digitisation of cable systems in Taiwan are other significant landmarks at STAR.

Leveraging the success of its television brands, STAR is aggressively creating the next generation of media connectivity in Asia: from the production and distribution of television channels to the development of enhanced television, from film production to radio content, from investing in cable infrastructure to partnerships with Internet companies. STAR has evolved into Asia's leading multi-platform content and services provider, setting the pace for Asian media.

TV joint ventures of STAR are: Phoenix Satellite Television Holdings Ltd., Channel [V] Music Networks Ltd., Partnership ESPN, STAR Sports, VIVA Cinema. Thus STAR has the following TV channels of different categories:

General Entertainment – Phoenix Chinese Channel, Phoenix CNE Channel, Phoenix North America Chinese Channel, STAR Chinese Channel, STAR World and STAR Plus.

Movies – STAR Movies (India), STAR Movies (Middle East), STAR Movies (Southeast Asia), STAR Movies (Taiwan), STAR Mandarin Movies, STAR Gold, Phoenix Movies, VIVA Cinema

Private and Foreign Channels

Music – Channel [V] Greater China, Channel [V] India, Channel [V] International, Channel [V] Australia, Channel [V] Thailand, Channel [V] Korea.

Sports – STAR Sports (Asia), STAR Sports (Taiwan), STAR Sports (India), ESPN (Asia), ESPN (Taiwan), ESPN (India), ESPN (Philippines)

News & Documentaries – STAR News, Phoenix InfoNews Channel, Sky News, Fox News, National Geographic Channel is also distributed by STAR.

Its websites are: STAR – www.startv.com; Channel [V]– www.channelv.com, www.vindia.com ESPN STAR Sports– www.espnstar.com, Phoenix Satellite Television\ www.phoenixtv.com.

The film properties include: Fortune STAR Pictures and Media Assets while cable partnerships are: Hathway Cable and Koos Cable. STAR has Internet partnerships with: baazee.com; explocity.com; indiaproperties.com; indya.com; netease.com; sinobit.com

ESPN STAR Sports is a 50:50 joint venture formed in November 1996 between two of the world's leading cable and satellite broadcasters, ESPN, Inc. and STAR. The reach is over 79 million households for ESPN and 56 million households for STAR Sports (as of August, 2001). Together, ESPN STAR Sports' nine channels (ESPN Asia, ESPN India, ESPN Taiwan, ESPN Philippines, MBC-ESPN, STAR Sports Asia, STAR Sports India, STAR Sports Taiwan and STAR Sports Southeast Asia) bring the world's premier live sports and leading regional events to viewers 24 hours a day. The ESPN STAR Sports Event Management Group, formerly Sports Corporation, stages, manages and promotes sporting events around Asia. ESPN STAR Sports combines the strength and resources of its ultimate parent companies, Walt Disney (ESPN, Inc.) and News Corporation Limited (STAR), two of the world's leading cable and satellite broadcasters. All of the ESPN STAR Sports' programming emanates from its company headquarters in Singapore, a 60,000 square-foot, state-of-the-art production facility. ESPN STAR Sports in all has over 500 experienced and professional staff in Singapore,

India, Taiwan, Beijing and Hong Kong. ESPN STAR Sports has long-term agreements with sports associations such as the National Basketball Association, UEFA, English Premier League, US Golf Association, Wimbledon, US Tennis Association, Major League Baseball, the English and Wales Cricket Board, the West Indies Cricket Board, the Asian Football Confederation, the Asian PGA, the International Table Tennis Federation, and the FIQ-WTBA Asian Zone.

ESPN

Back in 1978, ESPN began bringing the world's most exciting live sports action to die-hard sports fans in the US. Today, its proven mix of international and regional programming, customised specifically for local viewing audiences, has made ESPN the worldwide leader in sports. ESPN's phenomenal success, however, is not just due to its non-stop, action-packed programming. ESPN's combination of innovative production techniques and state-of-the-art equipment provides each of its predominantly younger, active life-style viewers with the best seats in the house – all from the comfort and privacy of their own homes. And sitting right there with them is ESPN's first-string team of knowledgeable and insightful commentators, sharing the passion and excitement of the fast paced, competitive action that is destined to make tomorrow's sporting headlines. Just as it has done for the past twenty years, ESPN continues to offer serious sports fans the inside track on the world's most exciting sports.

Today ESPN, Inc. is 80 per cent owned by ABC, Inc. which is an indirect subsidiary of 'The Walt Disney Company'. The Hearst Corporation holds the remaining 20 per cent interest in ESPN.

ESPN, Inc. includes the following entities: The flagship sports television network since its September 1979 launch, ESPN now reaches more than 76 million homes (and 77 per cent of American TV households). Reaching more than 64 million homes, ESPN2 was launched on October 1, 1993. It is anchored by the live event programming and the 2-night sport-specific news shows. A 24-hour sports news network launched on November 1, 1996,

Private and Foreign Channels

ESPNEWS features continuous scores, highlights, analysis, interviews, live press conferences and breaking news. ESPN Classic presents the greatest games, stories, heroes and memories in the history of sports, with current perspective and commentary. Launched in May, 1995 and now in 20 million homes, it was acquired by ESPN, Inc. in October 1997. In virtually every country with its networks and syndicated programmes, ESPN International wholly owns or has equity interest in 20 networks and distributes US and international sports programmes to more than 150 million households in 21 languages.

Launched in March 1998, the biweekly ESPN The Magazine utilises ESPN's sports news resources combined with timely, in-depth commentary and opinion. Offering round-the-clock programming to more than 650 affiliates, ESPN Radio includes The NBA on ESPN Radio, Major League Baseball on ESPN Radio and a wide variety of sports talk and news. The most popular sports site on the Web, ESPN.com (part of GO Network) delivers the latest sports stories, statistics and scores, along with interactive features, real-time game coverage, live chats, multimedia and exclusive, in-depth analysis from ESPN experts.

ESPN Enterprises develops new products and businesses using the ESPN brand and assets, such as pay subscription programming, digital games, home video, compact discs (platinum-selling Jock Jams I, II and III), ESPN Zone (themed dining and entertainment), the ESPN Club at Disney's BoardWalk in Orlando, ESPN – The Store, apparel, retail distribution and more. ESPN Zone, a sports-themed dining and entertainment complex, opened in Baltimore on July 11, 1998. Developed by Disney Regional Entertainment in conjunction with ESPN, nationwide expansion was planned with Zones in Chicago and New York opened in 2002.

Channel [V]

Initially M-TV was part of the STAR fare like Zee in India but then it was replaced by Channel (V). The channel features the latest chart-topping music videos, popstars and trends, popular VJs and youth culture. Locally-produced programming, packaging and local presenters ensure that Channel [V] reflects the humour, tastes and attitudes of its huge youth audience. Channel [V] is available in the following markets: Hong Kong India, Indonesia, Mainland China Malaysia, Middle East, Philippines, South Korea, Taiwan and Thailand.

MTV

Music Television launched in August 1981 is the world's most-watched television network, reaching 384 million households around the globe. MTV is an advertiser-supported, basic cable service of MTV Network targeted at the age group of 12-34 years-olds. MTV is a multidimensional youth brand that extends across virtually all media.

MTV Networks owns and operates many of the most popular basic cable television programming services, including MTV. It also owns Nickelodeon, which is seen in over 471 million households worldwide via localised channels, branded blocks, and individual programmes; VH1 reaching over 100 million households around the world; and The New TNN, which serves 84 million homes in North America with the tops in pop culture programming. Other services include MTV2, Nick at Nite, TV Land, CMT, and The Digital Suite from MTV Networks. MTVN is also involved in a variety of entertainment businesses that extend its brands, including films, books, online, and consumer products.

The Suite from MTV Networks is the company's offering in the digital universe. The Suite is made up of nine music and kids programming services: MTV 2, which serves as the flagship channel for the music services; MTV "X," which offers hard rock, active rock and heavy metal; MTV "S," featuring Spanish-language music videos for US Spanish-speaking young adults; VH1 Classic, which relives the renaissance of rock music from the '60s and '70s; VH1 Soul, offering classic R&B and adult urban music; and VH1 Country, featuring music from artists defining today's country music; Noggin, the first-ever educational channel for kids; Nickelodeon GAS, a game and sports channel; and Nick Too, a time-shifted feeds of the original Nickelodeon channel.

Internationally, MTV reaches more than 340 million households in 140 countries via 31 localised TV channels and 17 websites. Following MTV's "think globally, act locally" philosophy, each international channel—MTV Asia, MTV Australia, MTV Brasil, MTV Europe, MTV Latin America, and MTV Russia—adheres to the overall style, programming philosophy, and integrity of the MTV trademark while promoting local cultural tastes and musical talent.

MTV Asia reaches over 124 million households in 21 territories. MTV Asia consists of three regional channels: MTV Mandarin, MTV Southeast Asia, and MTV India. Launched on April 21, 1995, Chinese-language MTV Mandarin serves up a playlist consisting of 60 per cent Mandarin music videos with the balance made up of international videos to viewers in China, Hong Kong, Taiwan, and Singapore. The English-language MTV Southeast Asia, launched May 5, 1995, can be seen throughout Asia, including Brunei, Hong Kong, Indonesia, Malaysia, Papua New Guinea, Singapore, Thailand, Vietnam, and the Philippines. MTV Southeast Asia offers a customised mix of music in Bahasa Indonesia, Bahasa Malaysia, Thai, and Tagalog, as well as popular international hits.

On October 28, 1996, MTV Southeast Asia was split into a third channel, MTV India, which is seen in Bangladesh, India, the Middle East, Nepal, Pakistan, and Sri Lanka. MTV India's programming consists of a mix of 70 per cent Indian film and pop music, with the balance made up of international music videos. All three 24-hour services are uplinked from headquarters in Singapore. Ending 2000 as its most successful year ever, MTV Networks International rang in the New Year with the launch of MTV Japan, a 24-hour, Japanese-language advertiser-supported music television channel and website. Distributed via cable and satellite platforms, MTV Japan replaced music channel Vibe, one of Japan's most widely distributed cable and satellite channels reaching 2.8 million households. MTV Japan features original Japanese programming targeting the age group 16 to 34. In addition to MTV Japan, MTV also launched a new 24-hour terrestrial MTV channel to 2 million households in the Philippines in January 2001. On July 1, 2001, MTV and Korea's leading media company 'On* Media' launched a new 24-hour, Korean-language music channel for the Korean audiences. The new 24-hour MTV Korea channel replaced the four-hour daily MTV programming on OnGameNet, another channel carried by the On* Media, and features original, locally produced content customised for the Koreans aged between 15-to-34.

Through a multi-year licensing agreement, MTV Australia launched on the Optus Vision cable platform on March 20, 1997, and will soon be available on Optus Vision's satellite service. MTV Brasil launched on October 20, 1990, and is currently seen in over 16 million households, 24 hours a day. The Portuguese-language network, hosted by the Brazilian VJs, features video music by the Brazilian and international artists. MTV Brasil is a joint venture of MTV Networks and Abril S.A.

MTV Latin America is a 24-hour Spanish language network that offers music programming for the age group 12-to-34 in approximately 11.5 million households in 21 territories in Latin America and selected US Hispanic markets. MTV Latin America, a wholly-owned venture of MTV Networks, was launched on October 1, 1993.

MTV Russia was launched on September 26, 1998, and reaches more than 18 million homes. The free, over-the-air service is available to households in Moscow, St. Petersburg, Omsk, Voronezh, Novosibirsk, and Ekaterinburg, among other cities. Through a multi-year licensing agreement with BIZ Enterprises, the launch of MTV Russia marked the first time a western television network which has been customised specifically for Russian youth. In January 2000, MTV Networks International acquired an equity position in MTV Russia.

Zee TV

Zee TV is watched daily by an average of 180 million viewers across the world and is the pioneering force in the cable and satellite revolution in India. ZEE TV's programming meets the prime time requirements of both the Eastern and Pacific Time Zones. Aimed at serving the needs of South Asians living abroad, the channel airs 24 hours a day and includes movies, dramas, children's programmes, talk shows and special interactive programmes involving social issues.

Programming highlights: General programming covers a wide area of interest: movies, sitcoms and game shows, children's programmes, regional and mythology, detective, suspense and horror, news, reports and discussions, cookery and health. ZEE TV's local programming is committed to delivering a cultural message to South Asians leaving abroad, with a powerful distribution system and global resource network. ZEE TV offers extensive coverage of cricket, the biggest craze in Asia. The channel's appeal consists of programmes from the Indian subcontinent in Hindi and other South Asian languages.

Incorporated in 1982, Zee Telefilms Ltd. (ZTL) has a market capitalisation of USD 2.8 billion as on November 8, 2000. It launched in 1992 Zee TV, India's first private Hindi satellite channel. Zee Network today has a bouquet of 14 satellite TV channels over the Indian subcontinent and enjoys a 220 million worldwide viewership. The footprint covering the entire Southeast Asia offers versatile content ranging from general entertainment, current affairs / business, regional languages (under the Alpha brand), movies (including the 24-hour, Zee MGM movie channel in joint venture with MGM) music and sports. Zee Network also hosts a kids channel (Nickelodeon from Viacom). Another one from the Zee Creative Studios would be the production of India's first feature film in animation. Zee satellite TV channels are also serving the Indian Diaspora in the USA (on Echostar platform), Europe (BSkyB/ SES-Astra), Southeast Asia, Africa, Australia and New Zealand.

Zee Education, set up in 1994 transformed into Zee Interactive Learning Systems (ZILS) in 1999 with an aim to provide technology-driven learning (e-learning) via strong network of creation and distribution of knowledge through Zed TV, zeelearn.com portal, ground learning centres and virtual classrooms. The eZee Retail Network distributes learning solutions directly to the consumer.

It has also succeeded in building the single largest cable distribution network in India, Siticable Network Pvt. Ltd. With a reach of over 5 million subscribers across 43 cities, Siti-Cable runs two local channels that cater to region-specific audiences. Keeping in line with its objective of information dissemination through technology, Zee Interactive Multi-media Ltd. is rolling out Hybrid Fibre Coaxial (HFC) broadband network in a number of Indian cities that envisages provisioning of broadband services in a phased manner. Zee TV has tied up with a leading infotech group to launch, a DTH satellite TV service in India that brings a number of private satellite TV broadcasters on to a common DTH service platform.

Asianet

Asianet Satellite Communications Ltd. is the largest cable network services company in the southern Indian state of Kerala. Started on 30 August 1993, Asianet Satellite Communications has today grown in size and reach. Its cable network services operate from over 40 centres spread throughout Kerala and touch over half a million homes and establishments. The Asianet cable network carries upto 70 channels. It includes eight exclusively-owned channels which are only cable-cast over Asianet network, namely Asianet Cable Vision (ACV, a news, events and movie channel), Jukebox and Medley (interactive video music channels), Swathi (audio music channel), CCC (cine cable channel) Rosebowl (digital infotainment channel), Gamestation (interactive gaming channel) and Jyothi (education channel).

Asianet's exclusive portal, keralaonline.com features latest news, reviews and updates on local events, neighbourhood information and topics of general interest, with dedicated channels for travel, health, matrimonials, chat, photo album, and music downloads. Asianet provides high quality CATV access. In keeping with worldwide developments towards convergence in video, voice and data technologies, Asianet is on the road to becoming a genuine provider of broadband network services.

Asianet Satellite Communications Ltd. is also an Internet Service Provider (ISP) in the state of Kerala. With a view to ensure high bandwidth availability, Asianet has set up its own International Satellite Gateways at Trivandrum and Cochin. Asianet Internet Service is already available in Trivandrum and Cochin. The company is also geared to implement an ambitious plan to create an

Information Highway by laying an optical fibre backbone that would provide statewide connectivity and also interlink the company's various local networks. Asianet's ISP operations would also help create a great deal of synergy for its CATV services. The ongoing upgradation of the network into a hybrid fibre coaxial one would enable the company to offer up to 500 channels in the near future and open up new vistas in the form of the Web TV and Interactive multimedia services. As an ISP, Asianet looks at being a user-friendly provider of Internet access, Web-services, e-commerce services, data and voice connectivity services. Asianet Global was launched on 6 August 2002.

BBC World

BBC World is the BBC's international news and information channel broadcasting 24 hours a day around the world from its base at BBC Television Centre in London. BBC World, under the original name of BBC World Service Television, was set up in 1991 to serve Asia and the Middle East. It rapidly expanded to Japan, Africa and Europe, and in 1996 to Latin America and the Carribean. Europe had earlier been served by a channel called BBC TV Europe, set up in 1987, largely comprising domestic entertainment programming from the BBC. This channel in turn evolved into BBC Prime, providing a 24-hour entertainment television programming service to the continental Europe. BBC World reaches over 200 million homes across 200 countries and territories. BBC World provides news, business and weather reports 24 hours a day, plus the best of the BBC's current affairs, documentary and lifestyle programming. BBC World provides dedicated local programming for the channel's substantial audiences in Europe and India; plus 60 hours per week of Japanese translation.

BBC World dedicated a 24-hour fully digital newsroom and studio located at London's BBC Television Centre. This is the world's first all digital 24-hour newsroom. The channel is marketed and distributed by BBC Worldwide, the commercial and international arm of the BBC.

BBC World is a commercial channel funded by advertising and subscription. BBC Worldwide commissions the channel from BBC News. A venture in Hindi launched in India in 1995 did not last long.

NBC

America's first broadcast network, NBC has evolved into a diverse, international media company. NBC has the exclusive rights to every Olympic Game through 2008. It owns and operates more than 13 stations, along with CNBC, a leading business-news network. In partnership with Microsoft, NBC operates MSNBC. NBC has recently acquired Telemundo, the second-largest Spanish-language broadcaster in the US.

An industry pioneer for seventy-five years, the National Broadcasting Company was founded in 1926 by General Electric, RCA, and Westinghouse. RCA became the sole owner of NBC in 1932. In 1986, RCA was purchased by General Electric, which today wholly owns and operates NBC. Starting off as a radio network in the 1920s, NBC evolved into a television broadcaster in the 1940s.

In addition to the NBC Television Network and the NBC Television Stations Division, the company owns CNBC, which is the global leader in business news, reaching 198 million homes worldwide. In April 2002, the NBC purchased Telemundo, the second-largest US Spanish-language television network. In partnership with Microsoft, the NBC operates MSNBC, which is a leading cable-news channel and the world's preeminent news site on the Internet. NBC's operations include additional investment and programming activities, including CNBC Europe and CNBC Asia; equity investments in Arts & Entertainment, the History Channel, ValueVision, Inc. (ShopNBC), Rainbow Media Holdings, Inc., and Rainbow Media Group; and a non-voting interest in Paxson Communications Corporation.

NBC Digital Media, part of the Business Development and Interactive Media group at NBC, is responsible for NBC's new media strategy, including developing new growth businesses and ventures and supervising many of NBC's established Internet interests, which include MSNBC.com, CNBC on MSN Money, NBCSports.com, NBCOlympics.com, Polo.com, enhanced television initiatives, and the NBC Internet Strategic Investment Portfolio. In August 2001, NBC acquired the NBC Internet, Inc., a publicly traded Internet portal in which NBC held a minority interest since its formation in 1999. After the acquisition, the NBC's site was converted from a portal to a "jump page" that provided access to all of NBC's affiliated websites.

NBC's Enhanced Broadcast Group has been in existence for over six years. During that time NBC has produced interactive television applications for a variety of platforms, including Wink, WebTV, Microsoft, Intel's digital TV initiative, Replay, Tivo, and Gemstar's interactive programme guide. Today NBC produces over 350 hours weeks of enhancement across sports, finance, and late-night programming. NBC's EBG also developed and maintains Channel 488 on DirecTV, a virtual news and finance data channel. These and other technological developments keep NBC a leader among media companies in the interactive field and in the convergence of traditional television and new media. NBC also holds strategic investments in a number of Internet and new media companies.

CNBC

9 December 1997 saw two of the world's leading media companies, Dow Jones & Company and NBC, coming together. This global alliance created a powerful combination of strengths: Dow Jones produces vital world business and financial news and information; NBC is the leading television network in the US and the only US network with global reach and vision. This move put together the world's most recognised business news brands including The Wall Street Journal, CNBC and Dow Jones. CNBC and Dow Jones teamed up to provide business news programming that is unparalleled in scope. CNBC is available to households worldwide.

Headquartered in the financial heart of Singapore, CNBC Asia Pacific uses full-time the virtual reality broadcast studio, giving it the ability to create computer-generated, custom-designed sets, and take an innovative lead in the presentation of complex data. With global editorial and network resources, viewers can expect the latest and most up-to-date information from anywhere in the world that has an impact on their business.

CNBC is the recognised global leader in business news, providing real-time financial market coverage and business information to more than 198 million homes worldwide throughout the business day. In the US and Canada, CNBC is distributed to more than 82 million households, providing business news as a joint service of its parent, NBC, and Dow Jones, publisher of *The Wall Street Journal*. In addition to its headquarters in Fort Lee, NJ, CNBC has news bureaus in midtown Manhattan, Washington, DC, Chicago, Los Angeles, London, Palo Alto, Singapore, the Nasdaq MarketSite, and the New York Stock Exchange. CNBC also has news and studio operations in several Wall Street Journal bureaus, including San Francisco and Seattle.

In Japan, Nikkei-CNBC is an alliance between CNBC Asia Pacific and the television news service of Nihon Keizai Shimbun Inc. (Nikkei), the leading business news and market information provider in Japan. In India, CNBC Asia Pacific and Television Eighteen India Ltd. (TV18) produces programming for the dedicated India feed of CNBC India. TV18 also markets the channel to advertisers in India. Sony Entertainment Television India Ltd. (SET) manages cable distribution for CNBC India. In China, CNBC Asia Pacific and Shanghai TV co-produce World Economic Finance Report which airs on Sundays at 8:30 pm on Shanghai TV channel 1.

MSNBC

MSNBC is a partnership between NBC, a leading provider of news and information, and Microsoft, the leader in personal computer software and a major provider of Internet online services. Built on the worldwide resources of NBC News, MSNBC delivers breaking news and in-depth coverage to 74 million households on cable 24 hours a day and up to 20 million unique users a month on the Internet. MSNBC has established itself as America's news leader on cable and the preeminent Internet news site by providing comprehensive breaking news, as well as reporting the day's top stories. MSNBC premiered in July 1996 to 22 million subscribers, the biggest subscriber base ever for a new cable service. By developing programming simultaneously for cable and the Internet, MSNBC offers truly integrated television, interactive news, and dynamic discussion of topical events.

CNN and Turner Broadcasting System

The CNN News Group is one of the largest and most profitable electronic news and information companies in the world. The hub of the CNN News Group is the Cable News Network (CNN), distributed to 73 million US households. Altogether, the CNN News Group is available to more than 800 million people worldwide with six cable and satellite television networks (CNN, Headline News, CNN International, CNNfn, CNN/SI and CNN en Español), three private, out-of-home networks, two radio networks, eight websites and CNN Newsource, the world's most extensively syndicated news service.

As earlier mentioned, CNN was the first foreign satellite channel that attracted the attention of the Indian elite during the Gulf War. It is now an AOL Time Warner company. In fact, Turner Broadcasting System, Inc. now operates many of the most powerful and well-established brands in entertainment and news. It has today the following businesses – TBS Superstation, Turner Network Television (TNT) Cartoon Network, Turner Classic Movies, Turner South Boomerang, TCM Europe, Cartoon Network Europe ,TNT Latin America, Cartoon Network Latin America, TCM & Cartoon Network / Asia Pacific, Atlanta Braves, Atlanta Hawks, Atlanta Thrashers, Philips Arena, The WB Televisions Network, Kids' WB! CNN/US, CNN Headline News, CNN International, CNNfn, CNN en Español, CNN Airport Network, CNNRadio, CNNRadio Noticias, CNN Newsource, CNN.com, CNNMoney.com, CNN Student News, CNNSI.com, CNN.com.br (Portugese), CNN.com Europe (English), CNN.de (German) CNNenEspanol.com (Spanish), CNNItalia.it (Italian) CNN.com Asia (English), CNNArabic.com. Joint Ventures, Cartoon Network, Japan Court

TV (TWE-owned) CETV, NBC/Turner, NASCAR Races, Viva+, CNN+, CNN Turk, n-tv.

Thus, Turner Broadcasting System had three of the top five basic cable networks in total-day household rating and delivery in the US: TBS Superstation, TNT and Cartoon Network. In 2001, TBS Superstation was the most-watched basic cable network for the 25th consecutive year, airing 8 of the 10 highest-rated theatrical movies on basic cable—led by the number one film, New Line Cinema's Rush Hour. TBS Superstation reaches approximately 87 million US households. TNT's Louis L'Amour's Crossfire Trail was watched in 7.7 million households, making it the most-watched movie in basic cable history. TNT reaches approximately 85 million US households. Cartoon Network reached nearly 150 million households around the world and in the US reaches more viewers aged 2-11 during prime time than any other network, broadcast or cable. The Powerpuff Girls has generated $700 million in merchandise sales to date and has spawned a feature-length animated film to be distributed by the Warner Bros.

Available worldwide to more than 1 billion people, CNN reached more than 85 million US homes at the close of 2001 and was the top cable news network in households, total viewers and all key sales demographics. The WB broadcast network attracts the youngest median-age viewers of all networks and was the number one network among female teens for the fourth consecutive season.

CNN.com is among the world's leaders in online news and information delivery. Staffed 24 hours, seven days a week by a dedicated staff in CNN's world headquarters in Atlanta, Georgia, and in bureaus worldwide, CNN.com relies heavily on CNN's global team of almost 4,000 news professionals. CNN.com features the latest multimedia technologies, from live video streaming to audio packages to searchable archives of news features and background information. The site is updated continuously throughout the day.

Home Box Office

Home Box Office is now part of AOL Time Warner. It has the following businesses:– HBO, HBO 2, HBO Signature, HBO Family,

Private and Foreign Channels

HBO Comedy, HBO Zone, HBO Latino, Cinemax, MoreMAX, ActionMAX, ThrillerMAX, WMAX, @MAX, 5StarMAX, OuterMAX and HBO Independent Productions, HBO Downtown Productions. Joint Ventures Comedy Central, HBO Asia, HBO Brasil, HBO Czech, HBO Hungary, HBO India, HBO Korea, HBO Ole, HBO Poland, HBO Romania, A&E Mundo E! Latin America, SET Latin America, WBTV Latin America, Latin America History Channel.

Its two 24-hour services, HBO and Cinemax, have grown to serve approximately 38 million US subscribers. Offering blockbuster movies, innovative original programming, provocative documentaries, concert events and championship boxing, HBO is the highest-rated cable service during the day and in prime time. Cinemax, the second-highest rated pay service features award-winning documentaries and more than 1,600 movie titles a year.

Internationally, HBO joint ventures reaches 16 million subscribers in more than 50 countries in Latin America, Asia and Central Europe. At the 2002 Primetime Emmys, HBO won 24 Emmys in the 54th Annual Primetime Emmy Awards® competition, tied with NBC for the most awards. "Band of Brothers" won the Emmy® for miniseries, and tied with "Six Feet Under" for the most awards on the network, with 6. "Six Feet Under" won the most Emmys® of any drama series, while "The Gathering Storm" won 3 Emmys®, the most of any movie, including Made for Television Movie. "Sex and the City" also won 3 Emmys®. The September 2002 season premier of The Sopranos became the most watched original programme in HBO's 30-year history, and was the week's number one primetime programme among adults 18-34. In July 2001, HBO launched its subscriber video on demand service, HBO on Demand, in Time Warner Cable's Columbia, SC system, providing digital HBO subscribers the convenience of watching over 150 titles including the best of HBO original programming and movies whenever they choose and with VCR functionality. The service has since been launched in 35 additional markets, with rollout continuing in 2002.

Nickelodeon

Nickelodeon, launched in April 1979, is an advertiser-supported basic cable service of MTV Networks targeted at 2-11 year-olds, has been the highest-rated basic cable network in the US since 1995. It has a larger kids' audience than the three major broadcast networks combined. The industry's leading producer of original programming for kids, the network offers an incredible line-up of original animation, known as Nicktoons; variety and game shows; as well as adventure and news magazine shows. Additionally, Nick Jr., Nickelodeon's programming for preschoolers, includes educational, sing-along, puppet, and variety shows, and the enormously successful Blue's Clues. On September 16, 2000, Nickelodeon began programming CBS's Saturday morning children's schedule with six half-hour series from Nick Jr. CBS's 2000-2001 children's lineup, "Nick Jr. on CBS" will feature Blue's Clues, Little Bill, Little Bear, Franklin, Kipper, and new series Dora, the Explorer. Nickelodeon is a global entertainment brand with businesses in programming, production, consumer products, online, recreation, publishing, and feature films that are substantially increasing Nickelodeon's presence and impact on children's entertainment worldwide.

Disney

The Walt Disney Company is a diversified worldwide entertainment company with operations in four business segments: Media Networks, Parks & Resorts, Studio Entertainment and Consumer Products. Media Networks is comprised of the ABC Television Network having 226 primary affiliated stations; and the ABC Radio Networks, which consist of more than 8,900 programme affiliations on more than 4,600 radio stations. In October 2001, the Company acquired Fox Family Worldwide. Among the businesses purchased are The Fox Family Channel, which will be renamed ABC Family, a 76% ownership interest in Fox Kids Europe, which will eventually be recast under the Disney brand, Fox Kids channels in Latin America, and The Saban Library and Entertainment Productions business. The transaction also includes the television rights to Major

League Baseball games two nights a week during the regular season, plus several first-round playoff games.

The Company's cable and international broadcast operations principally are involved in the production and distribution of cable television programming, the licensing of programming to domestic and international markets and investing in foreign television broadcasting, production and distribution entities. The Company owns Disney Channel, Toon Disney, SoapNet, 80 per cent of ESPN, Inc., 37.5 per cent of the A&E Television Networks, 50% of Lifetime Entertainment Services, 39.6% of E! Entertainment Television and has various other international investments.

The Walt Disney Company also develops, produces and distributes television programming to global broadcasters and cable and satellite operators, including the major television networks, Disney Channel and other cable broadcasters, under the Buena Vista Television, Buena Vista Production, Touchstone Television and Walt Disney Television labels. The Company is producing original television movies for the wonderful world of Disney. The Internet operations of the media networks groups develop, publish and distribute content for online services intended to appeal to broad consumer interest in sports, news, family and entertainment. Internet websites and products include ABC.com, ABCNEWS.com, Enhanced TV, ABCSports.com, ESPN.com, Disney.com, Family.com and Movies.com.

Disney Online, a business unit of the Walt Disney Internet Group, was founded in 1995 to develop the company's presence in the online world. Headquartered in North Hollywood, California, with satellite offices in New York, Chicago, San Francisco, and Detroit, Disney Online's in-house development studios produce a variety of innovative, award-winning, and highly trafficked destinations on the World Wide Web.

Sun Network

The flagship company of Sun Network, Sun was one of the first regional channels of India that now serves the Tamil-speaking population across the globe. Started in 1993, the channel changed the cable network concept in Southern India. The group now has several channels. Another Tamil channel is KTV. Gemini TV offers entertainment and information to the Telugu-speaking population across the world. Surya TV serves entertainment and information to the Malayalam-speaking population across the world. Udaya TV and Ushe TV are in Kannada while Teja TV is in Telugu. Sun Pictures offers the telefilms customised to regional tastes, offers entertainment to the south Indian population across the world.

A new era in television entertainment began with the arrival of Sun Cable Vision in Chennai and Coimbatore. Now you can access more than 65 channels of quality Channels including the Sun TV, KTV, Gemini TV, Surya TV, Udaya TV, Sun News, 24-hour news channel, Teja TV, Ushe TV, Raj TV, Vijay TV, Star Network Channels, Zee Network Channels, Sony Entertainment, DD Channels, HBO, MTV, Discovery Channels, and many more including the cable channel SCV, covering entertainment, news, movies, sports, music and education. SCV is planning to give its subscribers Internet through cable. SCV's broadband network is based on a design known as the hybrid fibre coaxial (HFC) where optical fibre links the system headend to network nodes which serves between 500 to 2000 subscribers, and coaxial cables connecting individual homes to each node. Inside the home, cable signals can be split between various TV or PC-based devices like a cable TV set-top box and a cable modem. The HFC architecture automatically results in a network that offers a greater channel capacity, improved signal reliability and far-superior two-way transmission capabilities. With the completion of its city network, SCV is now ready to rollout services beyond cable TV, such as high-speed Internet access. In the near future, SCV will also be in a position to deliver other broadband applications such as: • High-speed Internet access on both TV and PC – Besides the PC, surfing and e-mailing on the TV will be possible through enhanced set-top boxes. Electronic programme guides (EPG) service integrates broadcast information and material from the Internet. Delivered with the help of state-of-the-art set-top boxes, EPG services include alerting users when their favourite programmes are coming up, setting the video recorder to record automatically and also allowing parental control over children's viewing options. Other possibilities include:

Telecommuting:– The home office concept will become more cost-efficient and accessible with full local area network (LAN) access via the cable modem. • Videoconferencing – In future, the videoconferencing will no longer need to be done in a specialised location. The future home will be equipped with an advanced set-top box that will allow the user to enjoy this service in the comfort of his home.

Distance learning:– Subscribers will be able to tap into the vast universe of interactive multimedia sites on the Web for research and educational purposes.

Interactive home-shopping and games:– Interactive television will be a commonplace in the future with services that will allow for virtual online shopping and easy access to graphic-rich game servers. News and entertainment-on-demand users will download movies, news and sports highlights or enjoy other pay-per-view services offered on the Web.

Telephony:– Telecommunications using cable will be a possibility in the future, whether through remote access via the set-top box, modem or a wireless connection. The myriad of services available in the future will not only enhance our entertainment and communication experience but also change the way we live, work and play. In the future, every household in the city will be able to experience the full potential of the broadband network, all through a single coaxial cable in the comfort of their home.

Jaya TV

On 22 August 1999, Jaya TV, a Tamil channel, was floated by close associates of Tamil Nadu Chief Minister J. Jayalalitha, to counter Sun Network run by Kalanithi Maran, son of the late Murasoli Maran, Union Commerce Minister and a nephew of 78-year old president of the Dravida Munnetra Kazhagam (DMK) and former Chief Minister Karunanidhi. Jaya TV is managed by T.T.V. Dinakaran, AIADMK leader, Lok Sabha member, and nephew of Sasikala Natarajan, a close associate of Jayalalitha. Jaya TV by its own admission was the only instrument of poll campaign during the assembly elections that brought Jayalalitha to power in Tamil Nadu. According to a former member of Jaya TV staff, it was great to work for it when Jayalalitha was in opposition, but when she is in power, it is worse than Doordarshan with routine stories.

Raj TV

The Raj Television Network was started in 1994 to provide wholesome entertainment for the entire family. With programmes targeted at young and old, male and female alike, the Network has positioned itself as The People's Channel. Through its two channels – Raj TV and Raj Digital Plus, the network reaches Tamil viewers in urban and rural India but also those outside India. The Network runs a number of popular serials presented by some of the best names in Tamil films today. These in combination with a number of popular chat shows and game shows give the network an edge with the viewers. In addition, the Network has built up a library of over 2000 films, some of the best in Tamil films from the nostalgic old favourites to the box office hits of today. It is also going in for other language channels, the first one being in Telugu.

Eenadu TV

(Eenadu TV) ETV was launched on 27 August 1995 by Ramoji Rao, owner of Eenadu Group of newspapers in Hyderabad. The various business activities of the group are: Ramoji Film City: the film production complex, Eenadu and Newstime: the Telugu and English newspapers, ETV: the satellite television channels, Ushakiron Televison: producing television software, Ushakiron Movies: creating movies in Indian languages, Ushakiron Movies International: creating movies for international viewers, Mayuri Film Distributors, Margadarsi Chit Funds, Dolphin Hotels, Priya Foods, Kalanjali and Margadarsi Apparels.

Ramoji Rao entered into the media business in 1974 with the launch of Eenadu, the Telugu newspaper, with its current circulation is more than a million. The satellite television venture ETV began in 1995 with launch of a Telugu channel. Today they have 11 channels in various Indian languages.

ETC Networks

ETC Networks Ltd. owns two channels *etc* Hindi and *etc* Channel Punjabi. ETC Networks Ltd. is a listed company with Bombay Stock Exchange. Initially *etc* Channel was launched on 26 August 1999 as a 24-hour Indian Music Channel with the punch line of *"Aakhir Dil Hai Hindustani"*. Within a short span of six months, *etc* was rated as the no.1 Indian music channel. It was listed on the Bombay Stock Exchange in May 2000.

To increase interactivity with the viewers the channel has added road shows and SMS services. Films and Indi Pop music still remains the heart of the channel and constitutes 95 per cent of the programming. The channel has also added a show on astrology. *etc* channel Punjabi was launched in June 2000. Within a short span of 3 months, *etc* channel Punjabi became the no.1 Punjabi channel amongst stiff competition from 3 other channels of its genre. *etc* Channel Punjabi has bagged exclusive rights for eleven years to telecast *Gurbani* live from the Golden Temple, Amritsar. Zee Telefilms holds 51 per cent shares in ETC Networks Ltd.

B4U Network

B4U Network is a channel that is based on Bombay's film industry (Bollywood). A vertically integrated company, B4U Network is involved in all aspects of the Bollywood film industry from film making to film distribution and merchandising. B4U is the world's first 24-hour South Asian Premium Digital Bollywood Movie Channel, launched in August 1999 in the UK. This was followed by a global launch within six months. Other than UK, B4U is currently available in the Middle East, US, Canada, Europe, Mauritius, India and South Africa. The main driver and unique selling proposition (USP) of B4U is its symbiotic affiliation with Eros International, the largest distributor of Bollywood films worldwide. This enables B4U to screen new movies within six months of their theatrical release in countries other than India. B4U guarantees five films every day, a mega blockbuster movie every month and comes with a blockbuster promise every Sunday night. It also broadcasts exclusive star interviews, behind-the-scenes, making of films, music-based programmes, news and interactive programmes. This includes features like 'Movie On Demand' whereby a movie is shown as per viewer's choice, voted through its website www.b4utv.com.

B4U Network launched a second channel B4U Music in May 2000 in the UK – a free to air channel, which has caused much excitement amongst the satellite digital audience. The channel not only shows latest and forthcoming song sequences from Bollywood films but an array of music. B4U Music was simultaneously launched in India. Other than India and UK, this value-based service from B4U is now available in South Africa, Middle East, Europe, and Mauritius too.

B4U Music is set to be a global channel with beams covering the Asian region, Middle East and the Western hemisphere. B4U claims the distinction of being the first on many counts. It is the world's first 24-hour premium digital movie channel for South Asians. It is the first Asian channel to launch pay-per-view in most parts of the world. It is the first Asian channel to go global within 6 months of its launch and to be launched as a premium service in the Middle East.

AXN

Launched on 21 September 1997, AXN now reaches over 70 million households across Asia. Featuring action and adventure lifestyle programming, AXN is the home of fast-paced, dynamic entertainment to viewers around the world. Backed by Sony Pictures Entertainment, AXN delivers young adult viewers (18-35) a round-the-clock fix of blockbuster features, action and reality series and specials, first-run alternative sporting events and the latest in cult CGI animation.

AXN is the first 24-hour cable and satellite TV channel in Asia exclusively dedicated to action and adventure programming. AXN is 100 per cent owned by Sony Picture Entertainment, the parent company of Columbia TriStar, the company that produced hit action movies such as Crouching Tiger, Hidden Dragon, Final Fantasy: The Spirits Within, Charlie's Angels, Black Hawk Down, Spiderman, and Men in Black 2. Sony Pictures Entertainment (SPE) is a division of Sony Corporation of America (SCA). SCA is a subsidiary of Tokyo-based Sony Corporation. SPE's global operations encompass motion picture production and distribution, television production and distribution, worldwide channel investments, home entertainment acquisition and distribution, operation of studio facilities, development of new entertainment products, services and technologies, and distribution of filmed entertainment in 67 countries.

Sony

Sony Entertainment Television dedicated to Hindi family entertainment was launched in October 1998. It has programming from the supernatural to the lighthearted, from talk-shows to lifestyle, from the most glamorous events to the legendary blockbusters.

Sony Entertainment Television in India is the first venture of Sony Pictures Entertainment, the biggest entertainment powerhouse of America. As part of the Sony family, the channel has access to a wide variety of international software from film and television divisions of Sony Pictures Entertainment. Sony Entertainment Television is seen in over 28 million households throughout India, Pakistan, Sri Lanka, Bangladesh and the Middle East.

MAX, the premium films, cricket and events channel was the second satellite offering from the Sony Entertainment Television network, and was launched in October 1999 keeping in mind the huge popularity and impact that blockbuster Hindi films, events and cricket have on the people of India.

MAX is committed to taking the best of Hindi Cinema to its millions of viewers and has a library of over 1000 films. MAX has aired some of the biggest titles from Indian Cinema including the best films of Shah Rukh Khan, Aamir Khan, Amitabh Bachchan, Salman Khan, Sanjay Dutt, Anil Kapoor, Jackie Shroff, Dev Anand, Raj Kapoor, Yash Chopra and others. Amongst the blockbusters, MAX has aired hits like *Kaho Na Pyar Hai, Kuch Kuch Hota Hai, Dilwale Dulhaniya Le Jaayenge, Border, Mohabbatein, Mission Kashmir, Champion, Rangeela*, and others.

MAX's mix of films and cricket gives it an unparalleled and cutting-edge uniqueness in the marketplace. MAX has been showing premier international cricket matches, which included Sri Lanka Cricket, Sharjah Cricket, Singapore Cricket, and innovative contests like the Hong Kong Sixes. At all times, MAX actively seeks to acquire new properties in cricket and leading sports when available.

MAX is a division of Sony Entertainment Television, a completely independent business unit and profit centre. Its vision statement is "To be the leading movies and events channel and preferred destination of the Indian movie buff delivering the highest value to its viewers and associates in the Indian entertainment space".

National Geographic

The National Geographic Society is the world's largest nonprofit scientific and educational organisation. It was created on the evening of January 13, 1888, Thirty-three men travelled on foot, horseback, and in horse-drawn carriages through the streets of Washington to the Cosmos Club, then on Lafayette Square across from the White House. They convened around a large mahogany table to discuss "the advisability of organising a society for the increase and diffusion of geographical knowledge." The entity they created has become the largest nonprofit scientific and educational institution in the world. It publishes flagship magazine *National Geographic* and other magazines *Adventure, Traveler, World* and new classroom magazine *National Geographic for Kids* along with books and CD-ROMs.

The National Geographic Channel is a business enterprise of National Geographic Television (now National Geographic Television & Film) with Fox Cable Networks in the US. In September 1997, NBC and National Geographic Television formed a partnership creating National Geographic Channels International, a partnership with BSkyB/Fox. NGCI is distributed in 18 languages to over 100 million households in 129 countries throughout Europe, Asia, Australia and Latin America. These 24-hour channels feature new National Geographic Television programming and past specials, and also showcase a variety of documentaries by distinguished filmmakers.

On 15 January 2002 National Geographic Television has changed its name to National Geographic Television & Film (NGT&F). The new name reflects the continuing expansion of National Geographic's world-renowned production into additional multi-platform entertainment platforms, including feature and large-format film.

The National Geographic Channel is a business enterprise of NGT&F and Fox Cable Networks Group in the US, and is joined abroad by NBC.

Through its Los Angeles-based National Geographic Features Films NGT&F is developing and producing nonfiction stories whose theme and scope naturally lend to dramatic treatment on the big screen. NGT&F is producing television programming for its weekly cable series, EXPLORER, on MSNBC; acclaimed specials and limited series on PBS; and the National Geographic Channel in the US and abroad. NGT&F has several long-form television dramas in development including a four-hour miniseries based on Stephen Ambrose's *Undaunted Courage* with Hallmark Entertainment and TNT. NGT&F is a wholly-owned subsidiary of National Geographic Ventures, which also manages National Geographic's businesses in interactive, online, merchandising, travel expeditions, and related businesses. *National Geographic Beyond the Movie,* an innovative, multi-media initiative anchored in documentary television was launched in the spring of 2001. National Geographic successfully worked with Touchstone Productions to produce a *National Geographic Beyond the Movie* complementary programme to its summer blockbuster, *Pearl Harbor,* and has just completed a programme for New Line Cinema's critically-acclaimed *The Fellowship of the Ring.* Worldwide, NGT&F's programming can be seen on the National Geographic Channel, MSNBC, and PBS, home video and DVD, and through international broadcast syndication. The National Geographic Channel is received by more than 130 million households in 23 languages and 136 countries, including the US and India.

Nationalgeographic.com, which launched the National Geographic Society into cyberspace on June 20, 1996, delivers adventure and exploration with the click of a mouse for Web visitors interested in travel, photography, maps, scientific discovery, and news. Today, the site averages more than 30 million page views per month and has been honoured with virtually all the industry's leading awards.

Discovery

Discovery Communications, Inc., a global real-world media and entertainment company has emerged from the Discovery Channel created by John S. Hendricks in 1982 as the first cable network in the United States designed to provide high quality documentary programming. John S. Hendricks is the founder, chairman and CEO of Discovery Communications, Inc. Earlier Hendricks founded and served as president of the American Association of University Consultants (AAUC), a private consulting organisation specialising in television distribution and marketing of educational programmes and services.

DCI's current ownership consists of four shareholders: Liberty Media Corporation (NYSE: L), Cox Communications, Inc. (NYSE: COX), Advance/Newhouse Communications and John S. Hendricks, the Company's Founder, Chairman and CEO. Its current global operations span 155 countries with over 700 million total subscribers. DCI's stable of networks now encompass 33 networks of distinctive programming representing 14 entertainment brands including TLC, Animal Planet, Travel Channel, Discovery Health Channel, Discovery Kids, and a family of digital channels. DCI's other properties consist of Discovery.com and 170 Discovery Channel retail stores. The expansion is the result of the acquisitions of TLC in 1991 and the Travel Channel in 1997, the launches of Animal Planet in 1996 and the Discovery Health Channel in 1999, and the development of six targeted channels. The strategic partnerships around the world including DCI's global alliance with the BBC, and a major joint venture with The New York Times Company to co-own the Discovery Civilisation Channel. DCI's retail services were expanded by acquiring The Nature Company stores in 1996, creating a chain of Discovery Channel Stores.

Few media companies have the distribution, impressions and cross platform capability that Discovery has around the world. In 2002, Discovery Networks, US will produce more than 3,000 hours of original programming. The Discovery Channel is one of the two most widely distributed cable networks in the United States, with over 85 million subscribers, and the most widely distributed television brand in the world, reaching over 400 million households in 155 countries.

Discovery successfully transformed Discovery.com's operations into an integrated information, entertainment and marketing tool for Discovery Networks, US in 2001. Delivering the online experience of the Discovery brands, with cutting-edge, high quality content that is "the best of the best," Discovery.com reaches 4.4 million viewers a month.

On 17 June 2002, DCI launched Discovery HD Theater, a new 24-hour high-definition television (HDTV) network on HD platforms being rolled out by EchoStar Communications Corporation on its DISH Network satellite TV service nationwide, AT&T Broadband's Greater Chicago Market (where plans are set to launch HDTV service, and in numerous other markets by Charter Communciations, Inc. (Nasdaq: CHTR) and Cox Communications, Inc.

Discovery Communications, Inc. has created a Discovery Radio service to be carried by the two new satellite radio services, XM Satellite Radio and Sirius Satellite. A customised Discovery-branded channel will offer a range of programming, including news, health, travel, science, kids and specials. Discovery Satellite Radio will be transmitted directly to consumers via vehicle, home and portable radios.

Animal Planet

Animal Planet is entertainment for viewers of all ages. The network's original programming taps into the deep emotional connection between people and animals and provides a diverse mix of original movies, fiction, reality programming, adventure series, sports, drama and sitcoms. Animal Planet has grown to reach over 78 million homes throughout the United States since 1996, making it one of the fastest growing networks in cable television history. Animal Planet's international growth continues to increase rapidly as well, with the channel now available to 69 million homes outside the United States in more than 71 countries.

Animal Planet is literally all over the map—consumers can find the Animal Planet brand in numerous venues off the television screen. A global partnership with Toys 'RUs brought the first specially branded Animal Planet section to 1,500 Toys 'R Us outlets around the world. As the first licensed property in the history of Discovery, 'Crocodile Hunter' branded toys can be found in Wal-Mart, Toys 'R Us, Kohl's and Shopko.

Animal Planet claims commitment to promoting awareness of conservation, biodiversity, and the need to preserve endangered species and their habitats. These issues are recognised through World Animal Day programming and through partnerships with United Nations (UN) agencies including the UN Environment Program (UNEP), and the UN Development Program (UNDP); and, the Earth Communications Office (ECO). These partnerships educate millions of people about issues such as species conservation, habitat protection, and the importance of biodiversity to the future of our planet.

Gurjari and Lashkara

On 14 April 1999, Reminiscent India Television Pvt. Ltd. launched two of its regional language channels with an eye on global Asian audiences. These were Gurjari in Gujarati and Lashkara in Punjabi. RITV is part of RTV UK – a global network which showcases channels of various South Asian languages such as Gujarati, Punjabi, Hindi, Bengali, Urdu and Tamil. Apart from this, RTV also operates a terrestrial channel – MATV and Raag, its Music channel. RTV reaches South Asians in Southeast Asia, Africa, UK, Europe, Australia and New Zealand.

In India, Gurjari and Lashkara enlightens its viewers through a unique blend of programming that portrays the culture, tradition and beliefs of the Gujarati and Punjabi communities.

Lashkara is one of the most successful regional language channels in India. It commands a large viewership base not only in Punjab and Delhi, but also in a large measure in the northern belt and wherever Punjabis have settled in India. The channel claims to have a vast and varied line up of programmes with a mix of religion, soaps, dramas and comedies – a healthy mix for people of all age groups.

Sahara TV

Sahara India Pariwar, a diversified group with interests in aviation, TV software production, real estate, mass communication has also launched a television channel – Sahara TV. As an infotainment channel it aims for a strong reach in 30 million homes in over 66 countries worldwide. Uplinked from Singapore and beamed to India and 65 countries via the regional hot-bird AsiaSat-3S satellite, Sahara TV programmes promise innovative programming and fewer commercial breaks.

On 12 January 2002, Sahara India Pariwar, announced its plans to launch a bouquet of 38 news channels – a national news channel and 37 independent city-based regional news channels covering several north Indian states and Mumbai. With the launch of these 38 news channels, Sahara TV aims to focus on a unique concept of providing not just national and international news but also in-depth, high-quality city-based and regional news coverage. Sahara had earlier announced on 5 July 2000 to introduce a news and current affairs channel.

IN Network

IN Network Entertainment Ltd., is a 100 per cent subsidiary of Hinduja TMT Ltd., an established name in the IT sector. The main activity of the company is in film and content finance, production and distribution. The subsidiaries combine distribution with infrastructure spanning a cable television network, a Hindi movie channel, a local television network, and fully integrated media commerce channel for merchandising. The diverse interests of IN Network in the entertainment business combined with the wide spectrum of activities of its parent, has provided the company with a unique positioning to implement an integrated entertainment business model in India; in line with the success stories of the international media conglomerates.

IndusInd Entertainment Limited (IEL): IEL produces TV content and operates a bouquet of popular local cable TV channels under the IN umbrella brands, e.g. IN Mumbai, IN Bangalore, IN Delhi, etc. Its IN Time's news bulletin gives comprehensive coverage to all cities where IN CableNet operations are underway. IEL is India's leading multi-carrier digital content provider and is already streaming its In Mumbai Channel Live on Forindia.com. Digital content will soon be made available on a variety of platforms, e.g. Cable, Satellite, Internet, Wireless Aided Protocol and Digital Satellite Radio. Planet E-shop is a virtual shopping portal with a suite of shop-front designs, virtual shopping carts, logistics and fulfilment operations.

Cable Video India Limited (CVIL) operates as CVO, a Hindi Movie Channel, with a reach of over 6 million households. It has a big library of Hindi films including black and white classics, children's specials, musical hits, social, historical and mythological hits and the best of action among others. It showcases the latest Hindi movie on a continuous basis. CVO was launched simultaneously in six cities – Mumbai, New Delhi, Bangalore, Belgaum, Ahmedabad and Hyderabad on 15 November 1996. It has since expanded its network to more than hundred centres of India through cable distribution systems. CVO provides a value-addition to its viewers with a wide range of film-based programmes interspersed between the films. These have been conceived and are being produced in-house by a team of professionals. The range of film-based shows include countdown of popular songs, movie trailors, clippings of forthcoming releases, song requests, thematic songs, interviews with film stars and many more programmes based on the film world. CVO continuously showcases new titles on securing telecast rights. The channel is committed to acquire telecast rights for new movies, from time to time, depending upon their availability for viewing on cable.

Shop 24 Seven, a joint venture with Planet E Shop Inc., USA was launched in November 2001, and is India's first integrated, interactive e-commerce initiative using television, Internet and franchised points of presence for an exclusive range of Indian and imported products. ForIndia.com, the premier one-stop portal, is a part of IndusInd Entertainment Limited, a wholly owned venture of Hinduja Group, providing content to wide range of media enterprises. Comprehensive coverage is the credo that guides forindia.com. Committed to evolving creative content that meets the needs of users worldwide, the portal provides the most up-to-date communication services and technology, interest-specific channels catering specifically to the Indian online user. The focus of these channels ranges from local and regional news, business and sports, to global interests and events. With its wide-ranging multi-media content, forindia.com adds value to HTMT's reach worldwide.

Aastha

Since the popularity of epic-based serials was established with *Ramayana* and *Mahabharata* on Doordarshan many channels in India have put some epic-based or religious discourses as part of regular programming. But some channels came up exclusively depending on such fare and Aastha is one of them.

Aastha Television and CMM Music Television have been promoted by Kirit C. Mehta, the Chairman and Managing Director, who discovered the enormous potential that exists in the Indian Media industry while producing a TV serial on Jainism. On 18 June 2000, Aastha Television Channel was launched with the objective of networking the global community to enable them to partake in the spiritual and religious happenings in India and other Indian cultural pockets across the globe. It is a 24-hour channel, dedicated to broadcasting India's rich socio-spiritual and divine cultural-heritage on a premium digital platform. Alongside Aastha Television was launched CMM Music Television, a healthy entertainment channel that incorporated all the elements of fun, staying clear of any form of vulgarity. About a year later, Web venture – Aasthasansar.com was launched. Recently the parent company CBNL has linked up with Pentamedia Graphics Ltd, Chennai, for Webcasting Aastha Television and CMM Music Television. Through this venture both these channels are now available all over the globe on the Internet.

Sanskar TV

A similar satellite channel on Indian culture 'Sanskar TV' started transmission in June 2000. This digital channel is on Thaicom 3 Satellite and puts out a 24-hour fare based on religion and culture including songs, pilgrimages, discourses by various well-known orators and saints.

TV18

Television Eighteen India Limited (TV18) was launched in 1993 by Raghav Bahl and Sanjay Ray Chaudhury. It now calls itself a content provider. TV18 went public with listings on the Indian bourses in 1999. TV18 tied up with the CNBC Asia to launch CNBC India as a full-fledged business news and information channel in late 1999. Its latest foray is in cyberspace with the establishment of an Indian business and finance portal moneycontrol.com. Dow Jones, GE, ICICI, News Corp, SET are some of the reputed clients of TV 18 which has bureaus in Mumbai, Delhi, Calcutta, Chennai, Bangalore and the full-fledged studios in Mumbai and Delhi.

UTV

Incorporated in 1990, the UTV Group started as a television production house has now diversified into in-flight entertainment, events, dubbing, ad films, motion pictures, broadcasting, post-production and animation. UTV takes pride in having a pedigreed shareholding of powerful media and investment companies from around the world, including News Corporation and Warburg Pincus.

Balaji Telefilms

Balaji Telefilms Limited (Balaji) is amongst India's most prominent and successful media companies. Headquartered in Mumbai, the company is primarily engaged in the production of television software in Hindi, Telugu, Tamil and Kannada. The company has been promoted by actor Jeetendra, Shobha Kapoor and Ekta Kapoor.

Balaji commenced operations in 1994 with the production of a fiction thriller called 'Mano ya na mano' for Zee TV. Thereafter, Balaji's programmes have been aired regularly on Star Plus, Doordarshan, DD Metro, Sony Entertainment, SABe, Metro Gold, Zee, Sun, Gemini and Udaya channels.

SABe TV

Sri Adhikari Brothers Television Network Limited (SABTNL) is an integrated Television content production house and a broadcaster. The company commenced operations over 13 years ago as a Television Software Production House producing programming for India's National Broadcaster – Doordarshan. The era of liberalisation ushered during the early 90's resulted in the growth of Cable and Satellite Television Channels providing opportunities for SABTNL to provide content to privately-owned television channels like Zee TV, EL TV, Home TV, etc. The company continues to produce content for Doordarshan and markets airtime for these related programmes. Currently, the company provides about 10 hours of programming per week for Doordarshan's Hindi and Marathi language channels. The company launched its very own Television Channel – SABe TV on April 23, 2000. SABe TV is a 24 hours Hindi language General Entertainment Channel, transmitted digitally through the Asiasat 3S Satellite. SABe TV provides a mix of programming that include game shows, sitcoms, soaps, chat shows, mythologicals and a variety of entertainment programmes.

Al-Jazeera

Al-Jazeera is the only Arabic news channel in the Middle East offering news coverage 24 hours a day from around the world. Nicknamed the CNN of the Arab World and also Bin Laden TV, it was founded in 1996, and is based in Qatar. It was born from the ashes of BBC Arabic, a BBC partnership with a Saudi company and was, at least initially, funded by the Emir of Qatar and other Arab moderates. It is the fastest growing network among Arab communities and Arabic-speaking people around the world. Al-Jazeera's programmes are available worldwide through various satellite and cable systems.

While political programmes tend to be the most popular, the other shows covering news about business, culture, sports, health also get their share of audience. Interactive programming that involve audience participation are also highly popular since they are considered ground-breaking in that region of the world.

Launched in January 2002, aljazeera.net is owned by Al-Jazeera Satellite Channel and managed by Afkar Information Technology, a Web-services firm in Doha, Qatar, where both the high-profile TV station and the website are based. According to Mahmood Abdulhadi, the site's general manager, "We cover news in Arabic, about the Arab region mainly and the world in general. The main categories we have are the Arab world, Europe, the Americas, Asia Pacific, Africa; economics; sports; science and technology; health; and culture and arts. We have ... in-depth analysis ... special coverage and book reviews. We have also categories for interactivity, like quick vote and discussion forums where the user can express his opinion directly without pre-censorship. We provide the full script of Al-Jazeera Satellite Channel's main programmes, attached with its audio file within 24 to 36 hours from the time of the first broadcasting." It made its mark in giving different versions in Afghan and Iraq wars.

PTV

Pakistan Television can be viewed in some parts of India. PTV is available as satellite channel – PTV World – as it is using Asiasat-3 and Thaicom. PTV World satellite channel is meant for South Asia and the Middle East. Prime TV in UK also transmits PTV signal.

Pakistan Television Corporation Limited (PTV) is a public limited company. All its shares are held by the Government of Pakistan. The decision to establish a general purpose television service with the participation of private capital and under the general supervision of the Government of Pakistan was taken in October 1963. Subsequently the Government of Pakistan signed an agreement with Nippon Electronic Company of Japan, allowing it to operate two pilot stations in Pakistan. The first of these stations went on air in Lahore on 26 November 1964. On the completion of the experimental phase, a private limited company, called Television Promoters Limited was set up in 1965 which was converted into a public limited company in 1967. A Board of Directors appointed by the Government of Pakistan manages its affairs.

Television centres were established in Karachi and Rawalpindi/ Islamabad in 1967 and in Peshawar and Quetta in 1974. PTV satellite transmission is round the clock. The transmission includes ETV (Educational TV) and PTV World transmission. Mideast Time, an extension of PTV World, targets Pakistani expatriates in the Middle East. Programmes are cleared by PTV Censor Board which was first formed in 1968. It was separately instituted within PTV on the approval of Secretary, Ministry of I&MD in December 1980 to clear and certify bulk of imported and locally acquired programmes with speed and efficiency. There is another Censor Board for commercials constituted by the Ministry of I&MD functioning at the PTV headquarters since June 1990, which examines and certifies all advertisement material for telecast. There are four sub-Censor Boards for commercials functioning at Karachi, Lahore, Peshawar and Quetta.

TV5
The international network of French programmes, the 24-hour TV5 satellite programming, featuring French shows like *"Bouillon de Culture"* or *"Paris Chic Choc"* can also be seen in India. TV5 is French-language network with programming from five different countries where French is the main language.

FTV
Fashion TV (FTV) is the first and only international TV channel dedicated to fashion – 24 hours a day. A global leader in the fashion niche since 1997, FTV is broadcast on 31 satellites on thousands of cable systems; reaching over 300 million households on all five continents.

In May 1997, FTV leased digital transmission to Eutelsat and Intelsat and broadcasting 24 hours started on Eutelsat. In July 1997, FTV signed contract with CanalSat France and started broadcasting

24 hours on Astra digital. In August 1997, FTV was launched in Bangkok, HongKong and on cable in Munich (Germany). In September 1997, FTV started on Vienna Cable (Austria) and London Cable (UK). In October 1997, it began broadcasting 24 hours on Eutelsat Analog. In December 1997, FTV was launched on DirecTV Japan.

In January 1998, FTV went on Internet www.ftv.fr and the next month it broadcast for the first time Rio's carnival. FTV has the worldwide exclusivity for Rio's carnival broadcasting outside Latin America. In March 1998, FTV was launched on different cable systems through Europe: Poland, Hungary, Russia, Denmark. In April 1998, it put out terrestrial programmes in Italy.

Celebrating its first anniversary in May 1998, FTV launched itself in USA on Time Warner in New York area and Charter Cable in Miami. In June 1998, started 5-6 hours per night on TM3 (German analog cable) and Astra Analog satellite FTV signed distribution agreement with CanalSatellite (Spain) and TV Cabo (Portugal). In July 1998, signed a distribution agreement with several East European cable operators. In November 1998, launched 24 hours covering Asia. In February 1999, Internet presence launched with Yahoo, Broadcast.com and 4 channels via Broadband Internet. In March 1999, launched in Argentina. In April 1999, launched on cable systems in Israel. In June 1999, FTV was on RNN (Regional News New York). Since July 1999, FTV is on T-Online, Deutsche Telekom, Microsoft, Media player, Broadband launch started in New Zealand on Sky TV. In August 1999, launched on Hong Kong satellite, on PDM and Videoland in Taiwan. FTV launched on various Turkish cable operators. In Nov. 1999, FTV in Canada on Express Vu platform. In Dec. 1999, Medya Grubu started FTV on Turkish cable 12 hours a day. In Jan. 2000, launched on UPC Hungary (1,000,000 new viewers). In Feb. 2000, first step in Australia through Neighbourhood Cable and various cable systems first diffusion of the "India Fashion Window". In March 2000, launched on Multichoice Digital Platform, 600,000 new viewers in South and in sub-Saharan Africa. In April 2000, launched on DigiTurk, digital platform in Turkey. 6,000,000 new homes were connected. In May

2000, launched on Primacom (Germany). FTV is telecasted 24 hours a day on Turkish cable. In July 2000, SpeedCast delivered FTV streaming content to PC's worldwide. In Aug. 2000 launched on different cable systems in Russia. In Sept. 2000 on Nova, Greek digital platform. In Dec. 2000 launched on Foxtel digital platform (Australia) and thus became the first French channel broadcast in Australia. Launched on Pehlva, ART's bouquet on Nilesat for the Near and the Middle East. Launched on TECSAT cable networks all over Brazil.

Hallmark

Hallmark Channel is a 24-hour cable television programme service that claims to provide a diverse slate of high-quality entertainment that is family-friendly, has an audience of nearly 45 million subscribers in the US. The programme service is distributed through 1,700 cable systems, DirecTV (Channel 312) and EchoStar (DISH Channel 185) Direct-to-Home satellite services and C-Band dish owners across the country. Crown Media Holdings, Inc. (NASDAQ NM: CRWN) owns and operates the Hallmark Channel which, in addition to the US, is distributed worldwide to 110 countries. The combined channels reach nearly 92 million subscribers globally and is also available in India. With a mix of original programmes, movies and miniseries from the creative auspices of Hallmark Entertainment – as well as their award-winning libraries – the Hallmark Channel offers a lineup that is compelling and contemporary. An upcoming original productions on Hallmark Channel include: "Mark Twain's Roughing It," a four-hour miniseries based on Mark Twain's book of the same title, starring James Garner, Robin Dunne, Adam Arkin, Ned Beatty and Jill Eikenberry; "Snow Queen," a four-hour miniseries based on Hans Christian Andersen's classic story of the same title, starring Bridget Fonda; "Stranded," a four-hour miniseries inspired by Johann David Wyss' 1813 literary classic, Swiss Family Robinson; and "Adoption," a one-hour reality series, produced exclusively by Hallmark Entertainment, examining the trials, tribulations and joys of the adoption process. The network's lineup also includes programmes from the Hallmark Entertainment library of nearly 4,500 hours of programming, which has been honoured with nearly 200 Emmy Awards. Among the titles airing on the network: "The Titanic," "The Odyssey," "Gulliver's Travels," "Merlin," "Lonesome Dove" and "Animal Farm." Hallmark Channel is also the exclusive home of the prestigious Hallmark Hall of Fame Collection of movies, including "Sarah, Plain and Tall" and "What the Deaf Man Heard."

This account of private and foreign channels is neither comprehensive nor representative but gives a reasonable idea of the television scene and trends in India and the world. Major players like RTL, TV Globo, Televisa are not touching the Indian market. Like many mentioned above, the Grupo Televisa SA, is the largest media company in the Spanish-speaking world, and a major player in the international entertainment business. It has interests in television production and broadcasting, programming for pay television, international distribution of television programming, Direct-to-Home satellite services, publishing and publishing distribution, music recording, cable television, radio production and broadcasting, professional sports and show business promotions, paging services, feature film production and distribution, dubbing, and the operation of a horizontal Internet portal. The Grupo Televisa also has an unconsolidated equity stake in Univision, the leading Spanish-language television company in the United States. Similarly, the Globo International programming service provides the top rated Globo programming broadcast in Brazil. The TV Globo International Programme Grid consists of the world famous Globo Tele-Novelas, independent productions from Rede Globo de Televisão, news, variety programming and talk shows. TV Globo International also has a highly rated drama and documentaries.

Competing media companies do not hesitate to cooperate in different markets. For example, Discovery India and Sony Entertainment Television have created a distribution alliance for six entertainment channels in India in 2002. The partnership happily distributes Discovery's quality nonfiction brands, Discovery Channel and Animal Planet, with Sony Entertainment Television's local Indian brands.

4

Some Technical Aspects

During the last two decades broadcast technology has become more and more sophisticated and user friendly. Once what was impossible for broadcasters is now possible with a touch of button. Convergence has led to a creation of sophisticated workstations, systems and solutions where sometimes several companies work together. Despite all these developments some basics have remained unchanged.

One cannot think of a broadcast system without a studio, which can be defined as a controlled acoustical environment. A room is said to be 'dead' if there is no reflection of a sound wave from the walls and the ceiling. A location in the room is called 'dead' if any sound originating from there never returns to it in the shape of a reflected wave.

A microphone (an acoustic-electric transducer, generating electric voltage from air pressure waves) placed in the 'dead' position picks up only the sound emanating directly from the source. The effect is usually displeasing, as the sound is perceived as flat and shallow.

A 'live' room is the one in which a great deal of reflection takes place and the sound returns to its source several times with diminishing intensity and an acoustical environment which is too live, leads to less clarity and poor articulation of spoken word.

Reverberation, the persistence of a sound generated after the sound stimulus has ceased, is effectively controlled by varying the absorption caused by the wall surfaces within the studio. This is achieved by affixing absorbing material on the walls as well as the ceiling and by judicious arrangement of furnishings so that the best effect is obtained. This process is called acoustic treatment and involves soundproofing, the rejection of unwanted extraneous sounds.

Even after the optimal adjustment of room acoustics, it is necessary to employ special techniques in the placement of microphones and in seating of artists before the microphones so as to achieve the best balance. These techniques aim at building up a proper volume relationship and time lag between the original and the reflected sound. This is achieved by adjusting the distance between the sound and the microphones.

While the multi-microphone pick-up is not unusual in broadcasting, it is most often preferred to use as few microphones as possible. An improperly placed combination of microphones may tend to create problems, which in effect are akin to poor acoustics.

A studio should obviously be well insulated from external noise. There are two ways in which the external noise enters the studio: the structure-borne sound vibration conveyed through the fabric of the building along with water pipes, etc, and the air-borne noise. A good initial design of the building is often the only sure way to ensure satisfactory insulation against the structure-borne sound. When the structure-borne sound is unacceptable the only solution may be to stop the noise at source, for example swathing off water pump during recording or transmission.

A high proportion of the external noise is air borne. Sound insulation improves as the mass of partition (walls, floors, ceilings) is increased. Thin flimsy structures have poor sound insulation. To prevent the external noises from being heard when people enter the studio/control rooms, etc. small sound-absorbent cubicles are introduced, known as sound locks. Ideally, ordinary doors should never have direct access into the studio. The doors should close as tightly as possible to prevent sound leakage. In addition to closing mechanisms (door closures, securing levers, etc.) all studio doors should have magnetic seals at the edges to help ensure firm sealing. Care should be taken to make sure that entry points for cable ducts, water pipes, etc. must be effectively sealed.

Studio ventilation system can be a source of noise. A good studio ventilation system must have large cross-section trouncing so that the air is moved relatively slowly. Bends in the trunking should be of large radius to reduce turbulence and the inside walls of the trunking should be lined up with a sound absorbent material.

Acoustic resonances (standing waves) can occur as the sound reverberates to and fro between non-absorbent surfaces. These can be avoided by sound diffusion. This is usually achieved by introducing deliberate irregularities in the surfaces involved so that sound waves are scattered when they are reflected. Presence of technical equipment and scenery provides adequate scattering.

Reverberation time (RT) is the time taken for a sound in a studio to decay through 60 dB. Roughly speaking this means the time it takes for a fairly loud sound to die away to inaudibility). It affects the final quality of the sound considerably. If it is too short, speech tends to sound dry and orchestral music lacks 'warmth' and 'blend'. Too long a reverberation time, however, makes speech distant and 'echoey'. In open air RT is nearly zero, in usual radio talk studio it is 0.4 second, in average sitting room it is 0.5 second, in theatre 1.0 second, in large TV studios it ranges from 0.7 to 1.1 second and in concert halls it is usually between 1.5 to 2.2 seconds. It is always better to aim at low RT in studio because reverberation can always be added artificially to the sound output but it can never be taken away.

The size of studio varies according to the purpose for which it is to be used. In radio, for news broadcasts a studio could be just a small cabin, but for recording a radio play or musical concert much bigger studio is needed. In television the studio size has to take care of lighting and camera movements also. Necessary fittings to put up and connect additional equipment would be required accordingly. Broadcast stations normally have several studios for different purposes and available facilities may vary according to the size and purpose for which the studio is to be used. Some stations have one or two multi-purpose studios of relatively bigger size and one relatively small studio for news and current affairs programmes.

A studio is connected to a control room, which has necessary equipment to control and manipulate the output of the studio before passing it on for recording or transmission. Sometimes there is a master control room, which is connected to all control rooms and can monitor there output. In radio, the control room only needs audio control facilities while in television the control room has more complex equipment dealing with the audio and video both.

Outside Broadcast (OB) Vans are sometimes described as studio on wheels. In fact, these are control rooms that can be connected on one side with a microwave or satellite link to the master control facility of the broadcast station and on the other with the pick-up devices (cameras and microphones) which are carried in the vans to the site of event.

Microphones are common to radio and television as audio picks up devices. As a performer speaks sound waves are created and radiated in all directions from the source. When a microphone is placed close to the sound source, a portion of the sound waves strikes the transducing element causing it to vibrate sympathetically and transform the sound energy into electrical energy.

A microphone produces high fidelity electrical output only when it exactly follows the impinging sound impulses. For this the microphone must (1) respond equally well to all frequencies in the audio range; (2) not add extra frequencies which do not exist in the original sound (harmonic distortion); (3) not by itself generate electronic noise; (4) produce sufficient electrical output for the smallest perceivable value of sound; (5) be free from acoustic resonance; (6) be acoustically transparent so that it does not by its presence distort the wave front. A high-fidelity microphone is also called objective microphone. However, broadcasters do not always prefer completely objective reproduction; a good producer often desires a modification that heightens the effect intended to be created.

Microphones
Types of dynamic or moving-coil microphone: It consists of a coil attached to a flexible diaphragm, the coil moving freely in a transverse magnetic field and incident air pressure waves on the diaphragm generate voltage in the coil. This type of microphone is

the stronger and cheaper of the two. It can withstand heat and humidity better than the condenser type and is well suited to outdoor use and reporting. Generally it does not give the same sound quality as the condenser microphones.

Condenser or capacitance microphone: This is a structure consisting of a flexible metal diaphragm closely spaced from a solid metal surface. A DC voltage applied through a resistor is maintained between the two electrodes. The incidence of sound pressure waves causes the spacing between the two electrodes to vary and thus the potential difference between them. The generated AC voltage developed across the resistor is usually capacitance coupled to an amplifier stage. Condenser microphones give better sound quality but are more expensive and very sensitive to heat and humidity and in tropical climates their use should be restricted to air-conditioned studios. The condenser microphones are sensitive to handling, pops and breathing noises. Some types have built-in protection against this. For news broadcasts these are ideal studio microphones.

Carbon microphone: It is the one that utilises the property of variable contact resistance provided by carbon granules in loose contact. A chamber housing the granules has two electrodes for connection to current source that passes current through the granules. A flexible wall of the chamber is exposed to incident sound pressure waves that vary the resistance of the carbon path.

Ribbon microphone: It is the one in which the electrical output is developed between the ends of a thin metal ribbon suspended in a strong magnetic field. The ribbon is exposed to the air and with both faces exposed acts as a pressure-gradient transducer. With one face exposed it behaves as a pressure type.

Pressure microphone: It has a voltage output proportional to instantaneous pressure. Moving coil microphone is an example of this type.

Pressure gradient microphone or velocity microphone: It is the one with an electrical voltage output proportional to particle velocity of the sound wave. The ribbon microphone is an example of this type.

Cardioid microphone: It combines the omni-directional response of the pressure microphone with the output from a bi-directional velocity microphone, thus an over all cardioid (a heart-shaped) directional response can be obtained. Other microphone combinations can be used and some microphones have controls or switches to 'aim' a null in the polar diagram in a particular direction.

Omni-directional microphone: It picks up sounds coming from any direction with equal sensitivity.

Directional microphone: It has a main direction of sensitivity and should always be pointed to the sound source. This type of microphone helps to reduce sound reverberations inside the studio or background noises outside. Directional microphone has proximity and if the sound source is close to it the sound will be coloured. Low tones of voice get boosted and it gives a voice a warmer and closer blend. Many directional microphones have an M/S switch. In the S-position (S for speech) the proximity effect is cancelled. In M-position (M for music) the frequency response is flat. This position is used if you are speaking from far away or if you speak close and you want the 'close' effect.

For getting clear "dry" voice recordings (if the sound reverberations from the wall make the voice "wet" and less clear) and to decrease background noises, when recording outside a directional microphone should be used. The microphone should be closer to the speaker but he should speak over and not into it.

Lavalier microphone or personal microphone or neck microphone: This is a dynamic microphone built specifically to be hung around the neck or to be attached to clothing. For interviews in particular this is a very useful microphone. Care should be taken that it does not rub noisily against the clothing.

Shotgun or gun microphone or super-cardioid microphone: This is a highly directional type microphone and is usually covered in a light metal tube as protection against wind noise. The gun microphone picks up sound through a narrow angle over long range, which enhances its versatility.

Some Technical Aspects

Boom microphone: It is a moveable arm with a microphone at its end. The arm movement permits positioning of the microphone and when mounted on a television camera it ensures that the microphone is out of view and gives superior directional results. The boom is frequently telescopic.

Radio or wireless microphone: It comes in two parts – a personal type microphone clips on clothing and a transmitter slips into reporter's pocket. It makes interviewing and recording music from a distance possible. It is extremely effective but needs to be treated with care as some types are inclined to be temperamental.

All microphones are highly sensitive to wind noises. A windshield of metal or foam can be helpful in correcting this, though high wind noises can never be entirely eliminated.

Audio Recorders

Cassette recorder: There are plastic cases with a length of narrow recording tape ready for loading into a cassette recorder. Low noise C-60 type should be preferred for the C-120. "Long-play" tends to turn tape into spaghetti inside the recorder. For editing the cassettes are dubbed on to 1/4-inch tape.

Reel to reel tape recorders: These tape recorders use 1/4-inch tape on open reels. Single-track machines should be used for news work. Their recorders are reliable and rugged.

Cartridge machines: Cartridges are plastic cases containing endless loops of 1/4-inch tape on a single reel. Only half of the width of the tape is recorded with the sound signal, the other half is recorded with a brief pulse or "pip" automatically when the sound recording begins. Machine will hear its own pip when the tape loop has been completely through to where it began and will then stop immediately. The tape is thus "cued up" ready to play again at the correct point.

It is advisable that a broadcasting organisation should standardise the type of tape it uses and align all recorders to that tape. In many organisations various non-professional tapes are used in professional machines. If you record on just any commercial tape on a recorder that is factory adjusted for one make of professional tape, you lose most advantages of a professional tape recorder.

Every tape is recorded with either IEC or NAB equalisation. These are two different standards for an electronic procedure to reduce tape hiss. A broadcasting organisation should decide on a single standard. A tape should be played back according to the same standard as used when it was recorded otherwise a sound colouration will occur. Some tape recorders have IEC/NAB switch and can play back according to both the standards. In such a case it should be known which standard was used while recording.

Disc reproducers or grams are important in storing music and sound effects. Disc reproducers should have a high quality turntable and motor assembly for stability and inaudible rumble. It should have a well-designed arm to ensure good tracking, minimum disc wear, etc.

Level controls allow you to adjust the level of sound signal being recorded to the standard magnetisation level on the tape. Meters are either VU-meters (Volume Unit Meters) or PPM-meters (Peak Programme Meters). Competent use of controls ensures good sound quality.

VU-meters have a scale marked from -30 dB, over 0 dB to +3dB, the part from 0 to +3 dB is marked in red. For speech, you should adjust the meter so that the peak readings do not go over 0 dB. It is safe to adjust for peaks going no higher than -3 dB.

PPM-meters have a numbered scale from 1 to 7 or marked from -60 dB to +10 dB. Needle moves very fast when going up and slow when going down and it gives consistent peak readings. One should adjust the level exactly for peak readings of 0 dB or 6 dB on the numbered scale.

Level has to be readjusted with a new position of speaker or for a changing distance from the microphone or changes in the mean loudness. If you set the recording sound level too low you will get too much tape hiss when playing back and the sound on the tape will be 'drowned' in the tape hiss. If the sound level is too high the recording will be distorted and the sound will be damaged.

Automatic level control should be avoided, as the recorder cannot know what part of speech is meant to be soft or loud. If the

Some Technical Aspects

part is soft-spoken, the background noise will be amplified to disturb the recording.

Radio OB/Radio ENG or Wireless Link cars / vans are fitted with a two-way radio telephone for communication with headquarters, a car radio for receiving the public programmes (for cue purposes, etc.) and with a high quality transmitter which realises a programme link to the studio. It is also equipped to perform other functions such as mixing, recording and work over line links.

Such systems are useful in live coverage of events and can give live inserts to a news programme. Wireless links in FM band are also available.

The video pick-up device or the television camera is similar in principle to a standard photographic or film camera but it differs by using a pick-up tube in place of film emulsion to convert the image of a scene into electrical signals. In a film camera, the lens shutter that allows the light to enter is closed after the light has entered the lens and struck the film and the film is advanced to the next frame automatically. To transport the film through a film camera sprocket holes are made in the film. These perforations are spaced four holes to each frame on 35mm film along both the edges of the film. On 16mm film there is one hole to each frame along both the edges if the film is silent but along one edge only when a sound track area is incorporated on it. On Super 8 there is one perforation to each frame along one edge opposite the centre of each frame. All motion picture cameras are motor-driven at a governed speed and to transport the film a claw enters a perforation and pulls the film down one frame at a time. Geared to this claw is a shutter, which closes while the film is travelling and reopens while the film is momentarily held stationary for the exposure. At normal speed this action repeats 24 times each second but because the images are retained in the retina, the eye sees continuous movement when the film is projected.

In a video or television camera, light enters the lens and strikes the sensitive area of the pick-up tube called the target area which is located behind a glass at the front of the tube and is made of a photoconductor metal alloy (antimony trisulfide in Vidicons and oxides of lead in Plumbicons). The target area is stationary and there is no shutter in a video camera but there is an iris, which may be closed. Instead of the movement of the target area, there is a cathode-ray scanning circuit, which operates the pick-up tube's deflection or sweep system and is co-ordinated by external electronic sweep circuits. These circuits move an electron beam back and forth across the front of the pick-up tube, pick up the picture information and wipe or clear the surface of the target area a given number of times per second, preparing it each time for a new exposure. Each exposure is called a frame and each frame is composed of two fields, one composed of all even-numbered sweep lines in the frame and the other composed of odd-numbered sweep lines. The number of these lines and the sweep frequency differs from system to system while these lines are horizontal elements of the images, the vertical elements are light or dark or the colour changes.

Depending upon the pick-up tube used the television cameras are of the following types:

Vidicon camera: Vidicon tubes are used in both portable and studio cameras. The picture received through the lens sets up a charge on the image side of a target in a Vidicon tube. The charge travels through the target and is discharged by a Vidicon beam on the opposite side, the gun side of the tube. Deflection circuits move this beam – back and forth – across the backside of the target scanning the target image. This defection circuit reading is fed into a load resistor, which produces the video signal.

For a portable television camera the Vidicon tube measures one inch in diameter and about six inches in length. A colour television camera requires three or four tubes for a 3-V or 4-V system. The 3-V system consists of tubes receiving red, blue and green pictures having gone through the lens prism and then through a red, green or blue filters into the Vidicon tubes. The 4-V system adds a monochromatic (black and white) tube to improve the crispness of the picture and to eliminate a slight blurring around the edges.

Plumbicon camera: The Plumbicon tube is slightly larger but it produces a better picture at low light levels. It has less image retention or burn in than a Vidicon. The three tubes in the colour Plumbicon camera are sensitive to the light spectrum. There is a red tube, a green tube and a blue tube instead of optical filters used in the Vidicon camera.

Image-Orthicon camera: The Image-Orthicon tube is much larger than the Vidicon tube and therefore it was perhaps never used as a portable camera. The Image-Orthicon tube has an additional electron multiplier section, which produces larger video signals than do either the Vidicon, or the Plumbicon tubes. The Image-Orthicon tubes have a shorter life span. It is becoming virtually obsolete because of high cost and larger size.

Satin camera: In this camera the target area of the tubes is made of a compound of selenium (S), arsenic (A), and tellurium (T). However, the construction of the tube is similar to the Vidicon. Satin is a registered trademark of Hitachi. Many modern colour cameras in use today are using 2/3-inch Satin tubes with electrostatic focusing and electromagnetic deflection for red, green and blue. These cameras also use microprocessors that digitally control an automatic setup system, including black balance, white balance, centreing, pulse-cancelling and fault diagnostic functions.

CCD-cameras: In these modern cameras, there is no tube. The light is focused on a compact array of light sensitive solid-state elements on a small semiconductor chip. The chip is called a charge-coupled device or CCD. The theory of operation of a CCD imaging chip is that the photons strike the surface of the imaging chip, which is divided into individual elements (rather than the continuous photosensitive surface of an imaging tube). Each element samples the light at that point and converts the light to a charge, which is then read out to camera circuitry. The surface of the imaging chip therefore resembles a matrix of individual elements, which in turn defines the spatial resolution capability of the camera. The advent of CCD-charge-coupled display technology in recent years has made possible miniaturisation of cameras without loss of quality. It is proving important particularly in news and sports coverage.

BBC R&D and Gigawave have also developed cable-free digital radio cameras, that provide a flexible and safe way to get broadcast cameras into crowded areas and places previously not possible.

It is the function of the camera lens to collect light from a scene and to focus it on the photosensitive surface of the pick-up tube. A lens is defined as an optical device made of glass and used for bending light rays by employing the natural effect of refraction. It could be a simple lens composed of a single glass element or it could be a complex lens system with a combination of different elements. Lens systems are mounted in lens barrels, which keep the lens elements separated in specific relationships to one another, and have engraved markings, the knurled rings on their outer surfaces for lens adjustment.

There used to be as many as four separate lenses of different fixed focal lengths mounted on a revolving turret on the video cameras used in the earlier days of television. The cameraman would choose any one of these lenses for a specific shot by turning a handle at the back of the camera, which mechanically turned the turret at the front of the camera. However, all modern cameras employ zoom lenses, which are capable of continuously changing the image size or field of view of an object without moving the camera. The zoom lens has a variable focal length, as it is a multi-element lens whose elements are made to move within the barrel in relationship to one another by the use of various controls.

The principal advantage of a zoom lens is that it offers continuously variable angle of view between two fixed limits. Typical horizontal angles are 6 to 30 degrees (a 5:1 zoom) and 5 to 50 degrees (a 10:1 zoom). The later range is best suited for studio cameras. A servomotor may directly operate the zoom mechanically or electrically. The latter provides smoother zoom. Certain zoom lens designs have the facility for fitting range extenders that alter the actual angular range available though the zoom ratio remains the same, e.g. by using X2 extender 5 to 50 degree would become 2.5 to 25 degree.

Camera mountings: The camera can be mounted on the cameraman's shoulder which allows for all the flexibility of the

Some Technical Aspects

human body in its motion and even though cameras are being designed to be shoulder mounted and have soft contoured shoulder pad, it is much more stable on a fixed mount. To provide a firm support for the TV camera a mounting of some kind is invariably used in studio productions and for long shootings even outdoors. The TV camera head itself is fixed to a pan-tilt head, a device that can be swung from side to side and up and down, by using its pan-tilt handle. This in turn is bolted onto a camera mounting which may be a tripod, a three-legged device with independent adjustment of the length of each leg. Once set up the over all height is not easily changed. Tripod is lightweight and cheap but only allows the camera to be used in one static position. The tripods with wheels underneath (trolley) are also available as mountings. The tripods are commonly used in the field.

In studio camera can be mounted on a pedestal or a studio dolly where it can glide horizontally around on wheels and be cranked up and down a short distance. The pedestal is a highly sophisticated camera mounting which enables both subtle and marked changes in camera position and height to be made while on shot. It can be moved around the studio quickly and silently with minimum effort, guided by a steering-ring or a tiller-handle. Beneath the pedestal's base, mechanical linkages line up its three wheels either to point in the same direction or to enable one to steer while the others follow. Often at broadcast stations a dolly operator who leaves the cameraman free to frame and focus moves the studio dolly.

The other camera mountings include cranes, which can move to heights of 10 feet or more above or move down to near floor level.

A camera cable is the vital link between the television camera head and its control unit. The signal, video or audio, goes from the camera to its destination via camera cables and cable connectors at the end of these cables. It is a multi-way cable with a plug at one end and a socket at the other end, with keyway at both the ends to ensure that the cable locates correctly. The different types of wires within the camera cable carry various signals and supplies including the picture output from the camera, synchronising pulses, electrical power, talkback circuits to the camera and specialised voltage feeds to ensure correct operation of the pick-up tube.

There are several cabling points or distribution boxes on the studio wall into which the camera cable could be plugged. These are generally distributed on three of the four studio walls and are more than the number of cameras used in the studio. These help avoid long loops of cable around the studio floor and enable each camera to route its cable to meet the production requirements of a particular programme. These points are permanently routed to a communal patch panel near the camera control units.

Camera cables are often mishandled; they are stepped on, twisted and run into by heavy-wheeled pedestals. Cable connectors are often dropped on concrete floors or suffer attempted forced mating if their pins and sockets do not coincide resulting in bent pins. These mishaps should be avoided and when disconnected and stored both the ends should be covered to avoid entry of dirt or moisture into the cables. The cable should never be made to follow acute bends or twists to avoid internal damage.

Lighting used in television falls into two broad categories: (1) natural light (or sunlight) and (2) artificial light (or electric incandescent light).

Sunlight is also called available light and it can be controlled to some degree. Large panel reflectors can aim reflected light from the sun at a subject or scene when the need is to concentrate the available light. Its intensity for the pick-up tube can be reduced by the use of the camera lens aperture control and by the neutral density filter used to control the amount of light entering the lens.

Incandescent light available to video cameraman ranges from the small battery-pack-operated hand held or camera-top-mounted portable lamp; portable lightweight kits to massive high powered studio lights. The most prevalent type of studio light is the tungsten halogen incandescent lamp available in much wattage. Using dimmers or scrims can control light intensity of each lamp. Dimmers are used only for cyclorama lighting when the colour temperature is not critical. Scrims are diffusers placed in front of the lamp which soften and decrease the intensity of the light but maintain its colour

Some Technical Aspects

temperature at a steady 3200 to 3400 degrees Kelvin, the standard range to maintain accurate skin tones on colour television and optimum television results.

"Barn doors" are often clamped to the edges of the lamp fixture to adjust the field of light dispersion. The concentration of light from lamps is controlled by mounting the lamps in shaped reflectors behind the light source, by placing concentrating lenses called Fresnel lenses in front of the light source to provide spotlighting and by using some kind of control which moves the lamp in and out as the reflector changes the focus of the light. Thus the lighting fixtures fall in two categories; those that give focused light and the other that gives non-focused diffused or fill light.

In a studio situation a subject is lit by three lights: a key light, a fill light and a back light. The key light is the brightest light. The key light is often placed at a 45 degree angle from the camera. If the light is too close to the camera, the lighting will be too flat. If it is too great an angle, the key light will provide only side lighting. The key light is not focused narrowly. It lights the subject and the area around.

The fill light is used to fill shadows caused by the key light. A diffused light source placed near the camera may serve the purpose. The back light is used to light the subject's back and shoulders. It gives depth to the picture and helps separate the subject from the wall behind. Besides these main lights, there are possibilities of using additional lights to lighten specific areas, for example, and a small eye light may add sparkle to the subject's eyes.

To get the best out of the light source, it is necessary to control its placement and positioning. In the studios there are overhead support brackets, pole extenders, pantograph suspension systems with the light fixtures and mounting grids, etc. for this purpose. Well-equipped studios even have lighting bars on motorised hoists and other motorised telescopic systems. Besides, there are various types of lamp fixture stands with folding tripod legs for portable use and heavy bases for studios.

Studio lighting fixtures are often wired through a control panel or lighting console so that they can be switched on or off as needed from a central position rather than individually. These consoles can have programmed information for precise dimmer setting of all the lamps and can be used to provide different light effects such as day and night on the same set.

A *sound mixing* desk enables the operator to control the level of programme so that the reproduced sounds are neither too weak, relative to the background noise nor too loud overloading the system and causing distortion. Also relative outputs of sound sources such as, microphones, tape machines, etc. are mixed (balanced) to provide a combined sound signal artistically appropriate.

In a *sound mixing* desk each sound source is connected to a jack socket. Levels of the individual sound sources are adjusted by channel fades. Each channel can be switched to one of the two or more groups and the group faders act as sub-master controls. Finally, all the groups are combined and the overall balance is adjusted by the main (master) fader to keep the audio levels with the system's limits.

The *sound mixing* desks also provide the foldback, public address and clean feed. In the foldback one or more selected sources are fed to loudspeakers on the studio floor. The most common function of the foldback is to provide audible cues to performers in the studio. For example, a feed of telecine sound played over the studio foldback loudspeaker not only provides audible cues for the end of the film sequence, but also gives an indication of the pace and delivery.

The public address feed is taken to loudspeakers in the vicinity of a studio audience, as generally a studio audience is unable to hear much of the direct sound from the studio floor. Thus the PA feed through carefully placed directional loudspeakers is essential if the audience is to be able to hear properly and thus be able to react, ie applaud, laugh, etc.

A clean feed is a feed of the main desk output minus one or more selected sources. The clean feeds are essential facilities if we are simultaneously using two studios with contributions from each so as to ensure that the loudspeaker in each studio reproduces only the sound from the other studio to avoid howl-round or unwanted colouration.

In broadcast studio complex, particularly in television, talkback facilities are essential to co-ordinate the team effort. A microphone on the desk of the director (producer) relays his voice to cameraman through the camera cable, boom operators and to the other floor staff who wear headphones plugged into wall sockets distributed around the studio. A floor manager, who has to be extremely mobile often wears an earpiece connected to his small pocket receiver, which is tuned to the studio's radio talkback transmitter. Adjoining technical areas like VTR and telecine rooms are equipped with talkback loudspeakers. Where the production talkback is required to communicate outside the studio complex a sound line is used to feed a loudspeaker or headset there.

Key operated microphones enable the technical director, sound mixer or lighting director to talk on production talkback when necessary. A further key enables technical or production control room staff to speak on studio foldback loudspeakers, but this facility is made inoperative during transmission to prevent accidents. For certain types of productions, (e.g. news) the presenter wears a deaf-aid earpiece fed with a switched talkback which can be operated by a push-button switch by the director in the control room. This facility enables the director to pass instructions to the presenter even when the programme is on the air.

Besides, various private wire systems provide inter-specialist communication between the sound mixer and his studio assistant, between the lighting director and electricians and between the specialist control points (vision control, sound mixer and lighting) and the director.

Some communication on the studio floor has to be by signals that are easily comprehended by the professionals using them. For example, the cameraman can reply to talkback questions by camera movement. He can rapidly tilt his camera up or down to answer "yes" or pan it right to left to answer "no". A circular movement or zoom jerk means "I have a problem" and rapid in/out focusing shows that he cannot focus sharply on his subject due to limited depth of field. Similarly telecine and videotape operators do not usually need to talk to the director; they have a button, which operates a buzzer in the control room. One buzz in reply means "yes" and two buzzes mean "no".

Signals from the floor manager can provide a range of silent cues and instructions to guide the performers. For example, a circular 'winding up' motion of hand usually indicates the last 30 seconds. The final ten seconds are counted down separately with much exaggeration by finger signal. Frenetic cutthroat sign indicates over-running, finish immediately.

Telecine machines are special types of film projectors enabling the film image to be converted directly into video signal without the use of an intermediary screen. There are two basic designs of telecine – the flying spot design that employs a cathode ray tube (display tube) and the other Vidicon tubes.

Telecine machines have provision for corrections of various parameters of audio and video signals and the operator keeps on correcting these parameters when the film is running. The Vidicon telecine are in principal film projectors fitted with a suitable lens system which focuses the image of the film straight on the target of a Vidicon television camera.

Videotape recorder: A videotape recorder (VTR) is a machine of recording television pictures and sound onto a magnetic tape. The sound is recorded in the same way as in an audio tape recorder. However, recording the wide frequency band of television signals requires effective tape speeds much greater than those used in audio tape recording.

High effective tape speeds are achieved by rapidly moving the video heads across the magnetic tape as the tape is pulled forward by the tape transport mechanism. Stationary heads are used on the audio signal along a narrow band at the top of the tape and a control signal along the narrow band at the bottom of the tape.

There are two video-recording systems: the quadruplex (quad-head) and the helical-scan. In the quadruplex system four recording heads are equally spaced around the edge of a two-inch (5-cm) wheel that spins at 240 revolutions per second. In the helical-scan system two heads are usually used though some types have one head only. The heads are mounted on a short cylinder called the head drum. The tape follows a half-turn spiral path around the head drum so that the head drum spins and the heads record a series of slanting tracks across the tape. In case of two head helical-scan recorders the drum completes 30 revolutions per second while this drum speed is doubled in case of single head recorders.

Metal particle tapes and digital recording methods have been developed for producing recordings of superior quality. Digital recording consists of converting electrical signals from pick-up devices into signals representing numbers. The conversion is made by an electronic device that measures the characteristics of the signal with great precision many thousand times a second. Each measurement is given a numerical value and recorded on magnetic tape. In playback an electrical signal virtually identical to the original one is reconstructed from the measurements. High quality of digital recording is due to the fact that numbers can be recorded and played back from magnetic tape with almost complete accuracy.

Various recording systems not only utilise the different scanning arrangements but also use different width of tape. Following are the various formats and sizes of videotapes:

Two-inch quadruplex (transverse scan): This has been standard videotape used for broadcasting since 1956. Its basic problem is that there is no form of still frame or slow replay. In editing, therefore, one can only see pictures when the tape is running at its correct speed which makes accurate editing and fine adjustment difficult. Quad system is giving way to other systems as manufacture of this type of VTRs has been stopped. However, most broadcast systems are still using the old workhorse.

One-inch videotape (helical scan): This allows for still frame and slow speed replay and has now become standard type for broadcast use in place of quad.

3/4-inch high band videotape: This 3/4-inch size videotape is known as "High Band U-matic" and is of broadcast quality. It comes in cassette form and the location recorder is easily carried on the shoulder. General applications include ENG (Electronic News Gathering), EFP (Electronic Field Production) and PSC (Portable Single Camera) operations. A more recent development is "SP U-matic" also called Super High Band.

3/4-inch low band videotape: This tape is not broadcast quality. High band and low band systems are not interchangeable although cassettes of either system can be played back in the machines of the system for viewing purposes only. Low band is used in non-broadcast video, in off-line editing (when the master tape is transferred to a poorer quality tape for initial editing) and for viewing and exhibition purposes.

Half-inch broadcast quality videotape: This is used in broadcast quality systems such as Betacam. By using half-inch tape the recorder can be built into the camera giving shooting flexibility. Higher quality system such as Sony Betacam SP and Panasonic MII gives the same flexibility with performance comparable with one-inch systems.

Half-inch domestic videotape: Other than Betacam, half-inch tape is mostly used in home video systems which are used as cheap office viewing and for off-line editing also. The two main systems in current use are Video Home System (VHS) and Bateaux. These systems are not compatible though both use half-inch tape.

VTRs are becoming more and more sophisticated and easy to operate.

Television systems converter: Material recorded on one television system as opposed to format is not compatible with another system even if the make and type of machine is the same unless the tape is played through a standards converter.

There are basically three television systems in the world. The 625-line PAL system is used in the UK and Europe (except France), Australia, China and India; the 525-line NTSC system is used in the USA and Japan and 625-line SECAM system is used in France and the erstwhile USSR. There are modifications of these basic systems like NTSC 4.43 and PAL-M.

Television standards converters are available that not only convert the system on broadcast quality videotape but using a time base correction function they can assure clear stable images even when converting with half-inch home VCR.

Videotape editing on open real quadruplex machines was very difficult during early days. The tape was actually cut with a razor knife at editing points and spliced together. The vertical-interval edit point was found by moving a glass disk containing iron filings across the tape and observing as the tape's magnetism displaced the filings in a crude display of vertical interval. This was identified as the edit point.

The present practice is different. Videotape is dubbed or copied electronically from one tape to another at required edit points. The process requires (1) one or two videotape playback machines; (2) a time base corrector for each videotape playback machine; (3) a videotape recorder; (4) an editing controller and; (5) two or more video monitors, one for each tape machine.

Vision mixer or Production switcher: All video sources used in a production are fed into vision-mixing desk or a vision mixer. The outputs of all cameras, telecine, VTRs, caption scanners (film strips and slides and digital video effects are connected to the inputs of a vision-mixing unit or production switcher. Its function is to edit together by cutting, mixing, etc. all these various contributions to the production as desired by the director of the programme.

A switcher can be described in terms of its number of inputs and outputs; thus 8x2-switcher would have 8 inputs and two outputs. Video signals are combined in the switcher electronically by moving the video signal to and from buses or switch points. A bus is a line extension of a single point and a switching bus is a series of switch points, inputs, or intermediate points only one of which can be switched to the bus output at any given time.

Visual effects that require time, skill, and costly additional equipment in film can be achieved in TV at the touch of a button on a vision mixing panel:

Cut: It is an instantaneous switch from one picture to another.

Mix: Here the transition is less pronounced and as the faders are operated the established picture fades away while the new picture appears. Both the picture sources appear on the screen simultaneously. A mix can take several seconds or can be instantaneous.

Fade in/out: Here half of the split fader is used. A selected video source can be faded up or down (in/out) by moving the bus fader up or down. Fades are usually used as introductory or concluding changes in a programme.

Super: By fading in two or more picture sources together superimposition is obtained. This is generally used to add titles to an existing picture or generate some special effect.

Wipe: This is most common vision mixer special effect and can be described as a picture 'chasing' the earlier picture off the screen. The direction of entry can be horizontal, vertical, diagonal, circular or diamond shaped.

Split screen: It is a wipe frozen at a pre-determined point resulting in part of one picture inlaid into another.

Overlay: Brightness separation overlay generates tricks like white lettering on a black caption card which could be 'punched into' a scene from another source or a person before a black drop could be inserted and appear 'within' another scene. A special electronic switch effects this. Colour separation overlay does the same trick in the colour production.

Black edge facility: It adds thin black edges around the white lettering to make sure that there is clarity of caption. An electronic black edge generator artificially does this.

Electronic character generators: It generates letters and numerical that can be inlayed anywhere in a picture area. The output is connected directly to a vision mixer as a normal picture source and can be processed as such.

Control room: Attached to each studio is production control room where the programme producer or director sits and directs it. It has a group of labelled video monitors (cam 1, cam 2, telecine, preview, air, etc.); video control equipment at video technicians position; production switcher at switching position and audio console. Programme director's position has a talkback microphone and other associated equipment and with him there is a chair for the production assistant who assists him during the production.

In short, all the main control panels are placed in the control room and using them proceedings in the studio can be controlled and additional inputs from other sources can be incorporated into the programme.

Master control room: In large broadcast stations the studio complex invariably has a master control room which is connected to all the studios and various channels. What goes in the air can be controlled and monitored from here. It has the facilities to receive outside feeds from satellite or microwave links and pass it on to a relevant studio when required. It is connected to various transmitters and passes on signals to them for transmission via cables.

ENG/EFP: The video field shootings or productions or out of studio recording or telecast falls into two categories: electronic news gathering (ENG) and electronic field production (EFP). Except very important occasions when ENG coverage is directly sent to studio over microwave or satellite link for immediate telecast, ENG is usually videotaped on site for later editing and use in the newscast. ENG crew has a cameraman, a soundman and a light man, the crew may go and shoot the event or a reporter or producer who has to do the story may accompany it. With the availability of lightweight equipment the number of persons in ENG crew in more efficient organisations has gone down to two and in some cases even to one.

Electronic field production involves use of a full complement of transportable (not necessarily portable) studio/control room equipment with more than one camera in operation and their output is fed through a switcher.

Live coverage of important events and sports has been made possible by introduction of outdoor broadcast vans. In television OB vans have all the main processing facilities that are available in the control room of a well designed studio complex and have digital character generator and special effect generators. The output is sent to the master control room of the broadcast station by using microwave link and sometimes from long distances via satellite from where it is directly fed to the transmitter chain.

In India a public sector undertaking, Bharat Electronics Limited (BEL) has been associated in a big way in the development of broadcast hardware. The BEL entered the field of radio broadcasting in 1962 acquiring know-how for manufacture of transmitters and studio equipment from NEC, Japan. Within a decade BEL indigenised a large range of equipment. Initially it supplied studio equipment like tape recorders, consoles, etc. In 1972, BEL started designing studio equipment and transmitters for AIR. The products included transmitters in 100 KW, 10 KW and 1KW MW range and connected equipment. Mobile 10 KW MW transmitters, 3 KW FM transmitters, Mark II console tape recorders, 100 KW MW transmitters, 2x100 KW transmitters, 1 KW MW transmitters and 50KW SW transmitters are among the products that are currently being supplied. BEL's contribution of hardware to AIR during 1985-90 is expected to be Rs.900 million, which is ten times more than 1980-85. With the decision to have FM transmitters in most districts, BEL's supplies to AIR will increase substantially.

BEL started its activity in TV equipment manufacture when it acquired the technology of TV transmitters from NEC, Japan and the technology for TV studio equipment from Frenseh, West Germany during 1971. Over the years, BEL has not only developed the technology base to enable design and manufacture of state-of-the-art TV transmitters and studio equipment, but also successfully developed and supplied a large number of low power TV transmitters and TVROs for rebroadcast of TV programmes through satellite.

During this period BEL designed and manufactured OB vans for AIR and Doordarshan. BEL's OB van for colour TV EFP has all modern facilities and is comparable to those used in advanced countries. BEL also undertakes the setting up of modern colour TV studio and TV transmitting stations on a turn key basis.

Some Technical Aspects

Digital technology has revolutionised broadcasting and with the introduction of digital vision mixers fine tuning post-production has become a reality. A full range of effects can be carried out on recorded material and multiple picture generation is possible without loss of quality. A whole range of digital special effects generators is available in the market making film technique based special effects almost obsolete. Character generators provide comprehensive video lettering in a variety of typefaces, size and colouring. There is a large variety of computer based special effects generators that can store, retouch, re-size and reposition graphics and present them in the required order. These can provide some and all of the following features: multiple pictures, borders and matte effects, images of varying size, wipes, split screens, flips, cubes, re-sizing and repositioning of still pictures or freeze frames. These effects can be recorded and stored. There are also digital frame stores that electronically store any picture in desired order. It was at the 1976 Montreal Olympics a Quantel DFS 3000 transmitted a video image inset into the main picture showing a close-up of the Olympic torch as the runner entered the stadium. This was for many viewers the first experience of digital effects on television. In 1980s many companies started innovations in this area. Thomson Video Equipment introduced TTV 5650 digital vision mixer relying on all digital processing and accepting all types of conventional input sources while Quantel introduced Digital Production Centre that did everything a conventional suite could do and a lot more but all without the traditional bank of VTRs, edit controller or switcher.

Launched in 1981 Quantel's Paintbox still remains the graphics design tool of choice for broadcasters worldwide. Paintbox redefined the viewer experience, making digital graphics an integral part of any broadcast. Another radical leap was made in 1985 when Quantel invented Harry, the world's first non-linear editor. NLEs now proliferate and dominate the editing business, with linear editing suites now largely obsolete. Harry did for editors what Paintbox had done for graphic designers, moving them into another dimension. The concept of non-linear editing was taken online by Editbox, which is now an industry standard tool.

iQ is the single most exciting development in the last few years. Far more than just another product, iQ is an architecture, a new way of working, a whole new platform for content creation. iQ technology provides a completely integrated environment at the heart of which sits the powerful iQ platform where Quantel's purpose-built hardware meets the openness of standard platforms. All of the barriers to HD and 2K production have been swept aside. One can work in a fully uncompressed, top quality video of any resolution – in real time. iQ's unique resolution co-existence means that no matter what format and resolution your material is in, one can work with it all on the same timeline, in real time. There is no need to convert or compress, so there is never any loss of quality. When you have finished creating, simply choose your output format and iQ will do the rest. Fast versioning at the highest possible quality has never been easier. iQ is open – it is a completely integrated environment where Quantel's purpose-built hardware meets the openness of a standard (but very high specification) PC. iQ is also unrivalled when it comes to networking. Sitting at the heart of the facility, this platform will give you new levels of real time, interactive performance, enormous workflow flexibility and total creative freedom. iQ is new thinking in post-production.

QEdit Pro is a next generation multi-format editing and effects system that delivers a real 10 bit non-compressed quality and a high end-creative toolset into the mainstream finishing market. Resolution co-existence and a HD option make QEdit Pro the first PC-based NLE system to deliver real finishing performance across all SD and ASTC High Definition formats. The integrated toolset builds on the Henry Infinity and provides all the high end features found in iQ including tracking, sophisticated colour correction and the next generation Paintbox. The system's lightning fast pen and tablet, jog/shuttle unit, keyboard and hand controller is an ergonomic breakthrough for unmatched workflow efficiency.

Another important company in this area is Avid Technology, Inc., with corporate headquarters in Tewksbury, Massachusetts, USA. Avid delivers the solutions that make, manage and move media from video, audio and film to animation, special effects and streaming media. Avid's products are used to make television and news shows, commercials, music videos and CDs, corporate/industrial productions and major motion pictures. Avid provides powerful servers, networks and media tools to help customers search files, share media and collaborate on new productions, both locally and globally. Avid's solutions empower users to easily move media, whether on air, over cable or satellite or through the Internet. Avid's end-to-end solutions span the continuum of media creation, management and distribution.

Avid Unity for News is a media network for news that provides an open and expandable architecture for sharing, making, managing, and moving high-resolution video throughout the news production process – all in real time. It turns news production workstations into integral components of a true nonlinear workflow and makes newsroom far faster than tape, more efficient than linear processes, and more productive.

Avid NewsCutter Effects has full A/B functionality, advanced features and high-speed performance make this the right choice for a craft-editing news production suite. NewsCutter Effects systems support DV25, DV50 and D10 MPEG formats, can interface with both SDI and SDTI protocols, and are designed specifically for the demands of newsroom use, using only qualified hardware that has surpassed rigorous testing and integration standards in a broadcast-editing environment. It integrates with linear acquisition systems such as Betacam, Betacam SP, Betacam SX, DVCPRO, or S-VHS; fits into any existing linear or nonlinear news production environment. When connected to Avid Unity for News it allows editors and reporters unlimited access to all media. It links directly to Avid iNEWS, so one can view rundowns, write scripts, and drag-and-drop stories directly into the NewsCutter bin, eliminating retyping errors and streamlining the production process. Finished stories can be sent at speeds of up to 5 times faster than real time to play-out servers such as the Avid AirSPACE video server for broadcast within seconds of completion.

Avid iNEWS MultiByte is newsroom automation system for Asian-language broadcasters. This toolbox of separate but highly compatible applications includes Running-order Editor, Directory Viewer, Script Editor, assignment forms, instant messaging, and much more. This highly-reliable Asian language newsroom system built on 22 years of broadcast news automation experience has superior machine control technology that allows dynamic and instantaneous updating of devices from the running order. It uses a "building block" approach, so applications can be added, enhanced, or replaced independently. Avid iNEWS MultiByte's Directory Viewer enables viewing of edited news stories from any standard workstation and storage of hundreds of hours of video while maintaining links to written scripts

When ITN decided to move to a totally server-based newsroom it turned to Quantel. Quantel servers sit at the heart of Inspiration, a totally integrated tapeless newsroom from which ITN produces its wealth of programming, including a 24-hour news channel. With its browse capabilities journalists can now make editorial decisions for themselves, from their own desks. sQ is a completely new architecture for news and live production, offering complete scalability, industry standard compression schemes and with both broadcast-quality and browse images held on the same storage and controlled by a single database.

ENPS, Electronic News Production System, developed by Associated Press is another popular new newsroom system, supporting journalists working in more than 40 languages in more than 400 television, radio and network operations in about 40 countries. AP NewsCenter, with more than 200 installations worldwide, was the first newsroom computer system designed from the start for use with Windows—praised for its basic power and flexibility. AP NewsDesk, initially created to help stations more efficiently manage news wires and write scripts, is installed in more than 2,400 locations. More than two dozen companies are working with AP on MOS-related projects.

BBC also worked with AP but now it has launched its own company for the purpose. As part of the licence fee settlement in 2000, the British government tasked the BBC with generating £1.1bn in savings, efficiencies and increased commercial revenues, over

Some Technical Aspects

the next five years. The BBC Ventures Group of companies has been created with BBC Technology, BBC Broadcast and BBC Resources, wholly-owned commercial subsidiaries of the BBC. BBC Technology has been created in April 2001 to design, build and operate solutions for creating, managing and distributing content across all broadcast, digital media and interactive platforms – both for the BBC and the other global players. The company employs 1200 people at locations in London and Maidenhead in the UK and San Francisco, New York, and Atlanta in the US.

There are other solutions as well. When Murdoch's Star News Channel in India decided to produce its own content, it went to Autocue, which provided Star with a 55-seat QSeries newsroom system featuring fully integrated newsroom, media management, browsing, and automation capabilities in Bombay, Delhi and 21 other locations around India. In addition, Star also bought 14 Autocue prompting systems fully integrated with the QSeries newsrooms. The system integrated with a high-resolution server and editing system from Quantel, and with an on-air graphics system from Vizrt to create a seamless working environment for Star's journalists, to create and broadcast a 24-hour Hindi news service for the subcontinent. Ramsay Ismail, Autocue's Newsroom Systems Sales Director said on this deal, "We are happy to be able to demonstrate the full integration capability of the QSeries, from ingest and media management right through to scripting, running-order management, and on-air automation. And, of course, we must not forget prompting, where we are supplying Star with a number of separate systems all of which will be fully multilingual and all fully integrated with the newsrooms." Doordarshan is also using QSeries.

Autocue has been serving the broadcast industry since the mid-50s when Autocue Ltd. in London and in parallel QTV in New York produced and patented the very first prompters. Autocue and QTV merged in 1984 and have been serving clients like the Bloomberg, the BBC MTV Europe and Doordarshan in India.

The first prompters, consisting of a synchronised electric paper roller with one-inch jumbo type, used a mirror and a piece of semi-reflective glass to focus the image of the moving text over the lens of the camera into the presenter's eye line. This simple device transformed the way that presenters communicated, enabling them to maintain eye contact with viewers and to concentrate on delivery.

Since then Autocue has led the market in technical development, leading up to the fully integrated, PC-driven prompters now in use. Autocue have sold prompting hardware in nearly every country, estimating around 75% of the market worldwide. Since 1986 it has extended our reach into all aspects of television news production. Initially introducing scripting and newsroom systems, in 1997 it added transmission and master control automation as a natural extension of its services to develop the advanced production and automation systems it offers today under the name of the QSeries.

The QSeries has been designed to meet these fundamental challenges in news production: Software integration to provide a complete news and automation solution without reliance on a third-party software. Multi-lingual capability – allowing almost any language to be used. Comprehensive editing facilities – a flexible script editor suitable for applications from news to drama, with true multi-column facilities. Reliability-sharing critical data over several standard servers to provide load balancing and data mirroring. Scalability – any number of workstations connected with standard networking equipment. Active updating – to ensure that everyone sees the correct, current information. Easy of use – a simple, Windows-style approach that can be customised as much or as little as necessary. These challenges should be met by any newsroom system. QNews, QNet, QMedia and QTX form an integrated software family that provides flexible, innovative and seamless solutions for production office, newsroom and transmission facility.

TV Today has chosen a Swiss company Incite and its partners for its 24-hour news channel 'Aaj Tak' in Hindi and second news channel 'Headline News' in English. Incite, featuring multiple Incite editing and capturing stations, SAN-based (Storage Area Network) media-sharing, automated ingest and newsroom management based on MOS-protocol and Incite project configuration tools specifically designed for modern IT-network environments. Incite editor and

Incite remote producer are the core editing applications for this completely digital newsroom solution, with Incite remote producer being the newest addition to the production workflow. Incite editor is a hardware-based editor that accesses on-line material over the SAN, while Incite remote producer is a software-codec based editor, which accesses the same material over the gigabit. The result is a seamless blending of two types of networking, allowing increased scalability and versatility, at a much lower price and with a greater return on investment. Incite applications are fully integrated with the automated newsroom and with partners: The Octopus newsroom system, Aveco automated ingest and playout, and VizRT for real-time streaming graphics during playout.

Sony introduced DVCAM in 1996 and it has been successful in news broadcast market. Sony and Incite demonstrated the combined power of shooting directly on disk and then editing seamlessly in the field with laptops or home-type computers, using Sony's new DSR-DU1 portable Video Disk Unit and two new Incite products, Incite Remote Producer and Incite Newsmaker at IBC 2002, in Geneva. Sony's DSR-DU1 Video Disk Unit is a portable 40GB capacity, 2.5" hard-disk drive that attaches directly to professional quality DVCAM camcorders through i.Link (Firewire), recording up to 3 hours of video/audio signals in parallel with tape recording, and provides unique features for clip selection directly on the disk. The disk can then be attached to the editing station through the same i.Link connection, and coverage is ready to be edited without any transfer or copying needs. Incite Remote Producer and Incite Newsmaker are Incite's software-based editing applications for on-line editing of DV camcorder footage for laptops and PCs. Both programmes can take advantage of Incite's media management and editing tools to browse, preview and edit media directly from Sony's DSR-DU1 Video Disk Unit.

Sony also joined IBM to create for CNN a new digital asset management system aimed at putting CNN's videotape archive online, providing better protection for CNN's footage, and making it more easily accessible to CNN journalists worldwide. For CNN, the resulting system will reduce operational costs and provide greater opportunities to increase revenue by leveraging our digital assets across multiple platforms.

The joint IBM and Sony system is helping to change the way CNN stores and distributes content and marks the beginning of a complete transformation of CNN's traditional news production methodologies from analog to all new digital work-flows. The newly designed and customised system will digitise, catalog, store, distribute, and retrieve more than 120,000 hours of archival material, gathered during the past 21 years at CNN. The CNN production ramp-up is one of the biggest and most ambitious digital transformation projects ever undertaken.

Media Production Suite from IBM combines essential hardware and software components, including industry-leading applications. MPS includes built-in capabilities that allow companies to oversee workflow management; integrate production systems, manage production-quality video objects, and archive media; including the management of related physical tape libraries. Media Production Suite combines an open, standards-based foundation, with its scalable, robust architecture. Media Production Suite is fortified with a finely tuned set of functions and solutions, including creative; on-the-spot editing; advanced searches; sophisticated workflow management; media handling and playout to support realtime broadcasting.

Media Object Servers Communications Protocol (MOS) is an evolving protocol for communications between Newsroom Computer Systems (NCS) and Media Object Servers (MOS) such as Video Servers, Audio Servers, Still Stores and Character Generators. This protocol is supported and developed through cooperative collaboration among equipment vendors, software vendors and end users. The goal is to develop and implement a common communications protocol, which will allow integration of diverse NCS and MOS equipment.

Such cooperation is an important feature of the digital age and is best demonstrated by DVD.

DVD once stood for digital video disc or digital versatile disc, but now it just stands for DVD, the next generation of optical disc storage technology. DVD is essentially a bigger, faster CD that can hold cinema-like video, better than CD audio and computer data. DVD aims to encompass home entertainment, computers, and business information with a single digital format, eventually replacing audio CD, videotape, laser disc, CD-ROM, and video game cartridges. DVD has widespread support from all major electronics companies, all major computer hardware companies, and all major movie and music studios. With this unprecedented support, DVD has become the most successful consumer electronics product of all time in less than three years of its introduction.

It is important to understand the difference between the *physical formats* (such as DVD-ROM or DVD-R) and the *application formats* (such as DVD-Video or DVD-Audio). DVD-ROM is the base format that holds data. DVD-Video (often simply called DVD) defines how video programmes such as movies are stored on disc and played in a DVD-Video player or a DVD computer. The difference is similar to that between CD-ROM and Audio CD. DVD-ROM includes recordable variations DVD-R/RW, DVD-RAM, and DVD+R/RW. The application formats include DVD-Video, DVD-Video Recording, DVD-Audio, DVD-Audio Recording, DVD Stream Recording, and SACD. There are also special application formats for game consoles such as Sony PlayStation 2.

DVD is the work of many companies and many people. There were originally two competing proposals. The MMCD format was backed by Sony, Philips and others. The SD format was backed by Toshiba, Matsushita, Time Warner and others. A group of computer companies led by IBM insisted that the factions agree on a single standard. The combined DVD format was announced in September of 1995, avoiding a confusing and costly repeat of the VHS vs. Betamax videotape battle or the quadraphonic sound battle of the 1970s.

No single company "owns" DVD. The official specification was developed by a consortium of ten companies: Hitachi, JVC, Matsushita, Mitsubishi, Philips, Pioneer, Sony, Thomson, Time Warner and Toshiba. The representatives from many other companies also contributed in various working groups. In May 1997, the DVD Consortium was replaced by the DVD Forum which is open to all companies, and has over 220 members. Time Warner originally trademarked the DVD logo, and has since assigned it to the DVD Format/Logo Licensing Corporation. The term "DVD" is too common to be trademarked or owned.

Mention here should also be made of the Moving Picture Experts Group (MPEG), a working group of ISO/IEC (the International Standards Organisation/International Electrotechnical Commission) in charge of the development of international standards for compression, decompression, processing, and coded representation of moving pictures, audio and their combination. MPEG usually holds three meetings a year. These comprise plenary meetings and subgroup meetings on requirements, systems, multimedia description schemes, video, audio, synthetic natural hybrid coding test, implementation studies and liaison. MPEG meetings are attended by more than 300 experts from over 20 countries. So far MPEG has produced MPEG-1, the standard for storage and retrieval of moving pictures and audio on storage media (approved in Nov. 1992);MPEG-2, the standard for digital television (approved in November 1994); and MPEG-4, the standard for multimedia applications. (Its version 1 was approved in October 1998 and version 2 was approved in December 1999); MPEG-7, the content representation standard for multimedia information search, filtering, management and processing and has started MPEG-21 the multimedia framework.

5

Some Tricks of the Trade

While in radio one has to deal with only audio, in television the process is more complex because of an additional visual element. When one looks at the television programme production process, it incorporates audio element in it and is more akin to film production. The production team and their tricks described here are to give a general idea. In actual practice one person can perform the job of several and in very large productions there can be further subdivisions of responsibilities. A look at credits given in different productions will illustrate this idea.

The person who is generally in charge of the entire production is the producer. He/she comes up with the programme concept, lays out the budget for the production and takes major decisions. He/she is the team leader, the person who works with the writers, decides on the key talent, hires the director, and guides the general direction of the production. In smaller productions the director may also handle the producer's responsibilities. In this case the combined job title becomes a producer-director. Some productions may also have an associate producer who sets up schedules for the talent and crew, and who, in general, assists the producer throughout the production.

On a major production one of the producer's first jobs is to find a writer so a script can be written (the document that tells everyone what to do, say, etc.). The script is in fact a written plan or a blueprint for the production. The key talent for the production will normally be the next thing considered by a producer. In general, the talent includes actors, reporters, hosts, guests, and off-camera narrators, in short anyone whose voice is heard or who appears on camera.

The producer will also be responsible for finding a director, the person in charge of working out preproduction (before the production) details, coordinating the activities of the production staff and on-camera talent, working out the camera and talent positions, selecting the camera shots during the production, and supervising post-production (after the production) work. Thus, the director is the person in charge of taking the script to the very end of the production process. Assisting a director in the control room is typically a technical director (TD) who operates the 'video switcher' and is also responsible for coordinating the technical aspects of the production. Depending on the production facility, the specific responsibilities of production personnel can vary widely.

One or more production assistants (PAs) may be hired to help the producer and director. Among other things, PAs keep notes on ongoing production needs and changes. In dramatic productions, the continuity secretary (CS) carefully makes notes on continuity details as each scene is shot to ensure that these details remain consistent between takes and scenes. Once the production concerns are taken care of, the continuity secretary is responsible for releasing the actors after each scene or segment is shot.

Other people who may be involved in the production include the lighting director (LD) who designs the lighting plan, arranges for the lighting equipment needed, and sets up and checks the lighting. Some productions will need a set designer who, along with the producer and director, will design the set and supervise its construction, painting and installation. Their is usually a makeup person, who, with the help of makeup, hair spray, etc. sees that the talent looks as desired by the script. Major productions will have a wardrobe person also who is responsible for seeing that the actors have clothes that are appropriate to the story and script.

The audio director or audio technician arranges for the audio recording equipment, sets up and checks mics (*Mics stand for microphones*, and is pronounced *mikes*), monitors audio quality during the production, and then strikes (another production-type term meaning disassembles and, if necessary, removes) the audio recording equipment and accessories after the production is over.

The microphone boom/grip operator watches rehearsals and decides on the proper mics and their placement for each scene.

The videotape recorder operator arranges video recording equipment and accessories, sets up video recordings, performs recording checks, and monitors video quality.

The CG operator (electronic character generator operator) programmes (designs/types in) opening titles, subtitles, and closing credits into a computer-based device that inserts the text over the picture during the production. Camera operators do more than just operate cameras. They typically set up the cameras and ensure their technical quality, work with the director, lighting director, and audio technician in blocking (setting up) and shooting each shot. Depending upon the production there may be a floor manager or a stage manager who is responsible for coordinating activities on the set. He or she may be assisted by one or more floor persons, or stagehands. After shooting is completed, the editors use the video recordings to blend the segments together and add music and audio effects to create the final product.

The production process is commonly broken down into preproduction, production and post-production. The most important phase of production is preproduction. The importance of this is often more fully appreciated after things get messed up during a production and the production people look back and wish they had realised this before going into the second phase.

In preproduction, the basic ideas and approaches of the production are developed and set into motion. It is in this phase that the production can be set on a proper course, or misdirected to such an extent that no amount of time, talent, or editing expertise can save it. The producer has to clearly identify the goals and purposes of the production. If there is no clear agreement on the goal or purpose of a production, it will be impossible to evaluate success. In order for the programme to be successful, the needs, interests, and general background of the target audience (the audience the production is designed to reach) must be studied and kept in mind throughout each production phase. The producer and scriptwriter have to be fully aware of the audience's experience, education, needs and expectations. Thus to underestimate education or experience and inadvertently "talk down to" an audience insults them. To overestimate education or experience and talk over everyone's head is just as bad. In commercial television the "return on the investment" is generally in the form of increased sales and profits. But, it may take other forms, such as the expected moral, political, spiritual, or public relations benefit derived from the programme. Depending on the production, a storyboard may be developed. The storyboard consists of drawings of key scenes with corresponding notes on dialogue, sound effects, music, etc. At this stage a production schedule has to be developed depending upon broadcast or distribution deadlines. In some locations the controlling agency will limit exterior production to certain areas and to specific hours. Necessary access permits, licenses, security bonds and insurance policies must be arranged. Except for spot news and short documentary segments, permits are often required. Many semipublic interior locations, such as shopping malls, also require filming permits. Included in this category are a wide variety of clearances, which range from permission to use prerecorded music to reserving satellite time. If clearance cannot be obtained, alternatives must be quickly explored. If possible, existing stock footage is obtained from film or tape libraries.

During preproduction not only are key talent and production members decided, but all of the major elements are also planned. Since things such as scenic design, lighting, and audio are interrelated, they must be carefully coordinated in a series of production meetings. Once all the basic elements are in place, rehearsals can start. Depending on the type of production, rehearsal may take place either minutes or days before the actual shooting. A simple on-location segment may only involve a quick check of talent positions so that the camera moves, audio and lighting can be checked. A complex production may require many days of rehearsals. These generally start with a table reading or dry rehearsal where the talent, along with key production personnel, sit around a table and read through the script. Often, script changes take place at this point. Finally, there is a dress rehearsal. Here the talent is

Some Tricks of the Trade

"dressed" in the appropriate wardrobe and all production elements are in place. This is the final opportunity for production personnel to solve whatever production problems remain.

The production phase is where everything comes together in a kind of final performance.

Productions can either be broadcast live or recorded. With the exception of news shows, sports remotes, and some special-event broadcasts, productions are typically recorded for later broadcast or distribution. Recording the show or segment provides an opportunity to fix problems by either stopping the recording and redoing the segment or making changes during the post-production editing phase.

Tasks, such as striking (taking down) sets, dismantling and packing equipment, handling final financial obligations, and evaluating the effect of the programme are part of the post-production phase. Even though post-production includes all of these after-the-production jobs, most people only associate post-production with editing. As computer-controlled editing techniques and post-production special effects have become more sophisticated, editing has gone far beyond simply joining together segments in a desired order. Editing is now a major focus of production creativity. Armed with the latest digital effects, the editing phase can add much in the way of to a production. It is easy to become enthralled with the special effects capabilities of the equipment. All this high-tech stuff should only be considered a tool for a greater purpose: the effective communication of ideas and information. One should never confuse the medium with the message.

Like a motion picture, every television programme should be based on a shooting plan. It may consist of a few mental notes, scribbled suggestions, an outline, a story board or a detailed shooting script. A continuity or shooting script is a preliminary programme on paper – a continuous plan of photographing, editing and production.

A director has to think of a programme as a series of shots, comprising each sequence and a series of sequences make the programme. The terms scene, shot and sequence are sometimes misunderstood. Scene, an expression borrowed from the stage productions, defines the place or setting where the action is laid. A scene may consist of one shot or series of shots depicting a continuous event. A shot defines a continuous view filmed by one camera without interruption. If the set up is changed in any way – by the camera movement, change of lens or different action is recorded, it is not the same shot but the next shot. A sequence is a series of scenes or shots complete in itself which may occur in a single setting or in several settings.

In a script a scene is described which is a shot or take for a cameraman. In the case of a master scene script, however, there will be a number of shots designated as a, b, c, d, etc. Thus for practical purposes scene and shot are generally interchangeable. A shot or a portion of a shot is also referred to as cut. This term is derived from a portion of a shot which is cut out and used separately.

Each shot requires placing the camera in the best position for viewing a scene. Positioning of the camera, the camera angle, determines both the audience viewpoint and area covered in the shot. A carefully chosen camera angle can enhance the dramatic impact of the story and a carelessly picked camera angle may distract or confuse the audience.

A television programme is a series of continuously changing images in which the events are portrayed from a variety of viewpoints. Choice of camera angles can position the audience closer to the action to view a significant portion in a big close up; farther away to appreciate the grandeur of a vast landscape; higher to look down upon a vast construction project and lower to look up at the face of an important personality. In fact, the audience may be positioned anywhere instantly to view anything from anywhere from any angle at the discretion of the cameraman and the picture editor.

The camera angles are of three basic types based on viewpoint. In an *objective camera angle*, the camera shoots from a sideline viewpoint. The audience views the event through the eyes of an unseen observer. Since it does not present the event from the viewpoint of anyone within the scene, the objective camera angle is impersonal and therefore this treatment is also called an audience point of view.

Some Tricks of the Trade

In *a subjective camera angle* the shooting is from a personal viewpoint. The camera changes place with a person in the picture. The camera acts as the eyes of the audience to place the viewer in the scene. The viewer may see the event through the eyes of a particular person with whom he identifies. When the subjective shots are preceded by a close-up of a person looking off-screen, the viewer will comprehend that he is seeing what the player on the screen sees.

A newscaster looks directly into the lens to set up performer-viewer eye-to-eye relationship. Each viewer feels that the person on the television screen is speaking directly to him. This subjective treatment is ideal for documentaries on industrial or military subjects. Generals in the battlefield, for example, may be interviewed in a 'you-are-there' treatment. Survivors of an accident can tell their story directly to the television audience. An off-screen narrator taking the audience to the tour of a factory may stop a worker and question him on behalf of the audience. If properly used, this technique results in greater audience involvement because of added personal relationship it sets up.

Point-of-view (p.o.v.) camera angle is an objective angle but it records the scene from a particular player's viewpoint. Point-of-view shots are used whenever it is desirable to involve viewer more closely with an event and it often follows over-the-shoulder shots when two persons face each other and exchange dialogue. While dealing with this kind of shots it is advised that if a player looks off-screen then there is cut to what he sees and the camera pans around. In such a situation the pan should never reach the player whose point of view the audience is seeing through the camera because a person cannot see himself when he looks around.

The image size is determined by the distance of the camera from the subject and the focal length of the camera lens. It may vary during the shot by moving the camera or the subject or by using a zoom lens. These factors together determine the type of shot.

An extreme long shot (ELS) depicts a vast area from a great distance and is used to show the huge scope of the setting or event.

A wide angle static shot is more adaptable for extreme long shots. The pan should be used only when it increases the interest. This type of shots are best recorded from a high vantage point like the top of a building, a hill top, a mountain-peak or from a helicopter.

A long shot (LS) covers the entire area of action and presents the audience with the over all appearance of the place, people and objects involved. Because of the limited size of the television screen medium long shots or full shots that cover the players full length but do not depict the setting in its entirety are used more often.

A medium shot (MS) is also described as intermediate shot as it falls between a long shot and close-up. It covers the people above the knees or from just below the waist. An interesting medium shot is the two-shot in which two persons confront each other and exchange dialogue. It is sometimes called American shot as it originated in Hollywood. Two-shots may grow or progress out of medium or long shots.

A close-up of a person could be a medium close-up when the shot covers the subject midway between the waist and the shoulders to above the head; a head and shoulder close-up from just below the shoulders to above the head; a head close-up includes the head only; a choker close-up includes the facial area from just below the lips to just above the eyes.

Full screen close-ups of letters, telegrams, photographs, newspapers, posters or other written or printed material are called inserts.

A moving shot could be a pan shot if the camera revolves upon its vertical axis or dolly, crane or boom shot when it is mounted on one of these platforms. A moving shot can be further described as dolly where from a medium shot moves to a close-up. A shot in which the camera tracks along a moving subject is called a tracking shot or a follow shot. A low-shot is one in which the camera in angled upward at the subject. A high-shot is just the opposite with the camera looking down at the subject. A reverse shot is a scene made from the reverse direction of a previous shot.

A cut-in shot cuts directly into a position of the previous scene as in a cut-in close-up of a person or a thing. A cut-away shot is not

Some Tricks of the Trade

in the same scene, it is secondary event occurring elsewhere – a few feet away as in cut-aways in an interview (a cut-away close-up is close-up of someone just off the camera) or miles away if the story is switched to another locale.

A reaction shot is a silent shot usually a close-up of a person reacting to what is being said by another like noddies in an interview or thumping of desks or clapping by audience or someone in the audience.

Lens used may also become a art of the shot description: 'wide-angle shot', 'telephoto shot', or 'zoom shot' and the number of people covered could also be counted: 'two-shot', 'three-shot', or 'group-shot'.

Our world is three dimensional and therefore if a scene presented on the screen has to be effective it has to have depth effect. Whenever a subject presents only a single surface to the eye or camera it is said to be 'flat', because its depth is not apparent. A building, a face, a body is best judged from an angle which presents both the front and the side. There are many ways to achieve depth: with lighting, camera and subject movement, overlapping linear and areal perspective, use of short focal length lens. But the effective method is by selecting a proper camera angle. To achieve the depth effect the cameraman should try to position the camera at an angle, preferably a 45 degree which is usually called three-quarter angle to the subject. Such angling would record people and objects with roundness and two or more surfaces and converging lines which produce perspective suggesting three dimensions. Shooting square, so that only the front or side of people or objects are recorded, should be avoided.

The height of the camera shooting a scene is a very important factor as it influences the audience involvement and reaction to the event depicted, depending on whether the scene is viewed from eye-level or above or below the subject. Objective shots which present the scene as viewed by an observer should be framed from the eye-level of an average person about a five and a half feet high. However, the close-up of a person be shot from the subject's eye-level so that the audience sees that person on an eye-to-eye basis.

Point of view close-ups are recorded from the subject's eye-level when the persons in the scene who are relating with each other are approximately the same height, but from the opposing person's height when a difference in height exists, as in the case of a seated and standing person or when an adult relates with a child.

Level-angle shots are best for close-ups of people and to depict general scene. They provide frames of reference as they present an easily identifiable viewpoint because the audience sees the event as if on the scene. High angle does not necessarily mean that the camera is placed at a great height. All angles are relative and should be considered in relation to the height of the subject shot. A high-angle shot is one in which the camera is tilted downwards to view the subject. It may be even below the eye-level of the cameraman, if the subject being shot is small.

A high-angle shot may be chosen for esthetic, technical or psychological reasons as placing the camera higher than the subject and looking down may result in a more artistic picture as in case of a vast garden with patterned flower bed or a military base or an industrial complex. A high angle helps the audience with the geography of the setting and looking down provides map-like layout to orient the viewer.

Action occurring in depth such as field placing in a cricket match, a military formation or a production line may be viewed in its entirety from a high angle. A·level angle or a low-angle shot will record only foreground action, the camera can shoot across the entire area of action from front to back from high angle. It is useful in keeping sharp focus across the entire picture area. The high-angle shots reduce the height of a person or object. A tall person would look down at a shorter person or a child in a point-of-view shot. But the subjective camera may also place the audience higher so to look down on a person and his situation. Such high angle is excellent when a person should be belittled either by his surroundings or by his deeds.

A low-angle shot is one in which the camera is tilted upward to view the subject. Low angles should be used to inspire awe or excitement to increase a subject's height or speed, to drop the horizon and eliminate background, to position persons or objects against the sky. The low-angle shots of religious objects may inspire awe in the audience because the viewer is placed in a lowly position from which he looks up to the symbol of the Almighty. The same effect is useful in shooting important persons. A dominant character in a scene may stand out from a group if he is positioned slightly forward of the others and shot from a low angle. This will cause him to tower over others behind him. This simple trick gives him prominence and allows him to dominate the scene. The effect is more dramatic if the person steps forward during the scene to coincide with an increase in dramatic action.

An angle-plus-angle shot is recorded with a camera angled in relation to the subject and tilted either upward or downward. Such double angling will record the greatest number of facets and deliver the most forceful linear perspective and generate a three dimensional effect. Besides the front and side, the camera also looks up or down in this setting. The camera angle need not be high or low or full three-quarter angle, the trick is to prevent flatness by angling even slightly. The persons and objects will stand out more prominently in the setting and the separation between the subject and background will be greater if the camera records the scene at an angle depicting both the front and side and a tilt that reveals the top or bottom.

A three-quarter low angle, employing a wide angle lens, adds illusion of tremendous speed and power of moving vehicles. Rooms with ornate ceilings or patterned floors may be shot with a slightly lower or higher camera, that requires tilting upward or downward in addition to a three-quarter angling. Double angling in this manner will present the greatest number of facets to the camera.

A 'Dutch' angle is a crazily tilted camera angle in which the vertical axis of the camera is at an angle to the vertical axis of the subject. The dutch angle should be reserved for sequences when weird, violent, unstable or impressionistic effects are required. A catastrophe such as an accident, fire, riot or earthquake may employ such tilted camera angles for conveying violence or topsy-turvy effect to the audience. The Dutch-angle shots may also be used in montage sequences for creating an impression of passage of time or space. The angle of tilt is significant as the image that slants to the right is forceful while the one that slants to the left is weak.

The area covered is determined by the subject's image size in the frame. Progressive (or regressive) shots utilise a series of images increasing (or decreasing) in size. Sequences may proceed from long shot to medium shot to close-up or in reverse order. Contrasting shots utilise the pairs of different size images in opposition as a long shot may be contrasted with a close-up. Repetitious shots utilise a series of same size images. A sequence may begin progressively so that it moves in from establishing long shot to close-up and then it may move into repetitious series of close-ups such as reaction shots and the climax with a series of back and forth contrasting shots.

The viewpoint determines the subject's image angle or camera angle from which the audience views the scene. The viewpoint may also be progressive or regressive, contrasting or repetitious. In a progressive (or regressive) series each angle is greater (or smaller) than the preceding angle. Contrasting angles are pairs of shots employing camera angles in direct opposition to each other as a high angle may be followed by a low angle, a side angle such as an over the shoulder shot by an angle from the opposite side. Repetitious angles are series of similar angles applied in the same or different subject matter.

One should never try to tell the entire story in just one shot. A sequence is a series of shots and each shot should depict its particular portion of the story in the best possible way. First, think of the area required for the particular shot and then of the best viewpoint. The area and viewpoint should be considered from both esthetic and dramatic requirements. There should be a definite change in image size and viewing angle from shot to shot. This can be accomplished by changing camera angle, lens or both. Most rewarding results will be obtained when the camera is repositioned for the best possible angle for each shot. Most impressive effects occur when the camera height is adjusted to suit the subject and lens. Focal length is chosen to fit the individual shot. Each scene should be considered as part of a sequence or series of shots but must be given individual attention based on story requirements. The choice of camera angle should be decided by analysing the purpose of the shot and the effect wanted on the audience. Sun position, weather, terrain also influence the choice of the camera angle in outdoor shooting.

Signs, plaques, labels, etc should be filmed either straight-on or given three-quarter angle so that the lettering diminishes in size, as it reads from left to right. A lengthy sign recorded by panning or dollying camera movement must be shot in such a way that lettering enters from screen right and slides across from right to left.

Thoughtful use of camera angles can add variety and impact to story-telling. Proper camera angles can make the difference between audience appreciation and indifference.

Composition: A cameraman composes whenever he positions his camera in relation to the scene to be photographed. Good composition is arrangement of pictorial elements to form a unified harmonious whole. As composition involves artistic taste, personal likes and dislikes, experience and background of individual cameraman, there could be no hard and fast rules that could be applied to achieve good composition. A cameraman should always keep in mind that he is telling a story to an audience through his camera and should consider what composition helps most in this single object.

The main difficulty in composing for television or motion pictures is dealing not only with the shape of the people and objects but also the shape of motions. Thus, the elements of composition include lines, forms, masses and movement. They comprise compositional language which may convey the desired mood and atmosphere.

Compositional lines may be actual contours of objects or imaginary lines in space. People, buildings, trees, furniture, etc may all be expressed in straight, curved, vertical, horizontal, diagonal or any combinations of contour lines. On the other hand, while following action or moving in a scene the eye also creates transitional lines in space. Such imaginary lines suggested by eye movement or subject movement may be more effective than actual compositional lines. The viewer's eye may travel in a curved pattern to look at a group of persons, it may move in diagonal line to follow an aircraft take off or in a vertical line to look at an ascending missile. Thus the linear composition of a scene is dependent not only on actual contour lines but also on transitional lines created by eye movement.

For most effective composition, the real lines should not divide the picture in equal parts. Neither strong vertical nor horizontal lines should be centred. A pole or the horizon should not be placed in the middle of a frame. The frame should not be divided into two equal parts with a diagonal line from one corner to another. Unless formed by columns, trees or buildings as a part of repetitious pattern, straight lines should not parallel any side of the frame.

Meaning of compositional lines: Straight lines suggest masculinity, strength; tall vertical lines suggest strength and dignity; softly curved lines suggest feminity, delicate qualities; sharply curved lines suggest action and gaiety; long horizontal lines suggest quite and restfulness but they may also suggest speed because the shortest distance between the two points is a straight line; parallel, diagonal lines suggest action energy and violence and opposing diagonal lines suggest conflict, forcefulness; strong heavy sharp lines are more interesting than regular lines because of visual quality.

Meanings conveyed by lines are also influenced by gravity. Diagonals are dynamic and they usually suggest instability.

Straight angular or jagged lines such as lightening streak gives impression of speed, forcefulness or vitality. Unbroken lines make faster viewing than broken erratic lines.

All objects have form, while physical forms are easy to recognise, the forms created by viewer's eye movement from one object to another create many abstract forms in the viewer's mind. Eye movement from one person or object to another may have a triangular, circular or other form. A triangular form suggest, strength, stability and solidity. It is a compact closed form which causes the eye to continue from point to point without escape. A reverse triangle is also possible with the apex at the bottom. Two adults can thus be effectively composed with a child between them.

A circular or oval form also tends to tie in viewer's attention as this pattern causes viewer's gaze to wander without escape

Some Tricks of the Trade

from the frame. The cross is one of the few compositional forms that may be centred because its four arms radiate in all directions equally. The cross inspires a sense of unity and force and in many minds it symbolises the Almighty. The cross could be placed *off-centre* but never too close to the sides of the frame. Radiating lines are a variation of cross, there are many such excellent examples in nature – flower petals, tree branches, etc. The various L-shaped forms suggest informality and are flexible because they provide base and upright in combination. This type of composition is useful for landscape or establishing long shots.

Mass is the pictorial weight of an object, an area or a figure or a group made up of any or all of these. Lines, forms can dominate a composition by their esthetic or psychological value but masses capture and hold attention through heavy pictorial weight. Strength is added to an isolated mass. It is separated from its background by contrast, lighting or colour. Such treatment would cause a mass to stand out from a confusing, conflicting or otherwise "busy" background. A unified mass is strengthened when several figures or objects are tied together so that they combine into a dominant group. Wildly scattered groupings should be avoided. A dark mass will stand out against a light background and a light mass against a dark one through contrast. This is the simplest way to pull a figure or object away from the background to provide emphasis.

Predominating colour such as large blue shadow area or red-streaked clouds, illuminated by a setting sun can create a massive colour effect. Primary or highly saturated colours are most effective when used to dominate the scene.

Movements: The movements possess esthetic and psychological characteristics created by eye, going from one point to another within a scene or by following a moving object. The movements may change during a shot or a sequence of shots to match the changing characteristics of action. A horizontal movement suggests travel, momentum, displacement. A left to right movement is easy to follow, more natural and smoother as reading from left to right has pre-trained the audience to accept such movement and follow it effortlessly. A right to left movement is strong and against the nature of eye movement. It should be used where a stronger, more dramatic opposition has to be depicted.

An ascending vertical movement suggest aspiration, growth, freedom from weight, lightness, free flight, happiness, elevation may be conveyed by such movement. A descending vertical movement suggests heaviness, danger or destruction as portrayed by avalanche or waterfall. A diagonal movement is most dramatic and it suggests opposing forces, stresses and strains, power, overcoming obstacles by force. Such a movement may be suggested in static scenes by a Dutch tilt.

A curved movement suggest fear or fascination, fear as in curved snake. A circular or revolving movement suggest cheerfulness. A revolving movement also suggest mechanical energy as in wheels of industry. A pendulum movement suggests monotony, relentlessness such as back-and-forth pacing of a nervous person or caged animal.

It should be remembered that an interrupted movement or movement that changes direction attracts greater viewer interest than continuous movement or movement in constant direction. A movement towards the viewer is more interesting because it increases the size.

Balance is a state of equilibrium where all forces are equal or compensate each other. Unbalance upsets the viewer by disturbing his sensibilities and that is why some pictures just do not look right. A proper balanced composition is subconsciously agreeable. In television or motion picture balance is a series of pictorial compromises based on key positions of persons or objects and pauses in the action when these elements are at rest.

A pictorial balance is concerned with psychological weight which is influenced by relative eye attraction of various compositional elements in picture. Each element attracts according to its size, shape, tonal value, colour, movement and contrast with its surroundings and its placement in the frame. A large static object on one side of the scene can be balanced by a small moving object on the opposite side as they both have equal psychological or pictorial weight. A figure or object placed close to the centre of the frame possesses less compositional weight than one nearer the side. Therefore a lighter element should be moved further away from the centre while those of heavier weight should be positioned closer towards the centre to keep them in balance.

Here are a few general rules: A moving object possesses more weight than a stationary object and this is regardless of size. A relatively small moving object, particularly if light in tone, brightly coloured or contrasted against the background commands greater attention than a large stationary object. An object moving towards the camera becomes progressively larger and therefore carries more weight than a diminishing object moving away. The upper part of a picture is heavier than the lower one. Since eye movement is from right to left, the left side of the picture can support greater pictorial weight than the right side.

An isolated object has more weight than the one that is crowded or merged with others. An object will be heavier if placed at the side of the frame since the centre of the picture is compositionally the weakest. A large object may have more weight in static scene as it would dominate the picture regardless of position. Regularly shaped objects carry more weight than irregularly shaped objects. Peculiar or intricate objects are heavier because of additional interest they generate.

A compact object carries more weight than a loosely joined object. A vertically formed object will appear heavier than the oblique object. A bright object will possess more weight than a darker one. Warm colours such as red are heavier than cold colours such as blue. Bright colours carry more weight than dark colours.

Balance could be formal or informal. In formal or symmetrical balance, both sides of a composition are symmetrical or almost equal in attraction. It is usually static and suggests peace, quite or equality without conflict or contrast. A formal balance exists in popular profile, two-shots in which two persons sit or stand on opposite sides of the frame facing each other. Dominance switches from one person to another as each speaks in turn. It is also possible to favour one of them by better lighting, brighter colour costume or better separation from the background.

When both sides of a composition are asymmetrical informal balance is achieved. An informal balance is dynamic because it presents a forceful arrangement of opposing compositional elements where a dominant figure or object provides the centre of interest. Asymmetrical balance is employed subtly on close-ups where a single figure fills the frame by placing the head slightly off-centre so that slightly more space is provided in the direction in which the person looks and by association with whom the person in close-up is relating.

Smaller opposing compositional element can compensate for its size by additional weight acquired by its location, shape, brightness, colour value and movement. The dominant subject should not be placed in the same horizontal line with the lesser weight-opposing element but should be slightly higher or if lower should dominate the scene because of better lighting or better positioning in the frame.

Normally, a picture should have one centre of interest as two or more equally dominant figures, objects or actions in single scene compete with each other and weaken the effectiveness of composition. There are, however, occasions like scenes of roit panic or battle where more than one centre of interest could be justified. The centre of interest should not be centred in the picture. Audience interest may be attracted or switched during a scene by position, movement, action, sound, lighting, tonal values and colours and selective focussing.

In image placement or framing, the positioning of subject matter in the frame is important and in many scenes it requires continuous composing as the action progresses. A moving person should be framed in such a way as to give slightly more space in the direction of movement and similarly a statically positioned person should be given slightly more space in the direction in which he looks. Bottom frame line should not cut across joints: knees, waist, elbow, shoulders and the person particularly in close-up should be so framed that the frame line cuts between the joints.

It must be remembered that a viewer interprets the size of an unknown object in a picture in relation to an object of known size or with the background. For a cameraman, an action could be either

Some Tricks of the Trade

controlled when it can be directed or regulated and repeated by or for him; or it could be uncontrolled when the events cannot be staged for the camera. Most of what a television news cameraman covers is uncontrolled and in such a situation a cameraman has to adapt to prevailing conditions to record the best possible coverage.

A master scene is a continuous take of an entire event occurring in a single setting. It could be covered with a single camera or with multiple cameras. When shot with single camera portions of action are later repeated to obtain intercutting closer shots. When covered with multiple cameras intercutting closer shots are recorded simultaneously.

Single camera should be used on any staged action which can be precisely duplicated for closer shots while multiple cameras are used for sports events, quiz shows, panel programmes, round table discussions, press conferences, engineering tests or wherever the exact repetition of action is not possible and all angles have to be recorded simultaneously.

The other technique is triple take technique where there is an overlapping of the action at the beginning and the end of each shot. The cameraman thinks of three consecutive shots at any time, action at the end of the first shot is repeated at the beginning of the second shot and action at the end of the second shot is again overlapped at the beginning of the third shot. This is the simplest method of shot to shot continuity and is useful particularly when shooting without a script. The triple take technique can be used only on controllable action.

The direction in which a person looks or a vehicle or person moves can cause the most vexing problems of continuity. If a complete production could be photographed in a single shot there would be no directional problems. But it is seldom the case.

A simple method of establishing and maintaining the screen direction is to make sure that all cameras are positioned on one side of the action axis – line or travel or movement or straight line between two related objects or persons. Directional continuity must be maintained throughout a sequence depicting continuous action without a time lapse. The movement or looks of a person must be the same on each side of a match-cut, in which the action is continuous from shot to shot. Anything may change during a shot but nothing should be changed between the shots. It does not apply to scenes connected by dissolves or other optical effects.

Whenever the action is interrupted editorially or optically it is possible to assume that changes may have occurred in the meantime. Whenever a time lapse or a change in location within a sequence or between sequences is to be shown, various transitional devices may be employed to bridge time or space. Simplest method for achieving pictorial transition is by using introductory titles stating place and/or time to set the stage. Dateless elapsed time may also be conveyed with title like '10 years later'. A map may show progress at intervals during a journey or location of the event that follows the scene, may open on a place name at airport or railway station or it may open on a newspaper clearly focussing on date.

A fade-in, in which a black screen gradually brightens into an image is used to begin a sequence or story. A fade-out, in which the image gradually darkens to black is used to end a story or sequence. Sequences separated by fades are similar to acts of a play or chapters of a book. The fades between sequences in the same locale indicate a passage of time or fades may be used to indicate a switch to another setting.

A dissolve blends one scene into another and is exactly fade-out superimposed upon a fade-in, so that the loss of image density in the first scene is balanced by a gain in image density in the second scene. Dissolves are used to cover a time lapse or a change in locale or to soften a scene change that would be otherwise abrupt. Scenes that would appear as jump-cuts because of sudden shifting of the centre of interest may be dissolved.

Wipes are moving optical effects in which one scene seems to push another scene off the screen. The wiping motion may be vertical, horizontal or angular and demarcation between the two scenes could be a distinct line or a soft blend. Wipes may be shaped like stars, flames, lighting, hearts, spades, diamonds, etc. and may be expanding, contracting, swinging, spinning, rolling or twisting motion. Wiping pattern may be continuous, or broken up into several shapes within the frame.

Some Tricks of the Trade

A montage transition is a series of short scenes connected by straight cuts, dissolve or wipes used to condense time or space. This technique may depict portions of the story when events need not be shown in detail but must be included for continuity, editorial or narrative purposes. Superimposed images may be used as circus posters may be changed continuously over shots of speeding train or newspaper headlines spin into focus over a trial sequence. Many-imaged montage may be used for title background and several images may also be combined to show what is happening in several places simultaneously.

Sound transitions: Narration is a sound version of picture title and can cover a switch in locales or change of time. This is best demonstrated in newsreel where narration takes you from place to place and covers the lack of pictorial continuity. A documentary film may use simple narration to link sequences shot at different time and/or place.

A monologue may move a story forward or backward. For example, a police officer is playing back a tape-recorded confession and the picture dissolves to a flashback when the crime was being committed, or a scientist may imagine life on earth thousands of year ago from now and the picture dissolves to show how it progressed forward as he talks. The picture and sound may dissolve. A person speaking may dissolve to another he is seen writing a letter, while his sound can be heard and the picture can be dissolved to addressee who is seen reading the letter aloud or it may accompany the sound of the letter writer.

Telephone conversation provides excellent means of switching the story to another location. Radio, television, songs and sound effects, with or without music and/or dialogue, offer a variety of possibilities for imaginative sound transitions.

It is considered better to prepare the audience by introducing the sound before the picture appears, since the ear takes longer than the eye to note what is transpiring and therefore hearing should be given a headstart. An ambulance or a police siren can wail before the vehicle approaches the camera. However, the transitions should be handled with care in keeping with the event being depicted and should not attract undue attention to itself and distract the audience from the main story.

A close-up is a device that allows large-scale portrayal of a portion of action. A face, a small object, may be selected from the over-all scene and shown full-screen in a close-up. Close-up transports viewer into the scene, eliminates all non-essentials for the moment or/and isolates whatever significant incident should receive emphasis. A properly selected and effectively edited close-up can add dramatic impact and visual clarity to the event. But when used improperly it can confuse the audience and distract attention. However, employment of a close-up to distract audience in order to cover a jump-cut is as important editorially as its use for visual emphasis.

Close-ups of people, animals and objects require different treatment. In case of people, the close-up could be: medium close-up, from midway between the waist and shoulders to above the head; the head and shoulder close-up, from below the shoulders to above the head; head close-up covers the head only and the choker close-up is from below the lips to above the eyes. If not specified, a close-up of a person normally means the head and shoulder close-up.

In extreme close-ups, tiny objects or small portions of large objects or areas appear greatly magnified on the screen. Similar treatment is possible of portions of a person's head such as eyes, lips, ear or nose whenever the connected sense is of ultra-dramatic significance.

Over-the-shoulder close-up is the close-up of a person as seen over-the-shoulder of another person in the foreground. It provides an effective transition from objectively filmed shots to point-of-view close-ups. If over-the-shoulder close-ups are taken in opposing pairs, both the close-ups should appear uniform in size and similarly angled.

Close-ups could be cut-in or cut-away. A cut-in close-up is a magnified portion of the preceding larger scene. It is always part of the main action and continues the main action with a screen filling closer view of a significant person, object or small-scale action. Cut-in close-ups are used to play up narrative highlights such as an important dialogue, person's action or reaction; to isolate significant subject matter and to eliminate all non-essential material from view; to magnify small-scale action visually clarifying what is happening; to provide a time lapse in a lengthy process like typing where the beginning and cut-in close-up of fingers and keys on the key board can lead the audience to finished letter; to distract audience to cover jump-cut; to substitute for hidden action which cannot be shot for physical reasons.

A cut-away close-up is related to, but not a part of, previous scene. It depicts secondary action happening simultaneously elsewhere. Cut-away close-ups are used to present reactions of person(s) not involved in the main action; a cue to the audience on how they should react; to comment on the main event; to motivate a sequence as an engine whistles to hurry the passengers to get into a train; to replace a scene too gruesome or expensive to depict and to distract the audience to cover a jump-cut.

A cut-in close-up should always be established by a preceding long shot so that the audience is aware of its location in relation to over-all scene. However, cut-away close-ups need not be established since they are not a part of the main event and may occur anywhere. Where possible, one should prefer to use a cut-in close-up rather than a cut-away close-up as the cut-in close-up goes directly into the heart of an established scene, the cut-away close-up moves the audience outside the principal scene.

The close-ups should not be shot against a busy background, shiny surfaces, moving or otherwise distracting objects. Throwing the background slightly out of focus is effective. Whenever possible background should be nondescript, softly contrasting surfaces.

If it is desirable to startle, confuse, shock or surprise the audience, a close-up may be used as a sequence opener. Later the camera may be moved back to reveal the over-all picture.

Editing

After shooting is completed, the producer, director and videotape editor review the recordings and editing decisions are made. For major productions this has typically been done in two phases. First, there is off-line editing, using copies of the original tapes. The off-line editing decisions are usually made by editing a time-coded copy of the original footage. Time-code, sometimes called SMPTE/EBU time-code after the organisations that adopted it, refers to the eight digit numbers that identify the exact hours, minutes, seconds and frames in a video. By using these numbers, points on video recordings within at least 1/30th second can be specified. This level of accuracy can be quite important for a tightly edited show. One can see the time-code numbers in the picture on the left. In this case they are read as 0 hours, 1 minute, 16 seconds, and 12 frames. Using this edited tape and an EDL (edit decision list) as a guide, the production then moves to on-line editing where much more sophisticated equipment was used to create the edited master, the final edited version of the tape. During this final editing phase all necessary sound effects, colour balancing, and special effects are added. As high-quality nonlinear, digital editing is now widely used, the need for an off-line editing phase is being eliminated, or at least becoming optional.

Only good editing can give life to a production. The picture editor strives to impart visual variety by skillful shot selection, arrangement and timing. He recreates entire event to achieve a cumulative effect which is often greater than all actions in the individual scenes put together.

The famous Russian filmmaker Serge Eisenstein used to say that joining of two pieces of film results in three ideas: the ideas in each piece of film and the idea in their relationship.

Editing is called 'continuity cutting' where the story telling depends on matching consecutive scenes. It is compilation cutting, where the story telling depends on narration and the scenes merely illustrate what is being described.

Cross-cutting consists of parallel editing of two or more events in an alternative pattern. It may be used to heighten the interest by depicting simultaneously occurring actions in an alternative manner; to provide conflict by editing of two actions which will come together in a climax; to increase tension by alternate editing of two events which have direct bearing on each other; to heighten suspense and

Some Tricks of the Trade

to make comparisons to depict contrast. Cross-cutting may present events occurring simultaneously in different places or events separated in time.

Many picture editors prefer to make their cuts on movements so that the actual switch from one shot to another is marked by action and not as apparent as the cut between two static shots. However, the cameraman should never cut during any significant movement and all the moving action should be recorded to completion and the picture editor should always be provided with as much overlapped movement as possible in consecutive shots, so that he can study the action and make the most effective cut. Always move players into and out of close-ups to allow cutting on action. The camera should be started before a player enters the frame and stopped after he leaves to provide 'clean' entrances and exits.

A good screen story cannot be assembled from haphazard shots. The cameraman must shoot series of shots that match visually and technically. Action must match across straight cuts; exposure, lighting, colour and other technicalities must match from shot to shot. Unexplained gaps in continuity or technical variation will distract the audience and destroy the effectiveness of the presentation. Editorial and technical cheating can repair some mismatching but the cameraman should deliver visually perfect scenes. Changing both the camera angle and the image size will aid in obtaining smooth cuts between shots.

A series of moving shots will inter-cut without difficulty if the tempo of the camera movement is properly maintained. It may be the same object filmed from various camera angles and distances or different subjects recorded in repetitious manner. However, inter-cutting static and moving shots of static subject is generally difficult as the switch from static shot to a moving shot (or vice versa) is abrupt and jarring due to lack of subject movement. A pan, tilt or dolly shot of a static subject preceded or followed by a static camera shot should always be filmed with a static camera at the beginning and the end of the shot so that the cut will be across static frames.

The screen length of a moving shot is based on the time the camera is in motion while the screen length of a static shot is based on subject action. A moving shot must be used in its entirety (or any continuous portion) as it is difficult, if not impossible, to cut during camera movement. A static shot on the other hand can be generally trimmed shorter or cut into several shots. Thus camera movement should be used only where justified and providing that its length does not restrict the picture editor.

'Protection' or 'cover' shots are extra scenes shot to cover any unforeseen editing problems or to replace any doubtful scenes that may cause editing difficulties because of wrong timing, excessive length, possible mis-matching, lengthy pan or dolly shots, etc. Protection shots involve shooting a cover scene 'just in case' the original scene may not work for any reason. These can be added scenes not called for in the script that may help the editor in unforeseen ways. Examples of added protection shots are long shots of buildings, extreme long shots of industrial complexes or other vast areas, close-ups of signs, plaques, markers, scenes of general activity which many serve many editorial purposes and can serve to introduce, establish or bridge sequences. The cameraman should be on the lookout for such shots.

About poorly shot scenes some editors say, "If you cannot solve it, dissolve it." However, this tendency leads to excessive use of dissolves. To avoid this producers make the editor justify each dissolve.

More on Script

Script is plan or blueprint of how the action will be recorded and is the key element in the production process. Many productions are unscripted but even in such cases one can say that there is some kind of script in the mind of the director of the programme. There are semi-scripted shows and fully-scripted shows. In the first category are interviews, discussions, ad-lib shows, and many demonstration and variety shows. The scripts for semi-scripted shows resemble a basic outline, with only the show segments and their times indicated on the script. Although scripts for semi-scripted shows might be comparatively easy to write, this type of show puts pressure on the director and talent to figure things out as they go along. But the scripts for fully scripted shows list the complete

Some Tricks of the Trade

audio and video for every minute. In a fully scripted show the overall content, balance, pace and timing can all be figured out before the production starts and thus unpleasant surprises are minimised.

Documentary and hard news pieces should be reasonably concrete, should present information so clearly that the possibility for misunderstanding is minimised. A concrete news script would be quite different in approach and structure from the script for a feature story, a soft news piece, a music video, or a dramatic production where it is often desirable to not be too concrete and to allow room for personal interpretation.

A programme may have initially a rehearsal script which after rehearsal(s) will help in finalising the camera script. Once the camera script is finalised, camera cards are prepared for cameramen where each card contains only the information relevant to that particular camera keeping it brief and concise.

Scripts should be typed on one side of the page only. It should be typed on the right side of the page to enable the director (producer) to plot in his camera on the left. Plenty of space should be given between the lines of dialogue and stage directions should be easily distinguishable from the dialogue by typing them in capitals. Each scene should be started on a fresh page.

In a multi-camera production the director has to work out the visual and sound coverage well in advance of the studio day when the final programme is recorded. He needs to have assessed the number of cameras required, where these will be positioned initially and where they will move to during the course of action. He needs to have worked out the precise cutting points from one camera to another and to have thought out in advance the types of shots he wants. All this is worked out during the rehearsals and most directors note this information on their rehearsal scripts and this is normally passed on to the production assistant for typing the final camera script.

In the camera script the pages show the scenes listed in the order in which they are to be recorded. If fact, both the page numbers in the recording order and the page number in the original story order should be given and the latter should be put in brackets.

Each shot is numbered consecutively in the camera script. These numbers should be listed in the studio recording order and not in story order. Normally, the shot number is typed on the extreme left of the page. Every cut is a shot and should be given a shot number and the numbers should run consecutively in recording order starting from shot 1.

Cameras are numbered from one to as many as are employed on the production. Their output is available on monitors in the production control room. In the script it is identified which camera will be used for which shot. It should be seen that two consecutive shots should never be from the same camera. After the number of the camera comes the position it is allocated on the studio floor. This is referred to by a letter and corresponds with the same letter on the studio floor plan. Camera 1 will start in position A then move to position B and end up at position C. On the script it should be as 1A, 1B and 1C and the like. It should be checked that the time has been allowed for the camera to change position.

On the script directly beneath the camera and its position comes the cut line. It runs across the typed portion of the page and ends a slash upwards at precisely the point at which the director wishes the vision mixer to cut from one shot to another. The cut line should come at the end of the preceding word of the dialogue rather than just before a new line.

Each shot thus has a number, a camera and a camera position and then the shot description (the kind of shot and its content) is given in the script. This information is typed directly under the cut line in capital letters.

Recording breaks, VTR inserts and 'as directed' sequences are isolated from the main body of the script by means of drawing two lines across the page and the information about them is typed between these lines to make them stand out more clearly.

The right hand side of the page of the camera script contains all the dialogue and sound details.

Some Tricks of the Trade

Here is a list of commonly used camera script terms and abbreviations:

W/A	Wide angle shot
LS	Long shot
MLS	Medium long shot
3-s	Three shot (shot with three persons)
2-s	Two shot
2-s fav.X	Two shot, camera favouring X
o/s 2-s	Over the shoulder two shot
MS	Mid shot or medium shot
MCU	Medium close-up
CU	Close-up
BCU	Big close-up
X's POV	X's point of view shot
H/A	High angle shot
L/A	Low angle shot
Z/I	Zoom in
Z/O	Zoom out
A/B	As before
FAV	Favouring
F/G	Foreground
B/G	Background
F/WD	Forward
B/WD	Backward
CAM R	Camera right (as seen from the camera)
CAM L	Camera left
O/S	Over the shoulder
OOV	Out of vision
OOFL(R)	Out of frame left (or right)
Q	Cue
S/B	Stand by
F/U	Fade up
F/D	Fade down
MUTE	Without sound
V/O	Voice over
SOF	Sound on film
SOT	Sound on tape

SOVT	Sound on videotape
S & V	Sound and vision
MIC	Microphone
GRAMS	Music or sound effects from grams
F/X	Effects
SPOT F/X	Sound effects made in the studio
ATMOS	Atmosphere
F/O	Fade out
T/O	Take out
S/I	Superimpose
SUPER	Superimpose
DFS / DVE	Digital frame store or digital video effects
CPU	Caption projection unit
B/E	Black edge generator

WIPE, MIX and CUT

Camera script should be normally duplicated or photocopied on to a yellow paper which allows the type to be clearly read in the studio. But if scenes from a number of different episodes are to be shot on the same studio day, then each episode may be clearly identified by being duplicated on a different coloured paper.

Some TV news studios have overhead cameras connected to a monitor which is placed in front of the newscaster. Such script is typed in the middle between specified points that fall within the focussing range of the overhead camera, when the script is placed in the specific slot on newscaster's table. In such a system a separate copy for teleprompter is not required as the newscaster's copy appears on the monitor via overhead camera.

Though everybody working in television is not expected to know every trade perfectly but the need for co-ordination requires that all hands should have some idea of the tricks of various trades. The cameraman should know when the picture editor needs to avoid jerks or jump-cuts. The script-writer should know what kind of effect he should expect from which kind of shot and the director or producer should know all this and much more. Multi-skilling may also serve as insurance in these times when a major management emphasis is on reduction of manpower.

6

Broadcast News – Radio

Broadcasters all around the world are using various levels of automation in their news production systems. But the basics of news concept have not changed much in theory. All the new technology is there to help presentation and ease difficulties in the art of news presentation. The technology is also reducing manpower, which happens to be a costly input in the process.

News is one of the best known commodities in today's world. Everybody who understands a language and has access to mass media recognises it. The concept of news must have existed even before the beginning of the era of mass media. One may find relics of a primitive system in remote tribal areas where people exchanged local news during weekly markets just by talking to one another. When two friends meet after sometime they exchange information, which can be called personal news. Letters written to friends and relatives carry what they can describe as news. This kind of information exchange is continuing since early days of human society in one form or the other.

Everybody will agree that death makes news. If a person dies of a disease or an accident it makes news. The importance of this news is related to the importance of the person and/or deadliness of the disease.

Mrs. Indira Gandhi was assassinated. It was big news. If she had died of a heart attack or in an accident, even then it would have been a big news. That news was important because of the importance of Mrs. Gandhi—other factors were there, but the biggest news value of that event was the person involved.

If a person dies in a road accident in Bhopal it will be news in Bhopal; but if this person dies of AIDS or SARS in a Bhopal hospital it will become news of not only national but of international significance. In this case the importance of news is because of the disease. But even ordinary death of an ordinary old man will make news at least for those who know him and are related to him. It may not appear in a newspaper but it will be news to some people. Thus we can say that the concept of news in human society is as old as recognition of death as an event and its communication by any means to those whom the event would affect. Revolutions in transport and communication have led to various changes in significance and reach of the news but the basic concept is the same.

In this sense the concept of news may even be older than the concept of God. But as even today we do not have a universally agreed definition of God, there is no definition of news on which everybody agrees.

Before the era of newspapers and electronic media, news was communicated by word of mouth. Public announcements by those in power were communicated to the people by various kinds of drummers. Such announcements even now dominate the news coverage in the newspapers, radio and television in almost all countries irrespective of ideology. Radio and television stations become first targets in coups and those who snatch power from the old regime use these electronic drummers for their first announcements.

Though the concept is very old, the word 'news' is relatively recent in origin. In English it appeared as "newis" in 1423, "newyes" in 1485 and evolved to "newes" in 1523. It was only after 1550 that it became "news" and even in 1622 there was Butler's *Weekly Newes* in London while in 1685 we had such sentences as— "The amazing news of Charles at once were spread".

The four letters of the word news have been described as representing the four directions—North, East, West and South. News can come from any of these directions. But as we see every day all events do not make news. Only important and interesting events make news. Further, an event itself is not news—it becomes news when its account is available. Thus, famous Bhagalpur Jail blinding made news much after the event. Similarly, Clinton-Monica affair went on for quite some time before it made news—'when' the account became available.

History is also an account of important events. But it relates mainly to the past. News is in a way current history. Today's newspapers will be source materials for historians of tomorrow as today's historians consult old newspapers in the archives. What is happening today may go down in history, but its account which media gives now is news.

But if new facts about an event of historical significance are brought out today then it will make news. What Richard Nixon wrote about the Indo-Pak war of 1971 made news more than a decade later. Vijayalaxmi Pandit's account of the relationship of her brother, Jawaharlal Nehru with Edwina Mountbatten appeared in news columns throughout the world when both were dead and gone.

Not only events but opinions also make news. Opinion of important and famous people on Iraq war made news. An opinion expressed by a film personality during Oscar presentations about Iraq war made global news. The opinion of the man in the street about the budget makes news. Editorial comments by important newspapers can also make news for other newspapers. Coverage of the Indian prime minister's visit in the media of the country visited will make news in India. What the Pakistani press is publishing about an event in India may be news for the Indian press. What the US press wrote about the Bhopal gas tragedy was news for the Indian newspapers.

With these varying situations in mind we can attempt a definition of news: "News is an account of a recent event or opinion which is important or interesting".

Importance and *interest* are two factors that present unlimited variety and thus explain why an event is newsworthy for one newspaper or broadcasting station and not for many other newspapers and radio or TV networks; why one news item becomes world news while another may be fit for only a local daily or station.

News Values

Importance and interest are often described as news values but in fact, these represent the sum total of news values or intrinsic characteristics that distinguish news from non-news. Identifying and measuring these values is usually called news sense. It is commonly believed that reporters identify news by intuition. But this intuition, which should be called news sense, develops in newsmen who sub-consciously learn how to measure news values.

Change:- It is a basic news value. If nothing happens there will be no change. But the world is not static. Every moment things are different from the moment before. The bigger the change and the more the people affected by this change the more important it is from the news point of view.

Conflict:- Actual conflicts and even the danger of conflicts makes news, as they tend to bring about major change. All wars and threats leading to wars have proven record of news worthiness. But conflicts of smaller dimensions like group or personal conflicts resulting in crimes, strike and demonstrations, etc. also make news.

Even conflicting ideas and resulting debates make up news. *Tension* and *suspense* often associated with conflicts are also regarded as news values.

Disaster:- Be it a result of natural calamity like an earthquake or a volcanic eruption or be it a manmade event like the Bhopal gas tragedy or the Kanishka crash—disasters always make news. It is also true of disasters of lesser dimensions like boat tragedies, small acts of sabotage resulting in loss of life or property or both.

Progress:- Progress is also a news value as it is the positive result of efforts made by society. It improves quality of life. Through routine struggles of life frequently emerge shining successes. From laboratories after years of work emerge new devices, new inventions and new remedies. All this and its various dimensions make news.

Consequence:- The immediate and long-term consequence of an event also makes news. The more people it affects the greater the consequence. A fear of consequences of an event also makes news.

Thus, the possible consequences of a nuclear war makes news and all efforts to avert it and failures or successes in that direction make news.

Consequence also serves as a measure of conflicts, disaster and progress. The greater the consequence, the more the news value.

Cause:- Like consequence, the cause of a newsworthy event also makes news. Every event has consequences so has its causes also. The cause of a hotel fire may be known immediately. It will make news, but if it is not known all efforts to find out the cause and possible interpretations will make news. Similarly, various theories and interpretations of Punjab crisis will keep on making news from time to time.

Eminence and prominence:- Involvement of eminent personalities in an event adds to its news value and it is directly proportional to the prominence of the person. Thus, if an eminent scholar says something on a problem it will have a news value while the same remarks made by an ordinary person may go unnoticed. When Mulk Raj Anand fainted while speaking at Lucknow it became national news. If this would have happened to a less known figure the importance of that event would have been reduced to that order.

Prominence is many a time built up by the media. The media had a major role in bringing Jarnail Singh Bhindranwale, Charles Shobhraj, Billa and Ranga and Rajnarain into prominence. And then whatever they said or did, even if it did not have any other news value, got into newspapers just because of their prominence. People were interested in them because they were familiar. A big chunk of news in media is about those who are known.

Timeliness:- It is also a basic news value as old news is no news. In a highly competitive world of journalism every medium tries to be first with news. News is a highly perishable commodity and therefore every medium tries to give the latest available to score a point over the other.

Proximity:- News is meant for human beings. The prime concern of a man is himself then he is interested in his neighbourhood. If other things are equal, proximity becomes key news value. *A traffic jam in* Mumbai will be more important for a newspaper published from Mumbai but may not find a place in a Delhi newspaper. If the prime minister is visiting Chennai his activities will get more space in the Chennai edition of *The Indian Express* as compared to the Chandigarh edition of the same newspaper.

Novelty:- If a dog bites a man, it is not news, but if a man bites a dog, it is news. This old newspaper saying recognises the news value of the unusual—novelty.

Human interest:- Almost everything in news concerns human beings, but this particular news value is the emotional context of the news event. Anything that appeals to everybody not because of interest in the subject but because everybody shares human experience has news value. Human interest is the element with which the reader identifies anything familiar that stirs his feelings. Crime stories often have a human-interest angle that makes them readable.

Human interest content of stories is higher when ordinary persons are involved in extraordinary situations—an adventure, a disaster, a tragedy or a triumph. Human interest is also involved when it depicts extraordinary persons in ordinary situations.

An event may have many or all of these news values and taken together these values determine which news story is more important than the other, which should be printed or broadcast and which should be left out.

Print Vs Broadcast

With the emergence of electronic media, and now Internet, newspapers are not alone in the news market. Radio and TV stations all over the world also give news to their listeners and viewers and are feared as strong competitors of newspapers which may eventually push the latter out of market. But over the years, we have seen that newspapers have survived and in India we see expansion of newspaper industry along with the expansion of television network.

Reasons for this phenomenon can be explained in the characteristics of these media. Radio is audio-medium and television is audio-visual. One glances through headlines or a major story in a newspaper when it comes. Rest of the paper can be read at the time of one's choice. But in the case of radio, news bulletins are broadcast at fixed times and if one does not tune in then one cannot listen to it again. There are tape recorders and videocassette recorders (VCRs) but who records a news bulletin? Perhaps some media professionals or foreign mission officials whose job is to monitor what has been broadcast.

The advantage with TV and radio is that they can give spot news earlier than newspapers. Normally, what one sees in the night TV bulletin is read in newspapers in the morning? But why does one read newspapers even after listening to the news in the night? Those who have a TV set have not stopped buying newspapers.

In many cases the television news stimulates a desire to read a newspaper. It generates in the listener a desire to know more about the same news item, which has appeared on the TV screen and has vanished in a few seconds. It is another matter that the reader may be disappointed if he does not get enough information about the event which he comes to know through TV.

From his newspaper a TV listener expects more information and a thorough coverage. A good newspaper that wants to cater to the enlightened readership should keep this expectation in mind. The coverage should not be superficial. A newspaper reporter should get into the depth the subject. He should interpret and investigate where necessary. He should take care to give relevant details. Then only can his paper retain this readership.

Thus, the radio and television have added more responsibility on the shoulders of a newspaper reporter. Superficial coverage will not do now. The reporter will have to give as comprehensive a coverage as possible. The basic concept of news in radio and television is the same as in the case of newspaper. What is news for newspaper is news for television and radio as well. But because of limitations of the time available, a radio bulletin will carry what is more important and must be accommodated. On these most important events, radio or television correspondent will be able to give only the most essential information. All important items will be competing for the time in the bulletin and therefore it will not be possible to give as much detail as is possible in a newspaper.

A newspaper reader can read back a sentence if he fails to understand one in the first reading. This is not the case in radio and television news. The newsreader will read a sentence just once and if it is not clear to the listener, he will not be able to hear it again. Thus a radio and television reporter and the news editor will have to ensure clarity of each sentence. The language has to be very simple and meaning should be clear. The newsreader has to read it at a conversational speed and with right tone and pauses to ensure correct meaning and reception by the audience.

Radio and TV both use spoken language. When one listens to the radio or television, the message that one gets is in the language one is used to listening in conversation then one is more receptive. If the language is heavy or the speed is high or low a person listening to it gets tired or irritated quickly.

For example, in conversation while quoting somebody we do not change tense as is done in written English. The use of quotation marks is grammatically correct and while reading the quotation marks are not supposed to be read. This is what is meant by spoken language or radio language. In the spoken language long and difficult words are avoided. Sometimes certain words are changed to suit the newsreader's pronouncing capability.

In the general newsroom of All India Radio, editors select the news items which can be used and turned into broadcast language. The copy testing is done by the editor in-charge and he passes on the selected items to the other editors who turn it into what is called 'pool' copy. This 'pool' is circulated to all bulletin editors who select items according to the importance and the target audience.

The 'pool' copy is prepared in English and it is translated into other languages by a group of translator-cum-newsreaders for that language. When the same person or group of persons translate what they are to read, coordination of the reader and news writer is automatically achieved. But in some languages readers are different from translators and editors, the copy is then passed on to the reader who reads it for its readability and if he or she has any problem a word or phrase is changed.

Translation of news does not mean literal translation. It is basically rewriting the item in a different language. It, therefore, requires command over both the languages. In news translation care has to be taken that the meaning of the item does not change but the syntax should be changed according to the usage of the language in which the item is translated. Language should also be checked for readability and clarity. These are the general principles that apply to translation in news media.

Television newscasting, because of visual element in it, is a little more complicated. With the proper and clear language of the news and voice of the newsreader or anchor one has to ensure that the newscaster is presentable. Dry stories (stories without visuals) are like radio news items with newscaster in view. The newscaster should not smile while giving sad news. If the bulletin ends with sad news the natural smile of relief that comes at the end on the lips of a newsreader looks odd. Normally the editor should avoid putting sad news at the tail of the bulletin.

The visual when it is there should match with the words. Matching of words with visuals needs careful calculation of time and words and overall synchronisation. This requires maximum care while giving news of an award winning ceremony. Care with the use of stills (photographs) cannot be over emphasised. There have been instances when wrong visuals have been shown with a death story and the persons involved were members of Parliament.

Another major difference is in headlines. While in newspapers headlines are on the top of every story, in radio and television news headlines come in the beginning of the bulletin. In radio headlines there are just three or four sentences, each sentence usually dealing with a separate story. In radio bulletins headlines are sometimes repeated at the end. In television headlines are repeated usually at the end and also before the beginning of large segments like business or sports news in 24-hour news channels. The idea is to target the reader who has missed the main stories. There are sometimes headline bulletins on normally entertainment-oriented or radio and television stations. Thus, it can be safely said that there is no difference in the basic concept of news whether it is on radio, television or in a newspaper. The differences arise because of the characteristics of different media.

Radio news: News setups of various broadcast stations vary greatly, depending upon the area covered and the kind of network. Broadcast networks normally have a central news organisation and news is broadcast on all the stations of the network simultaneously. Many networks also have area specific bulletins that are different from central bulletins.

All India Radio is one of the largest networks in the world today. Until 1935, however, there were only two news bulletins a day: one in English and another in an Indian language from Calcutta and Bombay stations, based on a summary provided by Reuters. Centralised news operations from Delhi began in 1937. During the Second World War (1939-45) the Central News Organisation was responsible for five bulletins in English, four in Hindustani and three each in Tamil, Telugu, Marathi, Gujarati and Pusto.

At the time of Independence in 1947, AIR was broadcasting 74 news bulletins, 43 in the home service and 31 in the external services. In 1948, the Central News Organisation was split into News Services Division (NSD) and the External Services Division (ESD), but the news output of the ESD continued with the NSD. The centralised character of AIR news was slightly diluted when the Regional News Units came into being in 1954-55. About this time AIR also introduced Radio News Reel.

In 2003, News Services Division broadcasted everyday 364 news bulletins for a total duration of over 43 hours in its home, external and regional services. In the home service from Delhi 84 bulletins are put out for a duration of over 12 hours. The regional news units numbering 45 broadcast everyday, 187 bulletins for total duration of 19 hours and 45 minutes in 64 languages and dialects. External Services Division broadcasts 65 news bulletins in 25 languages. News Services Division also puts out 65 headline news bulletins daily on FM-I channel from Delhi, Mumbai, Chennai, Kolkata, Bangalore and Lucknow. Besides news bulletins, News Services Division is responsible for a number of current affairs programmes. Like newspaper, news sources of broadcast media include news agencies or wire services that keep on feeding news items all the time, some agencies have separate broadcast wires to cater to the need of broadcast stations. Broadcast stations have their own reporters and stringers who keep on feeding the news desk. Reporters are sent out on previously fixed events about which prior information is available. They are also rushed to cover accidents and other surprise events. There is also constant flow of handouts, some of which may find place in news bulletins. Bigger broadcast news organisations assign beats to their reporters and correspondents like newspapers and they are to keep track of developments in their respective beats.

Most broadcast stations also monitor other stations and this is another major source of news. All India Radio has a separate monitoring service, which has an elaborate arrangement for monitoring other stations in different Indian and foreign languages. Monitoring complex was located at Shimla and in April 1981 it has been shifted to Delhi. Besides this elaborate set up there is a small unit in the broadcasting house which monitors more important bulletins for the benefit of the News Services Division.

News coming to AIR from all these sources land in the General News Room (GNR), the nerve centre of the NSD, which operates round the clock. A computerised news gathering and processing system developed by Research Department of All India Radio and Doordarshan has been installed in Broadcasting House in New Delhi after the turn of the century. But as computers basically facilitate and speed up basic news operations, it is good to take real examples from pre-computer era.

In the GNR the editor-in-charge sitting at the head table functioned as copy taster. His function is like a chief-sub in a newspaper organisation. The editor-in-charge selects the newsworthy items and passes on the selected items to be turned into the radio style to a group of assistant editors called *pool editors*. Since it is neither possible nor necessary to prepare copies of each incoming item for all bulletin editors, a system of pooling all worthwhile items has been devised. The pool editors change the selected copy into pool items that are indexed and grouped into morning pool one, morning pool two, day pool, night pool, evening pool – one/two, evening pool sports, evening Parliament pool, etc. depending on subject and / time of the pool item.

To understand the functioning and various elements it is better to look at an interesting and busy news day with a heavy newsfall before computers took over from typewriters in the GNR of All India Radio. Here is 'Morning Pool One' of 24 March 1987:

Nikhil Sinha:A. P. Garg
K. C. Samal:M. P. Balan
Sadhana Agarawal:M. N. Shome
24-3-1987

MORNING POOL ONE

Index
1. Reporting Assignments
2. Advice
3. Elections
4. Revised Kerala Violence
5. ASLV
6. Dharna
7. Privilege
8. Revised ASLV
9. Maharashtra Assembly
10. Add Elections
11. Weather
12. Further Add Elections
13. Must Announcement
14. Punjab
15. Advice

End of Pool One

The first item of the Morning Pool One is 'Reporting Assignments'. Let us see what is in it.

MS:KLB MPI
24.3.87

Broadcast News – Radio

1. *Reporting Assignments:*

1000 a.m.	Mr. Makwana to inaugurate 4th Delhi Cooperative Congress	...*Khanna*
1300 hrs.	Chairman, Andhra Bank to meet the press.	...*Bahl*
3 p.m.	G.M. Mahanagar Telephone Nigam meets the press.	...*Khanna*
6:30 p.m.	President, Institute of Company Secretaries to meet the press.	...*Churchill*

XP ... *Bahl*
PIB ... *Khanna/Mohan Singh*
Congress ... *Das*

Morn. *(Khanna)*   Eve. *(Mohan Singh)*

As pool items go to all concerned, everybody knows who is doing what.

Item no. 2 and 15 are advices. Let us look at what is in no. 15.   *Nikhil Sinha: MPI 24.3 (15)*

15. *Advice*
In item MPI/3 'Elections', first page, last sentence is redrafted as follows:–

"Repoll has also been ordered in seven booths of Jorabagan constituency (deleting the words PTI says that)"

(PD: 0811)

Now let us see the original MPI/3 'Elections' in which the change has been made.

NS:GG MPI 24.3 (3)

3. *Elections*
Counting of votes begins this morning in the West Bengal, Kerala and Jammu and Kashmir Assembly elections. The first results are expected by the afternoon. All India Radio will broadcast special bulletins throughout tonight to announce the results.

Yesterday's polling in the three states was marked by unprecedented voter turn out. In Kerala, over seventy-five per cent of the one crore fifty seven lakh voters exercised their franchise. In Jammu and Kashmir, the turn out was over sixty-five per cent. Repolling will take place today in nine booths in the state while polling in nine booths of Tilail area in Bandipur constituency could not take place as the election personnel could not reach them due to heavy snowfall. In West Bengal too, the voter turn out was over sixty five per cent. Repoll has been ordered at one booth in Dinahata constituency where it will be held today. PTI says that repoll has also been ordered in seven booths of Jorabagan constituency.

m.t.f. (At the end "m.t.f." means "more to follow".)

There is another election item 'Add Elections' at no. 10.

NS:GG MPI 24.3 (10)

10. *Add Elections (The third sentence of para 1 of MPI/3 has been replaced.)*

The News Services Division of All India Radio has made special arrangement to announce the results. Today, the Hindi sports bulletin will be replaced by news in English at 1905 hours, while the English bulletin at 2000 hours has been converted to a Hindi one. Instead of the English sports bulletin at 2005 hours there will be an English news bulletin. A news bulletin in English has been introduced at 2205 hours.

Hourly news bulletins will continue even after midnight. While the English bulletins can be heard at one, three and five tomorrow morning, the Hindi news bulletins can be heard at two and four a.m.

At 8.21 in the morning, there will be the election commentaries in Hindi and English.

(CB: 0708)

At no. 4 is 'Revised Kerala Violence'. It is revising Kerala violence from earlier day.

NS:GG MPI 24.3 (4)

Broadcast News - Radio

4. *Revised Kerala Violence*
In Kerala, eight persons were killed and over eighty-two injured in post poll violence yesterday. Six people were killed and over forty injured in Thrikkerippur constituency. Two persons were stabbed to death in Kozhikode and Malappuram districts. Over 40 people were injured in tray clashes in different parts of the state.
(UNI:PTI:CB:0445)

Let us have a look at 'ASLV' at no. 5.
NS:GG MPI 24.3 (5)

5. *ASLV*
The country's first Augmented Satellite Launch Vehicle is scheduled to be launched any time after eleven this morning. The ASLV – a second generation launch vehicle – will put a 145 kilogram satellite into a four hundred kilometre near-Earth orbit. Our correspondent, Sheshachandrika, covering the launch, reports from Sriharikota that fuel-filling process for the all-solid five-stage launch vehicle started on schedule last evening. A network of stations at Sriharikota, Ahmedabad, Car Nicobar, Trivandrum, and Kavalor have been set up for tracking and commanding both the launch vehicle and the satellite. A successful launch will enhance the country's capability to put heavier satellites into orbit and usher in many high-technology areas.

Then we have at no. 8 'Revised ASLV'.
NS:GG MPI 24.3. (8)

8. *REVISED ASLV*
The country's first Augmented Satellite Launch Vehicle is scheduled to be launched any time after eleven this morning from the Shar range at Sriharikota on the Andhra Pradesh coast. The count-down for the launch is proceeding on schedule. The ASLV will put a 145 kilogram satellite into a four hundred kilometre near-Earth orbit. The satellite SROSS one is the first in the Stretched Rohini series. Our correspondent, Sheshachandrika, covering the launch, reports from Sriharikota that fuel-filling process for the all-solid five-stage launch vehicle started on schedule last evening. In a short while from now the mobile service tower will be moved about a 150

metre away from the ASLV which will then stand free with only the support of the umbilical mast. About eighty minutes before blast-off there will be a complete check up and the last ten minutes will be handled entirely by computer.

Our correspondent reports that the second-generation launch vehicle developed indigenously at the Vikram Sarabhai Space Centre employs a host of new technologies. The most important is its sophisticated guidance system which is essential for achieving the precision needed to put the satellite into the correct orbit. A network of stations at Sriharikota, Ahmedabad, Car Nicobar, Trivandrum, and Kavalor have been set up for tracking and commanding both the launch vehicle and the satellite. A successful launch will enhance the country's capability to put heavier satellites into orbit and achieve mastery in many high-technology areas.

The Prime Minister, Mr. Rajiv Gandhi, who arrived in Madras last night, is reaching Sriharikota this morning to witness the launch.

(Sheshachandrika phone: 0642)

A careful look at these items reveals that each carries date, time, item no., pool identification (MPI), slug ('ASLV', 'Advice', 'Election') identifying the subject and name or initials of those who were responsible for the item (NS:GG) and the source (UNI, PTI, Sheshachandrika phone) are indicated.

Let us look at the index of 'Morning Pool Two' of 24.3.87.

Nikhil Sinha: Sadhana Agarwal
Shome:Garg
24.3.1987

MORNING POOL TWO

Index
1. Advice
2. Chad
3. Revised Hockey Must Announcement
4. Morning Brandt Resigned
5. Explosion
6. New Hockey Must Announcement
7. Manoeuvres
8. Aids Warning

Broadcast News – Radio

  9. Sri Lanka
10. Warsaw Pact

End of morn. Pool Two

As a major English news bulletin is at 0810 hours it would be interesting to look at the last two items of this pool. 'Sri Lanka' and 'Warsaw Pact'.

NS:MNS MPII 24.3.87 (9)

9. Sri Lanka

In Sri Lanka, 32 persons were killed in violence in Trincomali and Jaffna yesterday.

In the eastern Trincomali district, Tamil militants attacked the Serunuwa village, killing 26 persons. An official spokesman told our Colombo correspondent Plaban Majumdar* that the dead were mostly civilians.

In the northern Jaffna peninsula, militants launched a pre-dawn attack on the Jaffna port camp with mortars. Five security personnel died in the incident and seven were reported missing. A number of buildings and shops have been damaged. The fighting was followed by fierce shelling from Port Pallaly, Mandativu and other army camps, accompanied by helicopter strafing.

*Plaban Majumdar:Colombo:Phone/0741
NS:GG MPII 24.3 (10)

10. Warsaw Pact

A two-day meeting of the foreign ministers of the Warsaw Pact countries begins in MOSCOW today. The main subject on the agenda ia expected to be the situation in Europe in the light of the latest Soviet proposal on the withdrawal of US and Soviet medium-range missiles from the continent. They will also discuss the Vienna talks on the reduction of conventional weapons and other initiatives aimed at strengthening peace and security in Europe.

(Tanjug pool:0750)

These item have been incorporated in the pool at 0741 and 0750 hours respectively and one of them finds place in the bulletin. Here is the bulletin as broadcast.

All India Radio
Esther Kar:N. M. Bhatia:Ratna Koul
News Services Division
24/3/87 English 0810 Hrs

This is All India Radio: The News Read by Sushil Jhaveri
- The country's first indigenously developed second generation satellite 'launch vehicle' is ready for blast off.
- Eight people have been killed in post poll violence in Kerala.
- The counting of votes in the assembly elections begins this morning.
- In Sri Lanka, 32 people have been killed in violence in the northern and eastern provinces.

And in Sports
- The semi-finals of the National Hockey championships are being played in Pune today; and
- India play Pakistan in the fifth one day International Cricket match at Nagpur.

The country's first Augmented Satellite Launch Vehicle is scheduled to be launched any time after eleven this morning from the Shar range at Sriharikota on the Andhra Pradesh coast. The count-down for the launch is proceeding on schedule. The ASLV-will put a 145 kilogram satellite into a four hundred kilometre near-Earth orbit. The satellite SROSS-1 is the first in the Stretched Rohini series. Our correspondent, Sheshachandrika, covering the launch, reports from Sriharikota that fuel-filling process for the all-solid five-stage launch vehicle started on schedule last evening. In a short while from now the mobile service tower will be moved about a 150 metre away from the ASLV which will then stand free with only the support of the umbilical mast. About eighty minutes before blast-off there will be a complete check up and the last ten minutes will be handled entirely by computer.

Our correspondent reports that the second-generation launch vehicle developed indigenously at the Vikram Sarabhai Space Centre employs a host of new technologies. The most important is its sophisticated guidance system, which is essential for achieving the precision needed to put the satellite into the correct orbit. A network of stations at Sriharikota, Ahmedabad, Car Nicobar, Trivandrum, and Kavalor have been set up for tracking and commanding both the launch vehicle and the satellite. A successful launch will enhance the country's capability to put heavier satellites into orbit and achieve mastery in many high-technology areas.

The Prime Minister, Mr. Rajiv Gandhi, who arrived in Madras last night, is reaching Sriharikota this morning to witness the launch.

In Kerala, eight persons were killed and over eighty-two injured in post-poll violence yesterday. Six people were killed and over forty injured in Thrikkerippur constituency. Two persons were stabbed to death in Kozhikode and Malappuram districts. Over 40 people were injured in stray clashes in different parts of the state.

The counting of votes begins this morning in the West Bengal, Kerala and Jammu and Kashmir Assembly elections. The first results are expected by the afternoon. All India Radio will broadcast special bulletins throughout tonight to announce the results.

Yesterday's polling in the three states was marked by unprecedented voter turn-out. In Kerala, over seventy-five per cent of the one crore fifty-seven lakh voters exercised their franchise.

In Jammu and Kashmir, the turn out was over sixty-five per cent. The Election Commission has ordered repoll in about two dozen polling stations in fourteen constituencies. The repoll will be held today or tomorrow between 7.30 a.m. and 4.30 p.m., subject to the availability of the election material with the polling parties.

The schedule of counting of votes for these constituencies would be revised in view of the repoll.

In West Bengal too, the voter turn-out was over sixty-five per cent. Repoll at one booth in Dinahata constituency will be held today. Repoll has been ordered in seven booths of Jorabagan constituency.

Polling was also held yesterday in the byelections to three Lok Sabha and eight Assembly constituencies spread over four states and the Union Territory of Pondicherry.

Our Lucknow correspondent reports that repolling has been ordered in one polling centre in the Hardwar Lok Sabha constituency and two polling stations of the Rath Assembly constituency in Uttar Pradesh. The repoll will be held today and the counting of these constituencies will be taken up tomorrow. Polling in eight stations in Patti Assembly constituency was postponed yesterday due to violence. Repolling in these stations will be held tomorrow. The counting of votes will be taken up as scheduled today in Kashipur Assembly constituency.

This is All India Radio giving you the news.

In Sri Lanka, 32 persons were killed in violence in Trincomali and Jaffna yesterday.

In the eastern Trincomali district, Tamil militants attacked the Serunuwa village, killing 26 persons. An official spokesman told our Colombo correspondent Plaban Majumdar that the dead were mostly civilians.

In the northern Jaffna peninsula, militants launched a pre-dawn attack on the Jaffna port camp with mortars. Five security personnel died in the incident and seven were reported missing. A number of buildings and shops have been damaged. The fighting was followed by fierce shelling from Port Pallaly, Mandativu and other army camps, accompanied by helicopter straffing.

The three-week Budget Session of the Maharashtra Legislature begins in Bombay today. The Governor, Shri Shankar Dayal Sharma, will address the joint sitting of both the Houses on the opening day. The Finance Minister, Mr. Sushil Kumar Shinde will present the Budget for 1987-88 tomorrow. The drought situation in the state and the strike by the resident doctor are likely to figure during the discussions in both the Houses.

The Gujarat Chief Minister, Mr. Amar Singh Chaudhury has said that the government is keen to resolve the farmer's problem through negotiations. Replying to the discussion on the demands of home and other departments in the State Assembly yesterday, Mr. Chaudhury said the government has already released the leaders of the Bhartiya Kisan Sangh arrested last Thursday during the *gherao* of the State Assembly. He, however, said the cases against those who have been chargesheeted cannot be withdrawn.

Meanwhile, the Bhartiya Kisan Sangh has reiterated its demand to release all the arrested farmers.

The Karnataka Assembly adjourned without transacting any business yesterday as the Congress (I) continued its six-day old *dharna*. As the House assembled, the Congress (I) members squatted in the well and pressed their demand for revocation of the suspension of one of the party members. The Chief Minister Mr. Ramakrishna Hegde turned down their demand saying that the member Mr. Adyantayya should tender an apology. Proceedings in the Legislative Council were also marred on the issue of nomination of Mandal Panchayats.

In the Rajasthan Assembly a privilege motion was tabled against the Chief Minister Mr. Harideo Joshi yesterday. Mr. Nathu Singh of the BJP who moved the motion said that the chief minister in his budget speech had announced that an open University would be set up in the state. He said the centre had, however, declared that it had no such proposal. The Speaker Mr. G P Tiwari assured the members that he would give his ruling on the motion later. A privilege motion is already pending in the House against Mr. Joshi for an alleged discrepancy in the budget speech.

The defending champions Indian Airlines take on Punjab and service clash with Railways, in the semi-finals of the National Hockey Championships in Pune today. All India Radio will broadcast running commentaries on the matches. These can be heard from 2.25 to 3.50 p.m. and from 4.10 to 5.50 p.m. on Delhi 'D'. AIR will also broadcast a running commentary on the final tomorrow from 3.40 to 5.05 p.m. on Delhi 'D'.

India and Pakistan play the fifth one-day international cricket match in Nagpur today. The visitors are leading 3-1 in the six match series. Chetan Sharma has been included in the team in place of Madan Lal.

All India Radio will broadcast a running commentary. This can he heard on Delhi 'B' from 8.55 a.m.
And now to end the news here are the main points again.
(Repeat headlines)
And that is the end of the news.

It is a major 10-minute bulletin. The other type is minor or headline bulletin of one or two minute duration. That kind of bulletin would have two or three sentences of each item selected for broadcast. In major bulletins some details are possible and it is advised that after the opening announcement it should have main points or headlines. The headlines should be repeated before the end of the bulletin.

The opening announcement in this bulletin is, 'This is All India Radio: The news read by Sushil Jhaveri.' And then there are headlines. One can see the difference between the broadcast headlines and the newspaper headlines. Broadcast headlines are complete sentences while this is rare in the case of print media headlines. Incomplete sentences can be used in headlines only rarely and to produce special conversational effect. Even those who prefer using incomplete sentences in the headlines are advised to use only complete sentences while repeating the headlines in the end.

The bulletin has to cater to the convenience of the listeners. For some headlines are enough, they may have no interest in details of any item. Many FM channels now use that format, the repeat headlines give an idea of the main events covered in the bulletin for the benefit of those who could not tune in from the beginning. One can see this technique used in most 24-hour news channels at the beginning of different segments like sports or business news.

Almost at the middle of the bulletin there is identification of the network. *"This is All India Radio giving you the news."* This serves two purposes – identifies the network and also helps change of subject. In this bulletin the identification ends election news and indicates a change in subject and after this the listener would not feel as if there is a sudden switch-over to events in Sri Lanka.

Regarding the language of broadcast one can see how present tense has been used in place of past and future tenses, 'is ready for blast off', 'have been killed', 'employs a host of', 'have been set up for', 'is reaching'. One can also observe how the place and date of the event is mentioned in the news story and how 'today', 'this morning', 'opening day', 'tomorrow' and 'yesterday' have been used for the purpose.

There is another point well illustrated in this bulletin. In radio news bulletin news must flow naturally. Newsreader should not seem to jump from one topic to another. There are two techniques that can be used to achieve this: (1) Departmentalisation, this is grouping of news items by subject or geography. (2) Transitional phrases, these are used to bridge separate sections or items. In the headlines 'And In Sports' has been used as a good transitional phrase. Departmentalisation is very clear. After all the news about ASLV, we have all the election news – election violence, polling, repoll and special election bulletins – are all grouped together. After the half-time network identification you have news from Sri Lanka and then news from various state assemblies is grouped together. And in the end you have all the sports news. As such the news fall is very heavy and hence several items that we find in the pool have not found their place in this main bulletin.

Now here is the index of 'Day Pool I'.

Surinder Kumar:H. I. Chadda
S. K. Sharma/Om Kedia:Ratna Koul
Jai Gopal/S. K. Sinha:Arvind Kumar 24/3/87
Vijay Singh/J. B. *Toppo
Rajinder Butt

DAY POOL I

Index
16. ASLV Must Announcement
17. Advice
18. Visit
19. Falerio
20. Cotton
21. Labourers
22. Must Announcement
23. Must Announcement – Hockey
24. ASLV
25. Temple
26. Reservoir
27. Died
28. Lead ASLV

29. Trains
30. Makwana
31. Blast Off
32. Revised Blast Off
33. Advice
34. Peace March

Item 24 'ASLV' and then 28 'Lead ASLV' illustrate how the story is being revised continuously with additional bits of information.

SK:HLC DPI 24.3.87 (24)

24. *ASLV*

The country's first ever Augmented Satellite Launch Vehicle, with the First Stretched Rohini Satellite on its top is parked at the launching pad with the support of the umbilical mast is about to be launched, from Sriharikota at 1210 hours today. Our correspondent Seshachandrika reports from the launching pad that the mobile service tower which includes a mammoth steel house was moved away a few minutes earlier. The scientists are looking forward for the last 10 minutes operation from 12 noon which will be done entirely by computer. The Prime Minister Mr. Rajiv Gandhi has already arrived in Sriharikota. He was taken around by the Chairman of the Space Commission, Dr U. R. Rao to various segments and other facilities of Shar.

Our correspondent reports that the second-generation launch vehicle developed indigenously at the Vikram Sarabhai Space Centre employs a host of new technologies. The most important is its sophisticated guidance system which is essential for achieving the precision needed to put the satellite into the correct orbit. A network of stations at Sriharikota, Ahmedabad, Car Nicobar, Trivandrum, and Kavalor have been set up for tracking and commanding both the launch vehicle and the satellite. A successful launch will enhance the country's capability to put heavier satellites into orbit and achieve mastery in many high-technology areas.

Seshachandrika:phone:1125
SK:HLC DPI 24.3.87 (28)

28. Lead ASLV

The country's first ever Augmented Satellite Launch Vehicle, with the First Stretched Rohini Satellite on its top is about to be launched, from Sriharikota in a shortwhile from now. It is scheduled to take off at 1205 hours. It is now parked at the launching pad with the support of the umbilical mast. Our correspondent Seshachandrika reports from the launching pad that the mobile service tower which includes a mammoth steel house was moved away a few minutes earlier. The scientists are looking forward for the last 10 minutes operation which will be done entirely by computer.

The Prime Minister Mr. Rajiv Gandhi along with the Chairman of the Space Commission, Dr U. R. Rao is watching the pre-launch operation from the satellite control centre. The Andhra Pradesh Governor, Miss Kumudben Joshi, the Chief Minister, Mr. N. T. Rama Rao and the Union Minister of State for Science and Technology Mr. K. R. Narayanan are sitting by the side of the prime minister.

(Here the second para of the earlier story has been picked up from the first para.)

Seshachandrika on phone:1155

Let us look at item no. 31 'Blast Off" and item no. 33 'Advice'

SK:HCL   DPI 24.3.87 (31)

31. Blast Off

The Augmented Satellite Launch Vehicle with the first Stretched Rohini Satellite blasted off from Sriharikota at 1209 hours today. The Prime Minister, Mr. Rajiv Gandhi was among the dignitaries who witnessed the maiden launch of the country's second generation launch vehicle.

UNI/PTI

33. Advice

Item 'Blast Off' DPI/31 ends on first page and source is UNI/PTI.

Item 31 leads to 'Revised Blast Off' which adds background information about ASLV.

SK:HLC   DPI 24.3.87 (32)

32. Revised Blast Off

The country's first ever Augmented Satellite Launch Vehicle ASLV was launched at 1209 hours this afternoon from Sriharikota launch site in East Coast of Andhra Pradesh. The 41-tonne, 23 metre-tall vehicle with 145 kilogram Rohini Satellite was blasted off exactly at 12 hours 9 minutes and 33 seconds as per schedule. Our correspondent Seshachandrika reports that the initial blast off upto 1.51 seconds was most successful.

The Prime Minister, Mr. Rajiv Gandhi, along with the Andhra Pradesh Governor, Miss Kumudben Joshi and the Chief Minister, Mr. N. T. Rama Rao watched the launching.

Our correspondent reports that the second-generation launch vehicle developed indigenously at the Vikram Sarabhai Space Centre employs a host of new technologies. The most important is its sophisticated guidance system which is essential for achieving the precision needed to put the satellite into the correct orbit. A network of stations at Sriharikota, Ahmedabad, Car Nicobar, Trivandrum, and Kavalor have been set up for tracking and commanding both the launch vehicle and the satellite. A successful launch will enhance the country's capability to put heavier satellites into orbit and achieve mastery in many high-technology areas.

(Seshachandrika:phone:1305)

Now it is interesting to look at the next main English bulletin which went on the air at 1400 hours.

All India Radio
News Services Division
Aditya Sen:Anup:GSB
1400 hrs (English)   24.3.87.
This is All India Radio. The news read by Harish Kashyap
The Headlines

- The country's first ever Augmented Satellite Launch Vehicle ASLV has been successfully blasted off.
- Counting is in progress in Kerala, Jammu and Kashmir and West Bengal where polling was completed yesterday.
- Early trends in Kerala show that the LDF candidates are leading in 45 and UDF in 35 constituencies.

Broadcast News - Radio

- In Jammu and Kashmir, the National Conference (Farooq)-Congress-I Alliance is in the lead in three constituencies in the Valley while in Jammu, the Congress is leading in three and BJP in one constituency.
- In Kerala, the Chief Minister, Mr. Karunakaran, the UDF Minister, Mr. K. M. Mani, Mrs. M. Kamalam and the Speaker Mr. Sudheeran, are ahead of their rival. In Kashmir, the Chief Minister Dr. Farooq Abdullah, was leading over his nearest rival by over 21,000 votes when reports last came in.
- At Nagpur, India face an uphill task for victory against Pakistan in the one-day International Cricket.

The country's first ever Augmented Satellite Launch Vehicle ASLV was launched at 1209 hours this afternoon from Sriharikota launch site in East Coast of Andhra Pradesh. The 41-tonne, 23 metre-tall vehicle with 145 kilogram Rohini Satellite was blasted off exactly at 12 hours 9 minutes and 33 seconds as per schedule. Our correspondent Seshachandrika reports that the initial blast off upto 1.51 seconds was most successful.

The Prime Minister, Mr. Rajiv Gandhi, along with the Andhra Pradesh Governor, Miss Kumudben Joshi and the Chief Minister, Mr. N. T. Rama Rao watched the launching.

Our Correspondent reports that the second-generation launch vehicle developed indigenously at the Vikram Sarabhai Space Centre employs a host of new technologies. The most important is its sophisticated guidance system which is essential for achieving the precision needed to put the satellite into the correct orbit. A network of stations at Sriharikota, Ahmedabad, Car Nicobar, Trivandrum, and Kavalor have been set up for tracking and commanding both the launch vehicle and the satellite. A successful launch will enhance the country's capability to put heavier satellites into orbit and achieve mastery in many high-technology areas.

Early trends from Kerala and Jammu and Kashmir show that the Left Democratic Front candidates have established lead in the Southern state and the Congress (I) and National Conference (Farooq) nominees are ahead in J & K in the Assembly elections held yesterday. No trends are available from West Bengal which also went to the polls. In Kerala, the Opposition LDF is leading in 45 constituencies while the ruling UDF is leading in 35 at the end of the second round of counting.

Prominent candidates who are leading include the Chief Minister, Mr. K. Karunakaran, the Speaker Mr. V. M. Sudheeran and the UDF Ministers, Mr. K. M. Mani and Mr. P. J. Joseph. The Deputy Speaker, Mr. Ahmed Haji, was leading by 10,000 votes over his CPI(M) rival. Important LDF candidates in the lead are Mr. Baby John, Mr. Chandrasekharan and Mr. Sivadas Menon.

Key UDF figures, who are trailing, are UDF Minister, Mr. R. Balakrishna Pillai, Mr. Sivadasan and Mrs. Kamalam. The Youth Congress (I) leader G Karthikeyan, was also trailing in Trivandrum North. The former Home Minister Mr. Vayalar Ravi, UDF is trailing by 1000 votes in Shertalai constituency.

The newly-formed CMP leader Mr. M V Raghavan is leading in Azhikode constituency.

AIR correspondent reported from Trivandrum that the final picture of the Assembly election is likely to emerge by this evening.

The Opposition LDF consists of CPI(M), CPI, Janata, Congress (S), Revolutionary Socialist Party, Lok Dal and Independents. The UDF consists of Congress (I), Muslim League, Kerala Congress (Mani), Kerala Congress (Joseph), National Democratic Party, Socialist Republican Party and Independents.

Early trends from Jammu and Kashmir indicate that the National Conference (Farooq)-Congress(I) alliance is leading in three constituencies in Kashmir valley. In Jammu division, the Congress(I) candidates have established early lead in three constituencies and BJP in one. The State Chief Minister and National Conference (F) leader Dr. Farooq Abdullah, is leading over his MUF rival by over 21,000 votes in the Ganderbal constituency. The Agriculture Minister, Master Beli Ram, and the state BJP President Mr. Baldev Singh, are also leading. In West Bengal, results of more than half of the 294 seats will be known today itself.

Reports reaching Calcutta say that the counting process began rather late at some centres following the delay in receipt of postal ballots.

Among the leaders whose political fortunes will become clear by tonight are the Land Revenue Minister, Mr. Binoy Choudhary the Commerce Minister, Mr. Nirmal Bose, and the Power Minister Mr. Prabir Sengupta.

The constituencies to be taken up for counting tomorrow include Satgachi where the Chief Minister, Mr. Jyoti Basu is seeking re-election.

Meanwhile, re-poll is taking place at one booth of Dinahata constituency in Cooch-Behar district.

In the byelections held yesterday, the Congress (I) has won Bahour reserved constituency in Pondicherry. The party candidate Mr. Rajalingam, defeated his nearest Janata Party rival Mr. P. Rajavelu, by a margin of 919 votes. The Congress (I) has wrested the seat from the Janata Party which it held for three consecutive terms from 1977.

In Uttar Pradesh repolling has begun in 8 polling stations in Patti Assembly constituency and two booths in Rath constituency in Assembly byelections. Repolling has also begun in Hardwar constituency in the Lok Sabha byelection. Polling at these places was suspended yesterday following incidents of booth capturing and violence. Counting of votes has begun in Kashipur Assembly constituency.

In Maharashtra, counting is on in the Nanded Lok Sabha constituency in the byelections held yesterday.

In Andhra Pradesh, the Congress-I has won the Polavaram reserved constituency in the Assembly byelection. The Party candidate, Mr. B. Durga Rao, defeated Telugu Desam candidate, Mr. Sirgannadora, by a margin of over 4,300 votes. Counting of votes in another Assembly constituency, Kalyan Durg, is on. Counting of votes in the Secunderabad Lok Sabha constituency will be held tomorrow. A re-polling is on in the two booths.

In Gujarat, counting has begun in the byelections to Modasa Assembly constituency.

Here is a Flash:

The first result from Jammu and Kashmir has gone in favour of the Congress(I)-National Conference(Farooq) Alliance. The Chief

Minister Dr. Farooq Abdullah, was declared elected from Ganderbal constituency. He defeated his nearest rival, Mr. Abdul Khaliq Sofi, of the Muslim United Front by a margin of over twenty-two thousand votes.

This is All India Radio giving you the news.
Cricket
At Nagpur, India were 27 for one in 11 overs when reports last came in, in the fifth one day international cricket match against Pakistan. They have to score 287 in 44 overs with an asking rate of 6.52 per over to win.

According to trends now available from West Bengal the left front is leading in 12 and Congress in 2 constituencies at the end of the second round.

To end the news here are the main points again.
- The country's first ever Augmented Satellite Launch Vehicle ASLV has been successfully blasted off.
- Counting is in progress in Kerala, Jammu and Kashmir and West Bengal where polling was completed yesterday.
- Early trends in Kerala show that the LDF candidates are leading in 45 and UDF in 35 constituencies.
- In Jammu and Kashmir, the National Conference (Farooq)-Congress-I Alliance is in the lead in three constituencies in the Valley while in Jammu, the Congress is leading in 3 and BJP in 1 constitueny.
- In Kerala, the Chief Minister, Mr. Karunakaran, the UDF Minister, Mr. K. M. Mani, Mrs. M. Kamalam and the Speaker Mr. Sudheeran, are ahead of their rivals. In Kashmir, the Chief Minister Dr. Farooq Abdullah, has been declared elected from the Ganderbal constituency.
- At Nagpur, India face an uphill task for victory against Pakistan in the one-day international cricket.

And that is the end of the news.

In this bulletin the News Services Division of All India Radio committed a blunder despite its more than fifty years of experience in broadcasting news. At the time when AIR was announcing the successful launch of the ASLV, parts of it had already reached the seabed in the Bay of Bengal. Well, the initial 'blast off up to 1.51 seconds' was 'most successful' but seconds later it turned downwards and went into the sea. This happened seconds after the correspondents of the news agencies (and perhaps AIR correspondent) told their desks on phone the story of the successful blast off from the site. The editors dealing with the story in the General News Room made use of this information and put out 'Revised Blast Off' in the 'Pool' which was incorporated in the 1400 hours bulletin without any change.

The GNR was alive to news fall even during the broadcast of the bulletin and therefore we have a FLASH on the victory of Dr. Farooq Abdullah. Thus, it appears that AIR correspondent at the launch site could not inform the GNR about the failure of the ASLV for two hours. The result was a disaster in the 1400 hours bulletin. Now with mobile phones and better connectivity such mistakes should not happen. However, even in those days it should have been possible to update the story. But perhaps the correspondents at the site waited for the official version, unmindful of the deadline for the major bulletin.

In the 'Day Pool' there is no story on elections while the bulletin is full of election news. AIR makes elaborate arrangements to cover elections. On the day when results are expected correspondents at various centres feed the GNR using dedicated hotlines specially hired from the telephone department for the purpose. Before elections a lot of hard work goes into identifying key constituencies and backgrounders are prepared with all the necessary information. This homework helps the GNR staff to prepare stories quickly as soon as results come on the hotline and to give due importance to the key contests despite great excitement and pressure of work. Election coverage of AIR can be an example of excellence for any network in the world.

The bulletin has an item on cricket sandwiched between the election news. Naturally, the item on trends in West Bengal has reached GNR and hence the newsreader only after the bulletin has started. Looking at the importance of news the editors have done well by including this item just before the end of the bulletin. They have also taken care that the change regarding Dr. Farooq Abdullah is incorporated in the repeat headlines, before the end of the bulletin.

The system of 'Pool' helps various bulletin editors as the items are converted into AIR style from the copy that comes from various sources. The bulletin editors need not have to deal with the entire news fall. They also get pre-selected new items in a form which can go on the air. Now their job is to select the items from the pool according to the requirements of the bulletin depending upon the duration and the target audience.

For languages other than English, bulletin items are supplied by GNR to various language units of the NSD where translator-cum-newsreaders translate and read the bulletins. In many languages final script is handwritten hence it is always good to have the same person or group doing the translation and newsreading. Hindi is an exception as there is a separate newsroom for Hindi which gets GNR POOL copy and also has wire services in Hindi from PTI (Bhasha) and UNI (Varta). The bulletin editors in Hindi compile their bulletins independently.

Here it should be mentioned that the system evolved in GNR was such that the stenographers typed the pool copy on stencils while the pool editors dictated. These stenographers were the first listeners of the item and they indicated if the language was difficult or vague. According to a former director of NSD some of the GNR stenographers did not even start typing until they were satisfied with the first sentence from the news editor and thus allowed him time to rephrase. As soon as the stencil was removed from the typewriter it went to the duplicating room and without any loss of time the copies were distributed to all concerned. Similarly copies of various bulletins were circulated to all who got the pool copy from GNR for ready reference while they were working on future bulletins. All this now has become cleaner and faster with the use of computers. Regional news units of AIR do not have pool system and work as any small station, which puts out limited number of news bulletins.

There was no use of voice reports, interviews and 'live' accounts from the place of event, now quite common in AIR, in the above examples of the bulletins. One of the earliest voice insert used in AIR bulletins was the voice of Mrs. Indira Gandhi announcing the surrender of Pakistani forces in Dacca. However, voice reports, actualities, interviews, on the spot features were used by AIR in its newsreel programmes since 1950s. Here is an actual example of a newsreel script, which gives an idea of the variety of item this format can include.

S.F.H. Naqvy: A.K.Kaul 19.4.88
All India Radio
News Services Division
Radio Newsreel
In this Edition

Pakistan's involvement in the terrorist violence in Punjab.
Prime Minister asks the industry to be more competitive.
President confers Arjuna Awards;
and
Punjab meet Kerala in the Santosh Trophy Football Final.

The Home Minister Mr. Buta Singh has strongly rebutted the Pakistan President, General Zia-ul-Haq's reported assertion that his country is not helping the terrorists in Punjab. Mr. Buta Singh declared in the Lok Sabha today that there is active participation of some of the government agencies of Pakistan in terrorist violence in Punjab. Our correspondent Vishwanath Ramesh interviews the Inspector General Border Security Force, Punjab Frontiers, regarding Pakistan's involvement in the terrorists activities.

(cut)

A National Conference on Transformation of Engineering Industry was held in New Delhi today. Addressing the valedictory session, the Prime Minister, Mr. Rajiv Gandhi emphasises the need for more competition to ensure quality.

(cut)

The prime minister asked the industry to shift its emphasis towards the areas where it has more export potential.

(cut)
The President R. Venkataraman today honoured thirteen sports persons with Arjuna Awards for their outstanding performance during 1986. The award winners are: Kumari Suman Rawat for Athletics, Jaipal Singh – Boxing, Kumari Sandhya Agarwal – Women Cricket, Joaquim Martin Carvalho – Hockey, Kumari Rama Sarkar – Kabaddi, Cyril C. Valloor – Volleyball, Naib Subedar Bhagirath Samai – Shooting, Prem Chand – Body Building, Lt. Col. K. S. Rao – Adventure Sports, Jag Mohan Sapra – Weight Lifting, and Kumari Arti Pradhan – Swimming. Mohd. Azharuddin – Cricket and Lt. Dhruv Bhandari – Yachting were not present to receive the Awards.

Our correspondent, Usha Singh interviewed some of the award winners. Joaquim Martin Carvalho of Hockey speaks about using new techniques in the game:
(cut)
Cyril C. valloor of volleyball
(cut)
Naib Subedar Bhagirath Samai, who won the award in shooting.
(cut)
Speaking on the occasion, the president stressed the need of spotting sports talent at the grassroot level:
(cut)
In Gujarat, a corporation has been set up to expedite the construction of the multi-purpose Narmada Project. Here is a report from our Ahmedabad correspondent, Digant Dave:
(cut)
And finally sports:

Punjab will meet Kerala in the final of the Santosh Trophy Football Championship. In the second semi-final today, Punjab defeated Maharashtra by a solitary goal. Our correspondent Rangarajan reports:
(cut)
And with that we end this edition of radio newsreel edited and produced by Fakhrul Naqvy.

'Cut' in the script indicates a voice insert. Newsreel is not presented live and live inserts in it are rarely used. It does not,

however, mean that AIR does not broadcast live programmes. Running commentaries of major sports events, and live broadcasts of important national functions like Independence Day address by the prime minister from historic Red Fort and live broadcast of Republic Day Parade from Rajpath have become routine features.

With the use of computers and broadcast techniques based on more sophisticated software the content of All India Radio bulletins has changed to accommodate more voice reports, etc. and the bulletins are also available on Internet.

Here is an example:
All India Radio: D. K. Ghosh:Elsie P.
News Services Division
English: 0815 hrs 20-05-2003

GOOD MORNING! I AM POONAM CHADHA
The Headlines
- India has rejected Pakistan's claim that terrorist groups operating in Jammu and Kashmir are not in its control.
- The Union Cabinet has decided to permit the conversion of industrial and commercial property in Delhi from leasehold to freehold.
- In Kolkata, the Narcotics Control Bureau has busted an international cartel dealing in banned drugs.
- A Special Court in Mumbai has attached two properties of the underworld don Dawood Ibrahim.
- The Tamil Nadu Government Doctors Association has withdrawn its proposed strike from tomorrow.
And in cricket
- New Zealand have clinched a 9-run victory over Sri Lanka in the fifth match of the triangular series at Dambulla.

(Hold for music)

India has rejected Pakistan's claim that terrorist groups operating in Jammu and Kashmir are not in its control. The External Affairs Minister, Mr. Yashwant Sinha said this in an interview to the BBC when his attention was drawn to his Pakistani counterpart Mr. Khurshid Mehmood Kasuri's statement that many of the terrorist groups are not under Islamabad's control. He said, Pakistan had handed over about 500 terrorists to the US authorities and similarly they can cooperate with India in dealing with the terrorist groups operating in Kashmir. We spoke to Pakistan Watcher General Afsir Karim on the issue.

(Sound bite – Afsir Karim)
As well as the infiltration continues to all along the LoC that means there are camps in various areas and it cannot be credible when somebody says that there are no camps and there is no infiltration. I think it has to be proved on the ground then only we can believe it.

Pakistan has not proposed any name for its envoy in New Delhi so far. The clarification came amidst contradictory statements from Islamabad about the appointment of a high commissioner to India. While Prime Minister Jamali reportedly told PTV that Pakistan's Ambassador to China, Riaz Mohammad Khan would be the new envoy to India, the Foreign office there said that Mr. Jamali was wrongly quoted.

New Delhi had named Mr. Shiv Shankar Menon as its new envoy to Islamabad.

The Union Cabinet has decided to permit the conversion of industrial and commercial property in the capital from leasehold to freehold. The facility already provided to the residential properties will continue. Talking to newsmen, the Urban Development

Minister Mr. Ananth Kumar said for Industrial and Commercial properties, a conversion charge at the rate of 10 per cent of the land rate will have to be paid. In case of original lessees, a rebate of 40 per cent will be given while general power of attorney holders will have to pay 33.3 per cent surcharge.

The prime minister is launching a mega 400 crore-rupee mega project to clean the river Gomti in Lucknow today. Our correspondent reports that Mr. Atal Behari Vajpayee will also lay the foundation of more than twelve projects at Kudia Ghat and inaugurate the much awaited sound and light show of the State Tourism Department.

(Voice cast – U.C.Roy)
(Gist)

Prime Minister Mr. Atal Behari Vajpayee's only engagement for the evening is that he will be addressing party workers and cadres at a local school. Tomorrow in the forenoon, he will honour the hindi poets and authors who have been awarded prices by the Uttar Pradesh Hindi Sansthan. In the afternoon, he will be dedicating certain projects worth one thousand one crore rupees at the banks of the Gomti.

The Commissioner for Railway Safety, Mr. Bhupinder Singh, investigating the Frontier Mail train fire has said that they have found valuable clues into the blaze, that killed 38 people near Ludhiana in Punjab recently. He said that forensic experts are examining a stove found in one of the coaches. Statements of witnesses are also being corroborated.

The Director-General of Jammu and Kashmir Police, Mr. A. K. Suri has been replaced by Mr. Gopal Sharma. A decision to this effect was taken by the state cabinet. Two senior police officials Mr. M. K. Mohanty and Mr. Rajam Bakshi are to be promoted to the rank of director-general. Some transfers in the civil administration have also been approved.

This is All India Radio giving you the news.

In Kolkata, the Narcotics Control Bureau has busted an international cartel dealing in banned drugs. Five foreigners have been arrested. Those arrested were residing as tenants in a house owned by the former CBI Additional Director, Mr. U. N. Biswas in the Salt Lake area.

The Director-General of the NCB, Mr. M. K. Singh told AIR that further arrests are likely to be made soon in this connection.

(Sound bite – Singh)

This is a raid to dismantle an ATS manufacturing facilities and probably this is the first case in the country. ATS is a synthetic drug not much known in this country. Although it is very much in vogue among the addicts, in Europe, in America, the South East, the Far East and Oceanea. So there in the raid we have found out not only raw material for manufacturing of these drugs as well as the equipment, the machinery for the manufacturing purpose. Now this is on a gang, a Chinese cartel. Earlier certain arrests were made in China itself and five of its members were arrested in New York.

All the accused were produced in the court at Barasat and have been remanded to judicial custody till the 2nd of next month.

The Rashtriya Janata Dal Chief, Mr. Laloo Prasad Yadav has demanded stringent action against Mr. U. N. Biswas

A Special Court in Mumbai, has attached the controversial Sara Shopping Centre and the Sahara Shopping Complex, reportedly belonging to the underworld don Dawood Ibrahim, his brother Iqbal and two others. According to police, the structures were illegally constructed by Dawood Ibrahim and his henchmen in connivance with civic body officials on CPWD land.

The Mumbai police says, it has evidence that Bollywood actress Shilpa Shetty's parents used the underworld to extort money from Industrialist Pankaj Agarwal, the owner of Praful Sarees. A top police official said in Mumbai that a Malaysian based gangster and his associate called Agarwal on behalf of Shilpa Shetty's parents asking him to pay two crore rupees.

The Tamil Nadu Government Doctors Association has withdrawn its proposed strike from tomorrow. The Association says the call would have caused inconvenience to the public. However, 5,000 medicos continue their strike. Our correspondent reports that the main demand of the striking Medicos is that the government should withdraw the order which facilitates coming up of new private medical colleges in the state.

(Voice cast – Sanjay Ghosh)

The Tamil Nadu government's decision to crack the whip has had a desired effect as the government doctors have called off the strike. The government had warned that they would invoke ESMA to deal with the strike. The ruling dispensation has taken a tough stand refusing to hold any further talks unless the students give up their strike. However, the students seem adamant despite the government suspending 5000 medicos. The director to medical education claims that some students were willing to return to classes. With the doctors falling in line, the medicos may find it difficult to prolong the nearly one month long strike.

(Sanjay Ghosh/Air/News/Chennai)

In Bihar, noted neurosurgeon Dr. Ramesh Chandra is yet to be traced. A delegation of the State Unit of the Indian Medical Association met the Chief Minister Ms. Rabri Devi and the RJD Chief Mr. Laloo Prasad Yadav and asked them to make efforts to secure the safe release of the surgeon. He was kidnapped on Saturday from Patna. Our Patna correspondent reports that of the two persons kidnapped in Patna on Saturday night, the police have found the jeweller Sanjay Dayal. The doctors have threatened to go on strike from tomorrow if the state government fails to secure the release of Dr. Chandra.

In Rajasthan, three senior officers are among 40 persons injured in stone-pelting and lathi-charge at Gajner in Bikaner district last night. The officers injured include a Divisional Commissioner and a Deputy Inspector General of Police. Our Jaipur correspondent, quoting official sources reports, the Police resorted to lathi-charge when some agitated Samajik Nyaya activists raised slogans and pelted stones at the Chief Minister Mr. Ashok Gehlot's public meeting.

(Voice cast – Anurag Vajpayee)

Samajik Nayay Munch now targets the Congress in Rajasthan for the last few days. The Munch have regularly been disrupting public meetings of the BJP State President, Mrs. Vasundhra Raje in her Parivartan Yatra. But this is the first incident when they disturbed Congress. The Munch is demanding reservation in upper castes. Yesterday night in Gujarat town of the Bikaner district clash began when police refused to allow the Munch activists to disturb Ashok Gahlot's meeting. When the activist insisted that they be allowed to meet the chief minister, the police resorted to lathi-charge and activists retaliated by throwing stones at the police and the gathering. Several police and administrative officials and 40 others were injured in this incident. After the clash, Chief Minister Ashok Gahlot addressed the meeting and said that there is no place of violation in democracy. He termed the incident a result of the BJP internal dispute. Mr. Gahlot said that he has always been advocating reservation to upper castes on economic basis. But this would be possible only if the Central Government amend the Constitution. Meanwhile, Mrs. Vasundhra Raje has asked the state government to refer the issue of reservation in upper caste to the centre.

Anuraj Vajpayee/Air/News/Patna

New Zealand have clinched a 9-run nailbiting win over Sri Lanka in the fifth match of the triangular cricket series at Dambulla in Sri Lanka yesterday. Left-arm spinner Daniel Vettori took his career best four for fourteen to lead New Zealand to victory. Earlier, put into bat, New Zealand scored 156 for 8 in their allotted 50 overs.

For details of these stories and more:

You can log on to our website: www.all india radio news.com

Now we have in the studios Prof. Sushila Ramaswamy of Delhi University and K. V. Prasad of The 'Hindu' to discuss some of the main newspaper stories.

Over to Mr. Prasad

(Hold for discussion)

Thank you Prof. Ramaswamy and Mr. Prasad for joining us in the studios.

(Hold for music)

Before we end here are the headlines.
- India has rejected Pakistan's claim that terrorist groups operating in Jammu and Kashmir are not in its control.
- The Union Cabinet has decided to permit the conversion of industrial and commercial property in Delhi from leasehold to freehold.
- In Kolkata, the Narcotics Control Bureau has busted an international cartel dealing in banned drugs.
- A Special Court in Mumbai has attached two properties of the underworld don Dawood Ibrahim.
- The Tamil Nadu Government Doctors Association has withdrawn its proposed strike from tomorrow.

Broadcast News - Radio

- And in cricket
- New Zealand have clinched a 9-run victory over Sri Lanka in the fifth match of the triangular series at Dambulla.

And that is the end of the morning news.

In this bulletin there are sound bites and voice casts. In some cases the full text is given where not possible the script has "gist". There is also a discussion on current topics featured in newspapers before the end of the bulletin. The headlines are repeated in the end for those who have missed them.

Most broadcasters are on Internet. There is usually a different team to handle the Internet version. The work of journalists in the net version is not very difficult. Software generates a form according to the design of the website. The journalists have to pick up various elements to be filled in that form and the software does the rest.

7
Television News

Because of the additional visual content, compilation and production of news bulletin is much more difficult in television. Compared to radio it involves much bigger production team and requires more coordinated effort. A reporting unit in radio consists of just one man who may carry with him a tape recorder. In television, a reporter has with him a cameraman to take the pictures, a recordist to capture the sound and where interior locations are involved possibly a lighting assistant to help artificial illumination to ensure a good quality picture. There are, of course, shortcuts where the camera crew is briefed to cover stories without reporters. With the development of 'camcorder', which combines camera and recorder has made one-man band a much more practical proposition but he has to do a lot more than a radio reporter. A television reporter with an outside broadcast (OB) van may have to report ad lib on camera, which may be broadcast directly using microwave or satellite uplink. A radio reporter may also use radio OB van but his job is much simpler as the audience does not see him. Before the rise of ENG, the recording of images and sound was just like film and had to go through similar time-consuming processing and then editing. It was the need for mobility and miniaturisation of equipment required by news programme makers that induced the lightweight revolution in television. The 16-mm film replaced the 35-mm film format in 1950s particularly when the American television teams used it successfully in covering the Korean War. For about 20 years, it was 16-mm film that ruled the television news gathering scene. Some organisations experimented with Super 8 but mainly as a way to cover such countries that do not permit normal television equipment and journalists but do not mind toy camera on a tourist.

A film had several problems. If something goes wrong while shooting no one can know until the film is processed. There were chances of loss of crucial pictures during the processing and also at the editing stage where one wrong decision could make an irreparable loss. Better equipment and techniques like 'phase reversal' were used to reduce the time consumed in processing.

Ampex began its research into magnetic tape recording for television in 1951 and by early 1956 demonstrated quadruplex technique on a two-inch wide tape. Coupled with new development in intercontinental communication systems the development of videotape opened a new era for television news gathering. The equipment was, however, very large and resembled an overgrown reel-to-reel audio recorder and with associated infrastructure could fill a small room. It was thus less manoeuverable than even the old 35-mm equipment. But research solved this problem in 1970s. First came the one-inch high quality tape for studio work and then Sony developed U-matic tape for broadcast quality recordings. The American broadcasters experimented with it and accepted it as perhaps the biggest advance in news gathering for television. It was in September 1974 in St. Louis, Missouri, "KMOX-TV" replaced its entire film equipment with ENG. By 1976 ENG started dominating the US while the European networks were cautious and slow in adopting the new technology.

In May 1977 the Japanese ENG coverage of London Economic Summit was beamed back to Tokyo by satellite and BBC used these pictures as part of its domestic output. BBC opened the 12-month trial of the new system with an interview of Margaret Thatcher, then leader of Conservative Opposition on 10 October 1977. This interview was recorded at the House of Commons and shown on the lunch-time news. The ITN began experimenting with ENG during April-May 1979 with the coverage of the general elections. By 1980 the switch from film to ENG was going ahead in Europe and other areas.

In India the Doordarshan started colour transmission and its news services started using the ENG from August 15, 1982. Using INSAT-1A the Doordarshan news showed the ENG pictures throughout the network on that Independence day. In the Ninth Asian Games, 1982, Doordarshan made full use of the ENG and OB vans. The ENG, also known as EJ (Electronic Journalism) or ECC (Electronic Camera Coverage), has become universally accepted mode of television news gathering. It consists of a portable camera and a portable videocassette machine on which picture and sound are recorded. The two pieces of equipment, usually linked together by a cable are operated separately by a cameraman and a sound recordist.

The advantage of the ENG is elimination of the process department and possibility of instant replay as well as instant transmission using microwave or satellite uplink from a site far away from the base. This versatility of the ENG is highly useful in television news work and has become the order of the day. Further miniaturisation of cameras and digitalisation has now led to many broadcasters using a tape-less newsroom system.

With ENG in the newsroom, most of the old style cutters which came from film industry newsreels have vanished and the film editors have become picture editors who can handle an entire range of visuals including input from the ENG teams. Many reporters now prefer to edit their own visual material without the help of a professional picture editor and then write their story accordingly. Where camera crew has gone to cover an event without a reporter, the news editor or news writer will have to write the story based on what has been brought back.

In the editing suite the raw material from the camera crew, the master tape or 'first generation' tape is never cut and the electronic image and sound from the videotape are re-recorded on a fresh tape leaving the original intact. A copy from the first generation tape is the 'second generation' from which a third generation copy can be obtained. It is not advisable to telecast beyond the third generation, as there is a loss of quality at each stage. Ampex in the late 1980s introduced a digital recording system where even the 20th generation is of broadcast quality.

The editing suite has two videocassette recorders with linked speakers and monitors, one set to display the 'rushes' and the other to build up the edited story. There is also a time code generator displaying in digital clock form and a time base corrector. Editing could be 'on-line' or 'off-line'. On-line when the editing is done from the master tape and off-line when the editing is done from a copy normally on a cheaper tape and the final edited version is produced later by using this off-line version as a guide. In news and current affairs programmes most of the editing is on-line as there is always a deadline pressure. Now nonlinear editing makes things much faster and simpler.

Besides the picture editor, production assistant and reporter or news writer or news editor may also be present when the ENG output is first seen on the monitor. While the picture editor looks at it to check the quality of recording, the news writer has to see it for its content. Together both of them decide the general outline and duration of various elements of the story.

Once the 'rushes' are seen and it is decided how the story has to be edited the editing proper begins. Now the second machine, the recorder, is loaded with a fresh tape and the insert-editing mode is selected. The picture editor presses 'play' on the machine with rushes and then pushes in the search dial into forward or reverse position to control the direction and speed of the tape while carefully looking for the first selected shot on the monitor. As soon as he gets the desired shot he stops turning the search dial and the monitor shows a single still frame.

Using the search dial in 'jog' mode he slowly moves the tape forward or backward to reach the exact point at which the edit is to be made. Pressing 'in' and 'entry' buttons on the panel together makes the machine to memorise the start time of the selected shot on the player's digital tape counter. To memorise the completion of the edit, 'out' and 'entry' buttons are pressed or simply 'stop' button is pressed. The editor now turns to the recording machine using in, out, and entry/stop buttons much the same way and then he selects 'preview' which allows him to rehearse the edit. Although the picture appears on both the monitors, the actual preview is checked on the recorder monitor only. If fine adjustment by a few frames is needed it is done by using the 'trim' button.

If the picture editor is satisfied with the preview he pushes 'auto edit' to record the selected shot from the rushes to the new tape. This is known as 'electronic splicing'. As this first scene is recorded, the editor can go ahead for selection and recording of the other shots in the desired sequence. It is possible to check the recorded story any time by using the 'review' button.

It is immaterial in what sequence the cameraman has recorded the news event. In the edited version the first shot, normally, should be a long shot establishing the location and giving the general view of the scene. Then there should be a mid-shot and then close-up of the main subject. If there is a deliberate change in this order, there must be a compelling reason or justification for this. Shots showing other participants, audience and crowds should also be shown to establish relationship between various shots and to give variety to the viewer and to show the atmosphere of the event.

When the whole story is assembled the production assistant prepares a shot-list. It consists of noting the details of the picture, sound, and length of each shot in seconds in an edited sequence. This information is vital to the news writer for writing the script of the story and therefore a copy of shot-list must be passed on to him. The PA (production assistant) has his/her own copy for future use of the production team. It is the responsibility of the PA to keep the original and edited tape safely and should pass it on to the VTR/VCR operator at the time of the bulletin and after the bulletin to the tape library. Other stories can also be build up on the same tape but the PA should know the order and note it down.

As radio news writing evolved from newspaper news considering the parameters of the new medium, the television news writing evolved from the radio news. When a news item has no pictures, the story is 'dry' and the newsreader is 'in vision' or 'on camera', such stories are not different from radio news items. But with the visual things change.

The basic principle of the television news writing is that the words and pictures should go together, the news copy should match the picture. And therefore, the news writer in television must see the visual input of the ENG with the picture editor and must see the final edited version before writing the story. He must have the shot-list of the finally edited version to time his word accordingly.

The television news writer has to make sure that he uses words to tell the story with the help of the visuals. Depending upon the duration and content of the various shots he can write the story taking three words a second as a general guideline for time calculation. This does not mean that he should cram the script with details while the visual is being shown and thus 30 seconds would mean 90 words. A television news writer must remember that the pictures also communicate and a picture is said to be equal to thousand words. Words should be used to help the picture communicate. For example, a person or object in medium shot or close-up must be identified the first time he/it appears on the screen and the viewer should not be left to wonder who/what he is looking at.

The news script should supplement the picture giving additional relevant information. It should not, however, repeat in detail what the viewer can see or hear for himself. Similarly, there is no point in giving details of something, which the viewer is not able to see. The best script is the one that uses minimum words but with the pictures that has the maximum impact.

There are some common pitfalls that a television news writer should avoid. To introduce a visual input he should not have phrases like, "Here we have..."; "We are looking at..."; or "Here is...". Even slightest difference in timing may become highly embarrassing. Words like, "The prime minister has this to say.."; "he added..."; or "Watch this scene..." should be avoided as they are redundant and insult the intelligence of the viewer, after all he is seeing or listening to what is being presented.

Obsession with the inverted pyramid style of news writing, which is a rule in newspaper journalism, creates problems in the television news writing. Many who came to television from the newspapers suffer from this disease. There are four elements of a television news story: hook, context, unfolding and wrap. The viewer has just one chance to understand what you have said. The story should be clear and easy to understand. Tell them, remind them and then remind them that you have reminded them.

Presentation is one of the most important elements for a broadcaster. If you ignore it you will be ignored. Many present day broadcasters seem to have lost site of an old golden rule; there must be a proper proportion of sight, sound and presentation. In television you are in the 'story-telling mode'. You are talking to the viewer and telling him the news. Here your story will not be shortened from behind for the want of space. It will go as it is. If there is a very important development, the story may be crowded out completely to accommodate the new development or the presenter reads out just the intro of your story. Thus the best way to write a television story is to make sure that the intro is the microcosm of the story and can stand without the visual.

A key element of television news is a mini production known as a 'package'. It is a two to three minute item usually reported by a journalist on location for inclusion in a full-length news bulletin or a current affairs programme. Despite shortage of time, it is still essential to know what is that you are reporting and what the facts mean. Observe the basics:- who, what, where, when, why and how. Research properly and choose the relevant facts.

The basic rule of writing for television is – keep it simple. A story must have a beginning, a middle and an end. A television reporter has only a hundred or so words to play with. The best way is to write a story in full. The first one or two sentences for the newsreader/anchor to introduce the story and adapt the last sentence or two as piece to camera, to summarise or act as reminder. A picture bridge is often used. It is a "piece-to-camera" that appears in the package serving to link two different thoughts with reporter emphasising the switch. It may provide emphasis by personal presence of the storyteller, or reporter may tell a short piece of the story, as there are no pictures to cover that part of the story.

It should be interesting and clear, devoid of unrelated details and in conversational language. The copy preceding the video should set up and indicate the overall content of the tape but should not have the words that are coming on tape. You are telling the story, you are not presenting the proof of what you have said in the news item.

For the first sentence the reporter should think how he would begin telling the story to a friend standing next to him. After this lead or intro there should be selected key facts to back that intro in a language that is simple and preferably in active voice. In any case the sentences should not be so complex that to understand one has to read several times. A reporter must make sure that he really understands what he is writing. After the first draft is ready the reporter must edit it ruthlessly. Avoid words like "today" as television is immediate and also sometimes the story is repeated the next day–as happens in most 24-hour channels. Avoid words like '*the*', '*an*' when possible. Use conversational language without jargon and clichés. Use strong simple words according to the spirit and meaning of the story. The reporter should check how the story reads once it is finished.

Here is a list of phrases that should be avoided:-put on hold, heated argument, hammer out a deal, around the clock, cold-blooded killers, bloody slaughter, campaign trail, hats in the ring, political football, damp squib, make or break, last-ditch, eleventh hour, do or die effort, pensioned off. Use the right word, not its second cousin.

The television news writer and the bulletin editor should keep in mind why the viewers switch on the news on television. They do not watch television only to get the latest news, radio perhaps does it better. They do not watch television to get all the news, local, national and international, the newspaper does it better. They do not see television news for the depth of coverage or analysis – a newsmagazine can do it better. Television viewers prefer the newscasts because they are taken to the scenes of action and shown what is happening or what has happened recently. Well-presented stories on television can move the viewers more deeply than radio or newspaper. The power of television lies in its appeal to two human senses and therefore a television news writer must use both in coordination to tell the story. The script and the tape should go together and not against each other as the later could result in chaos.

After the script is over the reporter should think how to cover it with pictures. A two-minute package could be, say, sound bite 40 seconds from expert or authorities, piece-to-camera 30 seconds, what reporter says on camera and voiced script 50 seconds. It may require a combination of library and on location footage to cover with pictures the 50 seconds. As no single shot should be less than three seconds, this can accommodate about 16 pictures. At the location first take static shots (no panning, pulling out and zooming in) of more than three-second duration and then take pans, pullouts, etc. The material recorded should be a part of pattern or sequence: wide or establishing scenes and then close-up, cutaways, etc. Pictures should be taken several times with different angles. As a general rule efforts should be made to have all pictures using a tripod, though it is not always possible. A hand-held camera invariably produces unsteady pictures, with wandering zooms and pans. The reporter is the team leader when out on a shoot, and should control the production irrespective of how experienced is the crew.

Reporters should select pictures to match the words and ideas in the script before going to edit suit. A well-planned piece should always have the script done and a picture sequence thought out. But when a reporter is send to cover a breaking story, one has to use all skills in command to cover the story to get the material back to base or a feed point. Once the techniques of stitching a story become second nature to reporters with experience and initiative, such panic situation can be handled with ease. But to reach that level practice – and more practice – is required when covering stories that allow time to do the job at a slower pace.

The voice-over or read is reporter's recording of the script, which can be marked up, so that the reporter can emphasise key words. A reporter at a news site can send newsroom what is called 'piece to camera' or 'stand-upper'. Here the reporter is in vision and is telling the story from the site. This kind of story immediately establishes the reporter's presence on the spot and he/she tells the story straight to the camera and through it to the viewer. Reading in monotone or putting stress on the wrong words destroys all the hard work. The reporter should look at the words used and try to put appropriate expression in the voice. If the word used is sad, sound should not be exciting. The reporter should be conversational and convincing, should talk to and not at the viewers. The reporter should use pauses and inflection to enhance presentation but should not bounce around through the piece. The reporter may be required to use autocue to read in front of a static camera in a studio, newsroom or on location. One should remember not to lean into the camera and not let eyes follow the words across the page. If a prompter is not available, the best way is to memorise the intro and then look at the notebook, occasionally speaking one or two sentences directly to the camera.

The importance about the framing by the cameraman is that the reporter should not stand against a wall or such backgrounds unless it is relevant to the story. It will look like a dry story from somewhere. The reporter should be seen at the scene of the event and should have something to show in the frame to that effect. Ideally, the reporter should be seen in the proximity of the most important action elements of the story being covered. A cameraman should not have the reporter in the centre of the frame but on one side so that he/she appears a part of the action and not a superimposition on it.

Something like 'piece-to-camera' in the studio is called 'studio spot' where somebody other than the newsreader comes in vision and presents a story with the help of visuals including stills, film or VCR. A reporter or specialist can be asked to do it where he can deal with a running story taking latest information up to the beginning of the bulletin. Unlike 'piece-to-camera', the person presenting the studio spot has all the comforts of the studio including the graphic aids and prompter.

Writing to pictures a reporter must always carefully think of the first shot, which should be a scene-setter. A story must be news-driven and should not be limited by the availability of pictures. When it is appropriate let the pictures do the talking. Reporters should not overwrite. Writing should be tight and should match with the pictures. This well writing to pictures adds to appreciation of the story by the audience. Details shown by the pictures should not be unnecessarily repeated in the script. Write out figures, values and dates in words. For example, 500 should always be written as five hundred and 5bn as five billion. Do not use $, % write dollar, per cent instead. Conjunction – that – may not be used. And above all, reporters should never bend the facts for artistic presentation.

Like the video, the reporter should take into account possible use of captions: stills, charts, graphs, maps and the like to help communicate the content of the story effectively. While using these visual aids the news writer should be in constant touch with the graphic artist or caption designer and should make sure that he has what he wants. All networks have examples where a wrong still or graphic did spoil the show. Doordarshan once showed photograph of a living member of Parliament (MP) while reporting the death of another. The correct picture was selected from a Lok Sabha publication and passed on to the graphics department for mounting it on a caption card. On the other side of the page was photograph of another MP who looked older than the one who died. The man who finally mounted the photograph on the caption card took this into account and corrected God's 'mistake' leading to a disaster in the bulletin. In-house graphic artists, now using sophisticated computer-based systems usually create graphics, but for that information must come from the reporter. The reporter should be aware of the capacities of the graphic unit, as he/she should be familiar with library.

The cell or inset is which appears over the shoulder of the presenter. It is a visual headline. It works best when it is bold and then it sets up the viewer even before the intro. It is a device that demands close coordination of image with a script. Such insets would not go with a teaser but with an intro of hard facts as image had already given out the story.

Interview is another important element of news stories. Interviews could be part of packages used in a bulletin or could be included live from OB vans and other stations near the event. Here are some tips.

Some reporters have developed reputation for using confrontationist technique in interviews. Tough questioning should be used when necessary, but it is usually better to put the interviewee at ease. It should be ensured that the interviewee talks to the reporter and not to the camera. A good interview calls for listening properly as well as asking relevant questions, that require homework and some come out from the answers. While phrasing a question care should be taken that a simple yes or no should not be the answer. Lousy answers usually stem from lousy questions.

There are five bad habits in interviews: (1) *Closed questions*—(with yes or no answers). Such questions are also called clip killers. Such questions begin with words like do, did, will, would, can, could, is, are and give the initiative to the interviewee. (2) *Non-question*—"That was a easy choice." "It was a tough decision." Such situation results when the reporter wants to show off his or her knowledge. (3) *Two for one*—It leaves the interviewee to choose one and ignore the other. Ask one at a time. (4) *Triggers*—Provocative words give subject a chance to react to a word rather than the question itself. Keep the language neutral. (5) *Never-ending questions*, questions that ramble on, confuse the interviewee and finally collapse under the weight of the words.

While conducting a research interview present yourself clearly and say why are you making contact. Explain that you need help. Ask simple open-ended questions: who, what, when, where, why and how? Know what information you want. Be polite, interested and curious. Do not be aggressive for you want information and not argument. Do not make it personal. Ask for clarification on anything that you are not sure of is related to the story. Before ending the conversation check names, titles, telephone numbers, near future whereabouts and suggestions about anyone else that should be talked to on the subject.

Thank and say you may call again. Try to remember these points always: Pay attention to details like double check names, addresses, titles, telephone numbers. Talk to interviewees – do not trust those who say he is a great talker. Think images what visuals would support the stories. Anticipate problems like noise, security, road closures, local customs. Keep notes. Do return all stills or documents you borrow. Check the credentials of experts. Cultivate contacts.

Define the purpose of the interview. Know where you want to get to. Plan simple questions to get you there. Keep the questions open ended. (begin with why or how or what…). Be specific. Vague questions get vague answers. Write your questions before you start your interview. Listen to the answer – do not be so busy preparing for the next question that you miss an important supplementary flowing from the answer. Do use a pause as a question. Use it with a nod or smile. Practice active listening. Do not commit to a preplanned question and be caught unawares by a surprise answer. Maintain eye contact at all times.

In a studio interview at the end shots where the interview and the interviewee nod and grin at each others – noddies – should be recorded. Such shots are very useful while editing. Reporter should make sure to know the correct name, title and functions of the interviewee. It should be flashed on the screen using character generator when the interviewee appears on the screen to avoid a clumsy introduction. While selecting sound bite (voice clip) for the package make sure the interviewee does not sound silly in any case. Finally, the reporter should never forget to use his commonsense and innovate when the situation so requires. Here is an anecdote from an Indian producer whose interviewee, a top corporate manager, was very tense before the camera and even after three re-takes he could not get good result. He told the interviewee, 'Let us rehearse' before the actual recording. After the 'rehearsal' he asked the crew to pack up as the 'rehearsal' was the actual recording that produced the right result.

In press conferences it should be made sure that the crew records the answers to their own reporter's questions. If the reporter wants to use answer to some other reporter's question, he should note that question and ensure that the crew records reply. A reporter should not wear too outlandish or esoteric dress unless the story demands that and should avoid red if the story has to go over satellite, as despite technological improvement in modern cameras the red tends to bleeds around the edges at the receiving end destroying the picture quality. A reporter while doing a piece-to-camera (PTC) should stand with a view behind that helps to tell the story, use tripod unless impossible and should not hesitate practising in front of the camera.

After the package is ready, a reporter should run it two or three times to ensure that it makes sense, there are no flash frames, bad edits or other technical problems. The reporter should make sure that the intro, tape and the script is delivered to the producer or editor responsible for using it. If the feed has to go to the broadcaster via landline, satellite or some other means, the reporter has to coordinate with VT editor, coordinator at the recipient's end and the master control unit linked to landline or satellite

Covering foreign assignment needed a lot more coordination before the arrival of new technologies like videophone. Even now everybody does not have the best of technology. In most cases the editing facilities were availed from local contacts but at times this equipment was also carried. Stringers or staffers posted in a foreign land have better local contacts and have arrangements for editing and sending the tape back to the home base. But if a camera crew goes to a foreign land to cover big event coordination becomes rather difficult. If an event is planned in advance normally a senior member of staff is sent in advance to work as 'fixer' and as the entire team arrives he has already laid down the rules of the game. The 'fixer' is in touch with the headquarters and feeds them the available facilities and required staff and equipment. Sometimes services of a local 'fixer' are also availed.

Most important consideration of a television news team is the arrangement to send the story back home before the deadline. Depending on the distance and the availability of flights the videotape can be sent to the headquarters by the air. Details should be communicated by phone or telex to the home base for speedy clearance at the airport. Sometimes the tape is hand-carried by a member of the air crew or cabin staff and sometimes by a willing passenger at times referred to as 'pigeon'. Besides informing the newsroom the details of the 'pigeon' and his flight the 'pigeon' should be armed with the telephone numbers of the newsroom so that in case of a communication gap between the news crew and the headquarters he could contact the newsroom on reaching the destination. Some government-owned networks use even the diplomatic bag for transporting the tape back home. In some cases a member of the team flies back with the tape. More and more television news crews now transmit their stories via satellite. Depending upon the bulletin deadline satellite time is booked. A margin should be provided for processing before the bulletin so that the 'feed' from crew should land on time.

But it is not always that a network will send its crew to cover stories. Costs are prohibitive. Therefore most of them also subscribe to international news film agencies and some, national corporations, are members of regional news exchange networks. Though now Reuters and AP dominate this market with their television services, at one time there were some other players of significance. CNN has arrangements where broadcasters can use the stories broadcast on CNN recording them off the air. BBC World is a possible competitor in this area.

Planning for news bulletins is a continuous process. There are a few regular meetings of the news staff everyday, while some other informal urgent meetings may be required to sort out various contingencies. Information about forthcoming events which the network may like to cover keep coming to the television just as in case of the other media. Planned stories are assigned in advance to reporters and camera crew. Some stories are research based and therefore each network has some research staff to look up references and to trace the relevant visual material from the tape library or other sources. Some stories may require studio recordings and therefore the production assistant concerned has to book studio for the purpose in advance.

There are some fire brigade operations where looking at the news agency output the producer comes to know of an accident or some unusual event and feels that his ENG team could shoot the story before the bulletin. One or two ENG teams are on some kind of emergency duty and they are rushed to the spot. If the event is very important and requires a bigger operation, then an OB van could be sent along with one or two reporters who may even ad lib the story during the bulletin or may arrange live interview.

Different broadcasters are at different stages of automation of news production. About two hours before the bulletin a rough shape of the bulletin is decided in the 'running order' or 'run down'. It is list of the sequence of the stories, which are to be transmitted, and has details of various elements of each story with the time required to transmit it. The running order is slowly compiled as the details of each story lands with the news editor. Each sheet of bulletin script has its running order number, no 1 being the headlines. The second sheet which may contain the lead story of the day will not be placed at no. 2 but with some gap in the running order so that if some bigger story lands from the news agencies it could be accommodated in the bulletin before the present lead. Similarly there are gaps after each story or group of stories so that if some related item comes it could be accommodated at proper place in the running order. In computer-based newsroom systems these sheets have vanished and the running order does not require any gaps as at given time and order any story could be added or deleted.

Before automation, the newsreader or anchor, the producer (director) and the production assistant keep on getting their copies as the script of each story is finalised and each of them marks the script according to the role he or she has in the production of the bulletin. The anchor or newsreader marks for the pauses while reading the script and checks pronunciation of proper names and sometime writes it in his/her own hand. If there are any difficult words in the copy he can request the news editor to change. While rehearsing the newscaster can also point out if a sentence is not clear in meaning. The production assistant also marks the script for his role in giving cues, and stand by commands. Similar markings are there on the producer's copy. These markings indicate the source of tape or still or graphic, the duration, the exact word when the command should be given to time it perfectly, counting the possible reaction time. In computerised newsrooms the final running order or run down and the final script is printed out minutes before the transmission. However, all the members of the production team can see the progress of the script using the VDTs (Video Display Terminals) and make their own contributions to the script through their VDTs.

It is interesting to look at the script of a major Doordarshan bulletin. Each page has initials of the editor and the stenographer, the time of the bulletin and the date. There is also the running order number which indicates where the story will be telecast in relation to the other stories in the bulletin. These indications and the slug are not read by the presenter.

GOOD EVENING
The Headlines
- The peacekeeping force in Sri Lanka resumed operations to recover arms and ammunitions.
- Government informed the Lok Sabha that negotiations with Union Carbide for seeking compensation for Bhopal gas victims to continue under the umbrella of the court.
- In Nagaland assembly elections, the remaining three results go in favour of the Congress (I).
- The US and the Soviet Foreign Ministers hold talks in Geneva on the treaty to ban medium-range nuclear missiles.
- Reports of two ships being attacked by the Iranian gun boats in the Straits of Hormuz.
- And, in SAF games India continue to dominate the medal tally.

mld/dks 2130 hrs (1) 23.11.87.

Sri Lanka – PKF
In Sri Lanka, the Peacekeeping Force resumed operations to recover arms and ammunition after a gap of 48 hours this morning. An official spokesman said in New Delhi that has been done in the absence of any positive response to the offer made by the Minister of State for External Affairs, Mr. Natwar Singh in Parliament on Friday. He regretted that the LTTE did not respond to the offer and is now insisting on a number of unacceptable pre-conditions prior to the consideration of laying down arms. The spokesman said that during the period since the announcement that the PKF will not fire on its own, the LTTE has been threatening to kill people assisting and supporting PKF.

mld/dks 2130 hrs (4-1) 23.11.87.

Sri Lanka – PKF (contd...2)

LTTE had also put out posters at various places saying that the Indian Red Cross should stop functioning and government offices and banks should not open.

In reply to a question the spokesman said there is no question of any discussion with LTTE under conditions other than those announced by Mr. Natwar Singh in the Parliament.

Meanwhile, curfew relaxation in Jaffna has been extended from 8 to 12 hours since Saturday. In Chunakam also shops have opened and local policemen have reported on duty. Air taxi services between Palaly and Colombo have been resumed.

mld/dks 2130 hrs (4-2) 23.11.87.

Casualties – PKF

Two hundred and sixty-two PKF personnel have been killed and 927 wounded during the operation in Sri Lanka till today. A press release issued by the Defence Ministry says that over 40 per cent of the wounded have been discharged from the hospitals. The press release refers to the highly exaggerated casualty figures published in a section of press and says that the publication of such exaggerated reports causes great concern and mental agony to the families of those serving the PKF. It also adversely affects the morale of the troops. The release also expresses regret that on a matter involving casualties of the peacekeeping force, the press should indulge in speculative reporting.

mld/rkp 2130 hrs (4-3) 23.11.87.

RYZHKOV

The visiting Soviet Prime Minister Mr. Nikolai Ryzhkov and Mrs. Ryzhkov visited Bhilai today. The Bhilai Steel Plant has been set up with the Soviet help three decades ago. The visiting dignitaries accompanied by the Chief Minister of Madhya Pradesh and Union Minister for Steel and Mines Mr. Fotedar visited various units of the plant. The Soviet prime minister and his wife who are both engineers, evince keen interest in the plant. They visited the blast furnace which was commissioned only last month.

Bhasin/RKP 2130 hrs (6-1) 23.11.87

RYZHKOV (contd...2)
Later they also went to the rolling mill where the widest steel plates are made in India. The 3600 mm plate mill so called to signify the length of its rolling barrel has the latest manufacturing techniques.

(hold)

The Soviet prime minister addressed a workers, meeting where he reiterated his country's commitment to further strengthen bilateral relations with India. He also conveyed greetings to the workers from the Soviet leader Mr. Gorbachev.

(hold)

mld/rkp 2130 hrs (6-2) 23.11.87

Czech Delegation
The visiting Czechoslovak Parliamentary delegation watched the proceedings of both the Houses of Parliament today. They were warmly greeted by the Speaker of the Lok Sabha Mr. Balram Jakhar when they called on him. The six-member delegation is led by the Chairman of the Federal Assembly of Czechoslovakia, Mr. Alve Indira.

(hold)

The delegation held discussions with various members of Parliament.

(hold)

In the evening the delegation called on the Vice-president and the Chairman of the Rajya Sabha Dr.Shankar Dayal Sharma. Dr Sharma wished them a fruitful stay in India.

(hold)

mld/wk 2130 hrs (9-1) 23.11.87

Czech Delegation (contd...2)
Earlier the visiting delegation met the Parliamentary Affairs Minister Mr. H. K. L. Bhagat.

(hold)

mld/rkp 2130 hrs (9-2) 23.11.87

Lok Sabha: Bhopal Gas

The Industry Minister, Mr. Vengal Rao told the Lok Sabha today that negotiations are under way with the Union Carbide Corporation to secure compensation for the Bhopal gas victims and these would continue under the umbrella of the Court. He, however, did not elaborate saying that the matter is subjudice. The minister was replying to a special discussion on the reported negotiations between the government and the Union Carbide for an out of court settlement in regard to payment of compensation for the victims of Bhopal gas tragedy. Mr. Vengal Rao assured the House that no efforts will be spared to secure compensation for the gas victims and their interests will be fully protected. Not satisfied with the Minister's reply, most of the opposition members present in the House staged a walk-out.

mld/dks 2130 hrs (10-1) 23.11.87.

Lok Sabha: Bhopal Gas (contd...2)

Earlier members from both the sides urged the government not to have any out of court settlements regarding the payment of compensation to the victims of the Bhopal gas tragedy.

mld/dks 2130 hrs (10-2) 23.11.87.

LS: Bhopal Gas (contd...3)

Replying to the questions, the minister said that the government has spent about fifty four crore rupees on the relief operations for the gas tragedy victims. He said, the government has rejected as mere pittance a sum of twenty one million rupees offered by the Union Carbide as interim relief for the rehabilitation of the victims. The state government is finalising a long term plan in this regard.

mld/acy 2130 hrs (10-3) 23.11.87.

Art Exhibition

Art born of the October Revolution was the theme of the Soviet Exhibition that opened in New Delhi today as part of the festival of the USSR in India.

The exhibition was inaugurated by the Soviet Minster of Culture, Mr. V. G. Zakharov. The Human Resource Development Minister, Mr. P. V. Narasimha Rao was present.

The exhibition traces the course of development of the Soviet visual arts in the fifteen Republics of the USSR. In the post-revolution period the Soviet art has been inspired by the slogans of Lenin that art belongs to the people.

(hold)

mld/acy 2130 hrs (12-1) 23.11.87.

Calling Attention

The Industry Minister, Mr. Vengal Rao assured the Lok Sabha today that the government will do its best to help the workers of the two units of ACC – Babcock Limited at Shabahad in Karnataka and Durgapur in West Bengal. Both the units involved in the manufacture of boilers for the power sector have been closed and workers laid off. The matter was raised through a calling attention notice, by Mr. Virendra Patil, Congress(I) and others in the House today. During the discussion, the members expressed concern over the closure of the units and urged the government to take necessary steps to revive the company and rehabilitate the workers. The minister said that the matter will be taken up with the Cabinet soon. The Secretaries' Committee has already examined the matter.

mld/uku 2130 hrs (13-1) 23.11.87.

Sathe

The 54th International Foundry Conference is currently on in the Capital. Over five hundred delegates from all over the world are attending the conference.

The Energy Minister Mr. Vasant Sathe inaugurated the conference this morning. In his inaugural address Mr. Sathe said that India is trying to catch up with the international developments in foundry. He said India has a rich history of foundry which dates back to the Mohanjodaro and Harappan period.

(hold)

Mr. Sathe released an international directory of foundry on the occasion.

(hold)

mld/acy 2130 hrs (14-1) 23.11.87.

Final Results

In Nagaland, all the remaining three results have gone to the Congress(I) raising its strength to 34 in the sixty-member state assembly. In the Longleng constituency, former Speaker, Mr. Chenlom Phome, defeated his nearest independent rival, Mr. Heong by 488 votes. The former minister, Mr. Banjak Phom, was elected from Tamlu. He defeated Mr. H. Nyemli of the NNDP by 251 votes. The last results from Koridang has also gone in favour of the party with its candidate Mr. Okzenketba defeating his independent rival Mr. Bendangtoshi by 519 votes.

(hold)
mld/dks 2130 hrs (15-1) 23.11.87.

Portfolio

Meanwhile, the portfolios of the members of the newly-constituted Hokishe Sema ministry have been announced. The chief minister will hold home, general administration, finance, revenue, food and civil supplies.

mld/rkp 2130 hrs (15-2) 23.11.87.

PM greetings

Mr. Rajiv Gandhi has congratulated the Nagaland chief minister on the victory in the assembly elections. In his message Mr. Gandhi said that the victory is vindication of the policies of Congress I. He said that the party is determined to spare no efforts for the welfare and uplift of the people of Nagaland.

mld/rkp 2130 hrs (15-3) 23.11.87.

Biswas

The mortal remains of noted Bengali folk singer and lyricist Hemanga Biswas were cremated in Calcutta last night after long illness. He was 75. Many film personalities were among others who attended the funeral.

Born in District Sylhet now in Bangladesh, Hemanga Biswas joined the freedom movement in 1930s. He was also associated with the Indian People's Theatre Association.

mld/acy 2130 hrs (16-1) 23.11.87.

Price Situation

Members of Rajya Sabha today urged the government to take urgent strong measures to check the rising prices. They were participating in a discussion initiated by Mr. N. E. Balram, CPI. He said the main reason for inflation has been the wrong economic policies of the government. A ruling party member said that inflation has been a worldwide phenomena but in India it is less in comparison to other developing nations. The debate is to continue.

mld/dks 2130 hrs (17-1) 23.11.87.

Visitors

In the Lok Sabha today, a person from visitors' gallery tried to raise slogans of Uttarakhand during the question hour. He was immediately nabbed by the watch and ward staff. Investigation is on to identify the person.

mld/acy 2130 hrs (17-2) 23.11.87.

Disarmament

The US Secretary of States Mr. Shultz and the Soviet Foreign Minister Mr. Shevardnadze had their first round of talks in Geneva today on some operational details of a treaty to ban medium-range nuclear missiles. The two have set aside two days for the talks. Their aim is to have the treaty ready for the President Regan and Mr. Gorbachev to sign in Washington at their summit on the 9th of next month. High level arms control aides are assisting them in their deliberations.

mld/uku 2130 hrs (18-1) 23.11.87.

Bangladesh

In Bangladesh, shops opened in the capital Dacca and the traffic was back on the road after the extended general strike ended at 2 p.m. today. Agency reports say para-military police in trucks mounted with machine guns continued to patrol the city's main streets. The liaison committee of the opposition alliances sponsoring the strike has announced that the strike would continue tomorrow also for eight hours. They are demanding the resignation of the government.

The reports say that earlier in the day riot police broke up an opposition rally of two thousand supporters of the Bangladesh Nationalist Party. The rally was held to protest against the government's ban on

mld/dks 2130 hrs (18-2) 23.11.87.

Bangladesh *(contd...2)*
newspapers publishing statements and photographs relating to violence during the strike. A BBC correspondent was arrested under the Special Powers Act.

mld/dks 2130 hrs (18-3) 23.11.87.

GULF
Reports from the Gulf say the Iranian boats have attacked two more ships in the Strait of Hormuz. The Iranian frigates are reported to have approached the ships for inspection of their cargo but were not allowed to do so. One of the two ships belonged to Taiwan and was flying Panamanian flag. The ship caught fire after it was hit by rocket-propelled grenades. The other ship was flying Romanian flag. Three of its crew members are said to have injured.

mld/uku 2130 hrs (19-1) 23.11.87.

GCC
The Gulf Cooperation Council countries will increase defence cooperation among its members in view of the recent escalation of war in the Gulf region. This was decided at the two-day conference of defence ministers from six GCC countries – The UAE, Saudi Arabia, Qatar, Bahrain, Oman and Kuwait. The statement issued at the end of the conference says that the member countries have decided to ensure collective action to face any threat to their security. The recommendations of the ministers will now be placed before the forthcoming summit of the GCC countries beginning on the 26th of the next month.

mld/uku 2130 hrs (20-1) 23.11.87.

Festival – Sports

A spectacular presentation by the Soviet gymnasts marked the opening of the sports programme as part of the festival of the USSR in New Delhi this morning.

The show was inaugurated by the Chairman of the Soviet Sports Committee, Mr. M.N. Gramov while the Minister of State for Youth Affairs and Sports Mrs. Margaret Alva was the chief guest.

Presentation of floor exercises and breathtaking acrobats kept the larger gathering in the Indira Gandhi Stadium spellbound for about an hour and a half.

(hold)
mld/rkp 2130 hrs (23-1) 23.11.87.

SAF Games

India continued to dominate in the medals tally in their South Asian Federation Games at Calcutta. They have so far claimed 23 golds.

Annavi of India claimed the gold when he leaped to 2.15 metres in the men's high jump event.

India's Golden Girl, P. T. Usha won the 400 metres Women's hurdles. She clocked 57.8 seconds below her personal best.

Others who won gold for India are: Surjit Singh in Discus, Bdhwa Oraon in the 800 metres for Men, Sanny Joseph in Women's Javelin, Tara Singh in the Men's 10,000 metres and S.S. Talwar in Pole Vault.

dm/acy 2130 hrs (26-1) 23.11.87.

SAF Games *(contd...2)*

Mohammad Saha Alam gave Bangladesh its first Gold Medal clinching the 100 metres sprint for men. He clocked 10.79 seconds.

In the swimming pool, Wilson Cherian of India created a new meet record in the 200 metres back stroke event. He claimed the gold clocking 2 minutes 7.92 seconds. Silver went to Surojit Ghose of India and Dim Islam claimed the bronze.

Julin Bolling of Sri Lanka created another meet record in 200 metres free style event. He clocked 2 minutes 2.92 seconds. Silver went to Sanjib Chakrabarty and bronze to P. Sal Kumar, both from India.

dm/acy 2130 hrs (26-2) 23.11.87.

SAF Games *(contd...3)*
Niyati Roy of India has won the Women's Singles Title in the Table Tennis event in the South Asian Federation Games. She beat Varsha Chulanin, also of India in straight sets 21-12, 22-20, 21-12.

mld/dks 2130 hrs (26-3) 23.11.87.

Aging
A two-day national symposium on Aging began in Bombay today to focus on the specific problems of the aged. The symposium will make positive recommendations to the government towards framing the national policy. The symposium was inaugurated by Mr. David Hobman, President, International Federation on Aging.

In his welcome address Mr. S. D. Gokhale, Chairman of the Indian Committee on Aging, Mr. S. D. Gokhale said that aged people should not be put in homes. He emphasised on evolving a new approach for the service of our senior citizens. One in every fifteen Indians is above the age of sixty. Most of them are still capable of contributing significantly to the society.

dm/acy 2130 hrs (27-1) 23.11.87.

Film
The Indian film "SWAMY" has been adjudged the best children feature film at the Fifth International Children Film Festival at Bhubaneshwar. It won the Golden Elephant Award. Child artiste Manju Nath was chosen the best actor. The awards were announced at a glittering function at the end of 11-day festival this evening.

mld/rkp 2130 hrs (28-1) 23.11.87.

Carpet Exhibition
An exhibition of Soviet carpets began in New Delhi today.

It was inaugurated by the Minister of Textiles, Mr. Ram Niwas Mirdha.

(hold)

The carpets were designed by Soviet designer, Mr. K. Aliev.

(hold)

mld/acy 2130 hrs (29-1) 23.11.87.

Weather

And now a look at the weather.

INSAT-1B picture shows scattered convective clouds over Kerala, Coastal Tamil Nadu and South Coastal Andhra Pradesh.

The Forecast: Rain or thundershowers are likely to be scattered over Coastal Andhra Pradesh, Tamil Nadu, South Interior Karnataka, Kerala and Lakshadweep. It is likely to be isolated over Andaman and Nicobar Islands and Coastal and North Interior Karnataka.

dm/acy 2130 hrs (31-1) 23.11.87.

The temperatures, recorded at four major cities are:

	Max. Temp.	Min. Temp.
Delhi	29.5	09.7
Calcutta	29.3	17.4
Madras	30.0	24.0
Bombay	33.3	23.4

This is a bulletin which has been presented by one newsreader or presenter. When the bulletin is presented by two newsreaders, the script has to identify who is presenting what. 'Hold' indicates that the newsreader has to wait here and wait for cue to read the next sentence as a VCR/VTR is being rolled or telecine is putting out something.

Television News

Running order (also called run down) of this bulletin was like this:

Bulletin 2130 hrs　　　　　　　　　　　　　　　Date: 23.11.87

	Editor X Titles and Signature Tune	Producer Y	Newsreader A
	(Slug)	(Pages)	(Visual)
1.	Headlines	1	
2.			
3.			
4.	Sri Lanka -PKF	3	Map
5.			
6.	Ryzhkov	2	VCR
7.			
8.			
9.	Czech Delegation	2	VCR
10.	Lok Sabha: Bhopal Gas	3	...
11.			
12.	Art Exhibition	1	VCR
13.	Calling Attention	1	...
14.	Sathe	1	...
15.	Final Results, etc.	3	...
16.	Biswas	1	VCR
17.	Price Situation; Visitors	2	...
18.	Disarmament; Bangladesh	3	...
19.	Gulf	1	...
20.	GCC	1	...
21.			
22.			
23.	Festival – Sports	1	VCR
24.			
25.			
26.	SAF Games	3	VCR
27.	Aging	1	VCR
28.	Film	1	...
29.	Carpet Exhibition	1	VCR
30.			
31.	Weather	1	Photo

There is no doubt that it is a poor bulletin and this is why it has been selected as an example. Obviously, a lot of ENG material has been used but all headline items, except sports, are without any moving picture. This indicates poor planning and production.

Though the map has been used in the lead story on Sri Lanka it could have filled only 3 to 5 seconds. ENG team could have recorded the official spokesman with the key announcement. Some file shots of the deployment of the PKF could have been used if fresh material from Jaffna or Colombo was not available.

The Indian Parliament did not allow photography inside and this would have been a good excuse for having Bhopal gas story dry. But nobody could have stopped the producer from using file shots of the tragedy and rehabilitation measures.

Items related to Nagaland elections and new cabinets there have all gone 'dry'. File shots of elections in Nagaland, still of the Chief Minister and a table showing the party position could have been shown without difficulty. Efforts should have been made to have some ENG material from Nagaland as the election and the formation of the new ministry was not an accident that occurred on the day of the bulletin.

The 'Price Situation', 'Visitors', 'Disarmament' are good examples of bad copy and wrong placement in the running order. The visitor who raised slogans must have been released when the bulletin was being telecast. The source of this story, a news agency item in the afternoon and perhaps nobody from the TV newsroom ever checked what happened to the man later. The price situation and disarmament both deserved better treatment, which does not appear difficult if effort would have been made.

Things are much clearer now with the introduction of computers and newsroom systems. A newsroom system on network keeps different elements in different columns of running order. Video input with a story does not need a description, it is just a number in a parallel column in the rundown. Graphics are also arranged in a parallel column with commands to be executed at a given time in the story. The script comes in front of news presenter and that has commands in brackets. For further instructions and changes at the

Television News

time when the bulletin is going live there is an earplug in anchor's or presenter's ear.

Here is another script of a major Doordarshan news bulletin: 14 May 2003: 07:30 a.m.

GOOD MORNING and welcome to Doordarshan News. I am Karan Singh.

In the next half hour, we will bring you the latest national and international news, as well as the headlines from newspapers across the country.

First up, are the headlines this morning.

- Riyadh explosions toll rises to 90, as George W. Bush vows to punish the guilty.
- Brajesh Mishra says a loose international coalition is not enough to fight international terror.
- Pakistani prime minister calls for enhanced economic cooperation with India for the prosperity of both nations.
- Slow moving cyclonic storm in the Bay of Bengal is likely to bring heavy rain along the Andhra and Orissa coast.
- The West Indies script a historic win against Australia in their Antigua test.
- US President George W. Bush has denounced the bomb attacks against Western targets in Saudi Arabia.
- He called them "despicable acts" and vowed to bring those responsible to justice.
- His comments came after Monday night's suicide bombings in the capital, Riyadh. Over 90 people are reported to have been killed in the attack.

(hold up sound)

The dead include 10 Americans and 9 suspected attackers, who shot their way past armed guards and rammed vehicles packed with explosives, into compounds that house mainly foreigners.

These co-ordinated blasts, which took place shortly before the US Secretary of State Colin Powell was to arrive in the Saudi capital, are being blamed on Al-Qaeda.

(hold up sound)

India's National Security Advisor Brajesh Mishra says a loose international coalition is not enough to fight terrorism.

Mishra, who was in the United States last week to meet the senior leaders there, including President Bush, was speaking at a function in New Delhi.

He said the terrorists were targeting democratic institutions, and that no single democracy could tackle the menace of terrorism on its own.

(hold up sound)

Mishra said the improvement in ties with the US does not mean India has become a client state.

(hold up sound)

Pakistani Prime Minister Zafarullah Khan Jamali says it is time for Pakistan and India to exchange political rivalry for economic cooperation.

Jamali told a conference of donors and lenders in Islamabad, that his ice-breaking phone conversation with Prime Minister Atal Behari Vajpayee last month had focused on the need to improve economic ties.

Jamali said he and Vajpayee, in the first high-level contact between India and Pakistan in more than a year, discussed how their economies could develop, but he gave no details.

(hold up sound)

There is currently no overland trade between the neighbours, and trade in many goods is banned.

Official bilateral trade via third countries stands at a paltry 204 million US dollars.

(hold up sound)

Similar sentiments were expressed by a member of the Pakistani MP delegation, which is now in Mumbai.

Salim Jaan Mazari, a member of Pakistan's National Assembly, told a business seminar there that lines of communication between the people, have to be established for better ties.

(hold up sound)

The 12-member Pakistani delegation is in India on a goodwill mission.

Television News

Defence Minister George Fernandes says infiltration of militants from across the border with Pakistan, is "looking down" at the moment.

Commenting on the fresh Indo-Pak peace initiative, Mr. Fernandes told reporters in Bangalore that confidence-building measures with Pakistan were being undertaken, but a time frame could not be set for normalcy.

(hold up sound)

Commenting on his recent visit to China, the defence minister said that both the countries were interested in having good relations.

Deputy Prime Minister L. K. Advani says the battle against proxy war is difficult, but India will succeed against it ultimately.

Mr. Advani was talking to reporters in New Delhi yesterday, after the special screening of a telefilm on last year's attack on the Akshardham temple in Gujarat.

28 people were killed by 2 terrorists, who opened fire with automatic weapons and burst grenades.

The attackers were later shot dead by commandos.

(hold up sound)

External Affairs Minister Yashwant Sinha has reached Moscow on a 6-day visit to Russia.

During his visit, Mr. Sinha will also hold talks with Colin Powell who is reaching the Russian capital today on a bilateral visit. They are expected to discuss the Indo-Pak relations.

And in Moscow, Mr. Sinha is scheduled to meet various Russian leaders, including Prime Minister Mikhail Kasyanov.

You are watching Doordarshan News. Coming up: 6 states get new governors.

This and more after a short break.

(hold)

Welcome Back. Here is a quick reminder of our headlines:
- Riyadh explosions toll rises to 90, as George W. Bush vows to punish the guilty.
- Brajesh Mishra says a loose international coalition is not enough to fight international terror.

- Pakistani Prime Minister calls for enhanced economic cooperation with India for the prosperity of both nations.
- Slow-moving cyclonic storm in the Bay of Bengal is likely to bring heavy rain along the Andhra and Orissa coast.

and

- The West Indies script a historic win against Australia in their Antigua test.

The provisions for imposing president's rule in a state are being made more stringent, to prevent its misuse.

The Standing Committee of the Inter-State Council, which met in New Delhi yesterday, accepted several recommendations of the Sarkaria Commission.

For instance, it was agreed that president's rule should be imposed only as a last resort, and that the state government should first be issued a show-cause notice, if immediate action is not required.

It was also agreed that all alternatives available to the centre under Article 355, should be exhausted first.

Briefing reporters after the meeting, Deputy Prime Minister Advani said the centre has agreed in principle, to incorporate into the Constitution the Supreme Court's pronouncement in the Bommai case.

(hold up sound)

There has been a reshuffle of governors.

The Governor of Bihar, V. C. Pande, has been shifted to Arunachal Pradesh.

According to a Rashtrapati Bhavan communiqué, 5 other governors have also been transferred.

The Governor of Jharkhand, Justice M. Rama Jois will take Mr. Pande's place.

The Arunachal Pradesh Governor Arvind Dave, now moves to Manipur, with the additional charge of Assam.

The Manipur Governor Ved Marwah has been shifted to Jharkhand.

The Tripura Governor Lt. Gen. K. M. Seth has swapped places with D. N. Sahay, the Governor of Chhattisgarh.

Now onto the West Bengal elections:
The Congress has managed to snatch Malda and Murshidabad Zila Parishads from the ruling Left Front.
Though the Left Front has retained the remaining 15 Zila Parishads, with an overwhelming majority.
The Trinamool Congress-BJP combine has been relegated to the third position.
Of the 711 seats that have been declared so far, the Left Front has won 616, the Congress 68, and the Trinamool-BJP combine 21 seats.
Sunday's elections to local bodies were marred by widespread violence in the state.

For the latest we spoke to our Kolkata correspondent.
1. Were these results entirely expected?
2. Whoever holds power at the local level, controls West Bengal. From these results, what can you say about the mood of the electorate?

The Gujarat Police arrested 4 more people from Ahmedabad yesterday, in connection with Haren Pandya murder case.
One was nabbed from Palanpur, and the others from Surat.
Our Ahmedabad correspondent Dhiraj Kakadia says the 4 allegedly supported Asgar Ali, who carried out Pandya's murder.
Congress President Sonia Gandhi has accused the NDA Government at the centre of dividing the society on religious lines and called upon the people not to get misled by its "false" promises.
She was addressing a farmers' rally at Sagwada village in the tribal dominated Doongarpur district yesterday.

(hold up sound)

It is time now for a look at the business highlights.

(hold)

The government detects irregularities of 455 crore rupees in FCI's rice exports.
ICAI to hear Sachin Tendulkar's case next month.
BSNL and MTNL roll back tariffs, hike free calls, and reduce fixed-to-cellphone call charges.

MTNL loses revenue of 300 crore rupees for not implementing TRAI tariff.

Canara Bank will lay stress on low deposits during 2003-2004.

Indian Railways plans to increase its share of freight traffic, from 38 per cent to 50 per cent in the coming years.

and

SAIL exports are up 5 times in April 2003.

Finally some good news for telecom consumers.

Public sector majors BSNL and MTNL have announced a partial rollback in tariffs.

The 2 PSUs have decided to increase the number of free calls, and reduce fixed-to-cellphone call charges.

(hold up sound)

Lets now have a look at the highlights from the world of sport.

(hold)

The West Indies score a record-breaking 418 to beat Australia by 3 wickets.

Sri Lanka beat New Zealand by 5 wickets in Tri-Series.

Serena Williams advances at Rome Masters. and

ACMilan edge out InterMilan to enter the Champions League final.

The West Indies have made a record-breaking score to win the final test of the 4-match series against Australia.

They have successfully thwarted Aussie hopes of a Caribbean whitewash.

The previous record of 406 runs in the fourth innings belonged to India.

Centuries by Sarwan and Chanderpaul and some gritty batting by Banks, saw Lara and his men salvaging some prestige, after having lost the first 3 tests series.

Doordarshan will telecast live the semifinals and finals of the French Open.

This is part of a 3-year deal Doordarshan has signed with Ray Media Limited, a London-based company that holds the terrestrial rights for this Grand Slam tennis tournament.

The matches, on June 5 to 8, will be telecast exclusively on DD Metro.

(hold up sound)

Besides this, Doordarshan also plans to telecast live the mixed doubles matches, if Mahesh Bhupathi and Leander Paes make it to the last four.

And now here are the headlines in the newspapers published from Delhi this morning.

(hold up sound)

We now go over live to Hyderabad, where Sanjeev Thomas has the local news.

Good morning, Sanjeev.

(hold up sound)

Thank you, Sanjeev.

Rizwana Akhtar now joins us from Bhubaneshwar.

Rizwana, what's the news from your city?

(hold up sound)

Thank you, Rizwana.

Now lets have a look at the events to take place today

(hold)

Yesterday's very severe cyclonic storm over the Bay of Bengal has moved slightly northwards, and was centred about 500 km east of Chennai this morning.

It is likely to intensify further, and move towards the north Andhra Pradesh and Orissa coasts.

The weather office has predicted heavy to very heavy rainfall and strong winds, along these coasts in the next 48 hours.

The sea will be very rough, and fishermen are advised not to venture out.

And now on to Mumbai, where the king of fruits held sway at a recent expo.

Mangoes in all their brilliant colours were on display, and needless to say, the visitors enjoyed every minute.

(hold up sound)

It is now time for a detailed look at the weather across the country.

(hold up sound)

Now let us take a look at the temperatures recorded at 5.30 this morning.

Delhi was 25.8 degrees celsius;
Kolkata—28.4;
Mumbai—27.6; and
Chennai—26.4 degrees celsius.

Before we go, here are the main stories once again:
- Riyadh explosion toll rises to 90, as George W. Bush vows to punish the guilty.
- Brajesh Mishra says a loose international coalition is not enough to fight international terror.
- Pakistani prime minister calls for enhanced economic cooperation, for the prosperity of both nations.
- Slow-moving cyclonic storm in the Bay of Bengal is likely to bring heavy rain along Andhra and Orissa coast.

and
- West Indies script a historic win against Australia in their Antigua Test.

That's the news this morning. Thanks for watching, Namaskar.

There are no sheets. Tapes are still there but days are not far when tape-less newsrooms will be a norm.

8

Trends and Issues

Towards the end of the last century when Internet was proclaimed as the medium for future many talked about the death of television or end of television. But it is an old story. In fact, new media never erases the existing media. Theater did not end when print arrived. Symphony orchestras did not disappear when recorded music appeared. When radio came it was supposed to have killed newspapers. When television came, it should have been doom for both radio and newspapers. But this never happened. Now it is clear that broadcasting is not crashing, not dying, not endangered, but it appears that in the new media world, the advantage belongs to broadcasters. It is the digital age, the Internet age, the interactive age, the age of personalised and customised content but most importantly it is an age of opportunity for traditional media companies. Because no one in the new media world had the resources, the experience and the creativity to match the quality of content of already existing and established media companies who owned enduring, powerful, and widely recognised brands. One must see mergers, acquisitions, and strategic alliances from this angle.

In fact, Neil Hickey wrote in *Columbia Journalism Review* about the merger of AOL and Time Warner, "In simplest terms, AOL Time Warner had thrown each other a life preserver in the effort to grow rationally in the new millennium. One of them needed more products on its shelves to increase its appeal to customers, and the other needed (after failed, fumbling attempts to construct it) a throughway to those millions of online eyeballs. Between them they could eventually offer fast, virtually instantaneous hook-up to

Internet over upgraded cable lines, and thus sell more of everything than either could alone. And they did be poised to offer the folks at home television, telephone, and Internet service in one package with one handy monthly bill." *(CJR March/April 2000)*. Despite difficulties there is no doubt that AOL Time Warner is the biggest media company in the world and is now growing more on the strength of Time Warner brands than on AOL. One of the positive results of dot-com bust is the realisation that the technological revolution is not eradicating traditional broadcast media but reshaping and realigning them.

Yet, if the new media do not destroy the existing ones, they most certainly change them. Printing changed the nature of oral cultures. Radio, movies and broadcast TV had an impact on publishing. Broadcast TV changed radio. Cable changed broadcast. The one common thread is that in every case, the audience size expanded. The top 3 news sites on the Web are products of leading broadcast or cable networks. The top music sites on the Web are part of MTV's portfolio again, the product of a leading network.

However, it does not mean there are no challenges— challenges to broadcasters come from rapidly evolving technology, from ever-expanding competition, from a business model in need of updating. The broadcasters who are mired in history and wedded to old ways will in fact follow the dinosaurs into extinction. Programming costs have skyrocketed, while fragmentation has made the prime time hit even more elusive. But in spite of all the challenges, the opportunities for broadcasters are immense. The content, brands, distribution – it all adds up to an incredibly powerful advantage in the age of expanding media and ever-more-fragmented audiences. As television and Internet converge, the number of news and entertainment options for consumers increase even more drastically than in the last decade. All this makes ability to reach a mass audience more and more valuable. Thus, the broadband revolution, far from sounding the death knell of traditional broadcast media, actually means that broadcasters and cable networks with established brand strength will reap disproportionate gains. When it comes to

Trends and Issues

technology, the opportunities far exceed the threat because the content is and will remain the driving force.

When it comes to Internet, the challenge is to translate the advantages into success in new platforms. This is what CBS has done, with its investments in Internet companies like CBS MarketWatch and CBS SportsLine. This is what MTV has done with the MTVi Group, the Web's leading source of music content. CBS has a broad portfolio of Internet investments, including a stake in MovieTickets.com, through which local CBS stations have the chance to share the revenues from online ticket sales. NBC, too, has been very creative about developing new initiatives with a variety of partners, from Ralph Lauren to the Washington Post.

The ten media giants in the early years of the twenty-first century are: AOL Time Warner, Disney, General Electric, News Corporation, Viacom, Vivendi, Sony, Bertelsmann, AT&T and Liberty Media. But one cannot get a glimpse of trends in media business unless one looks at actual assets

The merger of AOL and Time Warner that has created a corporate giant, the largest Internet and media company in the world was completed on 11 January 2001. (Now the merged corporate entity is called Time Warner). Around the time of merger, the AOL Time Warner basically operated businesses that fall in six categories

1. Interactive Services and Properties

America Online

Briefly, America Online, Inc., based in Dulles, Virginia, is the world's leader in interactive services, Web brands, Internet technologies and e-commerce services. America Online, Inc., operates: AOL, which has more than 29 million members worldwide and CompuServe, with more than 3 million members, the company's two worldwide Internet services; several leading Internet brands including ICQ, AOL Instant Messenger, Digital City and MapQuest; the new AOLbyPhone; the AOL Anywhere.com and Netscape.com portals; Netscape 6, Netscape Navigator and Communicator browsers; AOL Moviefone, the nation's no. 1 movie-listing guide and ticketing service; AOL@School, a free online learning tool for K-12 classrooms; and Spinner.com and NullSoft's Winamp, leaders in Internet music. i-Planet e-commerce Solutions, a Sun-Netscape Alliance, provides easy-to-deploy, comprehensive e-commerce solutions for the net economy. Here are some more details about the AOL Time Warner companies of this category:

AOL Service: AOL, the world's leading interactive service, is transforming the lives of its more than 29 million members with the most convenient, easy-to-use and valuable online features, content and other benefits available anywhere. AOL members average about an hour online daily, signalling how central the AOL experience is to their lives by enabling them to keep in touch, stay informed, shop, find entertainment, manage their finances and schedules, and much more.

AOL Anywhere: As part of the AOL Anywhere strategy, the AOL Anywhere portal gives members seamless access to the full spectrum of the AOL features and services, wherever and whenever they need them—including at work. And AOL Anywhere lets people access these services on a range of devices including pagers, cell phones and PDAs—using the same screen name and password.

AOL International: With the online medium now growing faster outside the US than within it, AOL International operates the America Online and CompuServe services in 16 countries and 8 different languages. The AOL International just completed its most successful year ever, adding a record-breaking 1.4 million new Net members for a total of nearly 4.6 million international AOL and CompuServe subscribers.

AOL@School: AOL@School is a unique online learning tool designed to help schools make the interactive medium a more effective part of the classroom experience. AOL@School applies America Online's hallmark focus on convenience and ease-of-use to help educators make the most of online learning and provides a series of safe, age-appropriate learning portals with easy-to-follow links to online content selected by educational experts.

CompuServe: The Internet value leader, CompuServe provides access to 3 million worldwide members at home and in the workplace. CompuServe's exciting new software upgrade,

CompuServe 2000 Version 6.0, offers powerful new features, such as expanded e-mail capabilities, new built-in audio and video player, new streamlined Toolbar and improved Address Book and My Calendar^{SM} service, now available from multiple locations; all of which add even greater value to the online experience.

Digital City: Digital City is the no. 1 local guide for America Online members and other Internet consumers, reaching more than 6 million unique users a month. Digital City products serve more than 200 markets—Digital City New York to Digital City San Jose—creating the first "local everywhere" coast-to-coast network. With its Entertainment Guide, Visitor's Guide, Local Shopping & Services Directory, "Local Experts" and "Best of the City," Digital City offers the leading portfolio of products to local consumers and local advertisers.

DMS: Digital Marketing Services is the leader in online marketing research and online rewards programs through the world's largest online service, America Online. Its online features include online quantitative marketing research services, the largest online respondent base with access to the opinions of 27 million AOL members, a state-of-the-art scientific approach that produces stable and reliable data, and a highly experienced staff of traditional researchers and computer specialists.

ICQ: ICQ, with more than 88 million registered users worldwide, is the most comprehensive instant messaging product. Its audience is global (two-thirds outside the US), Web-savvy and young (two-thirds between the ages of 18 and 35). On average, ICQ members have the service open on their desktops for three hours daily and in active use for 75 minutes each day. ICQ offers such free and compelling services as Instant Messenger, ICQ Web Mail, chat, ICQ Groups, IP telephony, SMS mobile messaging, Find a Friend Directory and ICQ Personal Assistant Tools. Every second of every day, someone around the world registers for ICQ. The software is free and available at ICQ.com.

iPlanet: iPlanet e-commerce solutions—AOL's strategic e-commerce alliance with Sun Microsystems, Inc. offers enterprises a highly scalable Internet software platform. iPlanet software provides a predictable base that allows enterprises to rapidly deploy new services and scale to accommodate the growing demand. The industry's broadest portfolio of e-commerce software and services includes solutions for wired and wireless communication and portal services, unified user management, application services and electronic commerce applications for electronic procurement, bill presentment and payment and dynamic trading.

MapQuest: MapQuest is the no.1 service in mapping and navigation, and is one of the best-known and most trusted brands on the Internet, reaching more than 7 million unique users a month. MapQuest provides unsurpassed online, voice and wireless mapping, directions, real-time traffic, and destination information to consumers any time, anywhere. MapQuest is one of the most popular mobile applications for consumers. Its business unit licenses its branded solutions to more than 1,750 business partners.

Moviefone: AOL Moviefone is the leader in providing online, telephone and wireless movie listings, information and ticketing to consumers anytime, anywhere. Through its online service Moviefone.com, its 777-film telephone service, and numerous wireless devices, the company serves approximately 5 million users each week with a complete, free directory of movies, showtimes, theater locations, the ability to purchase tickets, and other content of interest to moviegoers. Through its partnerships with film studios and movie exhibitors, the AOL Moviefone makes the movie-going experience more convenient and helps its partners promote movies and sell tickets. One in every five moviegoers uses Moviefone or Moviefone.com each week.

Netscape: Netscape has pioneered the development of world-class browsers, including, the most recently, the groundbreaking Netscape 6 browser, based on the small, fast, standards-compliant Netscape Gecko browser engine, which provides a compelling Web experience across traditional PCs and new computing devices. The newly-redesigned Netscape.com website provides consumers with convenient and easy access to a complete package of innovative Web-based applications, content and features. In addition, Netscape Netbusiness meets the needs of small businesses with a free one-stop home on Internet to enable them to better manage their everyday operations.

AOL Music: Easy to discover, experience, and buy music on the AOL Music brings together the AOL's leading music brands to reach the largest audience of online music fans in the world through a rich array of options making Internet.

2. Networks

Turner Broadcasting

It operates many of the most powerful and well-established brands in entertainment and news, including TBS Superstation, TNT, The WB, Cartoon Network, *Kids' WB!*, Turner Classic Movies, Turner South, CNN/US, CNN Headline News, CNN*fn*, CNN/SI, CNNRadio, and Boomerang, as well as the Atlanta Braves, Atlanta Hawks, Atlanta Thrashers, The Goodwill Games, and the Company's many international language-specific networks and other businesses.

Basic Cable

Turner Broadcasting is the leading revenue producer in basic cable, with three of the five top-rated basic cable networks. The Turner Broadcasting networks are ratings leaders in virtually all key demographics categories:

- TBS Superstation, the most watched network on basic cable for 24 consecutive years, became the first cable household to reach 80 million US households in fall 2000.
- TNT aired three of the top five original movies on basic cable in 2000.
- The global leader in animation, Cartoon Network draws from the world's largest animation library and now is available to more than 138 million households in 145 countries. In the US, the Cartoon Network is experiencing the fastest-growing ratings in basic cable and reached #1 last year for the first time in quarterly primetime household ratings among ad-supported cable networks.

Network Television
For the November 2000 sweeps ratings period, the WB Television Network scored the highest year-to-year increases of any network in almost every demographic category. It also recorded its highest adult men and women 18-34 ratings ever for any sweeps period. The WB continued its outstanding performance during the February 2001— leading all networks in growth among the advertiser-coveted adult 18-34 and 18-49 demographics. *Kids' WB!* is the no. 1 broadcast network in children's programming for the second straight year (2000).

News
CNN is the most watched 24-hour news network. Along with CNN Headline News and CNN International, the world's first global, 24-hour news network, CNN reaches more than a billion people worldwide, and the CNN websites generate more traffic than any other news competitor.

Home Box Office
It is America's most successful premium television network, whether measured by operating performance, subscribers, awards, ratings or critical acclaim. Its two 24-hour services—HBO and Cinemax— grew to 36.7 million US subscribers in 2000. Known for offering blockbuster movies, innovative original programming, provocative documentaries, concert events and championship boxing, HBO is the highest-rated cable service during the day and in prime time. The all-movie service Cinemax, the second-highest cable service after HBO, features more than 1,600 movie titles a year—more than any other premium service. Internationally, HBO joint ventures reach 12 million subscribers in more than 50 countries in Latin America, Asia and Central Europe.

3. Publishing
Time Inc. has a rich heritage of journalistic excellence and integrity dating back to *Time* magazine's founding in 1923. In its 75-plus years, Time Inc. has established itself as the foremost creator of publishing and information brands, including many of America's

most successful magazines. It is also a leading direct marketer of music and video products.

Publishing over 60 magazines with a total of 268 million readers, the company generates consistent growth through investing in its core product lines, developing brand extensions and new products, and seeking opportunities to build its brands in an online environment. Time Inc. is the only publishing company to have launched 9 major magazines in the past decade, and is the only company to publish four national weekly consumer magazines. In December 2000, Time Inc. acquired the Times Mirror Magazines from Tribune Company, including *Golf, Ski, Skiing, Field & Stream, Yachting* and other titles. Times Mirror Magazines, the largest publisher of men's-oriented special interest magazines, was renamed Time4 Media.

Time Inc. has launched several joint-marketing initiatives with America Online. Promotions of Time Inc. magazines on the AOL service continue to generate more than 100,000 gross magazine subscriptions per month, while Time Inc. has promoted the launch of AOL 6.0 with CD inserts in its magazines as well as retail distribution of CDs.

Time Warner Trade Publishing

Time Warner Trade Publishing's imprints, Warner Books and Little, Brown and Company, balance entertainment, quality literature and informative non-fiction.

Warner Books and Little, Brown and Company published newsmakers (like Jack Welch and Andy Grove in 2001), leading theorists (such as Malcolm Gladwell, author of The Tipping Point, in 2000), literary success stories (like Anita Shreve, Janet Finch, David Sedaris and Billie Letts) and popular commercial writers (including Nicholas Sparks, James Patterson, David Baldacci, Nelson DeMille, Sandra Brown and Michael Connelly).

iPublish.com

AOL Time Warner's digital publishing venture, releases more than 50 titles each month and is the online home of many best-selling and up-and-coming authors. This April, iPublish launched a groundbreaking online community in which authors and readers can submit work directly for publication consideration, get inside-the-industry-publishing tips, and purchase eBooks.(This venture did not last long and was closed down.)

4. Filmed Entertainment
Warner Bros:
Founded more than 75 years ago as a motion picture studio, Warner Bros. has evolved into a fully integrated global entertainment company. Warner Bros. stands at the forefront of every aspect of the entertainment industry, from feature films to television, home video, animation, product and brand licensing, interactive media and international theaters.

Warner Bros. Pictures: It has been at the forefront of the motion picture industry since its inception in 1923 and has held the top slot in annual market share, more often than any other studio. The company produces and/or acquires 25 to 30 films each year and is also one of the world's leading theatrical distributors, handling the distribution and marketing of all of its home productions, as well as those produced and financed by others. Warner Bros. is known as the creator of some of the most powerful worldwide franchises in movie history, including *Batman, Lethal Weapon, The Matrix* and the *Harry Potter*. The Warner Bros. film library consists of more than 6,500 feature films, including classic MGM and RKO titles obtained as a result of Time Warner's merger with Turner Broadcasting in 1996. Warner Bros. Pictures' recent franchise, *The Matrix*, became the studio's highest-grossing film ever, at more than $450 million at the worldwide box office, and won four Academy Awards in 2000. It also became the best-selling DVD of all time, with more than 3 million units sold in the US. Warner Bros. Pictures began production on *The Matrix 2* and *The Matrix 3* in early spring 2001.

Warner Bros. Television: This is one of the leading suppliers of primetime series on television, is responsible for such current hit shows as *ER, Friends, The Drew Carey Show, Whose Line Is It Anyway?* and *The West Wing*.

With its Time Warner partner, Toshiba, Warner Home Video has spearheaded the development of the DVD, now considered the fastest-growing new packaged-media format launch ever. Since their launch in 1997, the DVD players have significantly outsold the VCR and the CD player at comparable stages in their introduction

For the 2000-2001 season, WBTV is producing series for all six broadcast networks. Through its Warner Bros. Domestic Television Distribution, Telepictures Distribution and Warner Bros. Domestic Cable Distribution divisions, Warner Bros. Television is also one of the leading domestic distributors of first-run and off-network programming.

Warner Bros. International Television is one of the world's largest distributors of television programming, licensing some 40,000 hours of television programming and feature films dubbed in more than 40 languages to broadcasters in more than 175 countries. WBITV also has strategic co-production alliances with European broadcasters and production companies to create original international television programming.

Warner Bros. Animation: Warner Bros. Animation is a leader in television animation, creating, developing and producing original contemporary animation, as well as series, shorts, interstitial and commercials utilising classic animated properties from the Looney Tunes and Hanna-Barbera libraries. In 1994, Warner Bros. Animation also began producing animated full-length feature films. The Warner Bros. Animation library currently boasts more than 60 series, 12,000 animated titles and 1,500 classic shorts, including *Looney Tunes*, *Hanna-Barbera*, and 320 animated shorts from the MGM library.

Looney Tunes: Originating in the 1930s, the Looney Tunes and Merrie Melodies cartoons feature more than 100 characters, including such widely recognised and venerable stars as Bugs Bunny, Daffy Duck, Sylvester, Tweety, Road Runner, Taz and Marvin the Martian. Since 1960, these classic cartoons have been staples of children's television programming, with Bugs Bunny drawing top ratings on broadcast and cable television.

Hanna-Barbera: Hanna-Barbera's animation studio has produced more than 6,000 animated titles, and created such classic characters as the Flintstones, the Jetsons, Scooby-Doo and Yogi Bear. The legendary cartoon house, founded by Bill Hanna and Joe Barbera in 1957, became part of the Warner Bros. family as a result of Time Warner's merger with Turner Broadcasting in 1996.

Castle Rock Entertainment: Castle Rock Entertainment, the 14-year-old feature film and television production company whose hits include *The Green Mile, The Shawshank Redemption, In the Line of Fire, A Few Good Men, When Harry Met Sally, City Slickers* and the megahit television series *Seinfeld*, was founded by Alan Horn (now the President & CEO of Warner Bros.) and his partners Rob Reiner, Martin Shafer, Glenn Padnick and Andrew Scheinman. Castle Rock became part of the Warner Bros. family in 1996 as a result of Time Warner's merger with Turner Broadcasting.

Telepictures Productions: Telepictures Productions specialises in the development and production of reality and reality-based series and specials for the first-run syndication market. The company's production activities also include network and cable television programming for all day parts (daytime, prime time, access and late night). The company's 2000-01 line-up includes *The Rosie O'Donnell Show, Queen Latifah* and *Extra*.

Warner Home Video: With operations in 78 international territories, Warner Home Video (WHV) commands the largest distribution infrastructure in the global video marketplace. WHV's film library is the largest of any studio, offering titles from the repertoire of Warner Bros. Pictures, Turner Entertainment Company, Castle Rock Entertainment, HBO Home Video, New Line Home Video, Redbus Films (in the UK) and BBC Video (North America). WHV is also responsible for the sales, marketing and distribution of the Warner Bros. library to the domestic pay-per-view and video-on-demand markets.

In conjunction with its Time Warner partner, Toshiba, WHV has spearheaded the development of the DVD, considered to be the fastest growing new packaged media format ever. Since their launch in 1997, DVD players have significantly outsold the VCR and the CD player at comparable stages in their introduction.

Warner Bros. Consumer Products: Warner Bros. Consumer Products is one of the leading licensing and retail merchandising organisations in the world. With over 3,700 active licensees, Warner Bros. Consumer Products handles the licensing and merchandising for all the intellectual properties in Warner Bros.' vast film, television and publishing libraries. These include such world-renowned brands and franchises as *Looney Tunes* (over 100 characters including, of course, Bugs Bunny, Daffy Duck, Porky Pig and Tweety, to name but a very, very few); DC Comics (from Batman to Superman to Wonder Woman); MAD Magazine, Hanna-Barbera (including Scooby-Doo, the Flintstones, the Jetsons); Cartoon Network properties; classic films such as *Casablanca* and *The Wizard of Oz*; contemporary franchises like *Lethal Weapon* and *The Matrix*; plus current hit primetime series (including *ER* and *Friends*), and the literary phenomenon and feature film *Harry Potter*.

Established in 1991, the Warner Bros. Studio Stores carry exclusive, top quality merchandise, as well as selected licensed products based on world-famous classic and contemporary characters drawn from the entire AOL Time Warner family.

Warner Bros. International Theatres: Warner Bros. International Theatres currently boasts some 120 multiplexes (1,125 screens) in seven territories outside the United States—the United Kingdom, Japan, Australia, Portugal, Spain, Italy and Taiwan. One of the pioneers of multiplexing in the international marketplace, Warner Bros. International Theatres is a world leader in the design, construction, development and operation of multiplex cinemas. Its strategic partners include Village Roadshow in the UK, Australia and Taiwan; Village Roadshow and Focus srl in Italy; Mycal Corporation in Japan; Lusomundo S.p.A. in Portugal; and Lusomundo and Sogecable in Spain.

Warner Bros. New Media: Warner Bros. New Media oversees the migration and convergence of traditional media with new media and is the driving force behind Warner Bros.' activities in the entire new media space, including the Internet, interactive television and wireless. The division's strategic focus is on creating content especially designed for the new media, optimising the use of Warner Bros.' brands and talent, and serving as the access point for new business opportunities and distribution platforms.

Warner Bros. Online: It is one of the preeminent Internet entertainment destinations, providing original innovative programming, and serves as the exclusive, official entry point to all Warner Bros. information, entertainment and programme-based venues on the Web.

DC Comics: It is the leading comic book publisher in the industry and creator of some of the world's most renowned icons, has a long history of innovative publishing and utilisation of its characters to support the marketing of products. From the classic "Superman" radio programmes to the first online service devoted to comics, DC has demonstrated its heroes' abilities to leap from the printed page and conquer all media. DC's signature characters (Superman, Batman, and Wonder Woman) continue to attract new readers and major media attention, while new titles and characters (such as Hitman, Preacher, The Invisibles and Gon) have broken new grounds.

MAD Magazine: Published by DC Comics, *MAD Magazine* is a monthly humour magazine that has brought its unique brand of social parody and political satire to readers since 1952. The magazine's "idiot mascot," Alfred E. Neuman, has been gracing *MAD*'s covers since 1956.

New Line Cinema

New Line Cinema is one of the largest independent producers, acquirers, and distributors of theatrical motion pictures in the world.

Founded in 1967, the studio has a domestic marketing and distribution organisation capable of releasing more than 30 films a year; a home video division capable of releasing more than 40 titles a year; a television production and distribution organisation with relationships with every broadcast and cable network, station groups and pay-per-view carriers; an international division that distributes films globally in every major medium; and merchandising, music and new media subsidiaries that fully exploit New Line's film properties and franchises. New Line's programming refreshes AOL Time Warner's libraries and provides valuable programming for its cable networks, in particular TNT, TBS and HBO.

New Line, in conjunction with Warner Music, has created a new music label, New Line Music, which is designed to identify and break new talent as well as develop soundtracks for New Line's feature films.

5. Music

The worldwide appeal of artists signed to Warner Music Group's (WMG) record companies—Atlantic, Elektra, London-Sire Records Inc., Rhino, Warner Bros. Records and Warner Music International—is at the core of its growth strategy. As the demand for local repertoire has increased, WMG is expanding its signing of local artists. In addition, it is devoting greater resources to marketing US artists overseas and to creating greater global marketing opportunities for artists with worldwide appeal. WMG operates in 68 countries through various subsidiaries, affiliated and nonaffiliated licensees. WEA Inc., WMG's manufacturing and distribution operation, is comprised of three companies: WEA Corp., a leading US distribution company; WEA Manufacturing, one of the world's largest CD manufacturers as well as the no. 1 DVD manufacturer; and Ivy Hill, an award-winning design and packaging firm. WMG's publishing division, Warner/Chappell Music, Inc., is one of the world's leading music publishers, controlling more than one million copyrights worldwide.

In 2000, WMG significantly expanded its online presence. The company announced plans to offer one of the industry's largest collections of music via digital distribution through leading online retailers.

WMG began working with AOL last year on several groundbreaking initiatives. Warner Bros. Records and AOL's music service Spinner launched Madonna's latest CD, *Music*, with a world-premiere global listening party in September, followed by Madonna's first-ever-live AOL chat, with 120,000-plus fans. The album debuted the following week at no. 1 on the Billboard best-selling album chart.

WMG became the first of the major music companies to offer albums in the DVD-Audio format. DVD-Audio is the most significant industry format launched since the introduction of the CD nearly 20 years ago.

6. Cable Systems

Time Warner Cable: It owns and manages the most advanced, best-clustered cable television operations in United States, with more that 90% of its more that 12.7 million customers in systems serving 100,000 subscribers or more.

Time Warner is a pioneer in the dynamic cable industry—bringing the digital age into America's living rooms and transforming the way Americans receive information and entertainment. Time Warner Cable is solidifying its technological leadership through the digital upgrade of its systems and the introduction of such innovative services as Road Runner™, its jointly owned high-speed online service.

By the end of 2000, Time Warner Cable had completed digital upgrades at approximately 92% of its cable plant.

The rollout of RoadRunner continued at a rapid pace in 2000. Time Warner Cable had approximately 946,000 high-speed Internet customers at the end of 2000, up to 187% compared to 1999.

Continuing the aggressive national rollout of its digital cable service, Time Warner Cable had more than 1.7 million digital video subscribers at the end of 2000, representing 305% growth over a year earlier.

In February 2000, Time Warner and AOL signed a Memorandum of Understanding ("MOU"), setting out the framework for Time Warner Cable to offer consumers a choice of multiple Internet Service Providers (ISPs), including AOL, on its broadband cable systems. Consistent with the MOU, Time Warner entered into an agreement with EarthLink, the nation's second-largest ISP, to enable EarthLink to offer high-speed Internet access, content, applications and functionality—including video streaming—over Time Warner Cable's broadband cable systems. The agreement with EarthLink represents the cable industry's most far-reaching partnership with an unaffiliated ISP and is expected to become a model for future agreements.

Since the merger there have been a number of changes at AOL Time Warner, but the above description of properties is indicative of the trends.

Heroes or Villains

Another way to look at the trends is to look at some controversial personalities who have contributed substantially to change the media scene for better or worse. Some may count them as heroes while the others may count them among villains. Given below are some such examples:

Stephen M. Case

Steve Case, born and raised in Hawaii, five years after graduating in political science from Williams College began on 24 May 1985 by incorporating Quantum Computer Services, registered in Delaware and grew to become the Chairman AOL Time Warner on 11 January 2001. This phenomenal success is really fascinating. In November 1985, Quantum's first online service, "Q-Link," launched on Commodore Business Machines. In August 1988, Quantum's "PC-Link" launched through a joint venture with Tandy Corporation. In October 1989, "America Online" service was launched for Macintosh and Apple. On 19 March 1992, America Online went public on the NASDAQ market at original price of $11.50, under symbol AMER. On 16 September 1996, AOL moved from Nasdaq to the New York Stock Exchange, where it was listed under symbol "AOL"

On 19 August 1994, AOL acquired Redgate Communications, a multimedia publishing company. In November 1994, it launched the Greenhouse to develop original content online. On 30 November 1994, it acquired NaviSoft, a developer of Internet publishing tools. On 29 December 1994, AOL acquired BookLink Technologies, a developer of Internet applications. On 17 February 1995, it acquired ANS, a commercial Internet access provider. On 6 August 1996 it acquired ImagiNation Network (INN) to expand multiplayer games offering.

On 22 May 1995, AOL acquired WAIS, an Internet publisher, and Medior, a developer of interactive media. On 1 June 1995, it acquired Global Network Navigator (GNN) as platform for direct Internet service and WebCrawler search tool. On 22 September 1995, it acquired Ubique, Ltd., creator of Virtual Places.

On 1 February 1996, AOL acquired Johnson-Grace, leading developers of data compression technology. On 10 March 1997, it acquired Lightspeed Media to create original content for Greenhouse Entertainment Network. On 8 September 1997, AOL announced intention to acquire CompuServe Online Services and on 2 February 1998, AOL completed acquisition of CompuServe. On 6 May 1998, AOL announced intention to acquire NetChannel and on 8 June 1998 AOL announced intention to acquire Mirabilis Ltd. and its ICQ Technology. On 11 November 1998, AOL announced acquisition of PersonaLogic, Inc. On 24 November 1998, AOL announced acquisition of Netscape. On 1 February 1999, AOL announced intention to acquire MovieFone, Inc., the top movie listing and ticketing service. On 1 June 1999, AOL acquired leading Internet music brands – Spinner.com, Winamp and Shoutcast. On 15 June 1999, AOL acquired Digital Marketing Services, Inc., the leader in online incentive marketing programmes and online custom market research.

On 1 March 1995, AOL announced a joint venture with Bertelsmann, AG to create European online services and on 28 November 1995 Bertelsmann, AG and America Online launched AOL Germany. On 31 January 1996, AOL launched AOL UK and AOL Canada and on 18 March 1996 it launched AOL France.

AOL announced joint venture with Mitsui and Nikkei to launch service in Japan on 8 May 1996 and on 15 April 1997 it launched AOL Japan. On 10 February 1998, AOL and CIC announced plans to launch online service in Hong Kong. On 7 October 1998, AOL and Bertelsmann launched AOL Australia.

On 12 March 1996, marketing distribution alliances announced with Apple and AT&T. Browser partnerships announced with Microsoft and Netscape Communications. Licensing and developing agreement announced with Sun Microsystems. On 25 November 1996 Excite becomes AOL's exclusive Internet search and directory service. On 25 February 1997, a multi-year, $100 million marketing deal announced with Tel-Save Holdings.

On 17 June 1997, AOL Studios launches WorldPlay Entertainment. On 24 June 1998, strategic partnership with Sun

Microsystems. On 12 January 1999, AOL and Bell Atlantic announced partnership to deliver high-speed DSL access.

These were the acquisitions, joint ventures, alliances and partnerships, with particular focus on technological developments and strategic investments, that were driving the global expansion of Steve Case's AOL with his bid to merge Time Warner as the ultimate attempt to converge the old and new media. The deal was announced on 10 January 2000 and the objective that created the largest Internet and media giant in the world was achieved, despite opposition from rivals and consumer groups, on 11 January 2001. Later as shares lost there value in May 2003 he resigned as Chairman but continues to be on the Board of Directors of AOL Time Warner.

Ted Turner

Robert Edward "Ted" Turner was born on November 19, 1938 in Cincinnati, Ohio. His business career began as an account executive for Turner Advertising Company (now Turner Broadcasting System, Inc.) and, in 1963 after his father's suicide, became president and chief operating officer, a position he held until the company's merger with Time Warner in 1996. He became Vice-chairman of Time Warner in October 1996, with the merger of Time Warner Inc. and Turner Broadcasting System, Inc.

Turner oversaw Time Warner's cable networks division, which included the assets of Turner Broadcasting System, Inc. (TBS, Inc.), the CNN Newsgroup, as well as Home Box Office, Cinemax, and the company's interests in Comedy Central and Court TV. He also oversaw New Line Cinema and the company's professional sports teams – the Atlanta Braves, Atlanta Hawks and Atlanta Thrashers. When Time Warner merged with AOL he became Vice-chairman of AOL Time Warner Inc, the position he resigned in May 2003 but continues to be a member of its Board of Directors.

Turner entered the television business in 1970 with the purchase of Channel 17, an Atlanta independent UHF television station. Six years later, in January 1976, Turner diversified the company by purchasing Major League Baseball's Atlanta Braves. Later in the same year, on December 17, he originated the "superstation" concept, transmitting the station's signal to cable systems nationwide via satellite.

In January 1977, TBS acquired the National Basketball Association's Atlanta Hawks. On June 1, 1980, Turner inaugurated CNN, the world's first round-the-clock news television network. A second all-news service, Headline News, began operation on Jan. 1, 1982, offering updated newscasts every half-hour.

Launched in September 1985, CNN International serves as the company's global news service and is distributed in numerous countries and territories worldwide. Turner started the Goodwill Games in 1985 as an international, world-class, quadrennial, multi-sport competition. The inaugural Goodwill Games were held in July 1986 in Moscow and were followed by the 1990 Games in Seattle, Washington, the 1994 Games in St. Petersburg, Russia, the 1998 Games in New York City, the first winter games in Lake Placid, New York in 2000, and most recently, by the 2001 summer games in Brisbane, Australia.

In March 1986, TBS acquired the MGM library of film and television properties. This library formed the initial programming cornerstone of TNT, which was launched on Oct. 3, 1988. Versions of TNT are customised for Latin America and the Caribbean, with programming available in English, Spanish or Portuguese. In December 1991, Turner acquired the rights, library and production facilities of Hanna-Barbera Cartoons. Cartoon Network, launched on Oct. 1, 1992, showcases the company's vast library of cartoons and original productions. Cartoon Network in Latin America was launched on April 30, 1993, offering viewers in Latin America and the Caribbean 24 hours of cartoons in three languages. TNT and Cartoon Network were launched in Europe on Sept. 17, 1993, offering classic films and animation programming in seven languages. TNT and Cartoon Network in Asia Pacific, launched Oct. 6, 1994, provides programming in English, with some programmes dubbed or subtitled in Mandarin and Thai. In January 1994, Turner Broadcasting merged with New Line Cinema. Films from New Line and the combined Turner and Warner Bros. library of *film greats* provide programming for Turner Classic Movies (TCM), a 24-hour commercial-free network launched in April 1994.

Turner Broadcasting continued to expand its news division with the creation of CNN Radio and CNN Airport Network, which provides programming for airline travellers in many US airports, and CNN.com, the division responsible for multimedia/on-line news production and distribution. Combining the resources of CNN and Sports, illustrated to create a 24-hour sports news network, Turner launched CNN/SI on Dec. 10, 1996. CNN en Español, which was launched on March 17, 1997, offers 24-hour Spanish-language news to viewers throughout the Americas.

Turner has been the recipient of numerous honorary degrees, industry awards and civic honours, including being named Time magazine's 1991 Man of the Year and Cable and Broadcasting's Man of the Century in 1999. Turner was inducted into the Cable TV Hall of Fame in 1999, and in June 2000 he received the World Ecology Award from the University of Missouri. He is also a superior yachtsman, having won national and world sailing titles, including a successful defence of the 1977 America's Cup, the 1979 Fastnet Trophy and four Yachtsman of the Year awards. In October 1995, Turner accepted the Atlanta Braves' first World Championship trophy on behalf of the team. In August 2000, he was inducted into the Atlanta Braves Hall of Fame.

Turner has also made his mark as one of the most influential philanthropists in the US. He directs most of his philanthropic activities through the Turner Foundation (turnerfoundation.org), which was founded in 1991, the United Nations Foundation (unfoundation.org), which was created in 1997, and the Nuclear Threat Initiative (nti.org), which was launched in January 2001. Turner is Chairman of the Turner Foundation, which grants up to $50 million annually to support the following efforts: 1) clean water and toxics reduction; 2) clean air through improved energy efficiency and renewables; 3) wildlife habitat protection; and 4) the development of equitable practices and policies designed to reduce population growth rates. The Turner Foundation has made grants to hundreds of organisations including: Advocates for Youth, Alliance for

Affordable Energy, American Bird Conservancy, Global Green USA, the Georgia Campaign for Adolescent Pregnancy Prevention, National Audubon Society, National Academy of Sciences, National Museum of the American Indian, National Public Radio, National Safe Energy Communications Council, Save the Bay, Self Reliance Foundation, Sierra Club, Thurgood Marshall Scholarship Fund, Union of Concerned Scientists, and the World Watch Institute. In addition, the Turner Community Youth Development Initiative provides support for locally designed youth development programmes in 30 rural communities near Turner's properties. The Turner Endangered Species Fund (www.tesf.org) is a core grantee of the Turner Foundation, which works to conserve biodiversity by emphasising efforts on private land, particularly on the Turner properties. Endangered species, which have been reintroduced or restored, include black-footed ferrets, condors, desert bighorn sheep, prairie dogs, Mexican wolves, red-cockaded woodpeckers and West Slope cutthroat trout.

In September 1997, Turner announced his historic gift of $1 billion over ten years to the United Nations Foundation. Since its inception, the organisation has granted approximately $100 million each year to support the goals and objectives of the United Nations to promote a more peaceful, prosperous and just world. UNF has identified four core priorities: women and population; children's health; the environment; and peace and security. In early 2001, Turner launched the Nuclear Threat Initiative, a foundation he co-chairs with former Senator Sam Nunn. The Nuclear Threat Initiative is working to close the growing and increasingly dangerous gap between the threat from nuclear, chemical and biological weapons and the global response. The Initiative is a place of common ground where people with different ideological views can work together to make real and significant progress to reduce the risk of use and prevent the spread of weapons of mass destruction. The Foundation is committed to increasing public awareness, encouraging dialogue, and catalysing action and promoting new thinking about reducing the danger from nuclear, chemical and biological weapons on a global basis. Turner has pledged at least $250 million over five years to the organisation. Through Turner Enterprises, Turner manages the largest commercial bison herd in North America, with approximately 27,000-head spread amongst his 14 ranches in Montana, New Mexico, Oklahoma, South Dakota, Kansas and Nebraska. In addition, Turner owns property in California, Florida, Georgia, South Carolina and Argentina. The mission of Turner Enterprises is to manage Turner lands in an economically sustainable and ecologically sensitive manner, while conserving native species. Turner also enjoys several outdoor sports, especially hunting and fishing.

Murdoch

Rupert Murdoch was born in Melbourne, Australia, on 11 March 1931. Murdoch studied at Oxford and worked at the *Daily Express* for 2 years. He returned to Australia in 1952, when he inherited *The Adelaide News* (his first paper) from his father Sir Keith Murdoch, a Melbourne publisher and a famous war correspondent.

Young Rupert transformed a rather small newspaper from a small town into a major success and boosted circulation by emphasising crime, sex, scandal, sports, and human-interest stories, while taking an outspokenly conservative editorial stance.

In the 60's, he did the same with the *Mirror* in Sydney as well as the *News of the World* and *The Sun* in London. In the 70's he turned *The New York Post* from a serious, stagnant paper into a provocative paper. Murdoch acquired *The Times* and *The Sunday Times* in London in the 1980's and he took on Hollywood by purchasing 20th Century Fox and Fox TV that same year. Asia was the next spot for Murdoch, where he purchased Star Television in the 90's. Today the News Corporation includes: a lion's share of the newspaper industry in Australia and approximately one-third of British newspapers and BSkyB (satellite television in Britain) and businesses in most media industries on three continents.

In addition to holdings in the media, Murdoch owns the LA Dodgers, the National Rugby League, Broadsystem, and Fox Interactive. He has successfully ventured into the Internet market as well, with his LineOne Service, among others.

HarperCollins Publishers

An American citizen since 1985, he is seen as having a right-wing political stance. It is also widely believed that he has lowered the quality of everything he has ever worked on. Although he has saved many publications, Murdoch believes that the main reason he receives so much criticism is because he embraces change and describes himself as a "catalyst for change". He is the man who reshaped Fleet Street in the 1980s by taking on the print unions and single-handedly created a pay TV market in UK in the 1990s.

His empire was at the risk of crumbling because of Murdoch's huge expenses during the recession of the early 90's. Luckily, because most of his bankers trusted Murdoch, they agreed to erase his debts incurred from the amount of loans he had taken all over the world. Chairman and CEO of a Corporation whose net worth is $5.3 billion, Murdoch has bounced back from whatever downfalls he has experienced in the past.

Thus, in about four decades, Murdoch has created the very model of the modern media mogul. He started in the '50s' with a small daily newspaper in Australia's hinterlands, and today leads one of the world's largest media empires. His News Corporation had total assets as of June 30, 2002 of approximately US$40 billion and total annual revenues of approximately US$15 billion. News Corporation's diversified global operations in the United States, Canada, continental Europe, the United Kingdom, Australia, Latin America and the Pacific Basin include the production of motion pictures and television programming; television, satellite and cable broadcasting; the publication of newspapers, magazines and books; the production and distribution of promotional and advertising products and services; the development of digital broadcasting; the development of conditional access and subscriber management systems; and the creation and distribution of popular on-line programming.

In his address to News Corporation's 2002 annual meeting on 9 October 2002, Chairman Murdoch reported, "In Asia, STAR was profitable for the second half of the fiscal year, a first-time achievement for our pan-Asian television platform. STAR Plus in

India was broadcasting an average of 19 of the top 20 cable shows every week by the end of fiscal 2002 and STAR is now making significant inroads in Southern China and Taiwan. We expect STAR to be modestly profitable for the current fiscal year, a sign that our faith in this platform is about to be rewarded".

Murdoch was under heavy criticism after his publishing company, HarperCollins, cancelled a book by former Hong Kong governor Chris Patten, that was critical of the Chinese leadership. Earlier Murdoch had been accused of placing profit before principle with regard to China. In 1994, he removed the BBC World Service from his satellite broadcasts into China at the request of the authorities there, who did not like a programme BBC aired about Mao Tse-tung. Murdoch had also been attacked for giving Deng Xiaoping's daughter a huge (reportedly $1 million-plus) HarperCollins book contract for a fawning – and historically flawed and commercially nonviable – portrait of her father at a time when Murdoch was seeking approval to expand his broadcasting ventures in China.

Murdoch's firing of editors Harold Evans of *The Times* (in 1982) and Andrew Neil of *The Sunday Times* (in 1994) were both widely felt to be over reporting by the papers that angered the Tory government, during a period when government decisions were massively enriching the tycoon. Murdoch is accused of using some of his media outlets for more than simple financial gain. HarperCollins has repeatedly paid stunning book advances to public figures who can be – or have been – enormously helpful on the political front. Since such books rarely earn back their advances, they appear to be outright gifts – or worse

In 1967, he married Anna Troy, whom he met while she was a trainee reporter on the *Sydney Daily Mirror*. After being married for 31 years, the couple got divorced in 1998. He is presently married to Wendy Deng, who formerly worked for Star TV in Hong Kong.

Disney

Walt Disney (Walter E. Disney) built first multimedia empire on animation. He was born in poverty on 5 December 1901 in Chicago. His father Elias was one of those feckless figures who wandered the heartland at the turn of the century seeking success in many occupations but always finding failure. Before leaving home at 16 to join the Red Cross Ambulance Corps during World War I, Walt, the youngest son, had attended art classes. In the service he kept drawing, and when he was mustered out, he set up shop as a commercial artist in Kansas City, Mo. There he discovered animation, a new field, and wide open to an ambitious young man.

He moved to Hollywood and opened a carton studio in 1923, which was managed by his brother Roy O. Disney. In 1928, Disney launched Mickey Mouse. Mickey owed a lot of his initial success to Disney's technological acuity, for Disney was the first to add a music and effects track to a cartoon, and that, coupled with anarchical inventive animation, wowed audiences, especially in the early days of sound, when live-action films were hobbled to immobile microphones.

Artistically, the 1930s were Disney's best years. He embraced Technicolor as readily as he had sound. Though he was a poor animator, he proved to be a first-class gagman and story editor, a sometimes collegial, sometimes bullying, but always hands-on boss, driving his growing team of youthfully enthusiastic artists to ever-greater sophistication of technique and expression. When Disney risked everything on his first feature, "Snow White and the Seven Dwarfs,", which premiered in 1937 it turned out to be a great success.

Artistically he strove for realism. There had been some good times in his childhood when the Disneys settled on a farm outside little Marceline, Mo., and he used his work to celebrate the uncomplicated sweetness of the small-town life and values he had only briefly tasted.

Though he enjoyed being a hero to the culturally conservative, his focus always was on new technologies. He became the first Hollywood mogul to embrace television. The show with him as host for over a decade became not just a profit centre for his company but also a promotional engine for his ventures. These included chuckle-headed live-action comedies, nature documentaries that relentlessly anthropomorphised their subjects, and, of course, Disneyland, which attracted his compulsive attention in the 50s' and 60s'.

Disneyland was another all out risk as Disney threw himself obsessively into the theme park's design, which anticipated many of the best features of modern urban planning, and into the "imagineering" by which the simulacrums of exotic, even dangerous creatures, places, fantasies could be unthreateningly reproduced. These attractions were better than any movie in his eyes—three dimensional and without narrative problems. They were, indeed, better than life, for they offered false but momentarily thrilling experiences in a sterile, totally controlled environment from which dirt, rudeness, mischance (and anything approaching authentic emotion) had been totally eliminated. All his other enterprises had to be delivered into the possibly uncomprehending world. When Disneyland opened in 1955 that changed: he now had his own small world, which people had to experience on his terms.

Before he died of cancer at 65 in 1966 in Los Angeles, he had at last devised a machine with which he could endlessly tinker. The little boy, envious of the placid small-town life from which he was shut out, had become mayor—no, absolute dictator—of a land where he could impose his ideals on everyone. The restless, hungry young entrepreneur had achieved undreamed-of wealth, power and honour. Asked late in life what he was proudest of, he did not mention smiling children or the promulgation of family values. "The whole damn thing," he snapped, "the fact that I was able to build an organisation and hold it."

An ugly 1941 labour dispute ended his dream of managing his studio on a communitarian basis with himself as its benign patriarch. Commercially, this worked out beautifully for him. Walt Disney Company (NYSE: DIS) is now a diversified worldwide entertainment company with operations in three segments: Creative Content, Broadcasting and Theme Parks and Resorts.

Disney Online, a business unit of the Walt Disney Internet Group, was founded in 1995 to develop the company's presence in the online world. Headquartered in North Hollywood, California, with satellite offices in New York, Chicago, San Francisco, and Detroit, Disney Online's in-house development studios produce a variety of innovative and highly trafficked destinations on the World Wide Web.

But the most significant thing Walt Disney made was a good name for him. It was, of course, long ago converted into a brand name, constantly fussed over, ferociously defended, first by Disney, latter by his corporate heirs.

Public Service Broadcasting

With the might of big corporations being felt, there is more and more stress on Public Service Broadcasting (PSB). It is an ideal that is difficult to realise, as it has to serve public independently of the state as well as commercial interests. National broadcasters getting funds from public exchequer have historically formed a vital component of the broadcasting sector in most countries. These broadcasters can offer alternative programming to that provided by the commercial sector. But in many countries the governing authorities exert control over such broadcasters

Quality public service broadcasting requires three elements: free and independent broadcasting organisations, with sufficient resources to provide quality news, information, education and entertainment programming, subject to public accountability for the way in which they fulfil their mandates and utilise public resources. The ideal public broadcasting system requires that the independence of public service broadcaster must be guaranteed by appropriate structures. The trend among governments is to cut budgets. It has resulted in increased pressure on these broadcasters for search of alternative sources of funding. And this in some cases leads to double disadvantage to independence, as they are obliged to mend their mandates to the tunes of the government and private sector both. In many countries it is difficult to find difference between the privately owned as well as partially public funded broadcasters.

National broadcasters, in theory, can become public service broadcasters if their independence from both the state and commercial interests is ensured by statutory provisions and providing sufficient funding. But in practice, it requires a lot of maturity among the ruling elite who do not succumb to temptation to use them for partisan ends, ensure plurality through wide variety of quality programming that adequately informs, educates and provides healthy entertainment to all sections of public. Media activists all over the world should work towards this end.

Children

Because children are seen as having special media needs and as being easily molded by television messages, a large number of scholars have taken up the issue of the impact of television on children and its possible policy implications.

TV has emerged as a formidable rival to the authority of parents over children and teachers over their pupils. The Lord Annon Committee in Britain noted, "Television might in some ways be taking the place of the family, church or school in influencing children's outlook."

Will the teachers and the parents find in TV a wholesome ally in shaping the consciousness of the growing child? Or will the TV result in moral and mental disorientation of children? Many parents feel that TV programmes over-expose the child to the glamour of modern life. Films depicting sex, crime and violence being viewed by children with their parents are creating new problems and new anxieties.

The Children's Television Act (CTA) was passed by the US Congress in 1990 in response to the failure of the broadcast television industry to serve the educational and informational needs of children. Broadcasters served "junk food for the mind," and featured many shows that were thinly disguised commercials for action toys and other products. The Act required stations to demonstrate how they were serving the educational and informational needs of children. Under the CTA, some of this programming had to be "specifically designed" to educate. Stations were obliged to inform the FCC, as part of their license renewal process, how they were fulfilling this new mandate. Another part of the CTA placed some limits on the amount of commercials that could air on children's television. Every eight years, stations are required to report to the FCC how well they have served the public in order to have their free licensed use of the airwaves renewed.

The FCC has also adopted rules requiring all television sets with picture screens, 33 centimeters (13 inches) or larger, to be equipped with features to block the display of television programming based upon its rating. This technology is known as the "V-Chip." The V-Chip reads information encoded in the rated programme and blocks programme from the set based upon the rating selected by the parent. Pursuant to the Commission's rules, half of all new television models, 13 inches or larger, manufactured after July 1, 1999, and all sets, 13 inches or larger, manufactured after January 1, 2000 must have V-Chip technology. Set top boxes that allow consumers to use V-Chip technology on their existing sets are now available.

In Section 551 of the Telecommunications Act of 1996, Congress gave the broadcasting industry the first opportunity to establish voluntary ratings. The industry established a system for rating programming that contains sexual, violent or other material parents may deem inappropriate and committed to voluntarily broadcast signals containing these ratings. The rating system, also known as "TV Parental Guidelines," was established by the National Association of Broadcasters, the National Cable Television Association and the Motion Picture Association of America. These ratings are displayed on the television screen for the first 15 seconds of rated programming and, in conjunction with the V-Chip, permit parents to block programming with a certain rating from coming into their home.

Women

A significant section of social scientists and media researchers is engaged in studies related to women in mass media. These studies cover all continents and show how media have been biased against women. International Association for Mass Communication Research has working groups that share research findings on gender issues. Media ethics studies also deal with issues relating to women.

There are two major concerns related to women in media. One, low employment of women in media particularly at decision-making levels and the other about the image of women projected through media.

Worldwide feminist research has pointed out that the employment of women in media is low and particularly so in decision-making levels. Men, who not only lead women in absolute numbers, but also constitute the bulk of the management or top-editorial ranks, dominate the world's media. If we are to focus on the media of developed as well as developing countries from their earliest history to the present time, we can hardly avoid the obvious conclusion that media have always been male dominated.

As the MacBride Commission has pointed out, "Journalists dealing with serious issues and political events are seldom women, and few women become editors or hold directing positions. In the USA out of 3000 film directors only 23 are women. Although extensively employed as production and continuity assistants, women rarely have the responsibility for taking broad decisions."

Employment figures of individual media institutions in the United States show that the common employment pattern is one in which proportionately more men are hired, especially at the top levels. Sexist bias is a conspicuous feature of the British media, which are accused of biased presentation of women and sex discrimination in hiring. The dominance of white males in some sections of media is defended by arguing that the major career ladders to top positions usually involve professional and educational skills, which are more common with men than women. According to Tunstall, "these factors which discriminate against women (in media) are also common to other occupations and especially in crafts and professions."

As regards portrayal of women the press and television have been identified as major culprits. In print media, the content researchers claim has been biased against women and responsible for projecting women as sex objects and propagate stereotyped roles and negative images. The advertisers emerge as main culprits of this crime.

According to the MacBride Commission, in both developed and developing countries, public attitudes regarding the role of women in society are major determinants in deciding the status of women. In shaping these attitudes, the media exert a strong influence. The media seldom depict women as significantly involved in work, in pursuance of careers, or in public life. A survey of Indian films found that out of 46 women who appeared as characters, only twelve were in employment and nine of these were in traditionally female jobs. A study of fiction in Soviet magazines found that no information about their employment was given in the case of 48 per cent of the female characters while the job status of only nine per cent of the men depicted went unidentified. Women are shown primarily as confined to the domestic sphere, or else as secretaries, assistants and in similar roles ancillary to those of men. Even in domestic and personal situations, women appear as incapable of making decisions without masculine guidance.

Reviewing the world scene the MacBride Commission said, "In general, inadequate attention is paid in the media to issues of specific importance to women: to the activities of the women's movement, or to social contribution made by independent and gifted women. Women appear, in magazine fiction and in television drama and comedy, as self-deprecating and dependent, irrational, superstitious and over-emotional. In advertising particularly, women are shown either as housewives whose interests are limited to domestic needs, or else as sexually alluring background which makes consumer goods more attractive by association... A number of studies conclude that the overall effect of the portrayal of women in the media is to reinforce, rather than reduce, prejudices and stereotypes. This distortion tends to justify and perpetuate existing inequalities."

Portrayal of women in radio has not attracted much research attention, probably because radio has been playing second fiddle to television which is not only newer but also more controversial. Indications are that radio is one of the least prejudiced media in portrayal of women's images. Butler and Paisley concluded that analyses of some radio content for the sex bias show that neither sex has the corner on goodness, badness or weakness.

Television, 'the most pervasive medium' and 'master of image and illusion' had been extensively studied. The consensus of the results is that both the programmes and commercials are highly biased against women.

In India the situation has been summarised by the Joshi Working Group on Software for Doordarshan, "Middle class ideologies of women's role as wives and mothers provide the underlying basis for most programmes. In a country where 36 per cent of the agricultural workforce is female, women continue to be projected as predominantly non-producers and as playing a limited role outside the home. Women are basically seen as performing a decorative function and as being marginal to national growth and development. Their primary place is seen as being within the home and this value is reflected in the content and setting of most television programmes. The plural nature of Indian culture and diverse role that women play is neither acknowledged nor communicated. This results in reinforcing of the stereotyped images and role specifications of women and in a unidimentional projection of their reality".

The negative stereotypes have been identified as: (1) A woman's place is in the home; (2) The most important and valuable asset of a woman is physical beauty; (3) A woman's energies and intellect must be directed to finding the right man and in "keeping" him; (4) Women are dependent, coy, submissive, they are masochistic in their response to indignities, humiliations and even to physical violence inflicted on them; (5) A good woman is the traditional housewife, long suffering, pious and submissive; the modern woman who asserts herself and her independence is undesirable and can never bring happiness to anybody nor find happiness herself; (6) Women are women's worst enemies; (7) The working woman is the undesirable exception who must be brought into the marriage fold and made to conform to social norms, etc. Awareness of these issues will certainly help to improve the programming.

The Joshi Working Group on Software had also deliberated on this issue. Its report pointed out, "Values form from the earliest ages. Girls are socialised to be passive, submissive, and docile because they grow up with such role models, which also define their lives as a preparation towards marriage and motherhood in almost total exclusion of any other aspect. Therefore it is important that the children's programme should be always conscious of projecting the values of equality and breaking those of sex stereotypes."

It recommended, "All advertisement shown on television must be scrutinised carefully by a special committee to ensure that they do not portray women in derogatory and stereotyped ways."

The bias against women should have decreased with increasing number of women now getting jobs in media but the situation has not changed much because of commercial considerations. In fact women are divided on issues like beauty contests as many spend lot of talent and resources to compete while others protest against such events.

The situation has been summed up in the document adopted by International Symposium: *'Women and the Media, Access to Expression and Decision-Making* – organised by Unesco at Toronto, *Canada (February 28 - March 3,* 1995), popularly known as Toronto Platform For Action. "In the past twenty years, the world has seen explosion in the field of communications. With advances in computer technology and satellite and cable TV, global access to information, when democratically used continues to increase and expand creating new opportunities for the participation of women in communication and media and for dissemination of information about women. However, all these developments bring about new threats. They may affect negatively the existing cultures and prevailing values of receiving countries. With the reemergence in some countries of reactionary beliefs, media are also becoming a weapon of domination and obscurantism. Finally the present global situation in media shows the perpetuation and reinforcement of negative images of women that do not provide an accurate or realistic picture of women's multiple roles and contributions to a changing world. Even more insidious are use by media of women's bodies as sex objects and the violence against women as "entertainment". Greater involvement by women in both the technical and decision-making areas of communication and media would increase awareness of women's lives from their own perspective."

The number of jobs given to women cannot be considered in absolute terms, as number of women looking for such jobs is still small as compared to men. The problem is with society at large and not just with media alone. The media are not the fundamental cause of the subordinate status of women, nor can the media alone remedy it.

There are many other factors for the situation, which should not be ignored while considering these issues. Saida Bano who was the first woman announcer at the Lucknow station of AIR in early forties, recalled the strong opposition of her orthodox family to her working at a place where she might come into contact with 'immoral professional singing girls'. She was able to get her way only when she assured them (not truthfully though) that such persons used a separate entrance to the studios. She later became the first woman newsreader of AIR. Women have been doing well in the area of news presentation on electronic media since then. Situation further improved when television came and spread.

Education and Rural Development

From the very beginning mass media, particularly radio and television, have been regarded very powerful as they can cross the frontier of literacy as well as national boundaries. Politicians and nation builders were attracted to them for the immense power they were supposed to possess for educating and mobilising the masses.

In India, even before Independence, the National Planning Committee (appointed by the Indian National Congress in 1938 with Jawaharlal Nehru as its Chairman) had realised the importance of broadcasting. Its subcommittee on communications observed (circa 1940), "Broadcasting, though it is of recent origin has developed so fast that from a luxury it has become a necessity in all advanced countries. It has now become a powerful tool in the hands of any government which knows how to use it. One cannot exaggerate its enormous influence in shaping the character and political views of a nation."

The NPC enumerated principal functions of broadcasting as follows:

1. Dissemination of news and useful information;
2. Adult education; fighting rural ignorance;
3. Propaganda by the state;
4. Entertainment.

"In planning for the development of broadcasting all the above aspects should be kept in view."

NPC emphasised, "It should not be forgotten that in view of the fact that the vast majority of the population is still illiterate and large sections of the women population do not go out in public, radio broadcasting is perhaps the most effective link between such sections and the progressive part of India. Radio also provides an easy channel for bringing to the masses useful information on agriculture, animal husbandry, current political thoughts, etc".

The NPC resolution of 25 June 1940 said regarding the future policy, "Communications and broadcasting are public utility services affecting the well-being of the community and are at present under the state control. They should be public monopolies and should be run on commercial lines and developed intensively, subject to the paramount consideration that they are social services and as such powerful agents in the task of national development."

The resolution advocated, "A fuller and more intensive use of broadcasting should be made for dissemination of news and useful information, education generally and more particularly adult education, publicity for social reforms and progressive measures and entertainment". This is an example of how the leaders of developing countries looked at broadcasting.

Radio and television are capable of transcending the literacy barrier and therefore could have become media for mass education. There have been efforts in this direction in all countries with variable effect. In India the national education policy (1986) has stressed, "Modern communication technologies have the potential to by-pass several stages and sequences in the process of development envisaged in the early decades. Both the constraints of time and distance at once become manageable. In order to avoid structural dualism, modern technology must reach out to the most distant areas and most deprived sections of beneficiaries simultaneously with the areas of comparative affluence and ready availability."

Radio has been extensively used for educational purposes all over the world. Countries, which have been anxious to spread language learning or to give formal or non-formal education at various levels have found radio to be an effective medium. Australia started using radio to teach children in the remote "outback" territories in 1932. In India there has been the Radio Pilot Project in the Centre for Educational Technology (NCERT) when radio lessons were used to teach Hindi in the primary schools of Rajasthan. It has given satisfactory results as revealed through the evaluation reports. The students gained in vocabulary and comprehension. The packaged lessons are now being distributed through audio cassettes by Central Institute of Educational Technology.

In distance education, radio has been used as an important component of multi-media approach. The advantage of the radio is that all over the world it is in the reach of the common man and can be carried from place to place easily. Open universities in the West and in Asia have relied on radio quite heavily. In British Open University a typical full credit course, a weekly unit, consisted of one text unit, some broadcast notes, one television programme of 25 minutes and one radio programme of 20 minutes. The radio programmes were meant to be heard directly as broadcast and each programme was broadcast twice to give more students the opportunity to listen to it at least once and also give some students the opportunity of listening to it twice. Andhra Pradesh Open University in India used radio for six hours a week while in Thailand STOU lessons are broadcast over radio for about 50 hours a week.

Television offers certain unique features of application in education that were not available earlier. Complex expensive experiments, field visits, microscopic observations, advanced technical equipment, archival films, interviews with distinguished people and authorities on the various subjects are some of the experiences that can be offered to students through TV. Language teaching can be effectively done through dramatised situations and pronunciation drills. The complete scientific experiment which may take a few hours can be shown in just a few minutes. In UK, the open university uses television for 35 hours a week. The Television and Radio University in China uses television as a lead medium making up 45% of the course, 15 hours viewing per week.

The Joshi Working Group on Software for Doordarshan discussed the ETV and said, "Under Indian conditions, ETV can be used to supplement and correct the deficiencies, inadequacies and gaps of routine instruction. It can help in highly specialised fields to meet the deficiencies of qualified and trained teachers by providing access to lectures by eminent instructors and teachers to pupils in all parts of the country. It can play a very important role in teacher training."

The Working Group on Software for Doordarshan emphasised the need for using television as an effective means for drive against illiteracy but also said, "Television which is an audio-visual medium is based on the principle of 'knowing through seeing and hearing' rather then 'knowing through reading'. Television programmes can educate the masses, up to a point without their first being literate. A peasant or an artisan or a labourer, therefore, can with the aid of television cross the barrier of literacy and grasp the fundamentals of first stage education related to his work and to improving his skills in his work."

In India, Delhi School Television Project was started in 1961 in which about 3000 television sets were installed in schools. SITE was perhaps the biggest ever experiment in ETV. Several organisations are now engaged in the task of producing educational television(ETV) programmes including: Central Institute of Educational Technology (CIET) and six State Institutes of Educational Technology at Ahmedabad, Bhubneshwar, Hyderabad, Lucknow, Patna and Pune; Technical Teachers Training Institutes at Bhopal, Calcutta, Chandigarh and Madras; Central Institute of Indian Languages, Mysore; Indira Gandhi Open University, New Delhi and University Grants Commission's audio-visual research centres and educational media research centres located in several universities.

Despite all this the use of radio and television in education in India is far from satisfactory. One major reason is lack of television sets in schools and colleges and at the homes of poor students. However, there is also a philosophic disagreement among many teachers traditionally accustomed to communication through talk-and-chalk. Some feel that the ETV programmes should be syllabus oriented while others feel that they should have enrichment orientation. As the programmes have fixed broadcast timings their usefulness is limited. As such the schools not only require TV sets there is a need for VCRs or VCPs for repeating the programmes if required or playing VHS tapes.

For the policy makers of developing world rural development is top priority and all efforts should be made to use modern means to achieve this target. One of the major reasons of poverty in countries like India is lack of information and education. Modern era has presented means to reach the masses more effectively. This is the age of information revolution and rural areas should not be allowed to remain distant form the changes in the global environment.

The MacBride Commission says, "In developing countries, radio is the only medium that can really be labelled "mass", where a large proportion of the population can be reached by radio broadcasts and possess the means to receive them." No other medium now has the potential to reach so many people so efficiently for information, education, cultural and entertainment purposes. Radio can be used easily and economically to reach outlying regions and for communication in many vernacular, often unwritten, languages existing in developing countries.

There is another reason why radio will remain very important mass medium in the developing world for a very long time to come. Production of radio programmes is much cheaper as compared to television and therefore radio is today the least transnationalised mass medium, both in terms of ownership and programme flows, because almost all countries have a certain capacity to produce radio programmes in line with their political needs, cultural patterns and basic values.

In India, even before Independence the National Planning Committee emphasised the use of radio as means for communication for rural development. During those days medium-wave radio broadcasting was supposed to be high quality and NPC advocated to cover the nation with a network of medium-wave transmitters.

These days FM broadcasting is being adopted increasingly as it provides the listeners with high quality signal, relatively free from interference. Moreover if employs hitherto unused high frequencies in overcrowded radio spectrum. FM broadcasting for local services is capable for expansion in a way which would relieve much of the present burden in the low, medium and high frequency bands and thus improve conditions for national, regional and international transmissions. The introduction of FM broadcasting is therefore of special interest to developing countries and particularly to tropical areas affected by solar interference. All India Radio has also taken to FM in a big way. Private FM stations are there but they are mainly for urban audience.

Thus, with the passage of time technology may keep changing and adapting to circumstances, but radio is here to stay. For developing countries like India where poverty abounds and is not likely to vanish early radio will continue to be the prime mass medium.

What Lord Irwin said in 1927 about radio holds true even today, "India offers special opportunities for the development of broadcasting. Its distances and wide space alone make it a promising field. In India's remote villages there are many who, after the day's work is done, find time hang heavily enough upon their hands, and there must be many officials and others whose duties carry them into out-of-the-way places where they crave for the company of and the solace of human companionship. There are of course, too, in many households those whom social custom debars from taking part in recreation outside their homes. To all these and many more broadcasting will be a blessing and a boon of real value. Both for entertainment and for education its possibilities are great, and as yet we perhaps scarcely realise how great they are."

Television has shown its worth for education and rural development during the famous SITE experience. Through SITE in

India villagers in about 400 selected villages had the experience of television much earlier than most city dwellers. However, as said earlier this medium has not been able to cross poverty barrier because of high cost of receivers. Unfortunately, urban-oriented programmes have taken over the wisdom box and made it an idiot box like the West.

The availability and maintenance of community sets in villages is poor. There are certain other problems because of the composition of Indian society relating to a variety of cultural and linguistic pattern. During the SITE these problems had been looked into. There are rural programmes no doubt but the usefulness of such programmes has been questioned. In broadcasting repetition is not immediately possible. It appears that to counter such problems educational and informative programmes on cassettes to be played in villages on community VCPs seems to be the only solution. Government can go for mass production of such equipment and programmes. With computers reaching some Panchayats and schools, even educational CDs would be useful. The multilingual experience of films division and field publicity units could be useful in this regard.

Community Media

Another alternative to supplement or to fill the void which is left uncovered by the state-funded and the commercial broadcasters is community media. With low cost broadcast technologies becoming available this seems to be a partial answer to the local needs. The concept of community radio developed in the West as an alternative to mainstream broadcast media. Pirate stations have been a major factor in motivating governments and national broadcasting systems to introduce legitimate local radio in Europe. In Latin America the thrust was to use radio as a medium to support education of the poor, the job that was not being done by private broadcasters that dominated the scene. In Africa, establishment of community radio became a kind of social movement as the wave of democracy and decentralisation swept large parts of the continent after the end of apartheid regime in South Africa. Unesco also played some role in putting some community radio stations on the ground. Community radio project in Homa-bay in Kenya and Mahaweli in Sri Lanka in the early 1980s are among some of the earliest Unesco efforts in this direction.

In 1986 the first Asian community radio was operational in Girandurukotte, in Sri Lanka under the Unesco-sponsored Mahaweli Community Radio project. In fact, the project was started in 1980 as a community programme service, serving the Mahaweli settlements under which nearly 60,000 families were resettled downstream the Mahaweli River. The purpose of this community radio was to cater to the needs of newly-settled families enabling them to exchange settlement experiences, learn skills from each other, to give timely information on day-today activities and help catalysing development in the new communities. It was complete a new experience where both young and mature members of the settler's families functioned as volunteer broadcasters, identified various settlement issues, animated the community through their own programmes, much of which also related to cultural expressions which they brought from their place of origins. A lively interaction between settlers and field officers responsible for various settlement administration matters broadcast over the community radio enabled the policy makers responsible for settlements to learn about problems and prospects of the settlements. Mahaweli community radio in Sri Lanka was administratively under the national broadcaster Sri Lanka Broadcasting Corporation. Three such radio stations are still functioning.

However, the first truly community-owned and operated Asian community radio stations were established in the Philippines with Unesco supported Thambuli Community radio project. "Thambuli Community Radio Project" set up a management and training team that co-operates with communities to organise independent community radio stations in less developed rural areas.

Then it was Nepal with community radio Sagaramatha, in its capital Kathmandu. The radio station was established with financial and technical assistance provided under Unesco's International Programme for the Development of Communication (IPDC). Unesco also intervened with the government to obtain the broadcasting licence for radio Sagaramatha after democracy was ushered in. Following this model six other such radios have come up.

Regional Unions and Exchanges

For the purpose of programme and news exchange, broadcasters have associated within regional unions such as the Arab States Broadcasting Union (ASBU), the Asia Pacific Broadcasting Union (ABU), the Caribbean Broadcasting Union (CBU), the European Broadcasting Union (EBU), the Union of National Radio and Television Organizations of Africa (URTNA), which arrange for inter-member transmissions. For example, the Unions lease national and international circuits for daily news exchange among their members, including reserve circuits as necessary.

International assistance has been instrumental in creating the operational networks of the unions of developing regions (**Afrovision, Arabvision, Asiavision, Caribvision**) which concentrate on news exchange. Innovative uses of ICTs, particularly low-cost multi-point satellite channels, have greatly improved the reach and sustainability of these activities.

The ASBU leases four Satellite channels on Arab Sat 2B – one dedicated for news and the other for programme and sports contribution feeds. Its Exchange Centre in Algiers receives three pre-determined daily news feeds via satellite from numerous Arab television stations, and re-transmits them by not switching to all its members including international networks, news agencies and sister unions.

Since its launch in 1984, Asiavision has been a major source of news for and about Asia. It brings together many of the continent's leading national broadcasters. Its members at present are those in Bangladesh, Brunei, China, India, Indonesia, Iran, Japan, Malaysia, Nepal, Pakistan, Singapore and Sri Lanka.

However, the most successful among these systems is the European one. The European Broadcasting Union (EBU) is an independent, non-governmental, noncommercial body which promotes cooperation in international radio and television broadcasting. It acts as a broker through which broadcasters worldwide can exchange radio and television services, and in particular, news footage and complete programs via Eurovision for television and Euroradio for radio. EBU has its administrative headquarters in Geneva. It also maintains a Eurovision control centre (which moved from Brussels to Geneva in 1993); TV news coordination bureau in New York, Washington and Moscow; and a bureau to the European Union in Brussels.

The EBU was formed in 1950 and is the biggest union of broadcasters in the world. Following the political change in Eastern Europe, 1993 marked the unification of EBU and OIRT (the former umbrella organisation of radio and TV services in Eastern Europe) and the formation of a single broadcasting organisation spanning East and West. In addition, the other broadcasting unions feed material into and take from Eurovision's news exchanges, including Asiavision, Arabvision, and OTI/SIN for Latin America. The same applies to the major news film agencies. The coverage of US news and other events in the Americas for Europe's televiewers and listeners is coordinated by EBU's TV news coordination bureaus in New York and Washington.

In addition to programme exchange, EBU is also concerned with organising pools for broadcasting major events – such as the Olympic Games and the World Football Cup – and negotiating rights for its members for such events. It has a programme of international live concert seasons, linking up countries as far apart as the United States, Japan and Australia for live stereophonic radio transmissions and for live opera seasons on television and radio. The EBU's members jointly finance the satellite circuits required for these exchanges. The television news items are then exchanged free of copyright between all participants, including contributions from the television news agencies. Individual news items are distributed on a dedicated Permanent News Channel. Live coverage, mainly intended for a growing number of national all-news channels, is assigned to the Permanent Events Network. News coverage is made available to participants as quickly as possible in news flashes.

The EBU has a permanent one-way satellite link across the Atlantic for channelling US news to Europe – primarily for injecting American news material (chosen by EBU's New York and Washington offices) into the Eurovision news service, but also for US-based correspondents of EBU member-broadcasters to feed material to Europe. The network also has a link to Asia which can be used for special events. The EBU uses 20 digital satellite channels and 6,000 km of terrestrial circuits to ensure the annual distribution to members of over 25,000 TV news items and 4,000 programmes on an average.

EBU-member broadcasting organisations pooled their resources and know-how to launch, on January 1, 1993, the first round-the-clock European news channel. Based in Lyon, France, Euronews is a public service programme brought free of charge to viewers in Europe.

Radio programmes exchanges via Euroradio take place according to demand rather than at a fixed time of day. The Euroradio satellite network carries, on an average, some 2,000 concerts and operas, 400 sports events, and 120 major news events each year.

NWICO Relevant

There has been a debate for about two decades in the last century, which called for removal of imbalance in information and communication among countries. This debate in Non-Aligned Movement, Unesco and UN finally resulted in walkout of UK and US from Unesco. The world did not get a New World Information and Communication Order (NWICO) which should have been more just and more balanced today.

"Big Ten" media giants, all Western – AOL Time Warner, Disney, General Electric, News Corporation, Viacom, Vivendi, Sony, Bertelsmann, AT&T and Liberty Media – with all their economic clout and cultural sway keep the world fully entertained and permanently half-informed.

They represent the grand convergence of the previously disparate US culture industries, many of them vertically monopolised already into one global superindustry, providing most of our imaginary "content." The monoculture, endlessly and noisily triumphant, offers, by and large, a lot of nothing, whether packaged as "the news" or "entertainment".

A media system that enlightens us, that tells us everything we need to know pertaining to our lives and liberty and happiness, would be a system dedicated to the public interest. Such a system would not be controlled by a cartel of giant corporations, because those entities are ultimately hostile to the welfare of the people. Whereas we need to know the truth about such corporations, they often have an interest in suppressing it (as do their advertisers). And while it takes much time and money to find out the truth, the parent companies prefer to cut the necessary costs of journalism.

The media's big bosses want big favours from the state, while the reporters are afraid to risk annoying their best sources. Despite the stubborn fiction of their "liberal" prejudice, the corporate media have helped deliver a punch or two to democracy the world over. Particularly on television news front people really felt the need for the NWICO more than ever before at the time of recent wars in Yugoslavia, Afghanistan and Iraq. Under AOL Time Warner, GE, Viacom et. al., the news is, with a few exceptions, yet another version of the entertainment that the cartel also vends nonstop. The news divisions of the media cartel appear to work against the public interest and for their parent companies, their advertisers and the US government.

The MacBride Commission Report, *Communication and Society Today and Tomorrow: Many Voices One World: Towards a New, More Just and More Efficient World Information and Communication Order* was published by Unesco in 1982. Though some parts of it have really become obsolete, this historic document is still relevant, as things have gone worse. The cold war had killed that effort and its end and the new media order that has emerged requires revisiting NWICO.

Media and War

The war in Iraq in 2003 and its coverage by CNN, BBC, AP and Reuters has once again highlighted the importance of media in modern warfare. As the armies all over the world must be analysing the use of various weapons and strategies in this war, it is essential to look at the media angle. As France was not party to this war the coverage provided by AFP and TV-5 was different and more balanced. Al-Jazeera also made its mark by covering the news from the Arab side. It had problems in US during the war.

The Vietnam War was the first to have the use of television and perhaps it could not be managed so well by the US generals and is usually blamed for the US defeat in Vietnam. There had been a lot of controversy about the coverage of Falkland War and also about the US invasion of Grenada when the media was not allowed to go to the war theatre with the invading troops. In the war in the Gulf in 1991, the media management was much improved and perhaps played a major role in projecting mainly the story of the US led forces. In fact, media have been turned into weapons of psychological warfare, which can justify a war and can continue the war of minds without even a formal declaration prior to, during and even after the actual war

During the Vietnam War, the propaganda was that it was a conflict of Vietnamese against Vietnamese into which the US threw their weight on the side of democracy and freedom. This assumption pervaded the media and was in fact quite false and dishonest like the Nazi propaganda when the Germans were overrunning the Czechoslovakia. But it was so insistent and so powerful and insidious that a great many people believed in the fundamental goodness of the US mission. There appeared to be a saturation in media coverage of Vietnam War but big story of the war was not reported until it was virtually over. In the Vietnam War atrocities were neither isolated, nor aberrations. But this was seldom judged to be news and therefore seldom told. With the assumption that the war was right, atrocities were reported as "mistakes" which were "blundered into".

The British term 'pacification', which they used in relation to Ireland, gained currency in Vietnam and became familiar to newspaper readers and television viewers in the West, but whose real meaning was seldom understood. Pacification meant killing as many people as possible in a given area within a given period of time. In 1971, the US Ninth Division killed 11,000 people in a pacification campaign named "Operation Speedy Express". Two diligent *Newsweek* reporters discovered that almost half of these were civilians and this was a mass slaughter condoned and covered up. The reporters wrote the story but six months later, a watered-down version appeared and no one was made responsible. In this sense even in Vietnam the management of media was quite a success.

The ultimate failure of the Vietnam enterprise (1961-1975) became undeniable by April 1975 when Saigon fell to North Vietnamese troops. So painful was the Vietnam experience that both the US Army and civilians seemed to want to put Vietnam out of memory. Many thought that journalists should not have been allowed at all and tried to put the blame of defeat on war coverage. Perhaps the Vietnam controversy led to the decision by the Reagan administration refusing permission for reporters to cover the US invasion of Grenada (October 25, 1983). Furious protests from the media led to a negotiated pool plan for coverage of future military actions. In the NBC Nightly News Commentary, John Chancellor termed the invasion "A bureaucrat's dream: Do anything. No one is watching." Gen. John W. Vessey Jr., Chairman of the Joint Chief's of Staff, appointed a commission to consider future press-military relations headed by retired Gen. Winant Sidle. The result was the "combat-correspondent pool" under which a small handful of physically fit reporters would be taken to combat zones. During the 1989 Panama invasion the scheme failed miserably as the pool was flown to Panama late, then virtually barred from witnessing any fighting for fear that details of civilian casualties would be reported.

By the 1991, during the Gulf War a lot more thought and preparation went in and twelve media combat pools were formed. Two of them, of 18 reporters each, specifically covered US Army and Marine Corps' ground combat activities; eight others, of seven reporters each, split their coverage among the four US armed services. There was a five-member pool to observe naval activities, and there was a "quick reaction" pool sent to areas of hostility on quick basis. Guidelines established by the Pentagon sought "to keep the public informed while protecting the safety of armed forces personnel in combat." Under these rules, reporters covered US combat activities as part of a group, or media "pool," and are escorted to those areas by a Department of Defense (DOD) official. The escort officer on the scene must approve any written or broadcast report before it was released to the other reporters covering the war. Most of the pool reporters covering US forces were those who worked for the US news organisations, although there was a slot for a Saudi reporter and another for a foreign journalist in each of the 18-member combat pools. If there was a disagreement about the contents of a pool report, the report was sent immediately to public affairs officials at the JIB in Dhahran for review by them and the appropriate media organisation. If no agreement was reached at that level, the disputed item was to be sent to Pentagon for review there by DOD officials in conjunction with the reporter's supervisor.

The opportunity to impartially record what happened in the Gulf War was lost; since almost all news came from military sources, independent reporting was virtually impossible and some of the most respected war photographers, including Don McCullin, were not given pool credentials to cover frontline activities.

Only journalists who signed an agreement to abide by US Defense Department restrictions on the coverage of the war were chosen to work in military pools; attempts to move independently were impeded by military roadblocks. Some of the correspondents have complained that they had been accompanied constantly even to the bathroom when on a warship to prevent unsupervised conversation with marines or pilots. Most of the journalists were lodged in a hotel in Riyad from the outbreak of war and were entirely dependent on military personnel for transportation and access to news. The detention of a *New York Times* journalist and confiscation of his credentials demonstrated the imposed constraints of 'pool' coverage after he interviewed local residents in a small border town in Saudi Arabia.

The use of propaganda and the disinformation during the Gulf War was widespread and effective in achieving its purpose. The coalition forces succeeded in giving and maintaining the impression that it was a "clean" war in which the use of high-tech weapons resulted in negligible human casualties. For this purpose wide use was made in press briefings of video films demonstrating the accuracy of the new weapons, military spokesmen avoided discussion on the human cost of the war and a new kind of jargon was introduced (using phrases such as 'collateral damage' for civilian casualties). In spite of the fact that up to 100,000 Iraqi soldiers and unknown number of civilians were killed in the war, there has been little coverage in the media of the unpalatable aspects of the war. There were other uses of media coverage of the Gulf War. It was serving as advertising to promote new weapons. The Patriot missile was advertised and was later sold to the South Koreans who had enough money to pay for the deployment of this new weapon system.

Another interesting feature which got consolidated during Yugoslav and Afghan wars and was also used to great success in Iraq war is multi-point briefings: official briefings from different centres of power. Central Command, Pentagon and White House gave briefings at different times so that television news channels could broadcast all these briefings live. CNN, BBC and Fox could take this one-sided message around the world. During this war even British Parliament became such a centre where Tony Blair and his defence minister could speak on the subject and get live coverage on news networks.

The "embedding" of media persons with US forces is the latest in the use of media in the Iraq war. The public affairs guidance on embedding of media during possible future operations/ deployments in the US Central Command (CENTCOM) area of responsibility were ready on February 3, 2003. The policy paragraph 2.a says, "The Department of Defense (DOD) policy on media coverage of future military operations is that media will have long-term, minimally restrictive access to US air, ground and naval forces through embedding. Media coverage of any future operation will, to a large extent, shape public perception of the national security environment now and in the years ahead. This holds true of the US public; the public in allied countries whose opinion can affect the durability of our coalition; and public in countries where we conduct operations, whose perceptions of us can affect the cost and duration of our involvement. Our ultimate strategic success in bringing peace and security to this region will come in our long-term commitment to supporting our democratic ideals. We need to tell the factual story – good or bad – before others seed the media with disinformation and distortions, as they most certainly will continue to do. Our people in the field need to tell our story – only commanders can ensure the media get to the story alongside the troops. We must organise for and facilitate access of national and international media to our forces, including those forces engaged in ground operations, with a goal of doing so from the start. To accomplish this, we will embed the media with our units. These embedded media will live, work and travel as part of the units with which they are embedded to facilitate maximum, in-depth coverage of the US forces in combat and related operations. Commanders and public affairs officers must work together to balance the need for media access with the need for operational security."

The media representative and the organisation he or she represents before embedding should sign an agreement. By paragraph 4(a) of this agreement the media employee agrees to "participate in the embedding process and to follow the direction and orders of the government related to such participation. The media employee further agrees to follow government regulations. The media employee acknowledges that failure to follow any directions, order, regulation, or ground rule may result in termination of the media employee's participation in the embedding process."

In the Iraq war there were about 500 embedded journalists giving out the US version from different theaters of war and this gave additional support to already established media manipulation practices. It was clear that the news management effort was not to allow the media to give the real picture of the war but to give the impression that enough is being told. However, many journalists also became tools of the authorities in making sure that media war was also won by the US led forces. After the Iraq war experience of 2003, the French are planning to put a French competitor to CNN.

9

Glossary

A

A&R person
The job at a record label of finding and nurturing new talent, working creatively with the artists to find producers and sometimes songs to record and generally overseeing projects. Stands for "artists and repertoire" and derives from the era in which labels helped artists find appropriate material to record.

ABC
American Broadcasting Corporation; also Australian Broadcasting Company

ABU
Asian Broadcasting Union

Access time
Interval between the selection of a computer function and its appearance on the screen.

Action area
Action region within a setting

Actuality
Real

Ad lib
Unrehearsed, unscripted action or speech

ADR (Automated Dialogue Replacement)
The process by which an existing dialogue is replaced with a new voice recording on video and animation.

AIBD
Asia Pacific Institute for Broadcasting and Development

AIR
All India Radio

AM (Amplitude Modulation)
A method of transmitting information by changing the amplitude (strength) of a high frequency carrier wave in proportion to the amplitude of the lower frequency signal. The amplitude-modulated carrier is subsequently detected (demodulated) and the original lower frequency signal is recovered.

AMPEX
Pioneers of videotape recording apparatus. Sometimes used as a generic term for all videotape equipment.

Analog signal
A signalling method that uses continuous changes in the amplitude or frequency of a radio transmission to convey information.

Anchor
Main presenter of a programme.

Animation
Artificially created apparent motion imparted by frame method in film and video, now made easy by computer graphics.

AP
Associated Press – a news agency

Aperture
F-stop, opening of lens diaphragm

Arc
Curved camera movement in the shape of an arc.

Arriflex
West German film camera. 16 mm sound and silent versions were very popular for TV news work before ENG.

ASBU
Arab States Broadcasting Union

Aspect ratio
Ratio between the height and width of a television picture, three units high by four units wide, 3:4.

Aston
Makers of caption-generating and other electronic equipment.

Atmosphere
Creation of a mood to make a scene appear more real.

Audio
Sound; the sound portion of a broadcast.

Glossary

Autocue
Tradename of field and studio-prompting device which enables performers to read from a written or electronically generated script while looking directly to the camera. Other makes include Portaprompt and Teleprompter. The company now also makes newsroom automation system QSeries.

B

Background
A set or sound used behind or below the action to help create an effect of realism.

Backing (protection)
Scenic planes beyond window doors, etc. that prevents the camera from seeing unwanted area outside the setting.

Backlight
The light from behind the subject providing tonal separation between this subject and its background. The backlight also reveals contours and edge texture.

Balance
A pleasing picture composition or well mixed audio.

Bandwidth
The range of frequencies encompassed by an electronic system transmitting television pictures (video) or sound (audio) signals. According to FCC it is the capacity of a telecom line to carry signals. The necessary bandwidth is the amount of spectrum required to transmit the signal without distortion or loss of information. FCC rules require suppression of the signal outside the band to prevent interference.

Barn doors
Four flaps fitted to a spotlight which are used to control the shape of the light beam.

Basic
Computer language, short for Beginners All Purpose Instructional Code.

Bashers
Simple floodlight consisting of 500W lamp in a reflector or shade.

Basys Broadcast Automation Systems
Makers of Newsfury newsroom computer system.

B & W
Black and white

BBC
British Broadcasting Corporation

Beam
The flow of electrons emitted from an electron gun in a television set or camera.

Beeper
A telephone interview recorded on audiotape. A special telephone circuit used emits a regular beep sound to inform the parties to the conversation that they are being recorded.

Betacam
Half-inch video format system introduced by Sony.

Betacart
Carousel system for the transmission of Beta videocassettes.

Big close up
Shot framing only a small part of the subject.

Bird
Communication satellite. So named after Early Bird, the first Intelsat satellite.

Black
Screen that has no picture information showing on it a blank screen.

Black edge
Facility for electronically creating a thin black edge around light overlayed lettering to improve legibility against backgrounds of similar tone.

Blanket license
A license granted to a performer by ASCAP (American Society of Composers, Authors and Publishers) and BMI (Broadcast Music Incorporated) in exchange for a fee. The license permits an artist the right to perform a song he or she did not compose

Blimp
A sound-absorbent cover made to cut down to acceptable limits the noise generated by mechanical equipment (notably film cameras).

Bloom (Block off, crush out, burn out)
Excessively light surface reproducing a blank white area.

Blow up
Greatly enlarged photograph.

Boom
A fixed or telescopic arm on a wheeled stand supporting a slung microphone.

Bridge
In a newscast, a few words tying one element of news to another.

BrightStar
Dedicated satellite linking the USA with the UK.

Glossary

Broadband
According to FCC broadband is a descriptive term for evolving digital technologies that provide consumers a signal-switched facility offering integrated access to voice, high-speed data service, video-demand services, and interactive delivery services.

Browser
A programme that displays the Web pages.

Burn in (Burn on)
An image of a bright area retained temporarily or permanently on a camera tube, defacing subsequent pictures.

Busy
An over-decorated, complicated or elaborate effect.

Buzz track
Unmodulated sound track made by recording silence with the microphone circuit open when commentary is recorded.

C

Cable TV penetration
Ratio of the number of customers to the total number of households with televisions that are passed by a cable system. Penetration is the basis of a system's profitability

Cache
A place on hard drive to store text and images from Web pages so that the pages come up quickly when you visit them more than once.

Camcorder
Combined lightweight videocamera and recorder.

Camera angle
A general term for the line the camera makes with the subject it is shooting.

Camera chain
A television camera, its camera control unit, and its power supply.

Camera tower
Scaffolding tower supporting TV camera for high shots (Slide chain).

Caption
Generic term for television news art work; also graphics.

Caption scanner
Apparatus for televising 35mm transparencies or small (12" by 9") graphics. It may incorporate a scanning tube (flying spot scanner) or a camera tube (eg. vidicon).

Cardioid microphone
A microphone with directivity pattern (polar diagram) heart shaped resulting in maximum sensitivity at the front and very low sensitivity at the rear.

CAS (Conditional Access System)
Uses set top box to receive channels of choice.

CATV (Community Antenna Television)
A service through which subscribers pay to have local television stations and additional programs brought into their homes from an antenna via a coaxial cable

CBA
Commonwealth Broadcasting Association.

CBS
Columbia Broadcasting System, a US network.

CCIR
International Radio Consultative Committee.

Ceefax (see facts)
BBC broadcast teletext system.

Cel
Transparent plastic sheet used as a base on to which animation art work is traced and painted.

Cellular technology
This term, often used for all wireless phones regardless of the technology they use, derives from cellular base stations that receive and transmit calls. Both cellular and PCS phones use cellular technology.

Channel
A general term for a succession of apparatus having a combined function. In a sound mixing system, for example, a section handling the output of one audio source, (e.g., microphone-amplifiers-fader-filtering, etc.) as opposed to a group of sources.

Character generator
Electronic generation of lettering or numbers for display on a TV screen. The output of the generator appears on the vision-mixing desk as a standard picture source, or on the studio output and is controlled from a form of typewriter type keyboard. A variety of type sizes and faces are available in a character generator.

Chroma (abbr.)
Chromakey, a process which places an electronic image on a screen behind the newscaster. The image may be a live remote, a still film or videotape.

Clarke belt position
22300 miles above the equator in which orbiting communications satellite appear to be stationary; after British science writer Arthur C. Clark who advocated the use of satellites in broadcasting.

Clean feed
This is a feed of the main sound-mixing desk minus one or more selected sources. The clean feed is an essential facility if contributions of two studios are used simultaneously. This arrangement ensures that loudspeakers in each studio reproduces only the sound from the other studio, thus howl-round or unwanted colouration can be avoided.

Clip
Short section excerpted from a film or VTR programme usually becomes an insert into another; also late or premature fade or cut resulting in missing of a word or syllable.

Closed captioning
A service for persons with hearing disabilities that translates television programme dialog into written words on the television screen.

Closed circuit
Not transmitted or broadcast. A programme fed (distributed) to limited selected points.

Closing (or close)
The standard concluding segment of a newscast according to format.

Close up
Framing which roughly speaking, includes just the head, or head and shoulders or an object seen at a close range.

Coaxial cable
Special wire used to transmit television signals from the studio or other originating point to the customer's television set. The term "coaxial" derives from the two conductive wires in a cable – a central "core" and an outer "jacket." Since they are concentric, they have the same "axis" and are "coaxial."

Collage
In a newscast, several photos, newspaper headlines or printed stories are pasted onto a card.

Commag
Combined magnetic system for recording sound onto a magnetic stripe bonded to one edge of a film during manufacture; also known as single system sound recording, now rare in television news.

Commercial leased access
A manner through which independent video producers can access cable capacity for a fee.

Common carrier
In the telecommunications arena, the term used to describe a telephone company.

Communication satellite
Manmade device positioned in space as a means of "bouncing" television or other signals from one part of the globe to another.

Comsat
Communication Satellite Corporation (US)

Contrast
Relationship between light and dark elements of a picture. High contrast has extremes of light and dark, low contrast has middle tones.

Control room
Room from which operations in a studio are directed and controlled.

Converter
Device that changes the frequency of a television signal. A home converter translates the signal from the frequencies at which they are sent over the cable to channels that the television set can pick up.

Cookie
A piece of information a Web page stores in your browser to use when you come back again. For example, a cookie might store your last entries in a particular form, so that you do not have to enter the same items again.

Copy
Written material for news

Copy taster
Journalist responsible for the first assessment of all incoming copy, specially from news agency sources.

Countdown
Time given in reverse order, usually spoken in the control room and given by hand signal in the studio to ensure smooth transition from one source to the next.

Cramming
A practice in which customers are billed for enhanced features such as voice mail, caller-ID and call-waiting that they have not ordered.

Credits
List of names of people that participated in the creation of a programme.

Glossary

Cropping
Trimming a still to a ratio of three units of height by four units of width to match the aspect ratio of a television screen.

Crossfade
To change sources of sound by steadily lowering the volume of the outgoing sound while raising the volume of the incoming sound.

Cross-posting
Posting a single message intended for several receivers.

Crawl
Graphics that move across the screen.

CSO (Colour Separation Overlay)
It is also known as chromakey. An electronic means of merging pictures from separate sources giving the illusion, for example that a performer in the studio is set against a pictorial background.

CU
Close-up

Cue
A visual or audible signal that starts the action in a scene.

Cue dot
Small circular dot made on an edited film usually in the top righthand corner, to indicate that it is coming to an end. Electronic cue dots are usually superimposed in the top lefthand corner to indicate the approaching end of one programme and to cue in the next.

Cut
Instant switch from one camera to another, or an order to stop action.

D

DBS (Direct Broadcasting Satellite)
System of transmitting broadcast signal to individual households using high powered satellites.

Dead
Not functioning

Deadline
That moment before each newscast when all copy and visuals should be prepared.

Deaf aid
Close fitting earpiece through which a performer in the studio or in the field can be given instructions by editorial or production staff.

Decibel or (db)
Unit measure of sound, volume or strength.

Defocus mix
A transition between two shots in which the first camera defocuses during the mix, while the second sharpens on its shot.

Depth of field
The area between the closest and the farthest objects that are in focus at a particular F-stop.

Diary story
News event covered by pre-arrangement

Dichroic mirror
A surface-coated glass filter which permits certain parts of the visible spectrum to pass through while reflecting others. Used in colour television cameras and telecine systems to analyse the full colour scene into red, green, blue components. A form of dichroic filter is used as a heat filter in projector systems to protect the film material from infra red and heat rays.

Digital
Signal with a finite number of discrete values, usually two. Advantages over analog signal transmission and storage include better immunity to noise and ease of computer processing (including signal compression, error detection and correction, and multiplexing).

DTV (Digital Television)
A new technology for transmitting and receiving broadcast television signals. DTV provides clearer resolution and improved sound quality.

Digital video effects
Video effects created by storing the complete television picture in digital form and then sampling this information selectively, reading this out to produce segmentation, inversion, wipes, reversal, inserts, magnification, diminution, multiplication, colour transformation, etc.

Dimmer
An electrical device for controlling the light output from luminaire (light fitting).

DBS/DISH (Direct Broadcast Satellite)
A high-powered satellite that transmits or retransmits signals which are intended for direct reception by the public. The signal is transmitted to a small earth station or dish (usually the size of an 18-inch pizza pan) mounted on homes or other buildings.

Directional
Particular pickup pattern of a microphone

Directivity pattern
A graphic plot representing the relative performance of a device at different distances and in various directions. It can show the sensitivity variations of a microphone or the variation in the output of a device (e.g. a lamp or a loudspeaker) with angle and distance.
Director
The person responsible for the organisation, creative interpretation and presentation of a particular programme. The function of a director varies from one organisation to another.
Dissolve
Transition between two pictures, one fades out while the next fades in, they overlap for a period. Can also apply to audio.
DNS (Director News Services)
It used to head the News Services Division of All India Radio. Now they have a DG News.
Dolly
A moving camera towards object (dolly-in) or away (dolly-out). The term "Dolly" is loosely used for any mobile mounting.
Dope sheet
Cameraman's detailed record of tape or film shot on location.
Double system
Separate magnetic system of recording sound on film. The sound is recorded separately on to a taperecorder run in synchronism with the film. Also known as Sepmag or sync sound.
Downstage
The activity area nearest to camera, to walk downstage means to walk towards the camera.
Dry run
Rehearsal without the camera.
Dub
To add or re-record sound to edited picture.
Dynamic microphone
Pressure-sensitive microphone.
Dynamic range
The range of sound levels which audio system can handle. At the top end of the scale it is limited by overload distortion and at the lower end by signal to noise considerations.

E

EBU
European Broadcasting Union.

Electrostatic microphone
A microphone in which the conducting diaphragm upon which the sound impinges forms one plate of a capacitor. Capacitance changes caused by diaphragm movements are converted into output signal.

Elevations
Drawings giving the dimensions and details of vertical planes, e.g. walls with doors, windows, pillars, surface treatment, etc.

E-mail
Also called electronic mail, refers to messages sent over the Internet. E-mail can be sent and received via newer types of wireless phones, but you generally need to have a specific e-mail account.

En banc
An informal meeting held by the Commission to hear presentations on specific topics by diverse parties. The Commissioners, or other officials, question presenters use their comments in considering FCC rules and policies on the subject matter under consideration.

ENG (Electronic News Gathering)
Lightweight video camera and sound recording system which has superseded news film.

Enhanced service providers
A for-profit business that offers to transmit voice and data messages and simultaneously adds value to the messages it transmits. Examples include telephone answering services, alarm security companies and transaction-processing companies.

ENS
Electronic News Room System; method of producing television news programmes with computers.

Establishing shot
Scene-setting shot of people or subject.

Eurovision
European International Network for the exchange of television programmes.

EVN (Eurovision News Exchange)
Exchange of television news items through Eurovision links.

EUTELSAT
European Telecommunication Satellite Organisation

Glossary

EXE files
A file with the extension EXE does something. Unlike text in document files, executable files run on the computer. EXE files usually contain a programme of some kind.

Eyeline
The direction in which the subject is seen to be looking by the camera.

F

Fade
The electronic equivalent of a film fade out. A dissolve from picture to darkness which is mid-grey rather than black.

Fader
General term for an intensity control, adjusting the strength of a signal. A fader may be used as a switch to introduce or remove sources to the main output ('Fade up' 'Fade down'). It may also be set at intermediate positions to adjust relative output of the sources (balance). Typical applications of fader include vision and sound-mixing consoles and lighting-control consoles.

FCC (Federal Communications Commission)
It is US agency responsible for broadcasting.

FDM
Form-driven mail. E-mail that is sent formatted like an application that you fill-in. Once you fill in the information directly on that form and then e-mail it back to the sender. The data that you input is collected in a spreadsheet

Feed
A news story or an entire programme electronically transmitted to other stations or broadcast to the public.

Fiber-optic cable
Hair-thin continuous glass fibers that allow the transmission of laser-generated light signals with low loss of power or interference.

Figure of eight
Type of microphone directivity pattern, the true three dimentional pattern would be two spheres in contact, with the microphone as the point of contact.

File footage
Archive / library material

Filler light
It is (usually diffused – "Soft") used to control the lighting contrast and to illuminate shadow areas cast by keylights.

First-run programming
Original programming created for the syndication marketplace.

Fish pole
Simple hand-held microphone boom. It consists of about 2m of suitable rod with a mounting at one end to support the microphone.

Fixer
Co-ordinator accompanying units in the field who often acts as the main point of contact between teams on location and the home base.

Flat
A basic scenic unit usually made of stretched canvas or hardboard on a flat wooden framework. Mainly used to form 'walls' of settings and vertical planes.

Floor manager
The person responsible for the production organisation (including performer cueing) in the studio. He is director's /producer's representative on the floor.

Floor men (Stage hands)
Studio crew who erect, dismantle scenery, handle captions and move scenery during the show.

Floor plan
Scale plan of the studio floor area with staging furniture, cameras, etc.

Fly
To suspend scenery or objects.

Fold back (F/B)
The reproduction of selected sound sources over studio loudspeakers as an aid to performers.

Foley
Process by which ambient sound effects (footsteps, door creaks, car horns) are added to video in postproduction. Named after sound effects genius Jack Foley.

Follow-up
News report based on previously broadcast or published material.

Foot print
Area covered by satellite transmission.

Format
(1) Overall style and look of a programme (2) Video tape size or recording pattern.

Glossary

Frame
A single still picture from a moving film or tape. There are 25 film frames to a second on the British TV system while 24 a second in the US.

Frame/picture Store
Electronic method of storing and displaying still pictures.

Franchise
Authorisation issued by a municipal, county or state government allowing the construction and operation of a cable television system within the bounds of its governmental authority.

Free puff
News item which publicises an event or product.

Freeze frame
A single frame of video tape or film held to stop the action.

FM (Frequency Modulation)
A method of transmitting information by changing the frequency of a high frequency carrier wave in proportion to the amplitude of the lower frequency signal we wish to transmit. The amplitude of the carrier wave remains unchanged. The frequency modulated carrier is subsequently demodulated to recover the original signal. A signalling method that varies the carrier frequency in proportion to the amplitude of the modulating signal.

FTP (File Transfer Protocol)
FTP is the Internet standard for uploading and downloading files and graphics. See KW: FTP for more information.

Futures file
Collection of information about items for possible future news coverage.

FX
Sound effects

G

Gain
Level of amplified sound or video.

Gel (pronounced "jel")
Semi-transparent heat-resistant material which is placed in front of a light source in order to modify its colour or other characteristics.

Geostationary orbit
Orbit in which satellites appear to remain in the same place relative to the earth.

GPS (Global Positioning System)
A US satellite system that lets those on the ground, on the water or in the air determine their position with extreme accuracy using GPS receivers.

Graphics
General name for art work including cards, charts, slides, photographs, etc.

Group
In a sound desk two or more channels may be faded together and so combined into a group, a single group fader then controls all these sources simultaneously.

Gun microphone
A type of microphone with an extremely narrow pickup angle, making it particularly useful for isolating individual sound sources.

GV
General view

H

Hammock
Programming slot between two hit shows, often used to launch a new programme.

Handback
Performer's form of words used to signal the end of his or her contribution.

Handout
Free publicity material given to news organisations.

Hand-over
Performer's form of words used by a newsreader or presenter, etc. as a cue for another performer, (e.g. 'Now with the home news...')

Hard focus
Sharply focused

HDTV
High Definition Television System of 1000 plus lines offering superior picture and sound quality. An improved television system which provides approximately twice the vertical and horizontal resolution of existing television standards. It also provides audio quality approaching that of compact discs.

Head
Device that transfers information to the tape from a recorder in the record mode and vice versa in play mode.

Headend
Electronic control centre of the cable system.

Glossary

Head gap
The magnetic gap between the poles in tape recorder heads.
Head shot
A still photo of a person's head or head and shoulders.
Helican scan
Recording format in which information is put on tape in a slanting or diagonal pattern; also called "slant track".
Hz (Hertz)
The unit of frequency (cycles-per-second).
Home page
A Web page that your browser opens each time it is run, or, the "main" page of a website
Hot
Overbright surface; equipment that is working, eg 'hot mike'.
HTML (Hypertext Markup Language)
The format of documents on the World Wide Web.
http (Hypertext Transfer Protocol)
The way computers exchange Web information. Internet addresses that begin with "http://" point to a Web page.
HUT (Homes Using Television)
Common television industry term for households watching TV, used to measure TV ratings.
Hyperlink
(Also links). Text or images that bring you to another place, either on the same page, another page, or another site entirely. Hyperlinks often appear as blue, underlined text. They can also be graphics. The mouse cursor usually changes to a pointing finger over hyperlinks.
Hypertext
Text documents that are linked to one another by hyperlinks.

I

Illumination
A measure of the amount of light incident on a surface.
IM
Instant Message; as in "Let me IM you."
In-betweener
Animation artist who works with the original animators' key poses, drawing more detailed movements to create actual "motion" from scene to scene and make the animation look fuller.

In-cue
Opening words of a news report.
Ink and paint artists
Animation artists who apply ink outlines to all of the characters and/or props within a scene. Ink and paint artists are also responsible for painting all drawings found within a scene.
Intelsat
International Telecommunication Satellite Organisation.
IVDS (Interactive Video Data Service)
A communication system, operating over a short distance, that allows nearly instantaneous two-way responses by using a hand-held device at a fixed location. Viewer participation in game shows, distance learning and e-mail on computer networks are examples.
ITFS (Instructional Television Fixed Service)
A service provided by one or more fixed microwave stations operated by an educational organisation and used to transmit instructional information to fixed locations.
Inter-negative (Dupe negative)
A negative derived from a print (positive) enabling further prints (dupe prints) to be produced.
Internet Explorer(tm)
A popular Web browser (a programme that displays Web pages), developed by Microsoft. Internet Explorer, also called MSIE.
Intervision
Eastern block counterpart of Eurovision.
Inject
'Live' contribution to a news programme from a distant source.
Instant lettering
The sheets of rub-on lettering used in non-electronic art work.
Interlace
System of sync that insures that lines of the second field will fall between the lines of the first field.
In-vision (story)
Item read by performer in studio without illustrations (also called 'dry story').
ITN (Independent Television News)
It is a company that provides national news to Independent Television in Britain.
IVN
Intervision News Exchange.

Glossary

J
Jiggle
Derogatory term for unwanted activity shown on the screen instead of a newscaster reading the news.
Jump cut
A direct cut to the same person or scene that destroys pictorial continuity by making a subject appear to jump from one position to another in consecutive shots.

K
Key grip
Person in charge of constructing and dismantling film sets and camera dolly tracks.
Keying colour
Colour chosen to activate colour separation overlay.
Key light
The main light source illuminating the subject; hard light sources (fresnel spotlights) are normally used as key lights.
Key shot
Master shot
Kill
Eliminate, cut out

L
Landline
Traditional wired phone service
Land mobile service
A public or private radio service providing two-way communication, paging and radio signalling on land.
Lay-on
Arrange coverage
Lavalier
Small mike hung round the neck on a cord.
Lead
(1) Opening item of a news bulletin; (2) Opening sentence of a story usually written for newscaster.
Lead in
Introduction or opening sentence of a story.

Leader
Position of a tape that precedes the first frame of picture, usually calibrated in seconds to aid count down.
Letterbox format
In video and television, the practice of placing black bars at the top and bottom of the frame, in order to simulate a wide-screen format (as if the viewer were looking through the slot in a letterbox).
Lift
An electronic adjustment in a camera or telecine channel, usually operated continuously for optimum picture quality, which moves all pictures, tones up or down the tonal scale.
Limbo
Strictly a totally neutral background for action.
Limiter
Electronic device for automatic control of sound programme levels, often used to present signals exceeding system parameters.
Linear source
A tungsten-halogen strip light used in soft-light sources and cyc light.
Line up
Technical adjustment of equipment to provide optimum performance particularly of camera channels, circuit checks, alignment, etc. just before a recording or transmission.
Lip flap
The result of cutting a film of a speaker to begin in mid-speech so that his lips are seen moving before he is heard.
Lip sync
Synchronised speech with picture and sound matching, frame by frame.
Live
Direct transmission of action as it happens.
Live-on-tape
A show video recorded in its entirety without editing.
Loop
A length of film or audio tape in which the ends are joined to permit continuous repeated performance (e.g. identifying announcements) or a continuous effect (e.g. rain or fog).
LPFM (Low Power FM Radio)
A broadcast service that permits the licensing of 50-100 watt FM radio stations within a service radius of up to 3.5 miles and 1-10 watt FM radio stations within a service radius of 1 to 2 miles.

Glossary

(LPTV) Low Power Television
A broadcast service that permits programme origination, subscription service or both via low powered television translators. LPTV service includes the existing translator service and operates on a secondary basis to regular television stations. Transmitter output is limited to 1,000 watts for normal VHF stations and 100 watts when a VHF operation is on an allocated channel.

LS
Long shot

Luminaire
The term used to describe complete light unit, i.e. housing and bulb.

Luminance
A measure of the amount of light which is reflected from a surface.

Lux
The practical metric unit of illumination.

M

M & E
Sound track with music and effects only without any dialogue.

MacGuffin
Term coined by Alfred Hitchcock. Refers to any situation in the unfolding of a story that motivates the action of a film, whether artificially or substantively.

Magazine programme
Programme which is a mix of hard news and feature items.

Magnetic (mag) track
A magnetic sound recording (single or multiple track) on a standard sprocketed film base. In **Sep-Mag** a separate recording is run in sync with the mute picture print. In magnetic stripe, the sound track is laid alongside the edge of the film, combines in one 'married' or 'combined' print both the picture and its sound.

Master
First generation tape or edited version from which dubs are made.

Master control
Switching and continuity centre to which various programme sources are fed.

Medium shot
Shot taken at normal viewing distance, usually cutting actors at the waistline.

MegaHertz (MHz)
Unit used to measure a broadcast of cablecast frequency.

Microphone, Mic or Mike
Instrument that converts sound waves to electric pulses.

Minicam
Mobile electronic camera unit with live capability.

Minimum focusing distance
The shortest distance from camera at which objects can be focused.

Mirror shot
Picture in which the camera shoots a subject via a mirror rather than by pointing at it directly.

Mix
The progressive fading out of one source and the fading up of a second. In vision, the first picture merges into the second.

Mixer
Device that mixes audio signals such as mikes and/or phonographs.

Modem
Modulator /demodulator which allows computer signals to be transmitted by telephone.

Monitor
Screen for displaying television pictures or computer-generated data; (verb) to listen and/or watch and take notes on output of broadcast stations.

Monochrome
Black and white

Monopod
Single extendible pole fitted to the base of a camera to keep it steady.

Montage
A rapid succession of moving or still pictures assembled to create an overall effect.

Move
Transmit copy or pictures by wire.

MS
Medium shot

MSO (Multiple System Operator)
A company that operates more than one cable system, also called multi-system operator.

Multiplexer
Vision and sound switch that allows several sources in succession to be routed at high speed on to one line for transmission.

Glossary

MW
Medium wave

N
Narrator
Off-camera voice on sound track.
Natural sound
Sound recorded on to tape at the same time as the pictures are taken.
NBC
National Broadcasting Company, a US network.
Neck mike
A small lightweight microphone which is hung from a cord round the neck.
Negative image
Reversed polarity of picture, white is black and vice versa.
Netiquette
The recommended conduct of individuals on the Internet
Netscape/ Netscape navigator
A popular Web browser (a programme that displays Web pages), developed by Netscape Communications Corporation
Network
Any connection of two or more computers that enables them to communicate. Networks may include transmission devices, servers, cables, routers and satellites. The phone network is the total infrastructure for transmitting phone messages.
News groups
Track an interest through an Internet Usenet Newsgroup. These worldwide discussion boards cover one small topic each.
News profiles
You can set up a news profile to automatically drop news articles on topics of interest to you—right into your e-mail box.
Noise
Unwanted video information generated by any electrical system. It looks like snow on the screen.
NTSC
National Television Standards Committee which gave its name to the US system of colour television.

O

O&O station (owned and operated)
TV stations owned and operated by one of the networks as opposed to those owned by station groups or individuals.

OB
Outdoor Broadcast

OC
On camera

Off-network (also off-net)
Television series running in syndication that were originally produced for airing on one of the networks.

OIRT
International Radio and Television Organisation based in Prague.

OOV
Out of vision.

Open video systems
An alternative method to provide cable-like video service to subscribers.

OSP (Operator Service Provider)
A common carrier that provides services from public phones, including payphones and those in hotels/motels.

Optical
General term encompassing mixes, fades, superimposition, double exposures, split screens, freeze frames, skip frames and other optical effects.

Oracle
Optical reception of announcements by coded line electronics, a British teletext service run by independent television.

Oscilloscope
A device used for alignment of electronic signal shows patterns on a display screen.

Out cue
Final words of a news report.

Over-crank
To run a camera motor at faster than normal speed. When seen, the picture appears to be in slow motion.

Overlay
An electronic switch enabling the pictures from two television sources to be integrated. A subject is placed in front of a special 'keying' tone or hue (not present in the subject itself). The overlay switch automatically substitutes for the key colour, a chosen background scene from another television camera, telecine, videotape, etc.

Glossary

P
PA
Production assistant
Paging system
A one-way mobile radio service where a user carries a small, lightweight miniature radio receiver capable of responding to coded signals. These devices, called "pagers," emit an audible signal, vibrate or do both, when activated by an incoming message.
Paint box
Electronic system for the creation of graphics.
PAL
Phase Alternation (by) Line. A colour television system.
Pan
Camera movement on horizontal or vertical plane.
PASB
Programme as broadcast is a detailed record of a programme for file and payments to contributors.
Patch
Interconnection between pieces of electronic equipment directly or by means of a patch board/panel.
PPM (Peak Programme Meter)
Meter for indicating peaks of sound levels, thus enabling an operator to avoid overmodulation, distortion, etc.
PCS (Personal Communications Service)
Any of several types of wireless, voice and/or data communications systems, typically incorporating digital technology. PCS licenses are most often used to provide services similar to advanced cellular mobile or paging services. However, PCS can also be used to provide other wireless communications services, including services that allow people to place and receive communications while away from their home or office, as well as wireless communications to homes, office buildings and other fixed locations.
Perspective (sound)
An illusion of distance of a sound source.
Perspective (vision)
An illusion of depth and space created by the use of decor, lighting, and lens angle selection. It is essential for picture and sound to maintain relative perspective to create a co-ordinated effect.

Phantom powering
A method of supplying power to electrostatic microphones along the three cord cable used for audio signals.

Phase distortion
Distortion arising when the relative phases of component parts of a complex wave are changed.

Pickups
Scenes shot after main production (TV and film) if continuity gaps are discovered in the editing process and need to be filled in.

Piece to camera
Report spoken directly to the camera in the field.

Pigeon
Traveller entrusted with passing film or tape between a camera unit and their base.

Pixel
Picture element

Plug-in
A small programme that adds to your browser's capabilities. For instance, the ShockWave plug-in lets your browser display small multimedia programmes that are embedded in some Web pages.

Presence filter
Circuit boosting a region of the frequency response of a sound channel. It can often convey the impression that a certain sound source stands out from its background.

Producer
Executive responsible for the overall planning, production and artistic shape of a series of programmes or part thereof.

Public address
In television, a feed of selected sources being reproduced by loudspeakers near a studio audience.

Q

Quadrature (quad) scanning
A videotape system using a rotating four-headed scanning mechanism.

Quadruplex
Videotape machine with four vision heads recording across a magnetic tape, two inches wide.

Quantel
Makers of electronic production equipment, particularly for computer graphics.

Quarter-cam
Quarter-inch format video system.
Quarter-inch tape
Quarter-inch wide audio recording tape.
Quartz-iodine
Very efficient, very bright, long lasting bulb used in lighting instruments.

R
Radio mike
Microphone used with a small transmitter, does not need cable link with recording equipment.
Random interlace
Unstable form of sync pulse that produces poor picture quality.
Raster
Face of a picture tube that picks up the stream of electrons from the electron gun coated with particles that will glow to create a picture.
Reaction shot
Specific type of close-up in which an actor or group of people respond to an event. The shot is supposed to convey the impact of the moment and is often accomplished with a cutaway from the primary action to someone viewing the occurrence
Ready
A warning given by producer or production assistant to indicate a command is eminent, e.g. 'Ready camera one' warns that the next command for a camera change will be a cut or dissolve to number one camera.
Rear projection (back projection)
Here film or slides are projected onto a translucent screen from behind and shot by cameras on the front side.
Reel
Film or tape spool.
Reflex projection
Front projection along the lens axis onto a finely beaded screen to provide a scenic background.
Reversal film
A motion picture film which develops as a positive print.
Reverse action
Action made to appear backwards in time sequence.
Reverse phase
A electronic means of changing (film) negative to positive for transmission purposes.

Reverse shot
Shot from the opposite direction to a previous viewpoint, eg., through a window inside-to-out and outside-to-in.

Reverberation
The prolongation of sound caused by repeated reflection from walls, floor, ceiling, etc.

Roaming
The use of a wireless phone outside of the "home" service area defined by a service provider. Higher per-minute rates are usually charged for calls made or received while roaming. Long distance rates and a daily access fee may also apply.

Roll
A command to start a tape machine.

Roller caption (crawl)
A mechanical device for displaying moving lettering, vertically or horizontally, across the screen.

Rostrum camera
A camera mounted on the photographic enlarger principle to control filming or taping of staic objects (maps, etc).

Running order
A order of transmission of items in a programme.

Run through
Rehearsal

Run up
Time considered necessary for technical equipment to reach its full operating speed.

Rushes
Exposed film or tape in its unedited form.

S
Satellite
A radio relay station that orbits the earth. A complete satellite communications system also includes earth stations that communicate with each other via the satellite. The satellite receives a signal transmitted by an originating earth station and retransmits that signal to the destination earth station(s). Satellites are used to transmit telephone, television and data signals originated by common carriers, broadcasters and distributors of cable TV programme material.

Glossary

SMATV (Satellite Master Antenna Television)
A satellite dish system used to deliver signals to multiple dwelling units, (e.g., apartment buildings and trailer parks).

Scanning
The movement of the electron beam from top to bottom and left to right.

Scanner
A mobile control centre serving outside a broadcast unit. A radio receiver that moves across a wide range of radio frequencies and allows audiences to listen to any of the frequencies.

Scene
The setting of a shot; or one shot; or a sequence of shots.

Script
The rehearsal script only contains the actors, lines (dialogue) and basic action (moves). A camera script also includes the operational, technical and staging information required for production treatment.

Search engine
A programme that looks for information that you request. On the World Wide Web, this has come to mean a Web page where you can search the entire Web. Some search engines search more limited areas, like newsgroups or phone books.

SECAM
Sequence Area Memoir colour television system.

Segue (pronounced seg-way)
When one piece of music effects, dialogue, cross fades into another often imperceptibly (fade out of one source during the fadein of the next). Sometimes this term is misused for 'sneak-in'.

Sepmag
A separate magnetic system of recording sound on film. The sound is recorded separately on to a tape recorder run in synchronism with the film.

Service provider
A telecommunications provider that owns circuit switching equipment.

Set
Surroundings in a scene as seen by a television camera, to put into required or rehearsed position. At the end of a rehearsal props, furniture, etc. are re-set in their opening position.

Shading
Contrast adjustment

Shot
An uninterrupted picture from one camera.

Shot list
Detailed written description of each scene in edited tape or film usually measured in seconds.

Sidebands
The band of frequencies on either side of a carrier frequency resulting from the process of modulation.

S/N ratio
Signal to noise. Ratio of power of picture signal to inherent noise in a system.

SIL
Silence

Single system
System of recording sound on to a magnetic stripe bonded to one edge of film during manufacture, also known as 'commag'.

Slamming
The term used to describe what occurs when a customer's long distance service is switched from one long distance company to another without the customer's permission.

Slant track
Helical scan

Slot
The position of a programme, news story or commercial.

SMATV Satellite Master Antenna Television.
System of sending satellite pictures to community dishes for distribution by cable.

Sneak in (or out)
To introduce (or remove) imperceptibly, unobtrusively.

Snow
Electronic interference in a picture, "noise".

SOF
Sound on film, film carrying its own sound track.

Soft shot
A shot that is slightly out of focus.

Soft source
A light source preferably of large area which produces diffused illumination.

Soft story
A news item considered interesting rather than important.

Solid state
Use of transistors instead of tubes.

Glossary

SOT
Sound-on-tape
Sound track
Area of tape on which sound is recorded.
Sound under
An audio level which permits background sounds to be heard but not so loudly that they interfere with the newscaster or reporter.
Soup
Processing plant for film, to develop film.
Special effects
Electronic and mechanical devices to create different illusions on the screen.
Spectrum
The range of electromagnetic radio frequencies used in the transmission of sound, data and television.
Splice
Physical joining of two pieces of tape.
Split focus
Focusing so that chosen subjects at different distances from the camera are equally and sharply focused, distributing the depth of field.
Split screen
A picture composed of two separate elements, each occupying half of the screen area.
Spot light
A type of lighting instrument that produces narrow beam, a popular current affairs programme of AIR.
Spread
To take more than allotted time.
SSL (Secure Sockets Layer)
A technology that encrypts (encodes) information that travels from your browser to a Web server. When you send and receive information within a secure server, your credit card number and any other information you send and receive is much harder for anyone to steal.
Stability
Measure of vtr or camera's life like abilities.
Stage brace
Extensible prop or stay used to hold up scenery.
Staging area
The main area of studio floor in which staging may be arranged.

Standupper
A report at the scene of an event with the camera focused on the reporter.
Steenbeck
A German-made film editing machine.
Stick mike
Stick-shaped microphone.
Still
A photograph, map or drawing or by definition just a photograph.
Still frame
Freeze frame – vtr scans one field continuously.
Stock
Raw unused tape or film.
Storyboard
Drawing of video next to audio in a fashion that details all elements of a programme. A visual script. In the process of planning a film, the narrative is often depicted, scene by scene, with materials and technicians that will be needed for the shoot. Storyboards are an overall, general depiction of the entire film sequence. They are also used in animation.
Stretching
Reading closely to fill a time gap.
Strike
Remove or dismantle scenery.
Stringer
A freelance contributor retained on a regular basis.
Stripe
Narrow band of magnetic sound track used in commag (single) system of recording sound on film.
Studio address
The use of loudspeaker to address studio performers or staff also called talk back.
Studio spot
A contribution made live in the studio by a performer other than the main presenter.
Superimpose (super)
The overlapping, simultaneous showing of two or more pictures on one screen.
Supply reel
Reel from which tape comes when going through a vtr.

Glossary

Surf
To move from one Internet location to another, usually by clicking a series of hyperlinks.
SW
Short wave
Sweeps
Month-long periods (usually in February, May, July and November) when Nielsen Media Research measures audiences in all TV markets. These periods are important to local stations and the networks as they help them determine their advertising rates, while providing an in-depth audience profile.
Swish pan
A very rapid, blurred pan indicating a change of scene.
Sync
The frame-for-frame matching of sound and picture. Out of sync means inexact union of sound and picture.
Syndicated programming
First-run and off-network series and specials sold to stations across the country, market by market, rather than provided by one of the networks.

T

Take-up reel
Takes up tape from supply reel after the tape has gone through the vtr.
Talk-back
One way sound link between control room and other technical area.
Talking-head
Any interviewee
Tally light
Red light on camera that goes on when that camera is on the "line".
Tap
A device installed in the feeder cable which connects the home TV set to the cable network.
Tape
A extremely thin plastic, one-quarter to two inches wide. Oxide formula on one side receives magnetic information from heads.
Tape guides
Grooved pins that guide tape around head assembly.
Telecine
Projector TV camera mechanism for transmitting film on television.

Tele lens
Short form for telephoto lens. A long focal length lens of specific design with reduced back focus.

Telephony
The word used to describe the science of transmitting voice over a telecommunications network

Teleprompter
A field and studio prompting device which enables performers to read from a written or electronically generated script while looking directly to the camera.

Tele-recording
The process of recording programmes or items by filming directly off high quality monitors.

Teletext
A broadcast videotex. On screen text information transmitted on unused lines within the television signal.

Terminal
Connectors, transformers and converter (if necessary) on the cable customer's set.

Test pattern
A special design of circles and lines that is used to properly focus and align television cameras.

Tie line
An inter-linking sound or vision connection routed between technical area.

Tight shot
Framing with little or no space around the subject, usually a close up.

Tilt
Vertical panning movement of the camera.

Time check
Synchronising clocks to ensure simultaneous starts.

Timing
Noting the length of time of each story or segment and its running time.

Title card
A card naming a story, sometimes used to begin a feature, may be illustrated.

Tracking
Adjusting the head-to-capstan distance of a videotape machine.

Tracking shot (dolly shot)
Extensive dolly movement, particularly when following alongside moving performer in a constant size shot.

Transducer
A device for converting one type of energy into another, e.g. loudspeaker converts electrical signal to sound waves.

Transponder
On board satellite equipment which receives and passes on a telecommunication signal.

Tripod
Adjustable three-legged stand fixed to the base of a camera to keep it steady.

Truck
Movement of the camera and tripod or dolly laterally to the left or right.

Tungsten Halogen (Quarter iodine) lamps
A lamp in which the evaporating filament burning in a halogen gas is redeposited on the filament itself rather than on the side of envelope, thus ensuring longer operating life without discolouration.

Turnaround
When the option on a project expires and the party holding that option chooses not to renew it, the project is said to be in turnaround and can move to another production company or simply go away.

Turret
Mounting for up to four lenses on front of camera.

TVRO
Television Receive Only

Two-shot
A shot that frames two people or any two objects.

TX
Transmission

U

UHF
Ultra high frequency, channels 14 through 83.

U-matic
A three-quarter inch videotape recording system first introduced by Sony.

Unbundling
The term used to describe the access provided by local exchange carriers so that the other service providers can buy or lease portions of its network elements, such as interconnection loops, to serve subscribers.

Under crank
To run a camera motor at slower speed than normal.

Universal service
The financial mechanism which helps compensate telephone companies or other communications entities for providing access to telecommunications services at reasonable and affordable rates throughout the country, including rural, insular and high costs areas, and to public institutions. Companies, not consumers, are required by law to contribute to this fund. The law does not prohibit companies from passing this charge on to customers.

Upcut
A loss of words at the start of a film or tape. A newscaster's delivery is also up-cut if his microphone is cut in after he begins a sentence.

Up on one
A command to the technical director to fade into the scene on number one camera.

Upstage
The acting area farthest away from the camera. To walk upstage is to walk away from the camera.

URL (Uniform Resource Locator)
An "address" pointing to a certain site on Internet. See '*Understanding Internet Addresses*' to read more on the parts of a URL.

URTNA
Union of National Radio and Television Organisations in Africa, established in 1962.

V

VDT/VDU
Visual Display Terminal or Visual Display Unit. Display screen linked to a computer.

VHF (Very High Frequency)
The part of the radio spectrum from 30 to 300 megahertz, which includes TV channels 2-13, the FM broadcast band and some marine, aviation and land mobile services.

Video
Picture portion of television signal.

Videocassette
A container which allows a tape to be threaded automatically into cameras and recorders.

Glossary

Video control (shading)
A continual adjustment of video equipment (exposure, black level, video gain, gamma, colour balance) to maintain optimum picture quality and match picture sources by the video engineer / vision operator / shader.

Video description
An audio narration for television viewers who are blind or visually disabled, which consists of verbal descriptions of key visual elements in a television programme, such as settings and actions not reflected in a dialogue. Narrations are inserted into the programme natural pauses, and are typically provided through the secondary audio programming channel.

Videotape
A magnetic tape specifically designed to pick up, store and play back television signals.

Videotex
A written information distributed to display screens from central computers.

Vidicon
A pickup tube used in portable television cameras.

Viewdata
Non-broadcast videotex accessed over telephone.

Viewfinder
A small monitor built in or attached to the top of a camera that allows cameraman to see what his camera is picking up.

Vision mixer
A control panel or console enabling picture sources (cameras, telecine, caption, scanners, etc.) to be selected individually or in groups by switches or faders. The term is also used for the operator of this apparatus.

Vision story
News item where the newsreader is in vision on camera.

Visnews
The international television news agency taken over by Reuters to start the Reuters TV service.

Voice over or VO
Commentary by unseen reader in the studio during the transmission.

VU meter
Volume Unit Meter, measures audio levels.

VTR
Video tape recorder

W

Wavelength
The length of one-signal cycle.

Webmaster
A person who manages a website

Whip pan
A very high speed panning movement of the camera.

Wide angle lens
A lens with an angle of field of 60 degree or more.

Wild track
Background sound recorded at the scene of an event by tape recorder or sound camera. The sound is not recorded to match any particular scene or to provide lip sync.

Windshield
A guaze or fabric shield, fitted over a microphone to reduce the audible effects of wind, breath, etc.

Wipe
Special effect, electronic or mechanical, that appears to push one image off the screen with another image either vertically or horizontally.

WTN (Worldwide Television News)
Formerly UPITN, television news agency.

Wrap (or wrap-up)
Conclude

X

Xenon lamp
A discharge type projection lamp having a colour temperature of about 65000 K (the standard for projecting colour film).

Z

Zip pan
A rapid panning movement, showing the scene clearly focused at the start and end of the panning with intermediate blurring.

Zoom lens
A lens with a variable focal length.

Zooming
An adjusting zoom lens, while on shot to produce varying magnification of the subject.

Appendix – 1

MacBride Commission Report:
Conclusions and Recommendations

The survey contained in this report has recorded a dramatic expansion of communication resources and possibilities. It is an expansion that promises great opportunities, but also raises anxieties and uncertainties. Everything will depend on the use made of the new resources – that is, on crucial decisions, and on the question of who will make the decisions. Communication can be an instrument of power, a revolutionary weapon, a commercial product, or a means of education; it can serve the ends of either liberation or of oppression, of either the growth of the individual personality or of drilling human beings into uniformity. Each society must choose the best way to approach the task facing all of us and to find the means to overcome the material, social and political constraints that impede progress.

We have already considered many suggestions for further development. Without repeating them it might be useful to begin our recommendations by summarising previous main conclusions:

Our review of communication the world over reveals a variety of solutions adopted in different countries – in accordance with diverse traditions, patterns of social, economic and cultural life, needs and possibilities. This diversity is valuable and should be respected; there is no place for the universal application of preconceived models. Yet it should be possible to establish, in broad outline, common aims and common values in the sphere of communication, based on common interests in a world of interdependence. The whole human race is threatened by the arms race and by the persistence of unacceptable global inequalities, both of which generate tensions and which jeopardise its future and even its survival. The contemporary situation demands a better, more just and more democratic social order, and the realisation of fundamental human rights. These goals can be achieved only through understanding and tolerance, gained in large part by free, open and balanced communications.

The review has also shown that the utmost importance should be given to eliminating imbalances and disparities in communication and its structures, and particularly in information flows. Developing countries need to reduce their dependence, and claim a new, more just and more equitable order in the field of communication. This issue has been fully debated in various settings; the time has now come to move from principles to substantive reforms and concrete action.

Our conclusions are founded on the firm conviction that communication is a basic individual right, as well as a collective one required by all communities and nations. Freedom of information – and, more specially the right to seek, receive and impart information – is a fundamental human right; indeed, a prerequisite for many others. The inherent nature of communication means that its fullest possible exercise and potential depends on the surrounding political, social and economic conditions, the most vital of these being democracy within countries and equal, democratic relations between them. It is in this context that the democratisation of communication at national and international levels, as well as the larger role of communication in democratising society, acquires utmost importance.

For these purposes, it is essential to develop comprehensive national communication policies linked to overall social, cultural and economic development objectives. Such policies should evolve from broad consultations with all sectors concerned and adequate mechanisms for wide participation of organised social groups in their definition and implementation. National government as much as the international community should recognise the urgency of according communications higher priority in planning funding. Every country should develop its communication patterns in accordance with its own conditions, needs and traditions, thus strengthening its integrity, independence and self-reliance.

The basic considerations, which are developed at length in the body of our report, are intended to provide a framework for the development of a new information and communication order. We see its implementation as an on-going process of change in the nature of relations between and within nations in the field of communications. Imbalances in national information and communication systems are as disturbing and unacceptable as social, economic, cultural and technological, both national and international disparities. Indeed, rectification of the latter is inconceivable

Appendix – 1

in any true or lasting sense without elimination of the former. Crucial decisions concerning communication development need to be taken urgently, at both national and international levels. These decisions are not merely the concern of professionals, researchers or scholars, nor can they be the sole prerogative of those holding political or economic power. The decision-making process has to involve social participation at all levels. This calls for new attitudes for overcoming stereotyped thinking and to promote more understanding of diversity and plurality, with full respect for the dignity and equality of people living in different conditions and acting in different ways.

Thus our call for reflection and action is addressed broadly to governments and international organisation, to policy makers and planners, to the media and professional organisations, to researchers, communication practitioners, to organised social groups and the public at large.

I. Strengthening Independence and Self-Reliance

Communication Policies

All individuals and people collectively have an inalienable right to a better life which, howsoever conceived, must ensure a social minimum, nationally and globally. This calls for the strengthening of capacities and the elimination of gross inequalities; such defects may threaten social harmony and even international peace. There must be a measured movement from disadvantage and dependence to self-reliance and the creation of more equal opportunities. Since communication is interwoven with every aspect of life, it is clearly of the utmost importance that the existing "communication gap" be rapidly narrowed and eventually eliminated.

We recommend:

Communication be no longer regarded merely as an incidental service and its development left to chance. Recognition of its potential warrants the formulation by all nations, and particularly developing countries, of comprehensive communication policies linked to overall social, cultural, economic and political goals. Such policies should be based on inter-ministerial and inter-disciplinary consultations with broad public participation. The object must be to utilise the unique capacities of each form of communication, from interpersonal and traditional to the most modern, to make men and societies aware of their rights, harmonise unity in diversity, and foster the growth of individuals and communities within the wider frame of national development in an interdependent world.

As language embodies the cultural experience of people, all languages should be adequately developed to serve the complex and diverse requirements of modern communication. Developing nations and multilingual societies need to evolve language policies that promote all national languages even while selecting some, where necessary, for more widespread use in communication, higher education and administration. There is also a need in certain situations for the adaptation, simplification, and standardisation of scripts and development of keyboards, preparation of dictionaries and modernised systems of language learning, transcription of literature in widely-spoken national languages. The provision of simultaneous interpretation and automated translation facilities now under experimentation for cross-cultural communication to bridge linguistic divides should also be envisaged.

A primary policy objective should be to make elementary education available to all and to wipe out illiteracy, supplementing formal schooling systems with non-formal education and enrichment within appropriate structures of continuing and distance learning (through radio, television and correspondence).

Within the framework of national development policies, each country will have to work out its own set of priorities, bearing in mind that it will not be the possible to move in all directions at the same time. But, as far as resources allow, the communication policies should aim at stimulating and encouraging all means of communication.

Strengthening Capacities

Communication policies should offer a guide to the determination of information and media priorities and to the selection of appropriate technologies. This is required to plan the installation and development of adequate infrastructures to provide self-reliant communications capacity.

We recommend:

Developing countries take specific measures to establish or develop essential elements of their communication systems: print media, broadcasting and telecommunications along with the related training and production facilities.

Strong national news agencies are vital for improving each country's national and international reporting. Where viable, regional networks should be set up to increase news flows and serve all the major language groups in the area. Nationally, the agencies should buttress the growth of both urban and rural newspapers to serve as the core of a country's news collection and distribution system.

National book production should be encouraged and accompanied by the establishment of a distribution network for books, newspapers and periodicals. The stimulation of works by national authors in various languages should be promoted.

The development of a comprehensive national radio networks, capable of reaching remote areas should take priority over the development of television, which, however, should be encouraged where appropriate. Special attention should be given to areas where illiteracy is prevalent.

National capacity for producing broadcast materials is necessary to obviate dependence on external sources over and beyond desirable programme exchange. This capacity should include national or regional broadcasting, film and documentary production centres with a basic distribution network.

Adequate educational and training facilities are required to supply personnel for the media and production organisations, as well as managers, technicians and maintenance personnel. In this regard, co-operation between neighbouring countries and within regions should be encouraged.

Basic Needs

All nations have to make choices in investment priorities. In choosing between possible alternatives and often conflicting interests, developing countries, in particular, must give priority to satisfying their people's essential needs. Communication is not only a system of public information, but also an integral part of education and development.

We recommend:

The communication component in all development projects should receive adequate financing. The so-called "development support communications" are essential for mobilising initiatives and providing information required for action in all fields of development—agriculture, health and family planning, education, religion, industry and so on.

The essential communication needs to be met include the extension of basic postal services and telecommunication networks through small rural electronic exchanges.

The development of a community press in rural areas and small towns would not only provide print support for economic and social extension activities. This would also facilitate the production of functional literature for neo-literates as well.

Utilisation of local radio, low-cost small format television and video systems and other appropriate technologies would facilitate production of programmes relevant to community development efforts, stimulate participation and provide opportunity for diversified cultural expression.

The educational and informational use of communication should be given equal priority with entertainment. At the same time, education systems should prepare young people for communication activities.

Introduction of pupils at primary and secondary levels to the forms and uses of the means of communication (how to read newspapers, evaluate radio and television programmes, use elementary audio-visual techniques and apparatus) should permit the young to understand reality better and enrich their knowledge of current affairs and problems.

Organisation of community listening and viewing groups could in certain circumstances widen both entertainment and educational opportunities. Education and information activities should be supported by different facilities ranging from mobile book, tape and film libraries to programmed instruction through "schools of the air".

Such activities should be aggregated, wherever possible, in order to create vibrant local communication resource centres for entertainment, education, information dissemination and cultural exchange. They should be supported by decentralised media production centres; educational and extension services should be location-specific if they are to be credible and accepted.

It is not sufficient to urge that communication be given a high priority in national development; possible sources of investment finance must be identified. Among these could be differential communication pricing policies that would place larger burdens on more prosperous urban and elite group; the taxing of commercial advertising may also be envisaged for this purpose.

Particular Challenges

We have focused on national efforts which must be made to lead to greater independence and self-reliance. But there are three major challenges to this goal that require concerted international action. Simply put, these are paper, tariff structures and the electromagnetic spectrum.

We recommend:

A major international research and development effort to increase the supply of paper. The worldwide shortage of paper, including newsprint, and its escalating cost impose crushing burdens upon struggling newspapers, periodicals and the publication industry, above all in the developing countries. Certain ecological constraints have also emerged. Unesco, in collaboration with FAO, should take urgent measures to identify and encourage production of paper and newsprint either by recycling paper or from new sources of feedstock in addition to the wood pulp presently produced largely by certain northern countries. Kenaf, bagasse, tropical woods and grasses could possibly provide alternative sources. Initial experiments are encouraging and need to be supported and multiplied.

Appendix – 1

Tariffs for news transmission, telecommunications rates and air mail charges for the dissemination of news, transport of newspapers, periodicals, books and audiovisual materials are one of the main obstacles to a free and balanced flow of information. This situation must be corrected, especially in the case of developing countries, through a variety of national and international initiatives. Governments should in particular examine the policies and practices of their post and telegraph authorities. Profits or revenues should not be the primary aim of such agencies. They are instruments for policy-making and planned development in the field of information and culture. Their tariffs should be in line with larger national goals. International action is also necessary to alter telecommunication tariffs that militate heavily against small and peripheral users. Current international consultations on this question may be brought to early fruition, possibly at the October 1980 session of the 154-nation International Telegraph and Telephone Consultative Committee, which should have before it specific proposals made by a Unesco-sponsored working group on "Low Telecommunication Rates" (November 1979). Unesco might, in cooperation with ITU, also sponsor an overall study on international telecommunication services by means of satellite transmission in collaboration with Intelsat, Intersputnik and user country representatives to make proposals for international and regional coordination of geostationary satellite development. The study should also include investigation of the possibility and practicalities of discounts for transmission of news and preferential rates for certain types of transmission to and from developing countries. Finally, the developing countries should investigate the possibility of negotiating preferential tariffs on a bilateral or regional basis.

The electro-magnetic spectrum and geostationary orbit, both finite natural resources, should be more equitably shared as the common property of mankind. For that purpose, we welcome the decisions taken by the World Administrative Radio Conference (WARC), Geneva, September-November 1979, to convene a series of special conferences over the next few years on certain specific topics related to the utilisation of these resources.

II. Social Consequences and News Tasks

Integrating Communication into Development

Development strategies should incorporate communication policies as an integral part in the diagnosis of needs and in the design and implementation of selected priorities. In this respect communication should be considered a major development resource, a vehicle to ensure real political participation in decision-making, a central information base for defining policy options, and an instrument for creating awareness of national priorities.

We recommend:

Promotion of dialogue for development as a central component of both communication and development policies. Implementation of national policies should be carried out through three complementary communication patterns: first, from decision-makers towards different social sectors to transmit information about what they regard as necessary changes in development actions, alternative strategies and the varying consequences of the different alternatives; second, among and between diverse social sectors in a horizontal information network to express and exchange views on their different demands, aspirations, objective needs and subjective motivations; third, between decision-makers and all social groups through permanent participatory mechanisms for two-way information flows to elaborate development goals and priorities and make decisions on utilisation of resources. Each one of these patterns requires the design of specific information programmes, using different communication means.

In promoting the communication policies, special attention should be given to the use of non-technical language and comprehensible symbols, images and forms to ensure popular understanding of development issues and goals. Similarly, development information supplied to the media should be adapted to the prevailing news values and practices, which in turn should be encouraged to be more receptive to development needs and problems.

Facing the Technological Challenge

The technological explosion in communication has both great potential and great danger. The outcome depends on crucial decisions and on where and by whom they are taken. Thus, it is a priority to organise the decision-making process in a participatory manner on the basis of a full awareness of the social impact of different alternatives.

We recommend:

Devising policy instruments at the national level in order to evaluate the positive and negative social implications of the introduction of powerful new communication technologies. The preparation of technological impact surveys can be a useful tool to assess the consequences for lifestyles, relevance for under-privileged sectors of society, cultural influences, effects on employment patterns, and similar factors. This is particularly important when making choices with respect to the development of communication infrastructures.

Setting up national mechanisms to promote participation and discussion of social priorities in the acquisition or extension of new communication technologies. Decisions with respect to the orientation given to research and development should come under closer public scrutiny.

In developing countries the promotion of autonomous research and development should be linked to specific projects and programmes at the national, regional and inter-regional levels, which are often geared to the satisfaction of basic needs. More funds are necessary to stimulate and support adaptive technological research. This might also help these countries to avoid problems of obsolescence and problems arising from the non-availability of particular types of equipment, related spare parts and components from the advanced industrial nations.

The concentration of communications technology in a relatively few developed countries and transnational corporations has led to virtual monopoly situations in this field. To counteract these tendencies national and international measures are required, among them are reform of existing patent laws and conventions, appropriate legislation and international agreements.

Strengthening Cultural Identity

Promoting conditions for the preservation of the cultural identity of every society is necessary to enable it to enjoy a harmonious and creative inter-relationship with other cultures. It is equally necessary to modify situations in many developed and developing countries which suffer from cultural dominance.

We recommend:

Establishment of national cultural policies, which should foster cultural identity and creativity, and involve the media in these tasks. Such policies should also contain guidelines for safeguarding national cultural development while promoting knowledge of other cultures. It is in relation to others that each culture enhances its own identity.

Communication and cultural policies should ensure that creative artists and various grassroots groups can make their voices heard through the media. The innovative uses of film, television or radio by people of different cultures should be studied. Such experiments constitute a basis for continuing cultural dialogue, which could be furthered by agreements between countries and through international support.

Introduction of guidelines with respect to advertising content and the values and attitudes it fosters, in accordance with national standards and practices. Such guidelines should be consistent with national development policies and efforts to preserve cultural identity. Particular attention should be given to the impact on children and adolescents. In this connection, various mechanisms such as complaint boards or consumer review committees might be established to afford the public the possibility of reacting against advertising which they feel inappropriate.

Reducing the Commercialisation of Communication

The social effects of the commercialisation of the mass media are a major concern in policy formulation and decision-making by private and public bodies.

We recommend:

In expanding communication systems, preference should be given to non-commercial forms of mass communication. Promotion of such types of communication should be integrated with the traditions, culture, development objectives and socio-political system of each country. As in the field of education, public funds might be made available for this purpose.

While acknowledging the need of the media for revenues, ways and means should be considered to reduce the negative effects that the influence of market and commercial considerations have in the organisation and content of national and international communication flows.

That consideration should be given to changing existing funding patterns of commercial mass media. In this connection, reviews could be made of the way in which the relative role of advertising volume and costs pricing policies, voluntary contributions, subsidies, taxes, financial incentives and supports could be modified to enhance the social function of mass media and improve their service to the community.

Access to Technical Information

The flows of technical information within nations and across national boundaries is a major resource for development. Access to such information, which countries need for technical decision-making at all levels, is as crucial as access to news sources. This type of information is generally not easily available and is most often concentrated in large techno-structures. Developed countries are not providing adequate information of this type to developing countries.

We recommend:

Developing countries should pay particular attention to: (a) the correlation between education, scientific and communication policies, because their practical application frequently overlaps; (b) the creation in each country of one of several centres for the collection and utilisation of technical information and data, necessary for within the country and from abroad; (c) to secure the basic equipment necessary for essential data processing activities; (d) the development of skills and facilities for computer processing and analysis of data obtained from remote sensing.

Developed countries should foster exchanges of technical information on the principle that all countries have equal rights to full access to available information. It is increasingly necessary, in order to reduce inequalities in this field, to promote cooperative arrangements for collection, retrieval, processing and diffusion of technological information through various networks, regardless of geographical or institutional frontiers. UNISIST, which provides basic guidelines for voluntary cooperation among and between information systems and services, should further develop its activities.

Developing countries should adopt national informatics policies as a matter of priority. These should primarily relate to the establishment of decision-making centres (inter-departmental and inter-disciplinary) which would *inter alia* (a) assess technological alternatives; (b) centralise purchases; (c) encourage local production of software; (d) promote regional and sub-regional cooperation (in various fields, including education, health and consumer services).

At the international level, consideration should be given to action with respect to: (a) a systematic identification of existing organised data-processing infrastructures in various specialised fields; (b) agreement on measures for effective multi-country participation in the programmes, planning and administration of existing or developing data infrastructures; (c) analysis of commercial and technical measures likely to improve the use of informatics by developing countries; (d) agreement on international priorities for research and development that is of interest to all countries in the field of informatics.

Transnational corporations should supply to the authorities of the countries in which they operate, upon request and on a regular basis as specified by local laws and regulations, all information required for legislative and administrative purposes relevant to their activities and specifically needed to assess the performance of such entities. They should also provide the public, trade unions and other interested sectors of the countries in which they operate with information needed to understand the global structure, activities of the transnational corporation and their significance for the country concerned.

III. Professional Integrity and Standards

Responsibility of Journalists

For the journalist, freedom and responsibility are indivisible. Freedom without responsibility invites distortion and other abuses. But in the absence of freedom there can be no exercise of responsibility. The concept of freedom with responsibility necessarily includes a concern for professional ethics, demanding an equitable approach to events, situations or processes with due attention to their diverse aspects. This is not always the case today

We recommend:

The importance of the journalist's mission in the contemporary world demands steps to enhance his standing in society. In many countries even today, journalists are not regarded as members of an acknowledged profession and they are treated accordingly. To overcome this situation, journalism needs to raise its standards and quality for recognition everywhere as a genuine profession.

To be treated as professionals, journalists require broad educational preparation and specific professional training. Programmes of instruction need to be developed not only for entry-level recruits, but also experienced personnel who from time to time would benefit from special seminars and conferences designed to refresh and enrich their qualifications. Basically, programmes of instruction and training should be conducted on national and regional levels.

Such values as truthfulness, accuracy and respect for human rights are not universally applied at present. Higher professional standards and responsibility cannot be imposed by decree, nor do they depend solely on the goodwill of individual journalists, who are employed by institutions which can improve or handicap their professional performance. The self-respect of journalists, their integrity and inner drive to turn out work of high quality are of paramount importance. It is this level of professional dedication, making for responsibility, that should be fostered by news media and journalists' organisations. In this framework, a distinction may have to be drawn between media institutions, owners and managers on the one hand, and journalists on the other.

As in other professions, journalists and media organisations serve the public directly and the public, in turn, is entitled to hold them accountable for their actions. Among the mechanisms devised up to now in various countries for assuring accountability, the Commission sees merit in press or media councils, the institution of the press ombudsman and peer group criticism of the sort practised by journalism reviews in several countries. In addition, communities served by particular media can accomplish significant reforms through citizen action. Specific forms of community involvement in decision-making will vary, of course, from country to country. Public broadcasting stations, for example, can be governed by representative boards drawn from the community. Voluntary measures of this sort can do much to influence media performance. Nevertheless, it appears necessary to develop further effective ways by which the right to assess mass media performance can be exercised by the public.

Codes of professional ethics exist in all parts of the world, adopted voluntarily in many countries by professional groups. The adoption of codes of ethics at the national and, in some cases, at the regional level is desirable, provided that such codes are prepared and adopted by the profession itself—without governmental interference.

Towards Improved International Reporting

The full and factual presentation of news about one country to others is a continuing problem. The reasons for this are manifold: principal among them are correspondents' working conditions, their skills and attitudes, varying conceptions of news and information values and government viewpoints. Remedies for the situation will require long-term, evolutionary action towards improving the exchange of news around the world.

We recommend:

All countries should take steps to assure admittance of foreign correspondents and facilitate their collection and transmission of news. Special obligations in this regard, undertaken by the signatories to the Final Act of the Helsinki conference, should be honoured and, indeed, liberally applied. A free access to news sources by journalists is an indispensable requirement for accurate, faithful and balanced reporting. This necessarily involves access to unofficial, as well as official sources of information, that is, access to the entire spectrum of opinion within any country.

Conventional standards of news selection and reporting, and many accepted news values, need to be reassessed if readers and listeners around the world are to receive a more faithful and comprehensive account of events, movements and trends in both developing and developed countries. The inescapable need to interpret unfamiliar situations in terms that will be understood by a distant audience should not blind reporters or editors to the hazards of narrow ethnocentric thinking. The first step towards overcoming this bias is to acknowledge that it colours the thinking of virtually all human beings, journalists included, for the most part without deliberate intent. The act of selecting certain news items for publication, while rejecting others, produces in the minds of the audience a picture of the world that may well be incomplete or distorted. Higher professional standards are needed for journalists to be able to illuminate the diverse cultures and beliefs of the modern world, without their presuming to judge the ultimate validity of any foreign nation's experience and traditions.

To this end, reporters being assigned to foreign posts should have the benefit of language training and acquaintance with the history, institutions, politics, economics and cultural environment of the country or region in which they will be serving.

The press and broadcasting in the industrialised world should allot more space and time to reporting events in and background material about foreign countries in general and news from the developing world in particular. Also, the media in developed countries—especially the "gatekeepers", editors and producers of print and broadcasting media who select the news items to be published or broadcast—should become more familiar with the cultures and conditions in developing countries. Although the present imbalance in news flows calls for strengthening capacities in developing countries, the media of the industrialised countries have their contribution to make towards the correction of these inequalities.

To offset the negative effects of inaccurate or malicious reporting of international news, the right of reply and correction should be further considered. While these concepts are recognised in many countries, their nature and scope vary so widely that it would be neither expedient nor realistic to propose the adoption of any international regulations for their purpose. False or distorted news accounts can be harmful, but the voluntary publication of corrections or replies is preferable to international normative action. Since the manner in which the right of reply and correction as applied in different countries varies significantly, it is further suggested that: (a) the exercise of the international right of reply and correction be considered for application on a voluntary basis in each country according to its journalistic practices and national legal framework; (b) the United Nations in consultation with all concerned bodies, explore the conditions under which this right could be perfected at the international level, taking into account the cumbersome operation of the 1952 Convention on the International Right of Correction; (c) media institutions with an international reach define on a voluntary basis internal standards for the exercise of this right and make them publicly available.

Intelligence services of many nations have at one time or other recruited journalists to commit espionage under cover of their professional duties. This practice must be condemned. It undermines the integrity of the profession and, in some circumstances, can expose other journalists to unjustified suspicion or physical threat. The Commission urges journalists and their employers to be on guard against possible attempts of this kind. We also urge governments to refrain from using journalists for purposes of espionage.

Appendix – 1

Protection of Journalists

Daily reports from around the world attest to dangers that journalists are subject to in the exercise of their profession: harassment, threats, imprisonment, physical violence, assassination. Continual vigilance is required to focus the world's attention on such assaults to human rights.

We recommend:

The professional independence and integrity of all those involved in the collection and dissemination of news, information and views to the public should be safeguarded. However, the Commission does not propose special privileges to protect journalists in the performance of their duties, although journalism is often a dangerous profession. Far from constituting a special category, journalists are citizens of their respective countries, entitled to the same range of human rights as other citizens. One exception is provided in the Additional Protocol to the Geneva Convention of 12 August 1949, which applies only to journalists on perilous missions, such as in areas of armed conflict. To propose additional measures would invite the dangers entailed in a licensing system since it would require somebody to stipulate who should be entitled to claim such protection. Journalists will be fully protected only when everyone's human rights are guaranteed.

That Unesco should convene a series of round tables at which journalists, media executives, researchers and jurists can periodically review problems related to the protection of journalists and propose additional appropriate measures to this end.

IV. Democratisation of Communication

Human Rights

Freedom of speech, of the press, of information and of assembly are vital for the realisation of human rights. Extension of these communication freedoms to a broader individual and collective right to communicate is an evolving principle in the democratisation process. Among the human rights to be emphasised are those of equality for women and between races. Defence of all human rights is one of the media's most vital tasks.

We recommend:

All those working in the mass media should contribute to the fulfilment of human rights, both individual and collective, in the spirit of the Unesco Declaration on the mass media and the Helsinki Final Act, and the International Bill of Human Rights. The contribution of the media in this regard is not only to foster these principles, but also to expose all infringements, wherever they occur, and to support those whose rights have been neglected or violated. Professional associations and public opinion should support journalists subject to pressure or who suffer adverse consequences from their dedication to the defence of human rights.

The media should contribute to promoting the just cause of people struggling for freedom and independence and their right to live in peace and equality without foreign interference. This is especially important for all oppressed peoples who, while struggling against colonialism, religious and racial discrimination, are deprived of opportunity to make their voices heard within their own countries.

Communication needs in a democratic society should be met by the extension of specific rights such as the right to be informed, the right to inform, the right to privacy, the right to participate in public communication—all elements of a new concept, the right to communicate. In developing what might be called a new era of social rights, we suggest all the implications of the right to communicate be further explored.

Removal of Obstacles

Communication, with its immense possibilities for influencing the minds and behaviour of people, can be a powerful means of promoting democratisation of society and of widening public participation in the decision-making process. This depends on the structures and practices of the media and their management and to what extent they facilitate broader access and open the communication process to a free interchange of ideas, information and experience among equals, without dominance or discrimination.

We recommend:

All countries adopt measures to enlarge sources of information needed by citizens in their everyday life. A careful review of existing laws and regulations should be undertaken with the aim of reducing limitations, secrecy provisions and other constraints in information practices.

Censorship or arbitrary control of information should be abolished. In areas where reasonable restrictions may be considered necessary, these should be provided for by law, subject to judicial review and in line with the principles enshrined in, the United Nations Charter, the Universal Declaration of Human Rights and the International Covenants relating to human rights, and in other instruments adopted by the community of nations.

Special attention should be devoted to obstacles and restrictions which derive from the concentration of media ownership, public or private, from commercial influences on the press and broadcasting, or from private or governmental advertising. The problem of financial conditions under which the media operate should be critically reviewed, and measures elaborated to strengthen editorial independence.

Effective legal measures should be designed to: (a) limit the process of concentration and monopolisation; (b) circumscribe the action of transnationals by requiring them to comply with specific criteria and conditions defined by national legislation and development policies; (c) reverse trends to reduce the number of decision-makers at a time when the media's public is growing larger and the impact of communication is increasing; (d) reduce the influence of advertising upon editorial policy and broadcast programming; (e) seek and improve models which would ensure greater independence and autonomy of the media concerning their management and editorial policy, whether these are under private, public or government ownership.

Diversity and Choice

Diversity and choice in the content of communication are a pre-condition for democratic participation. Every individual and particular groups should be able to form judgements on the basis of full range of information and a variety of messages and opinions and have the opportunity to share these ideas with others. The development of decentralised and diversified media should provide larger opportunities for a real direct involvement of the people in communication processes.

We recommend:

The building of infrastructures and the adoption of particular technologies should be carefully matched to the need for more abundant information to a broader public from a plurality of sources.

Attention should be paid to the communication needs of women. They should be assured adequate access to communication means and that the images of them and of their activities are not distorted by the media or in advertising.

The concerns of children and youth, national, ethnic, religious, linguistic minorities, people living in remote areas and the aged and handicapped also deserve particular consideration. They constitute large and sensitive segments of society and have special communication needs.

Integration and Participation

To be able to communicate in contemporary society, man must dispose of appropriate communication tools. New technologies offer him many devices for individualised information and entertainment, but often fail to provide appropriate tools for communication with his community or social or cultural group. Hence, alternative means of communication are often required.

We recommend:
Much more attention be devoted to use of the media in living and working environments. Instead of isolating men and women, the media should help integrate them into the community.

Readers, listeners and viewers have generally been treated as passive receivers of information. Those in charge of the media should encourage their audiences to play a more active role in communication by allocating more newspaper space, or broadcasting time, for the views of individual members of the public or organised social groups.

The creation of appropriate communication facilities at all levels, leading towards new forms of public involvement in the management of the media and new modalities for their funding.

Communication policy makers should give far greater importance to devising ways whereby the management of the media could be democratised—while respecting national customs and characteristics— by associating the following categories: (a) journalists and professional communicator; (b) creative artists; (c) technicians; (d) media owners and managers; (e) representatives of the public. Such democratisation of the media needs the full support and understanding of all those working in them, and this process should lead to their having a more active role in editorial policy and management.

V. Fostering International Cooperation

Partners for Development

Inequalities in communication facilities, which exist everywhere, are due to economic discrepancies or due to political and economic design, still others due to cultural imposition or neglect. But whatever the source or reason for them, gross inequalities should no longer be countenanced. The very notion of a new world information and communication order presupposes fostering international cooperation, which included two main areas: international assistance and contributions towards international understanding. The international dimensions of communication are today of such importance that it has become crucial to develop cooperation on a worldwide scale. It is for the international community to take the appropriate steps to replace dependence, dominance and inequality by more fruitful and more open relations of interdependence and complementarity, based on mutual interest and the equal dignity of nations and peoples. Such cooperation requires a major international commitment to redress the present situation. This clear commitment is a need not only for developing countries but also for the international community as a whole. The tensions and disruptions that will come from lack of action are far greater than the problems posed by necessary changes.

We recommend:

The progressive implementation of national and international measures that will foster the setting up of a new world information and communication order. The proposals contained in this report can serve as a contribution to develop the varied actions necessary to move in that direction.

International cooperation for the development of communications be given equal priority with and within other sectors, (e.g. health, agriculture, industry, science, education, etc.) as information is a basic resource for individual and collective advancement and for all-round development. This may be achieved by utilising funds provided through bilateral governmental agreements and from international and regional organisations, which should plan a considerable increase in their allocations for communication, infrastructures, equipment and programme development. Care should be taken that assistance is compatible with developing countries' priorities. Consideration should also be given to provision of assistance on a programme rather than on a strict project basis.

The close relationship between the establishment of a new international economic order and the new world information and communication order should be carefully considered by the technical bodies dealing with these issues. Concrete plans of action linking both processes should be implemented within the United Nations system. The United Nations, in approving the international development strategy should consider the communications sector as an integral element of it and not merely as an instrument of public information.

Strengthening Collective Self-Reliance

Developing countries have a primary responsibility for undertaking necessary changes to overcome their dependence in the field of communications. The actions needed begin at the national level, but must be complemented by forceful and decisive agreements at the bilateral, sub-regional, and inter-regional levels. Collective self-reliance is the cornerstone of a new world information and communication order.

We recommend:
The communication dimension should be incorporated into existing programmes and agreements for economic cooperation between developing countries.

Joint activities should be developed further in the light of the overall analysis and recommendations of this report. In particular, attention should be given to cooperation among national news agencies, to the further development of the news agencies pool and broadcasting organisations of the non-aligned countries, as well as to the general exchange on a regular basis of radio, TV programmes and films.

With respect to cooperation in the field of technical information, the establishment of regional and sub-regional data banks and information processing centres and specialised documentation centres should be given a high priority. They should be conceived and organised, both in terms of software and management, according to the particular needs of cooperating countries. Choices of technology and selection of foreign enterprises should be made so as not to increase dependence in this field.

Mechanisms for sharing information of a non-strategic nature could be established particularly in economic matters. Arrangements of this nature could be of value in areas such as multilateral trade negotiations, dealings with transnational corporations and banks, economic forecasting, and medium and long-term planning and other similar fields.

Particular efforts should be undertaken to ensure that news about other developing countries within or outside their region receive more attention and space in the media. Special projects could be developed to ensure a steady flow of attractive and interesting material inspired by news values which meet developing countries' information needs.

Measures to promote links and agreements between professional organisations and communication researchers of different countries should be fostered. It is necessary to develop networks of institutions and people working in the field of communication in order to share and exchange experiences and implement joint projects of common interest with concrete operational contents.

International Mechanisms

Cooperation for the development of communications is a global concern and therefore of importance to international organisations, where all member states can fully debate the issues involved and decide upon multinational action. Governments should therefore attentively review the structures and programmes of international agencies in the communications field and point to changes required to meet evolving needs.

Appendix – 1

We recommend:

The member states of Unesco should increase their support to the Organisation's programme in this area. Consideration should be given to organising a distinct communication sector, not simply in order to underline its importance, but to emphasise that its activities are inter-related with the other major components of UNESCO'S work—education, science and culture. In its communications activities, Unesco should concentrate on priority areas. Among these are assistance to national policy formulation and planning, technical development, organising professional meetings and exchanges, promotion and coordination of research, and elaboration of international norms.

Better coordination of the various communication activities within Unesco and those throughout the United Nations System. A thorough inventory and assessment of all communications development and related programmes of the various agencies should be undertaken as a basis for designing appropriate mechanisms to carry out the necessary consultation, cooperation and coordination.

It would be desirable for the United Nations family to be equipped with a more effective information system, including a broadcast capability of its own and possibly access to a satellite system. That would enable the United Nations to follow more closely world affairs and transmit its message more effectively to all the peoples of the earth. Although such a proposal would require heavy investment and raise some complex issues, a feasibility study should be undertaken so that a carefully designed project could be prepared for deliberation and decision.

Consideration might be given to establishing within the framework of Unesco an International Centre for the Study and Planning of Information and Communication. Its main tasks would be to: (a) promote the development of national communication systems in developing countries and the balance and reciprocity in international information flows; (b) mobilise resources required for that purpose and manage the funds put at its disposal; and (c) assure coordination among parties interested in communication development and involved in various cooperation programmes and evaluate results of bilateral and multilateral activities in this field; (d) organise round tables, seminars, and conferences for the training of communication planners researchers and journalists, particularly, those specialising in international problems; and (e) keep under review communications technology transfers between developed and developing countries so that they are carried out in the most suitable conditions. The Centre may be guided by a tripartite coordinating council composed of representatives of developing and developed countries and of interested international organisations. We suggest Unesco should undertake further study of this proposal for consideration at the 1980 session of the General Conference.

Towards International Understanding

The strengthening of peace, international security and cooperation and the lessening of international tensions are the common concern of all nations. The mass media can make a substantial contribution towards achieving these goals. The special session of the United Nations General Assembly on disarmament called for increased efforts by the mass media to mobilise public opinion in favour of disarmament and of ending the arms race. This Declaration together with the Unesco Declaration on fundamental principles concerning the contribution of the mass media to strengthening peace and international understanding, to the promotion of human rights and to countering racialism, apartheid and incitement to war should be the foundation of new communication policies to foster international understanding. A new world information and communication order requires and must become the instrument for peaceful cooperation between nations.

We recommend:

National communication policies should be consistent with adopted international communication principles and should seek to create a climate of mutual understanding and peaceful coexistence among nations. Countries should also encourage their broadcast and other means of international communication to make the fullest contribution towards peace and international cooperation and to refrain from advocating national, racial or religious hatred, and incitement to discrimination, hostility, violence or war.

Due attention should be paid to the problems of peace and disarmament, human rights, development and the creation of a new communication order. Mass media, both printed and audiovisual, should be encouraged to publicise significant documents of the United Nations, of Unesco, of the world peace movements and of various other international and national organisations devoted to peace and disarmament. The curricula of schools of journalism should include study of these international problems and the views expressed on them within the United Nations.

All forms of cooperation among the media, the professionals and their associations, which contribute to the better knowledge of other nations and cultures, should be encouraged and promoted.

Appendix – 1

Reporting on international events or developments in individual countries in situations of crisis and tension requires extreme care and responsibility. In such situations the media often constitute one of the few, if not the sole, link between combatants or hostile groups. This clearly casts on them a special role which they should seek to discharge with objectivity and sensitivity.

The recommendations and suggestions contained in our Report do not presume to cover all topics and issues calling for reflection and action. Nevertheless, they indicate the importance and scale of the tasks which face every country in the field of information and communication, as well as their international dimensions which pose a formidable challenge to the community of nations.

Our study indicates clearly the direction in which the world must move to attain a new information and communication order—essentially a series of new relationships arising from the advances promised by new communication technologies which should enable all peoples to benefit. The awareness already created on certain issues, such as global imbalances in information flows, suggests that a process of change has resulted and is under way. The power and promise of ever-new communication technologies and systems are, however, such as to demand deliberate measures to ensure that existing communication disparities do not widen. The objective should be to ensure that men and women are enabled to lead richer and more satisfying lives.

Appendix – 2

RTNDA Code

The Radio-Television News Directors Association, wishing to foster the highest professional standards of electronic journalism, promote public understanding of and confidence in electronic journalism, and strengthen principles of journalistic freedom to gather and disseminate information, establishes this Code of Ethics and Professional Conduct.

Preamble

Professional electronic journalists should operate as trustees of the public, seek the truth, report it fairly and with integrity and independence, and stand accountable for their actions.

Public Trust: Professional electronic journalists should recognise that their first obligation is to the public.

Professional electronic journalists should:
Understand that any commitment other than service to the public undermines trust and credibility.

Recognise that service in the public interest to create an obligation to reflect the diversity of the community and guard against oversimplification of issues or events.

Provide a full range of information to enable the public to make enlightened decisions.

Fight to ensure that the public's business is conducted in public.

Truth: Professional electronic journalists should pursue truth aggressively and present the news accurately, in context, and as completely as possible.

Professional electronic journalists should:
Continuously seek the truth.

Resist distortions that obscure the importance of events.

Clearly disclose the origin of information and label all material provided by outsiders.

Appendix – 2

Professional electronic journalists should not:
Report anything known to be false.
Manipulate images or sounds in any way that is misleading.
Plagiarise present images or sounds that are reenacted without informing the public.

Fairness: Professional electronic journalists should present the news fairly and impartially, placing primary value on significance and relevance.

Professional electronic journalists should:
Treat all subjects of news coverage with respect and dignity, showing particular compassion to victims of crime or tragedy.

Exercise special care when children are involved in a story and give children greater privacy and protection than adults.

Seek to understand the diversity of their community and inform the public without bias or stereotype.

Present a diversity of expressions, opinions, and ideas in context.

Present analytical reporting based on professional perspective, not personal bias.

Respect the right to a fair trial.

Integrity: Professional electronic journalists should present the news with integrity and decency, avoiding real or perceived conflicts of interest, and respect the dignity and intelligence of the audience as well as the subjects of news.

Professional electronic journalists should:
Identify sources whenever possible. Confidential sources should be used only when it is clearly in the public interest to gather or convey important information or when a person providing information might be harmed. Journalists should keep all commitments to protect a confidential source. Clearly label opinion and commentary.

Guard against extended coverage of events or individuals that fails to significantly advance a story, place the event in context, or add to the public knowledge.

Refrain from contacting participants in violent situations while the situation is in progress.

Use technological tools with skill and thoughtfulness, avoiding techniques that skew facts, distort reality, or sensationalise events.

Use surreptitious news gathering techniques, including hidden cameras or microphones, only if there is no other way to obtain stories of significant public importance and only if the technique is explained to the audience.

Disseminate the private transmissions of other news organisations only with permission.

Professional electronic journalists should not:
Pay news sources who have a vested interest in a story.

Accept gifts, favours, or compensation from those who might seek to influence coverage.

Engage in activities that may compromise their integrity or independence.

Independence: Professional electronic journalists should defend the independence of all journalists from those seeking influence or control over news content.

Professional electronic journalists should:
Gather and report news without fear or favour, and vigorously resist undue influence from any outside forces, including advertisers, sources, story subjects, powerful individuals, and special interest groups.

Resist those who would seek to buy or politically influence news content or who would seek to intimidate those who gather and disseminate the news.

Determine news content solely through editorial judgement and not as the result of outside influence.

Resist any self-interest or peer pressure that might erode journalistic duty and service to the public.

Recognise that sponsorship of the news which will not be used in any way to determine, restrict or manipulate content.

Refuse to allow the interests of ownership or management to influence news judgement and content inappropriately.

Defend the rights of the free press for all journalists, recognising that any professional or government licensing of journalists is a violation of that freedom.

Accountability: Professional electronic journalists should recognise that they are accountable for their actions to the public, the profession, and themselves.

Professional electronic journalists should:
Actively encourage adherence to these standards by all journalists and their employers.

Respond to public concerns. Investigate complaints and correct errors promptly and with as much prominence as the original report.

Explain journalistic processes to the public, especially when practices spark questions or controversy.

Recognise that professional electronic journalists are duty-bound to conduct themselves ethically.

Refrain from ordering or encouraging courses of action that would force employees to commit an unethical act.

Carefully listen to employees who raise ethical objections and create environments in which such objections and discussions are encouraged.

Seek support for and provide opportunities to train employees in ethical decision-making.

In meeting its responsibility to the profession of electronic journalism, RTNDA has created this code to identify important issues, to serve as a guide for its members, to facilitate self-scrutiny, and to shape future debate.

Adopted at RTNDA 2000 in Minneapolis September 14, 2000.

Appendix – 3

Airwaves Are Public Property
(Supreme Court Judgement)

Operative part of the Supreme Court judgement delivered by Justice P. B. Sawant and Justice S. Mohan on 9.2.1995 in the case between the Union of India and Cricket Association of Bengal. We, therefore, hold as follows:

(i) The airwaves or frequencies are a public property. Their use has to be controlled and regulated by a public authority in the interests of the public and to prevent the invasion of their rights. Since, the electronic media involves the use of the airwaves, this factor creates an in-built restriction on its use as in the case of any other public property.

(ii) The right to impart and receive information is a species of the right to freedom of speech and expression guaranteed by Article 19 (1) (a) of the Constitution. A citizen has a fundamental right to use the best means of imparting and receiving information and as such to have an access to telecasting for the purpose. However, this right to have an access to telecasting has limitations on account of the use of the public property, viz. the airwaves, involved in the exercise of the right and can be controlled and regulated by the public authority. This limitation imposed by the nature of the public property involved in the use of the electronic media is in addition to the restriction imposed on the right to freedom of speech and expression under Article 19 (2) of the Constitution.

(iii) The Central Government shall take immediate steps to establish an independent autonomous public authority representatives of all sections and interests in the society to control and regulate the use of the airwaves.

(iv) Since, the matches have been telecast pursuant to the impugned order of the High Court, it is not necessary to decide the correctness of the said order.

(v) The High Court will now apportion between the CAB and the DD, the revenue generated by the advertisements on TV during the telecasting

Appendix – 3

of both the series of the cricket matches, viz. the Hero Cup, and the international cricket matches played in India from October to December, 1994, after hearing the parties on the subject. The civil appeals are disposed of accordingly. In view of the disposal of the civil appeals, the writ petition filed by the Cricket Association of Bengal also stands disposed of accordingly.

Operative part of the Supreme Court Judgement delivered by Justice B. P. Jeevan Reddy on 9.2.1995 in the case between the U.O.I. and Cricket Association of Bengal.

Summary

In this summary too, the expression 'broadcast media' means the electronic media now represented and operated by AIR and Doordarshan and not any other services.

1. (a) Game of Cricket, like any other sports event, provides entertainment. Providing entertainment is implied in freedom of speech and expression guaranteed by Article 19 (1) (a) of the Constitution subject to this rider that where speech and conduct are joined in a single course of action, the free speech values must be balanced against competing societal interests. The petitioners (CAB and BCCI) therefore have a right to organise cricket matches in India, whether with or without the participation of foreign teams. But what they are now seeking is a license to telecast their matches through an agency of their choice – a foreign agency in both the cases – and through telecasting equipment brought in by such foreign agency from outside the country. In the case of Hero Cup matches, organised by BCCI, they did not ask for this facility for the reason that their foreign agent has arranged direct uplinking with the Russian satellite Gorizon . In both the cases, they wanted the permission to import the telecasting equipment along with the personnel to operate it by moving it to places all over the country wherever the matches were to be played. They claimed this license, or permission, as it may be called, as a matter of right said to be flowing from Article 19 (1) (a) of the Constitution. They say that the authorities are bound to grant such license/permission, without any conditions, all that they are entitled to do, it is submitted, is to collect technical fees wherever their services are availed, like the services of VSNL in the case of Hero Cup Matches. This plea is in principle no different from the freedom to the right to establish and operate private telecasting stations. In principle, there is no difference between a permanent TV station and a temporary one; similarly there is no distinction in principle between a stationary TV facility and a mobile one; so also is there no distinction in

principle between a regular TV facility and a TV facility for a given event or series of events. If the right claimed by the petitioners (CAB and BCCI) is held to be constitutionally sanctioned one, then each and every citizen of this country must also be entitled to claim similar right in respect of his event or events, as the case may be. I am of the opinion that no such right flows from Article 19 (1) (a).(b) Airwaves constitute public property and must be utilised for advancing public good. No individual has a right to utilise them at his choice and pleasure and for purposes of his choice including profit. The right of free speech guaranteed by Article 19 (1) (a) does not include the right to use airwaves, which are public property. The airwaves can be used by a citizen for the purpose of broadcasting only when allowed to do so by a statute and in accordance with such statute. Airwaves, being public property, it is the duty of the State to see that airwaves are so utilised as to advance the free speech right of the citizens which is served by ensuring plurality and diversity of views, opinions and ideas. This is imperative in every democracy where freedom of speech is assured. The free speech right guaranteed to every citizen of this country does not encompass the right to use these airwaves at his choice. Conceding, such a right would be detrimental to the free speech rights of the body of citizens in as much as only the privileged few powerful economic, commercial and political interests – would come to dominate the media. By manipulating the news, views and information, by indulging in misinformation and disinformation, to suit their commercial or other interests, they would be harming – and not serving – the principle of plurality and diversity of views, news, ideas and opinions. This has been the experience of Italy, where a limited right, i.e. at the local level but not at the national level was recognised. It is also not possible to imply or infer a right from the guarantee of free speech which only a few can enjoy.

(c) Broadcasting media is inherently different from press or other means of communication/information. The analogy of press is misleading and inappropriate. This is also the view expressed by several constitutional codes including that of the United States of America.

(d) I must clarify what I say, it is that the right claimed by the petitioners (CAB and BCCI) – which in effect is no different in principle from a right to establish and operate a private TV station – does not flow from Article 19 (1) (a); that such a right is not implicit in it. The question whether such a right should be given to the citizens of this country is a matter of policy for the Parliament. Having regard to the revolution in information technology and the developments all around, Parliament may or may not, decide to confer such right. If it wishes to confer such a right, it can only be by way

Appendix – 3

of an Act made by the Parliament. The act made should be consistent with the right of free speech of the citizens and must have to contain strict programme and other controls, as has been provided, for example in the Broadcasting Act, 1991 in the United Kingdom. This is the implicit command of Article 19 (1) (a) and is essential to preserve and promote plurality and diversity of views, news, opinions and ideas.

(e) There is an inseparable inter-connection between freedom of speech and the stability of the society, i.e. stability of a nation-state. They contribute to each other. Ours is a nascent republic. We are yet to achieve the goal of a stable society. This country cannot also afford to read into Article 19 (1) (a) an unrestricted right to licensing (right of broadcasting) as claimed by the petitioners therein.

(f) In the case before us, both the petitioners have sold their right to telecast the matches to a foreign agency. They have parted with the right. The right to telecast the matches, including the right to import, install and operate the requisite equipment, is thus really sought by the foreign agencies and not by the petitioners. Hence, the question of violation of their right under Article 19 (1) (a) resulting from refusal of license/ permission to such foreign agencies does not arise.

2. The government monopoly of broadcasting media in this country is the result of historical and other factors. This is true of every other country, to start with. That India was not a free country till 1947 and its citizens did not have constitutionally guaranteed fundamental freedom till 1950 coupled with the fact that our Constitution is just about forty five years into operation explains the government monopoly. As pointed out in the body of the judgement, broadcasting media was a monopoly of the government, to start with in every country except the United States where a conscious decision was taken at the very beginning, not to have state monopoly over the medium. Until recently, the broadcasting media has been in the hands of public/statutory corporations in most of the West European countries. Private broadcasting is comparatively a recent phenomenon. The experience in Italy of allowing private broadcasting at local level (while prohibiting it at national level) has left much to be desired. It has given rise to powerful media empires. This development is certainly not conducive to free speech right of the citizens.

3. (a) It has been held by this Court – and rightly – that broadcasting media is affected by the free speech right of the citizens guaranteed by Article 19 (1) (a). This is also the view expressed by all the Constitutional Courts whose opinions have been referred to in the body of the judgement. Once this is so, monopoly of this medium (broadcasting media), whether

by government or by an individual, body or organisation is unacceptable. Clause (2) of Article 19 does not permit a monopoly in the matter of freedom of speech and expression as is permitted by Clause (6) of Article 19 vis-à-vis the right guaranteed by Article 19 (1) (a).

(b) The right of free speech and expression includes the right to receive and impart information. For ensuring the free speech right of the citizens of this country, it is necessary that the citizens have the benefit of plurality of views and a range of opinions on all public issues. A successful democracy posits an "aware" citizenry. Diversity of opinions, views, ideas and ideologies is essential to enable the citizens to arrive at informed judgement on all issues touching them. This cannot be provided by a medium controlled by a monopoly – whether the monopoly is of the state or any other individual, group or organisation. As a matter of fact, private broadcasting stations may perhaps be more prejudicial to free speech right of the citizens than the government-controlled media, as explained in the body of the judgement. The broadcasting media should be under the control of the public as distinct from the government. This is the command implicit in Article 19 (1) (a). It should be operated by a public statutory corporation or corporations, as the case may be, whose constitution and composition must be such as it ensures their impartiality in political, economic and social matters and on all other public issues. It/they must be required by law to present news, views and opinions in a balanced way ensuring pluralism and diversity of opinions and views. It/they must provide equal access to all the citizens and groups to avail of the medium.

4. The Indian Telegraph Act, 1885 is totally inadequate to govern an important medium like the radio and television, i.e. broadcasting media. The Act was intended for an altogether different purpose when it was enacted. This is the result of the law in this country, not keeping pace with the technological advances in the field of information and communications. While all the leading democratic countries have enacted laws specifically governing the broadcasting media, the law in this country has stood still, rooted in the Telegraph Act of 1885. Except Section 4 (1) and the definition of telegraph, no other provision of the Act is shown to have any relevance to broadcasting media. It is, therefore, imperative that the Parliament makes a law placing the broadcasting media in the hands of a public /statutory corporate or the corporations, as the case may be. This is necessary to safeguard the interests of public and the interests of law as also to avoid uncertainty, confusion and consequent litigation.

5. The CAB did not ever apply for a license under the first proviso to Section 4 of the Telegraph Act nor did its agents ever make such an

application. The permissions, clearances or exemption obtained by it from the several departments (mentioned in judgement) are no substitute for a licence under Section 4(1) proviso. In the absence of such a license, the CAB had no right in law to have its matches telecast by an agency of its choice. The legality or validity of the orders passed by Shri N. Vithal, Secretary to the Government of India, Telecommunications Department, need not be gone into since it has become academic. In the facts and circumstances of the case, the charge of mala fides or of arbitrary and authoritarian conduct attributed to Doordarshan and Ministry of Information and Broadcasting is not acceptable. No opinion need be expressed on the allegations made in the Interlocutory Application filed by BCCI in these matters. Its intervention was confined to legal questions only.

6. Now the question arises, what is the position till the Central Government or the Parliament take steps as contemplated in para (4) of the summary, i.e. if any sporting event or other event is to be telecast from the Indian soil? The obvious answer flowing from the judgement (and Paras (1) and (4) of this summary) is that the organiser of such event has to approach the nodal Ministry as specified in the decision of the meeting of the Committee of Secretaries held on November 12, 1993. I have no reason to doubt that such a request would be considered by the nodal Ministry and AIR and Doordarshan on its merits, keeping in view the public interest. In case of any difference of opinion or dispute regarding the monetary terms on which such telecast is to be made, matter can always be referred to an arbitrator or a panel of arbitrators. In case, the nodal Ministry or AIR or Doordarshan find such broadcast /telecast not feasible, then they may consider the grant of permission to the organisers to engage an agency of their own for the purpose. Of course, it would be equally open to the nodal Ministry (Government of India) to permit such foreign agency in addition to AIR / Doordarshan, if they are of the opinion that such a course is called for in the circumstances.

For the above reasons, the appeals, writ petition and applications are disposed of in the above terms. No costs.

Appendix – 4

The Prasar Bharati (Broadcasting Corporation of India) Act, 1990

An Act to provide for the establishment of a Broadcasting Corporation for India, to be known as Prasar Bharati, to define its composition, functions and powers and to provide for matters connected therewith or incidental thereof.

Chapter – I

Preliminary

1. **Short title, extent and commencement**
    (a) This Act may be called the Prasar Bharati (Broadcasting Corporation of India) Act, 1990.
    (b) It extends to the whole of India.
    (c) It shall come into force on such date as the Central Government may, by notification, appoint.

2. **Definitions**
    In this Act, unless the context otherwise requires, –
    (a) "Akashvani" means the offices, stations and other establishments, by whatever name called, which, immediately before the appointed day, formed part of or were under the director-general, All India Radio of the Union Ministry of Information and Broadcasting;
    (b) "Appointed Day" means the date appointed under Section 3;
    (c) "Broadcasting" means the dissemination of any form of communication like signs, signals, writing, pictures, images and sounds of all kinds by transmission of electro-magnetic waves through space or through cables intended to be received by the general public, either directly or indirectly, through the medium

Appendix - 4

of relay stations and all its grammatical variations and cognate expression shall be construed accordingly;

(d) "Board" means the Prasar Bharati Board;

(e) "Broadcasting Council" means the Council established under Section 14;

(f) "Chairman" means the Chairman of the Corporation appointed under Section 4;

(g) "Corporation" means the Prasar Bharati (Broadcasting Corporation of India) established under Section 3;

(h) "Doordarshan" means the offices, *kendras* and other establishments, by whatever name called, which, immediately before the appointed day, formed part of or were under the Directorate-General, Doordarshan of the Union Ministry of Information and Broadcasting;

(i) "Elected Member" means a Member elected under section 3;

(j) "Executive Member" means the Executive Member appointed under Section 4;

(k) "*Kendra*" means any telecasting centre with studios or transmitters or both and includes a relay station;

(l) "Member" means a Member of the Board;

(m) "Member (Finance)" means the Member (Finance) appointed under Section 4;

(n) "Member (Personnel)" means the Member (Personnel) appointed under Section 4;

(o) "Nominated Member" means the Member nominated by the Union Ministry of Information and Broadcasting under Section 3;

(p) "Non-lapsable Fund" means the Fund created from the commercial revenues of Akashvani and Doordarshan to meet expenditure on certain schemes;

(q) "Notification" means a notification published in the official Gazette;

(r) "Part-time Member" means a Part-time Member of the Board appointed under Section 4, but does not include an ex-officio Member, the Nominated Member or an elected Member;

(s) "Prescribed" means prescribed by rules made under this Act;

(t) "Recruitment Board" means a board established under sub-section (I) of Section 10;

(u) "Regulations" means regulations made by the Corporation under this Act;

(v) "Station" means any broadcasting station with studios or transmitters or both and includes a relay station;

(w) "Whole-time Member" means the Executive Member, Member (Finance) or Member (Personnel);

(x) "Year" means the financial year.

Chapter – II
Prasar Bharati (Broadcasting Corporation of India)

3. **Establishment and Composition of Corporation**
   (a) With effect from such date as the Central Government may by notification appoint in this behalf, there shall be established for the purposes of this Act a Corporation, to be known as the Prasar Bharati (Broadcasting Corporation of India).
   (b) The Corporation shall be a body corporate by the name aforesaid, having perpetual succession and a common seal with power to acquire, hold and dispose of property, both movable and immovable, and to contract, and shall by the said name sue and be sued.
   (c) The headquarters of the Corporation shall be at New Delhi and the Corporation may establish offices, kendras or stations at other places in India and, with the previous approval of the Central Government, outside India.
   (d) The general superintendence, direction and management of the affairs of the Corporation shall vest in the Prasar Bharati Board which may exercise all such powers and do all such acts and things as may be exercised or done by the Corporation under this Act.
   (e) The Board shall consist of –
      (i) a Chairman;
      (ii) one Executive Member;
      (iii) one Member (finance);
      (iv) one Member (personnel);
      (v) six Part-Time Members;
      (vi) Director-General (Akashvani), ex-officio;
      (vii) Director-General (Doordarshan), ex-officio;
      (viii) one representative of the Union Ministry of Information and Broadcasting, to be nominated by that Ministry; and
      (ix) two representatives of the employees of the Corporation, of whom one shall be elected by the engineering staff from amongst themselves and one shall be elected by the other employee from amongst themselves.

(f) The Corporation may appoint such committees as may be necessary for the efficient performance, exercise and discharge of its functions, powers and duties:
Provided that all or a majority of the members of each committee shall be Members and a member of any such committee who is not a Member shall have only the right to attend meetings of the committee and take part in the proceedings thereof, but shall not have the right to vote.

(g) The Corporation may associate with itself, in such manner and for such purposes as may be provided by regulations, any person whose assistance or advice it may need in complying with any of the provisions of this Act and a person so associated shall have the right to take part in the discussions of the Board relevant to the purposes for which he has been associated, but shall not have the right to vote.

(h) No act or proceeding of the Board or of any committee appointed by it under sub-section (6) shall be invalidated merely by reason of–
  (i) any vacancy in, or any defect in the constitution of, the Board or such committee; or
  (ii) any defect in the appointment of a person acting as a Member or a member of such committee; or
  (iii) any irregularity in the procedure of the Board or such committee not affecting the merits of the case.

4. *Appointment of Chairman and Other Members*

(a) The Chairman and the other Members, except the ex-officio Members, the Nominated Member and the elected Members shall be appointed by the president of India on the recommendation of a committee consisting of –
  (i) the Chairman of the Council of States, who shall be the Chairman of the Committee;
  (ii) the Chairman of the Press Council of India established under Section 4 of the Press Council Act, 1978; and
  (iii) one nominee of the president of India.

(b) No appointment of a Member shall be invalidated merely by reason of any vacancy in, or any defect in the constitution of, the committee appointed under sub-section (1).

(c) The Chairman and the Part-time Members shall be persons of eminence in Public life; the Executive Member shall be a person having special knowledge or practical experience in respect of such matters as administration, management, broadcasting, education, literature, culture, arts, music, dramatics or journalism; the Member (Finance) shall be a person having special knowledge or practical experience in respect of financial matters and the Member (Personnel) shall be a person having special knowledge or practical experience in respect of personnel management and administration.

(d) The recommendations made by the committee constituted under sub-section (1) shall be binding for the purposes of appointments under this section.

5. **Powers and Functions of Executive Member**

(a) The Executive Member shall be the Chief Executive of the Corporation and shall, subject to the control and supervision of the Board, exercise such power and discharge such functions of the Board as it may delegate to him.

6. **Term of Office, Conditions of Service, etc. of Chairman and Other Members.**

(a) The Chairman shall be Part-time Member and shall hold office for a term of six years from the date on which he enters upon his office.

(b) The Executive Member, the Member (Finance) and Member (Personnel) shall be Whole-time Members and every such Member shall hold office for a term of six years from the date on which he enters upon his office or until he attains the age of sixty-two years, whichever is earlier.

(c) The term of office of Part-time Members shall be six years, but one-third of such Members shall retire on the expiration of every second year.

(d) The term of office of an elected Member shall be two years or till he ceases to be an employee of the Corporation, whichever is earlier.

(e) As soon as, may be after the establishment of the Corporation, the president of India may, by order, make such provision as he thinks fit for curtailing the term of office of some of the Part-time Members then appointed in order that one-third of the Members holding office as such Part-time Members shall retire in every second year thereafter.

(f) Where before the expiry of the term of office of a person holding the office of Chairman, or any other Member, a vacancy arises, for any reason whatsoever, such vacancy shall be deemed to be

Appendix – 4

a casual vacancy and the person appointed or elected to fill such vacancy shall hold office for the unexpired period of the term for which his predecessor in office would have held office if such vacancy had not arisen.

(g) The Whole-time Members shall be the employees of the Corporation and as such shall be entitled to such salaries and allowances and shall be subject to such conditions of service in respect of leave, pension (if any), provident fund and other matters as may be prescribed:

Provided that the salaries and allowances and the conditions of service shall not be varied to their disadvantage after their appointment.

(h) The Chairman and Part-time Members shall be entitled to such allowances as may be prescribed.

7. Removal and Suspension of Chairman and Members

(a) Subject to the provisions of sub-section (3), the Chairman or any other Member, except an ex-officio Member, the Nominated Member and an elected Member shall only be removed from his office by order of the president of India on the ground of misbehaviour after the Supreme Court, on a reference being made to it by the president, has, on inquiry held in accordance with such procedure as the Supreme Court may by rules provide, reported that the Chairman or such other Member, as the case may be, ought, on such ground, be removed.

(b) The president may suspend from office the Chairman or other Member, except an ex-officio Member, the Nominated Member or an elected Member, in respect of whom a reference has been made to the Supreme Court under sub-section (1) until the president has passed orders on receipt of the report of the Supreme Court on such reference.

(c) Notwithstanding anything contained in sub-section (1), the president may, by order, remove the Chairman or any Whole-time Member from his office if such Chairman or such Whole-time Member –

  (i) ceases to be a citizen of India; or
  (ii) is adjudged an insolvent; or
  (iii) engages during his term of office in any paid employment outside the duties of his office; or
  (iv) is convicted of any offence involving moral turpitude; or is, in the opinion of the president, unfit to continue in office by reason of infirmity of body or mind:

Provided that the president may, by order, remove any part-time Member from his office if he is adjudged an insolvent or is convicted of any offence involving moral turpitude or where he is, in the opinion of the president, unfit to continue in office by reason of infirmity of body or mind.

(d) If the Chairman or any Whole-time Member, except any ex-officio Member, the Nominated Member or any elected Member, is, or becomes in any way concerned or interested in any contract or agreement made by or on behalf of the Corporation or the Government of India or the Government of a State or, participates in any way in the profit thereof, or in any benefit or emolument arising therefrom than as a member, and in common with other members of an incorporated company, he shall, for the purposes of sub-section (1), be deemed to be guilty of misbehaviour.

(e) If a Part-time Member is, or becomes in any way concerned, or interested in any contract, or agreement made by or on behalf of the Corporation, he shall, for the purposes of sub-section (1), be deemed to be guilty of misbehaviour.

(f) The Chairman or any other Member may resign his office by giving notice thereof in writing to the president of India and on such resignation being accepted, the Chairman or other Member shall be deemed to have vacated his office.

8. *Meetings of Board*

(a) The Board shall meet at such times and places and shall observe such rules of procedure in regard to the transaction of business at its meetings (including the quorum at meetings) as may be provided by regulations:

Provided that there shall not be less than six meetings every year but three months shall not intervene between one meeting and the next meeting.

(b) A Member shall be deemed to have vacated his office if he absents himself for three consecutive meetings of the Board without the leave of the Chairman.

(c) The Chairman shall preside at the meetings of the Board and if for any reason he is unable to attend any meeting, the Executive Member and in the absence of both, any other Member elected by the Members present at such meeting, shall preside at the meeting.

(d) All questions which come up before any meeting of the Board shall be decided by a majority of the votes of the Members present and voting and, in the event of an equality of votes, the Chairman,

Appendix – 4

or in his absence, the person presiding, shall have and exercise a second or casting vote.

9. **Officers and Other Employees of Corporation**
   (a) Subject to such control, restrictions and conditions as may be prescribed, the Corporation may appoint, after consultation with the Recruitment Board, the director-general (Akashvani), the director-general (Doordarshan) and such other officers and other employees as may be necessary.
   (b) The method of recruitment of such officers and employees and all other matters connected therewith and the conditions of service of such officers and other employees shall be such as may be provided by regulations.

10. **Establishment of Recruitment Boards**
    (a) The Corporation shall, as soon as may be, after the appointed day and in such manner and subject to such conditions and restrictions as may be prescribed, establish for the purposes of Section 9, one or more Recruitment Boards consisting wholly of persons other than the Members, officers and other employees of the Corporation:
    Provided that for the purposes of Appointment to the posts carrying scales of pay which are not less than that of a Joint Secretary to the Central Government, the Recruitment Board shall consist of the Chairman, other Members, the ex-officio Members, the Nominated member and the elected Members.
    (b) The qualifications and other conditions of service of the members constituting the Recruitment Board and the period for which such members shall hold office, shall be such as may be prescribed.

11. **Transfer of Service of Existing Employees to Corporation**
    (a) Where the Central Government has ceased to perform any functions which under section 12 are the functions of the Corporation, it shall be lawful for the Central Government to transfer, by order and with effect from such date or dates as may be specified in the order, to the Corporation any of the officers or other employees serving in the Akashvani or Doordarshan and engaged in the performance of those functions:
    Provided that no order under this sub-section shall be made in relation to any officer or other employee in Akashvani or Doordarshan who has, in respect of the proposal of the Central

Government to transfer such officer or other employee to the Corporation, intimated within such time as may be specified in this behalf by the Central Government, his intention of not becoming an employee of the Corporation.

(b) The provision of sub-section (1) shall also apply to the members of the Indian Information Service, the Central Secretariat Service or any other service or to persons borne on cadres outside Akashvani and Doordarshan, who have been working in the Akashvani or Doordarshan immediately before the appointed day:

Provided that where any such member intimates, within the time specified in sub-section (1), his intention of not becoming an employee of the Corporation but to continue on deputation, he may be allowed to continue on deputation in accordance with such terms and conditions as may be prescribed.

(c) In making an order under sub-section (1), the Central Government shall, as far as may be, take into consideration the functions which Akashvani or, as the case may be, Doordarshan has ceased or ceases to perform and the area in which such functions have been or are performed.

(d) An officer or other employee transferred by an order under sub-section (1) shall, on and from the date of transfer, cease to be an employee of the Central Government and become an employee of the Corporation with such designation as the Corporation may determine and shall, subject to the provisions of sub-sections (5) and (6), be governed by such regulations as may be made as respects remuneration and other conditions of service including pension, leave and provident fund and shall continue to be an officer or other employee of the Corporation unless and until his employment is terminated by the Corporation.

(e) Every officer or other employee transferred by an order made under sub-section (1) shall, within six months from the date of transfer, exercise his option, in writing, to be governed –
  (i) by the scale of pay applicable to the post held by him in the Akashvani or Doordarshan immediately before the date of transfer or by the scale applicable to the post under the Corporation to which he is transferred;
  (ii) by the leave, provident fund, retirement of other terminal benefits admissible to employees of the Central Government in accordance with the rules or orders of the Central

Appendix – 4

Government, as amended from time to time, or the leave, provident fund or other terminal benefits admissible to the employees of the Corporation under the regulations, and such option once exercised under this Act shall be final: Provided that the option exercised under clause (a) by an officer or other employee shall be applicable only in respect of the post under the Corporation to which such officer or other employee is transferred and on appointment to a higher post under the Corporation he shall be eligible only for the scale of pay applicable to such higher post:

Provided further that if immediately before the date of his transfer any such officer or other employee is officiating in a higher post under the Government either in a leave vacancy or any other vacancy of a specified duration, his pay on transfer shall be protected for the unexpired period of such vacancy and thereafter he shall be entitled to the scale of pay applicable to the post under the Government to which he would have reverted or to the scale of pay applicable to the post under the Corporation to which he is transferred, whichever he may opt:

Provided also that when an officer or other employee serving in the Union Ministry of Information and Broadcasting or in any of its attached or subordinate offices is promoted to officiate in a higher post in the Ministry or office, subsequent to the transfer to the Corporation of any other officer or employee senior to him in that Ministry or office before such transfer, the officer or other employee who is promoted to officiate in such higher post shall, on transfer to the Corporation, be entitled only to the scale of pay applicable to the post he would have held but for such promotion or the scale of pay applicable to the post under the Corporation to which he is transferred, whichever he may opt.

(f) No officer or other employee transferred by an order made under sub-section (1) or sub-section (2), —
    (i) shall be dismissed or removed by an authority subordinate to that competent to make a similar or equivalent appointment under the Corporation as may be specified in the regulations;
    (ii) shall be dismissed or removed or reduced in rank except after an inquiry in which he has been informed of the charges against him and given a reasonable opportunity of being heard in respect of those charges:

Provided that where it is proposed after such inquiry to impose upon him any such penalty, such penalty may be imposed on the basis of evidence adduced during such inquiry and it shall not be necessary to give such person an opportunity of making representation on the proposed penalty:

Provided further that clause (b) shall not apply where an officer or other employee is dismissed or removed or reduced in rank on the ground of conduct which has led to his conviction on a criminal charge.

12. Functions and Powers of Corporation

(a) Subject to the provisions of this Act, it shall be the primary duty of the Corporation to organise and conduct public broadcasting services to inform, educate and entertain the public and to ensure a balanced development of broadcasting on radio and television. Explanation – For the removal of doubts, it is hereby declared that the provisions of this section shall be in addition to, and not in derogation, of the provisions of the Indian Telegraph Act, 1885.

(b) The Corporation shall, in the discharge of its functions, be guided by the following objectives, namely:-

   (i) upholding the unity and integrity of the country and the values enshrined in the Constitution;

   (ii) safeguarding the citizen's right to be informed freely, truthfully and objectively on all matters of public interest, national or international, and presenting a fair and balanced flow of information including contrasting views without advocating any opinion or ideology of its own;

   (iii) paying special attention to the fields of education and spread of literacy, agriculture, rural development, environment, health and family welfare and science and technology;

   (iv) providing adequate coverage to the diverse cultures and languages of the various regions of the country by broadcasting appropriate programmes;

   (v) providing adequate coverage to sports and games so as to encourage healthy competition and the spirit of sportsmanship;

   (vi) providing appropriate programmes keeping in view the special needs of the youth;

   (vii) informing and stimulating the national consciousness in regard to the status and problems of women and paying special attention to uplift their causes;

- (viii) promoting social justice and combating exploitation, inequality and such evils as untouchability and advancing the welfare of the weaker sections of the society;
- (ix) safeguarding the rights of the working classes and advancing their welfare;
- (x) serving the rural and weaker sections of the people and those residing in border regions, backward or remote areas;
- (xi) providing suitable programmes keeping in view the special needs of the minorities and tribal communities;
- (xii) taking special steps to protect the interests of children, the blind, the aged, the handicapped and other vulnerable sections of the people;
- (xiii) promoting national integration by broadcasting in a manner that facilitates communication in the languages in India; and facilitating the distribution of regional broadcasting services in every State in the languages of that State;
- (xiv) providing comprehensive broadcast coverage through the choice of appropriate technology and the best utilisation of the broadcast frequencies available and ensuring high quality reception;
- (xv) promoting research and development activities in order to ensure that radio and television broadcast technology are constantly updated; and
- (xvi) expanding broadcasting facilities by establishing additional channels of transmission at various levels.

(3) **In Particular, and Without Prejudice to the Generality of the Foregoing Provisions, the Corporation May Take Such Steps As it Thinks Fit –**
- (a) to ensure that broadcasting is conducted as a public service to provide and produce programmes;
  - (i) to establish a system for the gathering of news for radio and television;
  - (ii) to negotiate for purchase of, or otherwise acquire, programmes and rights or privileges in respect of sports and other events, films, serials, occasions, meetings, functions or incidents of public interest, for broadcasting and to establish procedures for the allocation of such programmes, rights or privileges to the services;
  - (iii) to establish and maintain a library or libraries of radio, television and other materials;

(iv) to conduct or commission, from time to time, programmes, audience research, market or technical service, which may be released to such persons and in such manner and subject to such terms and conditions as the Corporation may think fit;

(v) to provide such other services as may be specified by regulations.

(b) Nothing in sub-sections (2) and (3) shall prevent the Corporation from managing on behalf of the Central Government and in accordance with such terms and conditions as may be specified by that Government the broadcasting of external services and monitoring of broadcasts made by organisations outside India on the basis of arrangements made for reimbursement of expenses by the Central Government.

(c) For the purposes of ensuring that adequate time is made available for the promotion of the objectives set out in this section, the Central Government shall have the power to determine the maximum limit of broadcast time in respect of the advertisement.

(d) The Corporation shall be subject to no civil liability on the ground merely that it failed to comply with any of the provisions of this section.

(e) The Corporation shall have the power to determine and levy fees and other service charges for or in respect of the advertisements and such programmes as may be specified by regulations:

Provided that the fees and other service charges levied and collected under this sub-section shall not exceed such limits as may be determined by the Central Government, from time to time.

14. *Parliamentary Committee*

(a) There shall be constituted a Committee consisting of twenty-two members of Parliament, of whom fifteen from the House of the People to be elected by the Members thereof and seven from the Council of States to be elected by the Members thereof in accordance with the system of proportional representation by means of the single transferable vote, to oversee that the Corporation discharges its functions in accordance with the provision of this Act and, in particular, the objectives set out in Section 12 and submit a report thereon to the Parliament.

(b) The committee shall function in accordance with such rules as may be made by the speaker of the House of the People.

Appendix – 4

14. **Establishment of Broadcasting Council, Term of Office and Removal, etc. of Members Thereof.**
    (a) There shall be established, by notification, as soon as may be after the appointed day, a Council, to be known as the Broadcasting Council, to receive and consider complaints referred to in Section 15 and to advise the Corporation in the discharge of its functions in accordance with the objectives set out in section 12.
    (b) The Broadcasting Council shall consist of –
      (i) A president and ten other members to be appointed by the president of India from amongst persons of eminence in public life;
      (ii) four members of Parliament, of whom two from the House of the People to be nominated by the Speaker thereof and two from the Council of States to be nominated by the Chairman thereof.
    (c) The president of the Broadcasting Council shall be a Whole-time Member and every other member shall be a Part-time member and the president or the part-time member shall hold office as such for a term of three years from the date on which he enters upon his office.
    (d) The Broadcasting Council may constitute such number of Regional Councils as it may deem necessary to aid and assist the Council in the discharge of its functions.
    (e) The president of the Broadcasting Council shall be entitled to such salary and allowances and shall be subject to such conditions of service in respect of leave, pension (if any), provident fund and other matters as may be prescribed.
    Provided that the salary and allowances and the conditions of service shall not be varied to the disadvantage of the president of the Broadcasting Council after his appointment.
    (f) The other members of the Broadcasting Council and the members of the Regional Councils constituted under sub-section (4) shall be entitled to such allowances as may be prescribed.

15. *Jurisdiction of, and the Procedure to be Followed by, the Broadcasting Council.*
    (a) The Broadcasting Council shall receive and consider complaints from—
      (i) any person or group of persons alleging that a certain programme or broadcast or the functioning of the

Corporation in specific cases or in general is not in accordance with the objectives for which the Corporation is established;

(ii) any person (other than officer or employee of the Corporation) claiming himself to have been treated unjustly or unfairly in any manner (including unwarranted invasion of privacy, misrepresentation, distortion or lack of objectivity) in connection with any programme broadcast by the Corporation.

(b) A complaint under sub-section (1) shall be made in such manner and within such period as may be specified by regulations.

(c) The Broadcasting Council shall follow such procedure as it thinks fit for his disposal of complaints received by it.

(d) If the complaint is found to be justified, either wholly or in part, the Broadcasting Council shall advise the Executive Member to take appropriate action.

(e) If the Executive Member is unable to accept the recommendation of the Broadcasting Council, he shall place such recommendation before the Board for its decision thereon.

(f) If the Board is also unable to accept the recommendation of the Broadcasting Council, it shall record its reasons therefore and inform the Broadcasting Council accordingly.

(g) Notwithstanding anything contained in sub-section (5) and (6), where the Broadcasting Council deems it appropriate, it may, for reasons to be recorded in writing, require the Corporation to broadcast its recommendations with respect to a complaint in such manner as the Council may deem fit.

Chapter – III

Assets, Finances and Accounts

16. *Transfer of Certain Assets, Liabilities, etc. of Central Government to Corporation. As from the Appointed Day,—*

(a) All property and assets (including the Non-lapsable Fund) which immediately before that day vested in the Central Government for the purpose of Akashvani or Doordarshan or both shall stand transferred to the Corporation on such terms and conditions as may be determined by the Central Government and the book value of all such property and assets shall be treated as the capital provided by the Central Government to the Corporation;

(b) All debts, obligations and liabilities incurred, all contracts entered into and all matters and things engaged to be done by, with or for the Central Government immediately before such day for or in connection with the purposes of Akashvani or Doordarshan or both, shall be deemed to have been incurred, entered into and engaged to be done by, with or for the Corporation;

(c) All sums of money due to the Central Government in relation to Akashvani or Doordarshan or both, immediately before such day, shall be deemed to be due to the Corporation;

(d) All suits and other legal proceedings instituted or which could have been instituted by or against Central Government immediately before such day for any matter in relation to Akashvani or Doordarshan or both may be continued or instituted by or against the Corporation.

17. *Grants, etc. by Central Government*

For the purposes of enabling the Corporation to discharge its functions efficiently under this Act, the Central Government may, after due appropriation made by Parliament by law in this behalf, pay to the Corporation in each financial year, –

(a) The proceeds of the broadcast receiver licence fees, if any, as reduced by the collection charges; and

(b) Such other sums of money as that Government considers necessary, by way of equity, grant-in-aid or loan.

18. *Fund of Corporation*

(a) The Corporation shall have its own fund and all the receipts of the Corporation (including the amounts which stand transferred to the Corporation under Section 16) shall be credited to the Fund and all payments by the Corporation shall be made therefrom.

(b) All moneys belonging to the Fund shall be deposited in one or more nationalised banks in such manner as the Corporation may decide.

(c) The Corporation may spend such sums as it thinks fit for performing its functions under this Act and such sums shall be treated as expenditure payable out of the Fund of the Corporation.
Explanation – For the purpose of the section, "nationalised bank" means a corresponding new bank specified in the First Schedule to the Banking Companies (Acquisition and Transfer of Undertakings) Act, 1970 or a corresponding new bank specified in the First Schedule to the Banking Companies (Acquisition and Transfer of Undertakings) Act, 1980.

19. Investment of Moneys

The Corporation may invest its moneys in the securities of the Central Government or any State Government or in such other manner as may be prescribed.

20. Annual Financial Statement of the Corporation.
   (a) The Corporation shall prepare, in each financial year, an Annual Financial Statement for the next financial year showing separately –
      (i) the expenditure which is proposed to be met from the internal resources of the Corporation; and
      (ii) the sums required from the Central Government to meet other expenses, and distinguishing –
         (i) revenue expenditure from other expenditure; and
         (ii) non-plan expenditure from plan expenditure.
   (b) The Annual Financial Statement shall be prepared in such form and forwarded at such time to the Central Government for its approval as may be agreed to by that Government and the Corporation.

21. Accounts and Audit of Corporation
   (a) The Corporation shall maintain proper accounts and other relevant records and prepare an annual statement of accounts in such form and in such manner as may be prescribed.
   (b) The accounts of the Corporation shall be audited by the Comptroller and Auditor General of India at such intervals as may be specified by him and any expenditure incurred in connection with such audit shall be payable by the Corporation to the Comptroller and Auditor-General.
   (c) The Comptroller and Auditor General and any person appointed by him in connection with the audit of the accounts of the Corporation shall have the same rights and privileges and authority in connection with such audit as the Comptroller and Auditor General has in connection with the audit of Government accounts and, in particular, shall have the right to demand the production of books, accounts, connected vouchers and other documents and papers and to inspect any of the offices of the Corporation.
   (d) The accounts of the Corporation as certified by the Comptroller and Auditor General of India or any other person appointed by him in this behalf together with the audit report thereon shall be forwarded annually to the Central Government and that

Appendix – 4

Government shall cause the same to be laid before each House of Parliament.

22. *Corporation Not Liable to Be Taxed*
Notwithstanding anything contained in the Income-tax Act, 1961, or any other enactment for the time being in force relating to income tax or any other tax on income, profits or gains, the Corporation shall not be liable to pay any income tax or any other tax in respect of –
 (a) any income, profit or gains, accruing or arising out of the Fund of the Corporation or any amount received in that Fund; and
 (b) any income, profits or gains, derived or any amount received, by the Corporation.

Chapter – IV

Miscellaneous

23. *Power of Central Government to give directions*
 (a) The Central Government may, from time to time as and when the occasion arises, issue to the Corporation such directions as it may think necessary in the interests of the sovereignty, unity and integrity of India or the security of the State or preservation of public order requiring it not to make a broadcast on a matter specified in the direction or to make a broadcast on any matter of public importance specified in the direction.
 (b) Where the Corporation makes a broadcast in pursuance of the direction issued under sub-section (1), the fact that such broadcast has been made in pursuance of such direction may also be announced along with such broadcast, if the Corporation so desires.
 (c) A copy of every direction issued under sub-section (1) shall be laid before each House of Parliament.

24. *Power of Central Government to Obtain Information*
The Central Government may require the Corporation to furnish such information as that Government may consider necessary.

25. *Report to Parliament in Certain Matters and Recommendations As to Action Against the Board*
 (a) Where the Board persistently makes default in complying with any directions issued under Section 23 or fails to supply the information required under Section 24, the Central Government may prepare a report thereof and lay it before each House of Parliament for any recommendation thereof as to any action

(including supersession of the Board) which may be taken against the Board.

(b) On the recommendation of the Parliament, the president may by notification supersede the Board for such period not exceeding six month, as may be specified in the notification:

Provided that before issuing the notification under this sub-section, the president shall give a reasonable opportunity to the Board to show cause as to why it should not be superseded and shall consider the explanations and objections, if any, of the Board.

(c) Upon the publication of the notification under sub-section (2), –
  (i) all the Members shall, as from the date of supersession, vacate their offices as such;
  (ii) all the powers, functions and duties which may, by or under the provision of this Act be exercised or discharged by or on behalf of the Board, shall until the Board is reconstituted under this Act, be exercised and discharged by such person or persons as the president may direct.

(d) On the expiration of the period of supersession specified in the notification issued under sub-section (2), the president may reconstitute the Board by fresh appointments, and in such a case any person who had vacated his office under clause (a) of sub-section (3) shall not be disqualified for appointment:

Provided that the president may, at any time before the expiration of the period of supersession, take action under this sub-section.

(e) The Central Government shall cause the notification issued under-sub-section (2) and a full report of the action taken under this section to be laid before each House of Parliament.

26. *Office of Member Not to Disqualify a Member of Parliament*

It is hereby declared that the office of the member of the Broadcasting Council or of the Committee constituted under Section 13 shall not disqualify its holder for being chosen as or for being a Member of either House of Parliament.

27. *Chairman, Members, etc. to be Public Servants*

The Chairman and every other member, every officer or other employee of the Corporation and every member of a Committee thereof, the president and every member of the Broadcasting Council or every member of a Regional Council or a Recruitment Board shall be deemed to be a public servant within the meaning of Section 21 of the Indian Penal Code.

Appendix – 4

28. Protection of Action Taken in Good Faith
No suit or other legal proceeding shall lie against the Corporation, the Chairman or any Member or officer or other employee thereof or the president or a member of the Broadcasting Council or a member of a Regional Council or a Recruitment Board for anything which is in good faith done or intended to be done in pursuance of this Act or of any rules or regulations made thereunder.

29. Authentication of Orders and Other Instruments of Corporation
All orders and decisions of the Corporation shall be authenticated by the signature of the Chairman or any other Member authorised by the Corporation in this behalf and all other instruments executed by the corporation shall be authenticated by the signature of the Executive Member or by any officer of the Corporation authorised by him in this behalf.

30. Delegation of Powers
The Corporation may, by general or special order, delegate to the Chairman or any other Member or to any officer of the Corporation, subject to such conditions and limitations, if any, as may be specified therein, such of its powers and duties under this Act as it may deem fit.

31. Annual Report
(a) The Corporation shall prepare once in every calendar year, in such form and within such times as may be prescribed, an annual report giving a full account of its activities (including the recommendations and suggestions made by the Broadcasting Council and the action taken thereon), during the previous year and copies thereof shall be forwarded to the Central Government and that Government shall cause the same to be laid before each House of Parliament.

(b) The Broadcasting Council shall prepare once in every calendar year, in such form and within such time as may be prescribed, an annual report giving a full account of its activities during the previous year and copies thereof shall be forwarded to the Central Government and that Government shall cause the same to be laid before each House of Parliament.

32. Power to Make Rules
(a) The Central Government may, by notification, make rules for carrying out the provisions of this Act.

(b) In particular, and without prejudice to generality of the foregoing power, such rules may provide for all or any of the following matters, namely: –

(i) the salaries and allowances and conditions of service in respect of leave, pension (if any), provident fund and other matters in relation to the Whole-time Members under sub-Section (7) of Section 6;

(ii) the allowances payable to the Chairman and Part-time Members under sub-section (8) of Section 6;

(iii) the control, restrictions and conditions subject to which the Corporation may appoint officers and other employees under sub-section (1) of Section 9;

the manner in which and the conditions and restrictions subject to which a Recruitment Board may be established under sub-section (1) of Section 10;

(iv) the qualification and other conditions of service of the members of a Recruitment Board and their period of office under sub-section (2) of Section 10;

(v) the terms and conditions in accordance with which the deputation may be regulated under sub-section (2) of section 11;

(vi) the salary and allowances and conditions of service in respect of leave, pension (if any), provident fund and other matters in relation to the president of the Broadcasting Council under sub-section (5) of Section 14;

(c) the allowances payable to other members of the Broadcasting Council and the members of the Regional Councils, under sub-section (6) of Section 14;

(d) the manner in which the Corporation may invest its moneys under Section 19;

(e) the form and the manner in which the annual statement of accounts shall be prepared under sub-section (1) of Section 21;

(f) the form in which, and the time within which the Corporation and the Broadcasting Council shall prepare their annual report under Section 31;

(g) any other matter which is required to be, or may be, prescribed.

33. *Power to Make Regulations*

(a) The Corporation may, by notification, make regulations not inconsistent with this Act and the rules made thereunder for enabling it to perform its functions under this Act.

(b) Without prejudice to the generality of the foregoing power such regulations may provide for all or/any of the following matters, namely –

(i) the manner in which and the purposes for which the Corporation may associate with itself any person under sub-section (7) of Section 3;
(ii) the times and places at which meetings of Board shall be held and, the procedure to be followed thereat, and the quorum necessary for the transaction of the business at a meeting of the Board under sub-section (1) of Section 8;
(iii) the methods of recruitment and conditions of service of officers and other employees of the Corporation under sub-section (2) of Section 9;
(iv) the remuneration and other conditions of service, including pension, leave and provided fund in relation to an officer or other employee of the Corporation under sub-section (4) of Section 11;
(v) the authority competent to make certain appointments referred to in clause (a) of sub-section (6) of Section 11;
(vi) the services which may be provided by the Corporation under clause (f) of sub-section (3) of Section 12;
(vii) the determination and levy of fees and other service charges in respect of advertisements and other programmes under sub-section (7) of Section 12;
(viii) the manner in which and the period within which complaints may be made under sub-section (2) of Section 15;
(ix) any other matter in respect of which provision is, in the opinion of the Corporation, necessary for the performance of its functions under this Act:

Provided that the regulations under clause (c) or clause (d) shall be made only with the prior approval of the Central Government.

34. *Rules and Regulations to Be Laid Before the Parliament*

Every rule and every regulation made under this Act shall be laid as soon as may be after it is made, before each House of Parliament, while it is in session for a total period of thirty days which may be comprised in one session or in two or more successive sessions, and if, before the expiry of the session immediately following the session or the successive session aforesaid, both Houses agree in making any modification in the rule or regulation, or both Houses agree that the rule or regulation should not be made, the rule or regulation shall thereafter have effect only in such modified form or be of no effect, as the case may be; so, however, that any such modification or annulment shall be without prejudice to the validity of anything previously done under that rule or regulation.

35. Power to Remove Difficulties

If any difficulty arises in giving effect to provisions of this Act, the Central Government may, by order, published in the official Gazette, make such provisions, not inconsistent with the provisions of this Act, as it may deem necessary, for the removal of the difficulty:

Provided that no such order shall be made after the expiry of a period of three years from the appointed day.

Appendix – 5

Programme and Advertising Codes

Prasar Bharati

Programme Code: The General Broadcasting Code which is otherwise called Programme Code is for both wings of Prasar Bharati (Broadcasting Corporation of India) namely All India Radio and Doordarshan prohibits the following:
- (a) Criticism of friendly countries;
- (b) Attack on religions or communities.
- (c) Anything obscene or defamatory.
- (d) Incitement to violence or anything against maintenance of law and order.
- (e) Anything amounting to contempt of court.
- (f) Aspersions against the integrity of the president and Judiciary.
- (g) Anything affecting the integrity of the Nation, and criticism by name of any person.

Advertising Code: The Prasar Bharati Corporation consists of two wings namely All India Radio and Doordarshan. Commercials were introduced on AIR on 1 November, 1967 and on Doordarshan on 1 January, 1976. Both AIR and Doordarshan have served as an effective instrument for advertisers to publicise their goods and services. As a public service broadcasting organisation, AIR and Doordarshan have the responsibility to ensure that the advertisements, either in terms of contents, tone or treatment, do not mislead the listeners and viewers as well as the consumers or are not repugnant to good taste. The earning of commercial revenue is not the sole criteria of the Prasar Bharati. Thus the code has stricter provisions and the main features of the code are as follows:
- (a) Tobacco products including 'pan masala' and liquors are not permitted.
- (b) The goods and services advertised should be in consonance with the laws of the country enacted to protect the rights of the consumers.

(c) The commercial should never project a derogatory image of women and should not endanger the safety of children.

Programme and Advertising Codes for Broadcasting for Cable Operators (Rule 6 and Rule 7 of Cable Television Networks Rules, 1994).

Programme Code

6.(1) No programme should be carried in the cable service which:–
- (a) offends against good taste or decency;
- (b) contains criticism of friendly countries;
- (c) contains attack on religions or communities or visuals or words contemptuous of religious groups or which promote communal attitudes;
- (d) contains anything obscene, defamatory, deliberate, false and suggestive innuendoes and half-truths;
- (e) is likely to encourage or incite violence or contains anything against maintenance of law and order or which promote anti-national attitudes;
- (f) contains anything amounting to contempt of court;
- (g) contains aspersions against the integrity of the president and Judiciary;
- (h) contains anything affecting the integrity of the Nation;
- (i) criticises, maligns or slanders any individual in person or certain groups, segments of social, public and moral life of the country;
- (j) encourages superstition or blind belief;
- (k) denigrates women through the depiction in any manner of the figure of a women, her form or body or any part thereof in such a way as to have the effect of being indecent, or derogatory to women, or is likely to deprave, corrupt or injure the public morality or morals;
- (l) denigrates children;
- (m) contains visuals or words which reflect a slandering, ironical and snobbish attitude in the portrayal of certain ethnic, linguistic and regional groups
- (n) contravenes the provisions of the Cinematograph Act, 1952.
- (o) is not suitable for unrestricted public exhibition.
    Explanation – For the purpose of this clause, the expression "unrestricted public exhibition" shall have the same meaning as assigned to it in the Cinematograph Act, 1952 (37 of 1952);

(2) The cable operator should strive to carry programmes in his cable service which project women in a positive, leadership role of sobriety, moral and character-building qualities.

Appendix – 5

(3) No cable operator shall carry or include in his cable service any programme in respect of which copyright subsists under the Copyright Act, 1972 (14 of 1972) unless he has been granted a licence by owners of copyright under the Act in rest of such programme.

(4) Care should be taken to ensure that programmes meant for children do not contain any bad language or explicit scenes of violence.

(5) Programmes unsuitable for children must not be carried in the cable service at times when the largest number of children are viewing.

Advertising Code

7(1) Advertising carried in the cable service shall be so designed as to conform to the laws of the country and should not offend morality, decency and religious susceptibilities of the subscribers.

(2) No advertisement shall be permitted which –
   (a) derides any race, caste, colour, creed and nationality;
   (b) is against any provision of the Constitution of India;
   (c) tends to incite people to crime, cause disorder or violence; or breach of law or glorifies violence or obscenity in any way ;
   (d) presents criminality as desirable;
   (e) exploits the national emblem, or any part of the Constitution or the person or personality of a national leader or a State dignitary;
   (f) in its depiction of women violates the constitutional guarantees to all citizens. In particular, no advertisement shall be permitted which projects a derogatory image of women. Women must not be portrayed in a manner that emphasises passive, submissive qualities and encourages them to play a subordinate, secondary role in the family and society. The cable operator shall ensure that the portrayal of the female form, in the programmes carried in his cable service, is tasteful and aesthetic, and is within the well established norms of good taste and decency;
   (g) exploits social evils like dowry, child marriage.
   (h) promotes directly or indirectly production, sale or consumption of –
      (i) cigarettes, tobacco products, wine, alcohol, liquor or other intoxicants;
      (ii) infant milk substitutes, feeding bottle or infant food.
   (i) no advertisement shall be permitted, the objects whereof, are wholly or mainly of a religious or political nature; advertisements must not be directed towards any religious or political end;

(j) no advertisement shall contain references which hurt religious sentiments;

(k) the goods or services advertised shall not suffer from any defect or deficiency as mentioned in Consumer Protection Act, 1986;

(l) no advertisement shall contain references which are likely to lead the public to infer that the product advertised or any of its ingredients has some special or miraculous or supernatural property or quality, which is difficult of being proved;

(m) the picture and the audible matter of the advertisement shall not be excessively 'loud';

(n) no advertisement which endangers the safety of children or creates in them any interest in unhealthy practices or shows them begging or in an undignified or indecent manner shall not be carried in the cable service;

(o) indecent, vulgar, suggestive, repulsive or offensive themes or treatment shall be avoided in all advertisements;

(p) no advertisement which violates the standards of practice for advertising agencies as approved by the Advertising Agencies Association of India, Bombay, from time to time shall be carried in the cable service;

(q) all advertisement should be clearly distinguishable from the programme and should not in any manner interfere with the programme, viz. use of lower part of screen to carry captions, static or moving, alongside the programme.

Appendix – 6

DTH Guidelines

Guidelines For Obtaining License For Providing Direct-to-Home (DTH) Broadcasting Service In India

The Union Government has decided to permit Direct-to-Home (DTH) TV service in Ku Band in India. The prohibition on the reception and distribution of television signal in Ku Band has been withdrawn by the Government vide notification No. GSR 18 (E) dated 9th January, 2001 of the Department of Telecommunications.

The salient features of eligibility criteria, basic conditions / obligations and procedure for obtaining the license to set up and operate DTH service are briefly described below. For further details, reference should be made to the Ministry of Information & Broadcasting.

Direct-to-Home (DTH) Broadcasting Service, refers to distribution of multi channel TV programmes in Ku Band by using a satellite system by providing TV signals direct to subscribers' premises without passing through an intermediary such as cable operator.

Following are the eligibility criteria for applicants, conditions which will apply to DTH license and procedural details:

(1) *Eligibility Criteria:*
- The applicant company to be an Indian Company registered under Indian Company's Act, 1956.
- Total foreign equity holding including FDI/NRI/OCB/FII in the applicant company not to exceed 49%.
- Within the foreign equity, the FDI component not to exceed 20%.
- The quantum represented by that proportion of the paid up equity share capital to the total issued equity capital of the Indian promoter Company, held or controlled by the foreign investors through FDI/NRI/OCB investments, shall form part of the above said FDI limit of 20%.

- The applicant company must have Indian Management Control with majority representatives on the board as well as the Chief Executive of the company being a resident Indian.
- Broadcasting companies and / or cable network companies shall not be eligible to collectively own more than 20% of the total equity of the applicant company at any time during the license period. Similarly, the applicant company not to have more than 20% equity share in a broadcasting and / or cable network company.
- The licensee shall be required to submit the equity distribution of the Company in the prescribed Proforma (Table I and II of Annexure to Form-A) once within one month of start of every financial year.

(2) *Number of Licensees:*
- There will be no restrictions on the total number of DTH licenses and these will be issued to any person who fulfils the necessary terms and conditions and subject to the security and technical clearances by the appropriate authorities of the government.

(3) *Period of License:*
- License will be valid for a period of 10 years from the date of issue of wireless operational license by Wireless planning and Coordination Wing of Ministry of Communications. However, the license can be cancelled/suspended by the Licensor at any time in the interest of Union of India.

(4) *Basic Conditions/Obligations:*
- The license will be subject to terms and conditions contained in the agreement and its Schedule (Form-B)

(5) *Procedure for Application and Grant of Licenses:*
- To apply to the Secretary, Ministry of I&B, in triplicate, in the prescribed proforma (Form-A)
- On the basis of information furnished in the application form, if the applicant is found eligible for setting up of DTH platform in India, the application will be subjected to security clearance in consultations with the Ministry of Home Affairs and for clearance of satellite use with the Department of Space.
- After these clearances are obtained, the applicant would be required to pay an initial non-refundable entry fee of Rs.10 crores to the Ministry of Information and Broadcasting.

Appendix - 6

- After such payment of entry-fee, the applicant would be informed of intent of Ministry of I&B to issue license and requested to approach WPC for SACFA clearance.
- After obtaining SACFA clearance, within one month of the same, the Licensee will have to submit a bank guarantee (Form-C) from any Scheduled Bank to the Ministry of Information and Broadcasting for an amount of Rs.40 crores valid for the duration of the license.
- After submission of this bank guarantee, the applicant would be required to sign a licensing agreement with the Ministry of Information and Broadcasting as per prescribed proforma (Form-B).
- After signing of such a licensing agreement with the Ministry of Information and Broadcasting, the applicant will have to apply to the Wireless Planning and Coordination (WPC) Wing of the Ministry of Communications for seeking Wireless Operational License for the establishment, maintenance and operation of DTH platform.
- The Licensee shall pay an annual fee equivalent to 10% of its gross revenue as reflected in the audited accounts of the Company for that particular financial year, within one month of the end of that financial year.
- The Licensee shall also, in addition, pay the license fee and royalty for the spectrum used as prescribed by Wireless Planning and Coordination Authority (WPC), under the Department of Telecommunications.

(6) *Arbitration Clause:*
In case of any dispute, the matter will be referred to the sole Arbitration of the Secretary, Department of Legal Affairs, Government of India or his nominee, for adjudication. The award of the Arbitrator shall be binding on the parties. The Arbitration proceedings will be governed by the law of Indian arbitration in force at the point of time. Venue of Arbitration shall be India.

Appendix – 7

Foreign Investment and Uplinking Policy

There is no restriction on foreign equity in proposals related to production of software, marketing of TV rights, air times, advertisements, etc.

A decision on 25th July, 2000 liberalised the Uplinking Policy to permit the Indian private companies to set up uplinking hub/teleports for licensing/hiring out to other broadcasters. The new policy also permits uplinking of any television channel from India. It also allows the Indian news agencies to have their own uplinking facilities for purposes of news gathering and its further distribution. The salient features of eligibility criteria, basic conditions/obligations and procedure for obtaining the necessary permission for these services are briefly described below. For details, reference should be made to the relevant terms and conditions of licences/permission / approval.

1. **Licence for Setting Up of Uplink Hub/Teleports:**
   (a) *Eligibility Criteria:*
   - Company to be incorporated in India.
   - Foreign equity holding including NRI/OCB/PIO not to exceed 49%.

   (b) *Period Of Licence:*
   - 10 years.

   (c) *Basic Conditions/Obligations:*
   - To uplink only those TV channels which are specifically approved or permitted by the Ministry of I&B for uplinking from India.
   - To stop uplinking of TV channels whenever permission / approval to such a channel is withdrawn by the Ministry of I&B.
   - Can uplink both to the Indian as well as the foreign satellites. However, proposals envisaging the use of Indian satellite will be accorded preferential treatment.
   - To keep record of materials uplinked for a period of 90 days and to produce the same before any agency of the Government as and when required.

Appendix – 7

- To permit the Government agencies to inspect the facilities as and when required.
- To furnish such information as may be required by the Ministry of I&B from time to time.
- To provide the necessary monitoring facility at its own cost for monitoring of programme or content by the representative of the Ministry of I&B or any other government agency as and when required.
- To comply with the terms and conditions of the licensing agreement to be signed between the applicant and the Ministry of I&B.
- To comply with the terms and conditions of the Wireless Operational Licence to be issued by WPC.
- To uplink in C-Band only.
- The satellite to which uplinking is proposed should have been co-ordinated with Insat system.
- Failure to comply with the terms and conditions of the above licences would result in termination/cancellation of the licences.

(d) Procedure:
- To apply to the Secretary, Ministry of I&B, in triplicate, in the prescribed proforma (Form 1).
- On the basis of information furnished in the application form, if the applicant is found eligible for setting up an uplinking hub/teleport, its application will be sent for security clearance to the Ministry of Home Affairs and for clearance of satellite use to the Department of Space (wherever proposal is made for use of satellite).
- As soon as these clearances are obtained, the applicant would be required to sign a licensing agreement with the Ministry of I&B as per the prescribed proforma (Form-1 A).
- After signing the licensing agreement with the Ministry of I&B, the applicant can approach to the Wireless Planning & Coordination (WPC) Wing of the Ministry of Communications for seeking operating licence for establishment, maintenance and operation of uplinking facility.
- The applicant will pay the licence fee and royalty, as prescribed by the WPC Wing from time to time, annually, for the total amount of spectrum assigned to hub/teleport station, as per the norms and rules of the WPC Wing.

- The hub/teleport station owner will inform the WPC Wing the full technical and operations details of TV channels proposed to be uplinked through his/her Hub/Teleport in prescribed format.

2. Permission/Approval for Uplinking A TV Channel From India

(In case a TV channel proposes to set up its own uplinking facility/earth station, it has to apply separately for the same after following the procedure as in case of '1' above.)

(a) *Eligibility Criteria:*
- Any TV channel irrespective of its ownership, equity structure or management control which is aimed at Indian viewership.

(b) *Period of Approval/Permission:*
- 10 years.

(c) *Basic Conditions/Obligations:*
- To undertake to comply with the Broadcasting (Programme & Advertising) Codes laid down by the Ministry of Information & Broadcasting.
- To keep record of materials uplinked for a period of 90 days and to produce the same before any agency of the Government as and when required.
- To furnish such information as may be required by the Ministry of I&B from time to time.
- To provide the necessary monitoring facility at its own cost for monitoring of programme or content by the representative of the Ministry of I&B or any other Government agency as and when required.
- If the applicant hires its own transponder on a satellite, the same should be in C-Band and should have been co-ordinated with INSAT system.
- To comply with the terms and conditions of the permission/approval of the Ministry of I&B.
- Failure to comply with the terms and conditions of the permission/approval would result in withdrawal of such permission approval.

(d) *Procedure:*
- To apply to the Secretary, Ministry of Information and Broadcasting in triplicate in the prescribed proforma (Form-2) along with an affidavit in Form 2 A.
- After receiving the application and the affidavit as provided above, if the applicant is found eligible, the same will be sent for security clearance to the Ministry of Home Affairs and for

Appendix – 7

clearance of satellite use to the Department of Space (only in respect of those cases where the applicant proposes a use of a particular satellite instead of leasing it out from the uplink service provider).
- As soon as these clearances are obtained, the applicant would be permitted to uplink its channel(s) through a hub/teleport as requested.
- After receiving the permission for uplinking from India, the applicant can approach to the uplinking hub (teleports) owner for providing the necessary uplinking facility for their channel(s).

3. Licence for Uplinking to Indian News Agencies:

(a) *Eligibility Criteria:*
- The Company/Agency to be incorporated in India.
- Accredited by Press Information Bureau (PIB).
- 100% owned by an Indian with the Indian Management Control.

(b) *Period of Licence:*
- As per WPC licence.

(c) *Basic Conditions / Obligations:*
- To use uplinking for news gathering and its further distribution to other news agencies/broadcasters only.
- Not to uplink TV programmes/channels for direct reception by public.
- To keep record of materials uplinked for a period of 90 days and to produce the same before any agency of the Government, as and when required.
- To furnish such information as may be required by the Ministry of I&B from time to time.
- To provide the necessary monitoring facility at its own cost for monitoring of programme or content by the representative of the Ministry of I&B or any other Government agency as and when required.
- Conformity with the provisions of inter-system coordination agreement between INSAT and the satellite to be used.
- To comply with the terms and conditions of the 'No Objection Certificate' to be issued by the Ministry of Information & Broadcasting.
- To comply with the terms and conditions of Wireless Operational Licence to be issued by the WPC.

- Failure to comply with the terms and conditions of the 'No Objection Certificate' or the Wireless Operational Licence would result in withdrawal or cancellation of such certificate or licence.

(d) *Procedure:*
- To apply to the Secretary, Ministry of Information and Broadcasting in triplicate in the prescribed proforma (Form-3).
- On the basis of information furnished in the application form, if the applicant is found eligible for setting up the uplinking facility, its application will be sent for security clearance to the Ministry of Home Affairs and for clearance of satellite use to the Department of Space.
- As soon as these clearances are obtained, the applicant would be issued 'No Objection Certificate' for uplinking by the Ministry of Information & Broadcasting.
- After the issue of 'No Objection Certificate' by the Ministry of Information & Broadcasting, the applicant can approach the Wireless Planning & Coordination (WPC) Wing of the Ministry of Communications for seeking operating licence for establishment, maintenance and operation of its own uplinking facility or approach another licensee of uplinking for hiring or leasing the hub/teleport facility.
- The applicant will pay the licence fee and royalty as prescribed by the WPC Wing from time to time, annually, for use of spectrum, as per norms and rules of the WPC (in case of its own facility).

Guidelines for Uplinking of News and Current Affairs TV Channels from India

Preamble

The Union Government has revised the policy for uplinking of TV channels from India, insofar it relates to the News and Current Affairs channels. Accordingly, the guidelines for permission/approval for uplinking of News and Current Affairs TV channels from India, have been framed for immediate compliance.

Channels which do not have any news and current affairs content will, however, continue to be eligible to uplink from India, irrespective of ownership, equity structure or management control.

The use of all equipment/platforms for collection of footage/news by channels uplinked from outside for specific programme(s)/event(s) of temporary duration will be entertained on recommendation from the PIB

Appendix – 7

and permitted on a case to case basis, in consultation with the Ministry of Home Affairs and other ministries/departments concerned.

1. Applicability:

- These guidelines will apply to the existing News and Current Affairs TV channels uplinked from India as well as to those proposing to uplink from India.
- For the purposes of these guidelines (i) News & Current Affairs channel means a channel which has any element of news and current affairs in its programme content; and (ii) an existing channel means any channel which has been permitted by the Ministry of Information & Broadcasting to uplink from India. Existing channels will be required to conform to these guidelines within a period of one year from the date of issue of these guidelines.

2. Eligibility Criteria:

An applicant company desirous of uplinking news and current affairs TV channel(s) from India will be considered eligible, if it fulfils the following criteria:-

- It is registered/incorporated in India under the Companies Act, 1956.
- Foreign equity holding in the applicant company does not exceed 26% of the total paid up capital.
- Majority of its Board of Directors are Resident Indians.
- CEO of the applicant company, known by any designation, and/ or Head of the channel is a Resident Indian.
- News Editor(s) or authority(ies) exercising editorial control over news and current affairs programme (s) of the channel(s) are Resident Indians.

3. *Period Of Approval / Permission:*

- Ten (10) years.

4. *Basic Conditions / Obligations:*

- Permission for usage of facilities/infrastructure for live news/ footage collection and transmission, irrespective of the technology used, will be given to only those channels which are uplinked from India. To ensure compliance of this policy in respect of permissions/licences given/to be given for utilisation of VSAT/ RTTS/Satellite Video Phone and similar other infrastructure, which lends itself for use in uplinking/point to point transfer of content for broadcast purposes, separate guidelines will be issued by the Ministry of Communications & Information Technology.

- The channel/company will ensure that its news and current affairs content provider(s), if any, are accredited with the Press Information Bureau. Such accredited content provider(s) only can use the equipment/platform for collection/transmission of news/footage.
- The company/channel should ensure that it uses equipment which is duly authorised and permitted by the competent authority, or its content provider(s), if any, use equipment duly authorised by the competent authority,
- It will be obligatory on the part of the company to take prior permission from the Ministry of Information & Broadcasting, before effecting any alteration in the foreign shareholding pattern and/or in the CEO/Board of Directors.
- The company/channel will be liable to intimate to the Ministry of Information & Broadcasting the details of any foreigners/NRIs employed/engaged by it for a period exceeding 60(sixty) days,
- The company/channel shall undertake to comply with the Programme & Advertising Codes, as laid down in the Cable Television Networks (Regulation) Act, 1995 and the Rules framed thereunder.
- It shall keep record of the content uplinked for a period of 90 days and produce the same before any agency of the Government, as and when required.
- It shall furnish such information, as may be required by the Ministry of Information & Broadcasting, from time to time.
- The company/channel shall provide for the necessary monitoring facility, at its own cost, for monitoring of programmes or content by the representatives of the Ministry of Information & Broadcasting or any other Government agency as and when so required.
- The applicant company should use transponder on a satellite in C-Band only and the same should have been co-ordinated with INSAT system.
- The applicant company/channel shall comply with all the terms and conditions of the permission/approval prescribed by the Ministry of Information & Broadcasting and failure to comply with any of the terms and conditions will result in withdrawal of such permission/approval and suspension/cancellation of the Wireless Operating Licence issued by WPC.

Appendix – 7

5. Procedure:
- The applicant company shall apply to the Secretary, Ministry of Information & Broadcasting in triplicate in the prescribed proforma (Form 2.1) along with affidavits in Form 2A and 2B and shareholding pattern of the company as per annexures (Table I & II),
- On receipt of the applications and the affidavit as mentioned above, if the applicant company is found eligible, its request will be sent for security clearance to the Ministry of Home Affairs and for clearance of usage of satellite to the Department of Space,
- On receipt of these clearances, the applicant company will be permitted by the Ministry of Information & Broadcasting to uplink its channel(s) through an authorised hub/teleport.

6. Transitory Arrangements:
- Content providers/channels who are currently using VSAT/RTTS/Satellite Video Phone and similar other infrastructure, which lends itself for use for uplinking/ point-to-point transfer of content for broadcast purposes, will be allowed a maximum period of three months to come within the framework of these guidelines.

Guidelines for use of SNG/DSNG

(a) Conditions for use of SNG/DSNG in C-Band & KU Band
(i) The use of SNG/DSNG would be permitted to News and Current Affairs channels uplinked from India for live news/footage collection and point to point transmission.

(ii) PIB accredited content provider(s) if any, to the permitted News and Current Affairs channel(s) can use SNG/DSNG for collection/transmission of news/footage.

(iii) Entertainment channels who are uplinking from their own teleport, can use SNG/DSNG for their approved channels, for transfer of video feeds to the permitted teleport.

(iv) All foreign channels, permitted entertainment channels uplinked from India and companies/individuals not covered in (i), (ii) and (iii) as above will be required to seek temporary uplinking permission for using SNG/DSNG for any live coverage/footage collection and transmission on case to case basis.

(v) Only permitted teleport operators and Doordarshan may offer/ hire out SNG/DSNG equipments/infrastructures to other broadcasters who are permitted to uplink from India.

(vi) The uplinking should be carried in encrypted mode, so as to be receivable only in closed user group. The signal should only be down linked at the permitted teleport of the licensee and uplinked for broadcasting through permitted satellite through that teleport only.

(vii) Each company/channel desiring to use SNG/DSNG would have to apply to the Ministry of I&B and get permission before doing the same.

(viii) Uplinking from SNG/DSNG should be in SCPC mode only (only single feed can be uplinked from the SNG/DSNG at a time).

(ix) The channel would also give an undertaking that the feed collected through SNG/DSNG shall conform to Programme and Advertisement Codes.

(x) The use of SNG/DSNG would be permitted only in those areas/regions/states which are not specifically prohibited by MHA.

(xi) The company would submit the purchase documents of SNG/DSNG terminals and inform the Ministry of I&B about placement of these terminals at the various locations.

(xii) Period of permission:
    (i) for teleport owners – co-terminus with teleport licence;
    (ii) for permitted news and current affairs channels – for the period of the channel permission;
    (iii) for content providers to permitted channels – for the period of the channel permission;
    (iv) for other broadcasters having temporary uplinking permission – for periods as specified in the temporary uplinking permission;

(xiii) The company permitted to use SNG/DSNG shall apply to WPC for frequency authorisation of WPC. It should be renewed yearly in time and a copy should be submitted to this Ministry by the company every year.

(xiv) The permitted company shall maintain a daily record of the location and the events which have been covered and uplinked by SNG/DSNG terminals and down linked at their main satellite earth station and produce the same before the licensing authority or its authorised representative, which will include officers of Ministry of Home Affairs and the Ministry of I&B, as and when required.

(xv) The permitted company shall not enter defence installations.

(xvi) The equipment should not be taken in the areas cordoned off from security point of view.

Appendix – 7

- (xvii) The company/channel desiring to use SNG/DSNG would give an undertaking that it would be used for live news gathering and footage collection for captive use only.
- (xviii) Violations of any of the aforementioned terms and conditions would lead to revocation/cancellation of the permission to use SNG/DSNG.
- (xix) The permitting authority may modify the conditions laid down or incorporate new conditions, as and when considered necessary

(b) Additional Conditions for use of SNG/DSNG in KU Band
- (i) SNG/DSNG will not be used for DTH operation, directly or indirectly. Any such use would lead to the termination of licence/permission.
- (ii) Uplinking Dish used for SNG/DSNG operation would not exceed 2 meters.
- (iii) There would be no turnaround for broadcasting in KU band.

Appendix – 8

Community Radio Guidelines

Guidelines for Applying Licenses for Setting Up Community Radio Station:

Preamble

The Union Government has decided to grant Community Broadcasting licenses to well established educational institutions/organisations recognised by the Central Government or the State Government. These will include the universities and institutes of technology/management and residential school.

The salient features of eligibility criteria, basic conditions/obligations and procedures for obtaining license to set up and operate Community Radio service are briefly described below. For further details reference may be made to the Ministry of Information & Broadcasting.

2. **Technical parameters:**
   2.1 Licence will be granted for FM transmitters for power of 50 watts or less.
   2.2 Licence will be issued in the shared frequency band from 87.5 to 100 MHz. However, in the event of frequency not being available in this band, the exclusive broadcast band of 104 to 108 MHz may also be considered, as in case of private FM broadcasters. The frequency band from 100 to 104 MHz earmarked exclusively for the use of AIR, Prasar Bharati will not be disturbed.

3. **Procedure to be followed:**

Application

3.1 Any eligible institution/organisation desirous of setting up of community radio broadcasting service may make an application to the Ministry of I&B in the prescribed proforma. (Download application form).

Appendix – 8

- 3.2 The Ministry of I&B immediately on receipt of an application will consult the Wireless Advisor in the WPC wing of the Ministry of Communications and also the Prasar Bharati to determine the availability of frequency at the place requested by the applicant.
- 3.3 The Ministry of Information & Broadcasting will refer the eligible applicant case to the Ministries of Home Affairs, Defence, Human Resources Development and External Affairs and letter of intent and/or license will be issued only after getting the requisite clearances from these Ministries. The licensee will be required to sign a licence agreement after allotment of frequency by the WPC. The license agreement shall specify detailed terms and conditions under which the licence is to be operated.
- 3.4 Within one year from the date of signing of licence agreement, the applicant will complete all necessary formalities such as obtaining SACFA clearance, etc. set up the necessary broadcast facilities and obtain a Wireless Operating Licence from the Wireless Advisor in the WPC Wing of the Ministry of Communications and Information Technology.
- 3.5 In the event of more than one claimant for a single frequency at a given place, the licensee will be selected by a Committee constituted by the Ministry of I&B on the basis of standing commitment, objectives and resources of the applicant organisation.
- 3.6 Licensee will be charged only the spectrum usage fee as determined by the WPC. The Ministry of I&B will not levy any other licence fee.

4. Terms and Conditions:

- 4.1 The basic objective of the Community Radio broadcasting would be to serve the cause of the community in the service area of the licensee by involving members of the community in the broadcast of their programmes. For this purpose the community would mean people living in the coverage zone of the broadcasting service of the licensee.
- 4.2 The licence shall be for a period of three (3) years.
- 4.3 The licence shall not be transferable.
- 4.4 An applicant will not be permitted more than one licence.
- 4.5 The licensee shall provide its services on free to air basis.
- 4.6 The licensee shall not use its channel/broadcast services in whole or part for commercial purposes.

4.7 The programmes on the community radio service will focus on issues relating to education, health, environment, agriculture, rural and community development. The content must be confined to social, cultural and local issues and the format, subject, presentation and language must reflect and exude the local flavour and fragrance.

4.8 The licensee shall not be permitted to broadcast any news and current affairs programmes and shall not air election and political broadcasts.

4.9 The licensee shall not air any advertisement or sponsored programmes.

4.10 The licensee shall ensure that nothing is included in the programme of the licensee which:
  (a) offends against good taste or decency;
  (b) contains criticism of friendly countries;
  (c) contains attack on religions or communities or visuals or words contemptuous of religious groups or which promotes communal attitudes;
  (d) contains anything obscene, defamatory, deliberate, false and suggestive innuendos and half truths;
  (e) is likely to encourage or incite violence or contains anything against maintenance of law and order or which promote anti-national attitudes;
  (f) contains anything amounting to contempt of court;
  (g) contains aspersions against the integrity of the president and Judiciary;
  (h) contains anything affecting the integrity of the Nation;
  (i) criticises, maligns or slanders any individual in person or certain groups, segments of social, public and moral life of the country;
  (j) encourages superstition or blind belief;
  (k) denigrates women;
  (l) denigrates children.
  (m) may present/depict/suggest as desirable the misuse of drugs including alcohol, narcotics and tobacco or which may stereotype, incite, vilify or perpetuate hatred against or attempt to demean any person or group on the basis of ethnicity, nationality, race, gender, sexual preference, religion, age or physical or mental disability.

Appendix – 8

4.11 The licensee shall ensure that due care is taken with respect to religious programmes with a view to avoiding –
 (a) improper exploitation of religious susceptibilities; and
 (b) offence to the religious views and beliefs of those belonging to a particular religion or religious denomination.
4.12 That the licensee shall ensure that due emphasis is given in the programmes to promote values of national integration, religious harmony, scientific temper and Indian culture.
4.13 The licensee shall follow the Programme Code of All India Radio.
4.14 The licensee shall pay spectrum usage fee as determined by the Wireless Advisor in the WPC Wing.
4.15 Though the licensees will operate the service under the Ministry of Information & Broadcasting, Govt. of India, the licensing will be subject to the condition that as and when any regulatory authority to regulate and monitor the broadcast services in the country is constituted, the licensees will have to adhere to the norms, rules and regulations prescribed by such authority.
4.16 The licensee shall provide such information to the Government on such intervals as may be required. In this connection, the licensee is required to preserve tapes of programmes broadcast during the last six months failing which the Government will be at liberty to revoke the license.
4.17 The Government or its authorised representative shall have the right to inspect the broadcast facilities of the licensees and collect such information as considered necessary in public and community interests.
4.18 The Government reserves the right to take over the entire services and networks of the licensee or revoke/terminate/suspend the licence in the interest of national security or in the event of national emergency / war or low intensity conflict or similar type of situations.
4.19 All foreign personnel likely to be deployed by way of appointment, contract, consultancy, etc. by the licensee for installation, maintenance and operation of the licensee's services shall be required to obtain security clearance from the Government of India.
4.20 The Government reserves the right to modify at any time the terms and conditions if it is necessary to do so in the interest of the general public or for the proper conduct of broadcasting or for security considerations.

4.21 Government may revoke the licence at any time in public interest or for breach of any terms and conditions of the licence by giving a notice of 15 days.

4.22 Notwithstanding anything contained anywhere else in the licence, the Government's decision shall be final and conclusive.

4.23 The licensees shall furnish a bank guarantee for a sum of Rs.50,000/- (Rupees fifty thousand) only to ensure timely performance of the licence agreement.

4.24 If the licensee fail to commission services within the stipulated period, he shall forfeit the amount of the bank guarantee to the Government and the Government would be free to cancel the licence awarded to the licensee.

4.25 A licensee will be subject to such other conditions as may be determined by the Government.

Appendix – 9

The Cable Television Networks (Regulation) Act, 1995
No.7 of 1995
(25th March, 1995)

An Act to regulate the operation of cable television networks in the country and for matters connected therewith or incidental thereto. Be it enacted by the Parliament in the Forty-sixth Year of the Republic of India as follows:-

CHAPTER – 1

Preliminary

1. (a) This Act may be called the Cable Television Networks (Regulation) Act, 1995.
    (b) It extends to the whole of India.
    (c) It shall be deemed to have come into force on the 29th day of September, 1994.
2. In this Act, unless the context otherwise requires –
    (a) "authorised officer" means, within his local limits of jurisdiction;–
        (i) a District Magistrate, or
        (ii) a Sub-divisional Magistrate, or
        (iii) a Commissioner of Police,
and includes any other officer notified in the Official Gazette, by the Central Government or the State Government, to be an authorised officer for such local limits of jurisdiction as may be determined by that Government;
    (b) "cable operator" means any person who provides cable service through a cable television network or otherwise controls or is responsible for the management and operation of a cable television network;

(c) "cable service" means the transmission by cables of programmes including re-transmission by cables of any broadcast television signals;

(d) "cable television network" means any system consisting of a set of closed transmission paths and associated signal generation, control and distribution equipment, designed to provide cable service for reception by multiple subscribers;

(e) "company" means a company as defined in Section 3 of the companies Act, 1956;

(f) "person" means –
  (i) an individual who is a citizen of India;
  (ii) an association of individuals or body of individuals, whether incorporated or not, whose members are citizens of India;
  (iii) a company in which not less than fifty-one per cent of the paid-up share capital is held by the citizens of India;

(g) "prescribed" means prescribed by rules made under this Act;

(h) "programme" means any television broadcast and includes –
  (i) exhibition of films, features, dramas, advertisements and serials through videocassette recorders or videocassette players;
  (ii) any audio or visual or audio-visual live performance or presentation, and the expression "programming service" shall be construed accordingly;

(i) "registering authority" means such authority as the Central Government may, by notification in the Official Gazette, specify to perform the functions of the registering authority under this Act;

(i) "subscriber" means a person who receives the signals of cable television network at a place indicated by him to the cable operator, without further transmitting it to any other person.

CHAPTER– II

Regulation Of Cable Television Network

3. No person shall operate a cable television network unless he is registered as a cable operator under this Act:

Provided that a person operating a cable television network, immediately before the commencement of this Act, may continue to do so for a period of ninety days from such commencement; and if he it is proposed to confiscate such equipment and giving him a reasonable opportunity of making a representation in writing, within such reasonable time as may be specified in the notice against the confiscation and if he so desires of being heard in the matter:

Provided that where no such notice is given within a period of ten days from the date of the seizure of the equipment, such equipment shall be returned after the expiry of that period to the cable operator from whose possession it was seized.

(2) Save as otherwise provided in sub-section (1), the provisions of the Code of Civil Procedure, 1908 shall, so far as may be, apply to every proceeding referred to in sub-section (1).

15. (1) Any person aggrieved by any decision of the court adjudicating a confiscation of the equipment may prefer an appeal to the court to which an appeal lies from the decision of such court.

(2) The appellate court may after giving the appellant an opportunity of being heard, pass such order as it thinks fit confirming, modifying or revising the decision appealed against or may send back the case with such directions as it may think fit for a fresh decision or adjudication, as the case may be, after taking additional evidence if necessary.

(3) No further appeal shall lie against the order of the court made under sub-section (2).

CHAPTER – IV

Offences and Penalties

16. Whoever contravenes any of the provisions of this Act shall be punishable, –
    (a) for the first offence, with imprisonment for a term which may extend to two years or with fine which may extend to one thousand rupees or with both;
    (b) for every subsequent offence, with imprisonment for a term which may extend to five years and with fine which may extend to five thousand rupees.

17. (1) Where an offence under this Act has been committed by a company, every person who, at the time the offence was committed, was in charge of, and was responsible to, the company for the conduct of the business of the company, as well as the company, shall be deemed to be guilty of the offence and shall be liable to be proceeded against and punished accordingly;

Provided that nothing contained in this sub-section shall render any such person liable to any punishment, if he proves that the offence was committed without his knowledge or that he had exercised all due diligence to prevent the commission of such offence.

(2) Notwithstanding anything contained in sub-section (1), where any offence under this Act has been committed by a company and it is proved that the offence has been committed with the consent or connivance of, or is attributable to any negligence on the part of, any director, manager, secretary or order officer of the company, such director, manager, secretary or other officer shall also be deemed to be guilty of that offence and shall be liable to be proceeded against and punished accordingly.

Explanation: For the purposes of this section, –

(a) "company" means any body corporate and includes a firm or other association of individuals; and

(b) "director" in relation to a firm, means a partner in the firm.

18. No court shall take cognisance of any offence punishable under this Act except upon a complaint in writing made [8] "by any authorised officer".

CHAPTER – V

Miscellaneous

19. Where [9] "any authorised officer" thinks it necessary or expedient to do so in public interest, he may, by order, prohibit any cable operator from transmitting or re-transmitting [10] "any programme or channel if, it is not in conformity with the prescribed programme code referred to in Section 5 and advertisement code referred to in Section 6 or if it is" likely to promote, on grounds of religion, race, language, caste or community or any other ground whatsoever, disharmony or feelings of enmity, hatred or ill-will between different religious, racial, linguistic or regional groups or castes or communities or which is likely to disturb the public tranquillity.

20.[11](1) Where the Central Government thinks it necessary or expedient so to do in public interest, it may prohibit the operation of any cable television network in such areas as it may, by notification in the Official Gazette, specify in this behalf. [12](2) Where the Central Government thinks it necessary or expedient so to do in the interest of the–

(i) sovereignty or integrity of India; or

(ii) security of India; or

Appendix – 9

(iii) friendly relations of India with any foreign State; or
(iv) public order, decency or morality,

it may, by order, regulate or prohibit the transmission or re-transmission of any channel or programme.

[13] (3) Where the Central Government considers that any programme of any channel is not in conformity with the prescribed programme code referred to in Section 5 or the prescribed advertisement code referred to in Section 6, it may by order, regulate or prohibit the transmission or re-transmission of such programme".

21. The provisions of this Act shall be in addition to, and not in derogation of, the Drugs and Cosmetics Act, 1940, the Pharmacy Act, 1948, the Emblems and Names (Prevention of Improper Use) Act, 1950, the Drugs (Control) Act, 1950, the Cinematograph Act, 1952, the Drugs and Magic Remedies (Objectionable Advertisements) Act, 1954, the Prevention of Food Adulteration Act, 1954, the Prize Competitions Act, 1955, the Copyright Act, 1957, the Trade and Merchandise Marks Act, 1958, the Indecent Representation of Women (Prohibition) Act, 1986 and the Consumer Protection Act, 1986.

22. (1) The Central Government may, by notification in the official Gazette, make rules to carry out the provisions of this Act.

(2) In particular, and without prejudice to the generality of the foregoing power, such rules may provide for all or any of the following matters, namely:-

   (a) the form of application and the fee payable under sub-section (2) of Section 4;
   (b) the programme code under Section 5;
   (c) the advertisement code under Section 6;
   (d) the form of register to be maintained by a cable operator under Section 7;
   (e) any other matter which is required to be, or may be, prescribed.

(3) Every rule made under this Act shall be laid, as soon as may be after it is made, before each House of Parliament, while it is in sessions, for a total period of thirty days which may be comprised in one session or in two or more successive sessions, and if, before the expiry of the session immediately following the session or the successive sessions aforesaid, both Houses agree in making any modification in the rule or both Houses agree that the rule should not be made, the rule shall thereafter have effect only in such modified form or be of no effect, as the case may be; so, however, that any such modification of

annulment shall be without prejudice to the validity of anything previously done under that rule.

23. (1) The Cable Television Networks (Regulation) Ordinance, 1995 is hereby repealed.
    (2) Notwithstanding such repeal, anything done or any action taken under the said Ordinance, shall be deemed to have been done or taken under the corresponding provision of this Act.

Index

Aaj Tak 38,108
Aastha 71
ABC 8, 274
ABU 274
Advani, L. K. 16, 17
Afghan 270
Afghanistan 266
AFP 267
Afrovision 263
Akash Bharati 15
Akashvani 14, 16
Al-Jazeera 73,74, 267
All India Radio (AIR) 11, 25-26, 30-32, 152, 172, 273, 283, 339, 343, 387
Analog 2, 274
ANI 38, 39
Animal Planet 67
Annon Committee, 249
AOL 8-9, 221, 223, 237-239
AOL Time Warner 9, 220, 222, 223, 265
AP 106, 266, 274
Arabvision 263
Asianet 48-49
Asiavision 263
AT&T 9, 265
ATSC 5, 6
Audio recorders 85, 86
Australia 7, 32
Autocue 107, 108, 275
Avid 104-106
AXN 62

B4U Network 61
Balaji Telefilms 72
Balance 128, 129, 275

BBC 7, 49, 50, 106, 107, 185, 198, 266, 275
Bell 2
Bertelsmann 9, 265
Bolivia 7
Bose, Subhas Chandra 13
Brazil 7
Broadband 3, 222
Burkina Faso 7

Camera 87-89
Camera cable 91-92
Camera mountings 90-91
Camera angles 118-119
Canada 2, 7
Capital Cities/ABC 8
Caribvision 263
CAS 278
Case, Stephen M. 237
Chakravartty, Nikhil 30
Chanda Committee 14
Channel [V] 41, 43, 44
Chinoy, Rahimatuallah 13
Cinemax 55
CNBC 50-52
CNN 6, 9, 39, 53, 54, 109, 110, 198, 228, 240, 266, 272
Commercial radio 7
Commercial television 7,116
Community broadcasting 7
Community radio 10, 384
Composition 125-127, 129
Convergence 3, 79
Cote d'Ivoire 7
Czech Republic 7

Deregulation 8
Digital 2, 3, 282

Digital Video Broadcasting (DVB) 5, 6
Direct Broadcasting Satellite (DBS) 4, 281
Discovery 6, 37, 66, 67
Disney 8, 9, 56, 265
Doordarshan 11, 18-20, 33-35, 37, 39, 107, 186, 200, 213, 339, 343
Dow Jones 51
DRS 4
DTH 4, 29, 48, 371-373
Duggal, Kartar Singh 17
DVD 110, 111-112, 232, 235

Early Bird 2, 276
EBU 263-264
Editing 135-138, 187
Edmunds, P. J. 12
EFP 98,101
Eisner 8
Embedded journalists 271-272
ENG 98, 101, 185, 186, 198, 284
ENPS 106
ESPN 41-43, 57
ETC Network 61
ETV (Educational) 257-259
ETV (Eenadu) 60
Europe 7, 263, 264,
Eurovision 264, 284

Falkland 267
Fashion TV 75-77
FCC 250, 285
Fielden 12,13
Fiber-optic 3, 8, 285
Finland 7
Flash 171
Fox 270
France 7

Gandhi, Indira 14, 15, 143, 175
Gandhi, Rajiv 25, 167-169
General Electric (GE) 9, 50
Germany 7
Gill, S. S. 30
General news room (GNR) 153, 154
Gobal Village 1
Grenada 268

Gulf War 39, 268
Gurjari 68
Gutenburg 1

Hallmark 77
HBO 9, 54-55, 228, 234
HDTV 5, 288
Hum Log 39
Hungary 7

IBM 109, 110
Incite 109
India 4, 7, 11, 13
Indian Broadcasting Company 12
India Today group 38
IN Network 69, 71
INSAT 4, 35
Intel 6
Intelsat 1, 2, 290
Internet 1, 48, 183, 221
Intersputnik 1, 2
IPDC 262
ISBD 5
ITN 185, 290

Japan 45, 263
Jaya TV 59, 60
Joshi, P. C. 18, 26
Joshi, Uma Shankar 15
Joshi Working Group 18-21, 253

Kerala 48
KTV 58

Latin America 46, 264
Laser 2
Lashkara 68
Liberty Media 9, 265
Lighting 92

MacBride 9, 251, 252, 266, 311-333
Mahabharat 39, 71
Mahaweli 262
Mali 7
Marconi 2
Masani, Mehra 14
Master control 101, 293

Index

MAX 63-64
Mass 127
MCI 8
Microphone 79-80, 82-85, 114
Microsoft 6, 50
MIT 9
Moore 3
Morse 2
MOS 110
Movement (movements) 127, 128
MPEG 112
MSNBC 50, 54
MSO 294
MTV 44-46, 222
Murdoch 8, 36, 107, 243-245

NAB 5
Namedia feedback 21-22
National Geographic 64-66
National Planning Committee (NPC) 13-14, 255, 256
NBC 50-51, 268, 295
NDTV 36-37
Nehru 13, 14
Nepal 45, 262
News concept 143-145
News Corporation 8, 9, 265
News values 146-148
New Zealand 32, 182
Nickelodeon 56
Nigeria 7
NTSC 98, 295
NWICO 265, 266

OB van 87, 101, 102, 184, 296
Optic fiber 2

Package 190, 197
PAL 98, 297
Pakistan 7, 74-75
Parliament 16, 17
Paswan Committee 27-28
Pay TV 5
Peru 7
Piece-to-camera 190, 192, 196, 298
Pool 153, 154, 158, 268
Popoff 2

Prasar Bharati 16, 18, 25-27, 30, 344-366, 367
Press conference 196
Press Trust of India (PTI) 36
Production process 115-117
PTV 74-75
Public Broadcasting Service (PBS) 6
Public Service Broadcasting 6, 248, 249

QEdit Pro 104
Quantel 103, 104, 106, 107, 298
Qseries 107, 108
QTV 107

Radio Club 11
Radio-Locator 9
Raj TV 60
Ramayan (*Ramayana*) 39, 71
Regional unions 263
Reuters 38, 266
RTL 78
RTNDA 334-337
Russia 7

SABe 73
Sagaramatha 262
Sahara 69
Sanskar 72
Sarabhai, Vikram 18
Sarkaria Commission 22-25
Satellite News Gathering (SNG) 4, 381-383
Script 116, 118, 138-142, 189-191
SECAM 98, 301
Sengupta Committee 28
Shastri, Lal Bahadur 14
Shot (Shots) 110, 117, 119-125, 301, 302
Silicon chip 3
Singapore 7
Singh, V. P. 26, 27
SITE 4, 258, 260, 261
SMPTE 6
Sony 37, 63-64, 109, 110, 265
Sound mixing 94
South Korea 7
STAR 36, 37, 39-42, 107

Studio 79-96
Studio spot 193
Sun Network 57-59
Supreme Court 338-343

Telecine 96, 305
Telecom Act 7
Telegraphy 2
Teleprompter 306
Televisa 78
Time Inc. 228, 229
Time Warner 8, 221, 223, 229, 236
Turkey 7
Turner 8, 53, 227, 239-243
TV5 75, 267
TV18 52, 72
TV Globo 78
TV Today 37-38

Udaya TV 58
Uganda 7
Unesco 254, 261, 262, 265
United Kingdom 7, 107, 257
Uplinking Policy 374-383
USA 2, 4, 7, 107, 265, 270, 272
UTV 72

V-chip 250
Verghese, B. G. 15, 17, 19, 26
Viacom 9, 265
Videotape formats 97, 98
Vietnam 267-268
Vijay TV 58
Vision mixer 99
Visual effects 99, 100
Vivendi 9, 265
VTR 95-97

Warner Bros. 230-234
Walt Disney 6, 41, 56, 57, 245-248
WESTAR 2
Wheatstone 2
WMG 235
World Wide Web Consortium (W3C) 6

Yugoslavia (Yugoslav) 266, 270

Zee TV 46-48
Zee Telefilms Ltd. 47